GF
504
.D57
K57
1995

Kirby, Jack Temple.

Poquosin.

$17.95   21235

DATE		

BAKER & TAYLOR

POQUOSIN

POQU

STUDIES IN RURAL CULTURE *Jack Temple Kirby, editor*

OSIN

A STUDY OF RURAL LANDSCAPE & SOCIETY

Jack Temple Kirby

The University of North Carolina Press *Chapel Hill & London*

Manufactured in the United States of America

The paper in this book meets the guidelines for permanence
and durability of the Committee on Production Guidelines for
Book Longevity of the Council on Library Resources.

Library of Congress Cataloging-in-Publication Data
Kirby, Jack Temple.
Poquosin : a study of rural landscape and society / by Jack
Temple Kirby.
p.   cm.—(Studies in rural culture)
Includes bibliographical references and index.
ISBN 0-8078-2214-0 (cloth : alk. paper)—ISBN 0-8078-4527-2
(pbk. : alk. paper)
1. Man—Influence on nature—Dismal Swamp (N.C. and Va.)
2. Drainage—Environmental aspects—Dismal Swamp (N.C.
and Va.)   3. Reclamation of land—Environmental aspects—
Dismal Swamp (N.C. and Va.)   4. Wetland ecology—
Dismal Swamp (N.C. and Va.)   5. Dismal Swamp (N.C. and
Va.)—History.   I. Title.   II. Series.
GF504.D57K57   1995
333.91'8'09755523—dc20   94-48141
                        CIP

99 98 97 96 95   5 4 3 2 1

FOR SUSAN FORREST KIRBY

CONTENTS

ILLUSTRATIONS

Figures

Maps

PREFACE

Prefaces are skipped at comprehension's peril when a work is so odd and mysteriously titled as this one. *Poquosin* is an "environmental" history—a narrative of human-landscape interrelationships in the low country between the James River in Virginia and Albemarle Sound in adjacent northeastern North Carolina, from the arrival of Europeans and Africans until the present. The nineteenth century is disproportionately represented because it witnessed the principal human conflicts over the landscape's destiny. As subregions go, this one coheres rather well, in terms both physical and historical. (These terms are detailed in the Prologue and Chapter 4.) Coherence, however, includes a bifurcation of the country and its settlers into unreconciled parts—the cosmopolitan and hinterland—which, I believe, drove the subregion's history and must drive this book. A bifurcation so profoundly geographical implicates more than rivers and markets; it demands attention to the slippery matter of agency in history—that is, the power and initiative that amount to causation.

Environmental history seems always a narrative of pathos. The erect animals possessed of the largest brains and a capacity for sin act badly upon the rest of nature. They conceive of water, soil, forests, plants, and other animals as potential commodities, then manipulate them to optimize production; they extract, trade, degrade. This has been true in the Western Hemisphere, of course, for about five hundred years; but it is not all of the truth. Nature, too, has agency, beyond the spectacles of lightning, fire, storm, flood, and earthquake. Climate and geologic morphology are more persistent actors both in "natural" and human (unnatural?) history. They forbid, discourage, or invite human settlement; and invitation is seldom unlimited. The James-Albemarle low country has been mostly inviting. Aborigines made a Neolithic revolution of sorts there. Europeans and Africans incorporated much of Indian culture, but the landscape encouraged many British settlers to try to remake it in the image of Europe. This was truest among those who settled by the banks of Virginia's tidal rivers and Carolina's northern sounds. They had easiest access to the world's markets, to wealth and political power. Most of the subregion, however, remained remote from the market world for a very long time, in spite of its being subsumed, in outsiders' minds, under "the Tidewater," presumably a thriving commercial place. Dense swampy forests forbade transport of bulky commodities; rivers either were not navigable or, if they were, led to more wilderness. Here, in the hinterland, a culture barely commercial, one almost as Indian as European, endured until technological ingenuity overcame the inconveniences of nature's shape. Even then, even today, the hinterland's susceptibility to the cultivation of corn, peanuts, cotton, and especially the loblolly pine, renders it different from and subservient to the cosmopolitan sector. It has been the interaction of nature's and humans' agencies that made this so.

Partly because human agency has seemed so overweening in this countryside, and because my version of the saga features a variety of humans with memorable names and faces, I have chosen a compensatory title for this history. "Poquosin" was the spelling Englishmen devised early in the seventeenth century for the Algonquian word meaning "swamp-on-a-hill." At the beginning of the eighteenth century, John Lawson thought he heard "percourson" or "perkosan." "Poquosin" prevailed, however, until the twentieth century, when "pocosin" became standard. In my text I employ the most recent spelling, unless quoting the old usage. The antique spelling survives in the title out of respect for the dead—this is history, after all—and an eccentric affection for q's, which grow scarcer in our world.[1]

Real swamps, the English understood, are low, with water moving through them most of the year. Swamps-on-hills are sometimes covered with water, but the water stands still, gradually seeping downward; and of course they are higher than swamps. Pocosins, then, are the middle landscape between swamps and the higher ridges on which humans build farms and towns. As such, they have several important aspects. Among them—this the compensatory metaphor—is a vast capacity for the storage of carbon, the element of power.[2]

All of pocosins' known characteristics appeal to me, in fact. In addition to storing carbon, they moderate the subregion's hydraulic system. Pocosins store groundwater in deep peat, preventing rapid runoff and erosion, then filtering and cleaning the water before its descent into swamps and eventual return to the ocean. Pocosins also catch and store botanical detritus. Dead vegetative matter forms lush nurseries for infant fish that, like filtered water, ultimately descend to faster-moving vessels in the hydraulic circuit. Much of the once-alive detritus dissolves into carbon, however, and carbon, combined with hydrogen, oxygen, and other elements, creates life anew in many forms.[3] Yet pocosins have notoriously poor soils, they are frequently swept by wildfires, and they are virtually never occupied by humans. All three aspects are evocative of generalizations argued in this book.

First: "Poor" is a relative term, and pocosin soils are various. Whatever the measure, however, pocosins are nitrogen-starved—the chemical dissolves downward too quickly for agricultural production—and they are very acidic, usually supporting only acid-loving evergreen shrubs and pond pine trees in savannah-type assemblages.[4] Higher lands around pocosins have supported agriculture for more than a thousand years, but most of their soils, too, were and remain nitrogen-poor and acidic. Their relative poverty became apparent when richer clays and loesses in westerly places came under cultivation, more than two centuries ago. The acidic East's disadvantage produced a long crisis, then the modern, ameliorative agronomy of Edmund Ruffin. Ruffin was a native of the northwestern corner of the James-Albemarle country, and he figures large in this narrative.

Second: Pocosins' largely coniferous vegetation requires fire for regeneration. Nature herself initiated most fires through lightning. But Indians burned upland forests and pocosins on purpose, to clear land for farming and hunting, serving nature's ends very well.[5] Europeans and Africans in the subregion's hinterland adapted Indians' shifting fire culture to their own, more stationary, system on the upland ridges; and they persisted in burning the woods through the beginning of this century—longer than historians have supposed. This syncretic culture based on fire and corn—and its ultimate suppression—is also an important part of *Poquosin*.

Third: Periodic standing water surely discourages humans from inhabiting pocosins, but there is more. Pocosins are legendarily snaky places, provoking the aversive dread forever associated with venomous serpents. Swamps-on-a-hill probably *are* snaky; but in fact, no one knows for sure. For pocosins actually remain little-studied, especially their fauna. Pocosins nurture young fish, egrets and other waterfowl, almost certainly moccasins, rattlesnakes, and a host of nonpoisonous snakes. They seem to function as refuges—another good metaphor—for bears and other animals harried from nearby swamps by human depredations on their habitats.[6] Hardly more is observed or guessed, however, for pocosins have that fearsome capacity to protect mystery. Their mystery should command respect, so long after humans have outgrown the awe nature once commanded. I approve of this; pocosins are good for our imaginations and our moral beings.

Another instrumental virtue of pocosins, I think, is the vagueness of the name itself. It encompasses so many variations of wetlands higher than swamps that scientists ritually apologize for the usage.[7] Still, the scientists persist, as we all must. My choice of the Algonquian word as my title, then, may imply an attempt to co-opt critics: I must be vague here and there, good readers, for my subjects are miasmic. I prefer another reading—that mindful of the limitations both of research and my own capacity to understand and explain, vagueness acquires a certain wisdom as well as utility; call it restraint.

Finally, there is an irony in pocosins' recent history that instructs us again in nature's agency. Until after World War II, humans shunned pocosins like the dangerous serpents they are said to harbor. Occasional hunters in good boots may have been the sole exception. Then this last coastal frontier began rapidly to recede, before the bulldozer and backhoe. Thousands of acres were drained and, following generous applications of fertilizer, converted to pine plantations for the paper industry, and to soybean plantations for corporate agriculture. The wetlands' place in the hydraulic cycle was confounded, but not without visible revenge. During the 1970s, throughout much of the vast Chowan River drainage area, algae bloomed, choking a valuable fishery and spoiling riparian scenery men and women have loved for centuries. Nitrogen-rich fertilizer had run off pocosins hardened by drainage and the weight of heavy machinery. Mixing with the waters of the Nottoway, the Blackwater, the Meherrin, the Chowan, and dozens of creeks, the nitrogen engorged naturally occurring algae. Such enormous blooms prevent sunlight from reaching subaquatic vegetation, which is the basis of the food chain; and they deprive fish of oxygen, drowning them, in effect, by the millions.[8] The dead rose to the surface, to shine, rot, and stink. Grim retribution.

Yet the landscape is resilient, even with crippled function. Algae blooms subsided, riparian beauty revived. Nature lives on, though diminished, simplified. There is no happy ending, but no end, yet, either.

Having (in an earlier life) dug ditches, sawn boards without benefit of electricity, nailed roofing under summer sun, and soldiered a bit, I reaffirm my strong preference for scholarly research and writing. This labor is certainly lonelier, and it may produce results less permanent; but I find the physical demands agreeably light, the psychic ones large but commensurately rewarding. Solitary laborers also need help and accumulate debts, however—to institutions, colleagues, relatives—and acknowledging them publicly is as pleasurable as the work is privileged.

First the institutional: The taxpayers of Ohio provide me secure employment through Miami University, which in turn has supported this project in many ways for seven years. The W. E. Smith Professorship fund supplies much that is necessary to the dailiness of scholarship. The university also granted me two semester-long leaves, and the Committee on Faculty Research provided a summer research appointment and additional travel funds.

Among many pleasurable stays in Richmond, one was spent as a Mellon Research Fellow at the Virginia Historical Society; and I remain grateful to the Society for the appointment. The National Endowment for the Humanities made gift of a summer stipend as well, and the NEH also inadvertently aided the project while I directed two Summer Seminars for School Teachers on "critical texts" in environmental history. The teachers, probably more engagingly than my students in southern and environmental history, tested my understanding, and certainly inspired good thinking.

Libraries and archives in Virginia and North Carolina hold the principal sources for this work. The richest manuscript collections for my enterprise I found at the Virginia Historical Society, the Southern Historical Collection at the University of North Carolina, and the North Carolina State Archives in Raleigh. But the manuscript collections of Perkins Library at Duke University, Alderman Library at the University of Virginia, Swem Library at the College of William and Mary, and the Virginia State Archives were also important. Local history files—sometimes including manuscript collections—at city and county libraries are priceless. This is especially so in Norfolk and Portsmouth, but also in Suffolk and Courtland, Virginia, and in Elizabeth City and Windsor, North Carolina. The affiliation of county historical societies with such libraries—especially in poor rural counties—is a boon much appreciated.

Then individuals: My good friend, colleague, and department chair Allan Winkler created an intellectually stimulating work atmosphere and facilitated other institutional support. Jeri Schaner, our ingenious administrative secretary, accomplishes both the routine and the extraordinary expertly and with a speed that is the envy of other faculties. Chris Peterson of our paper science and engineering department, a veteran of the wood products industry, generously advised me on methods of estimating sizes of forests and in the elementary chemistry of papermaking. Orie Loucks, our eminent professor of zoology and ecology, sent marvelous works, old and new, on wetlands, works that I might not have discovered on my own. And Dean Karl Mattox, a botanist by trade, supplied contemporary literature on the chemistry of wood ashes and confirmed my historical use of these and other scientific sources.

During the late 1980s, Allen Plocher, then a doctoral student in ecology at Old Dominion University and a forestry intern with the Union Camp corporation, introduced me to the Blackwater Ecologic Preserve (surrounded by Union Camp's loblolly plantations) in Isle of Wight County near Franklin, Virginia. Plocher taught me the elements of "reading" pine forests—identifying species, estimating ages, spying evidence of turpentine extraction on old longleaf stumps, recognizing ruins of turpentine distilleries. And he showed me longleafs, which number among nature's loveliest creatures.

At the National Museum of American History in Washington, Lu Ann Jones permitted me to read typescripts of her invaluable collection of oral histories of peanut farmers. At the Virginia Historical Society, every administrator, archivist, and clerk is smart, resourceful, and sociable; but I feel particularly favored by Frances Pollard, Nelson Lankford, and by the blessed Howsom Cole, who introduced me to the irreplaceable Richard Eppes diaries. In Chapel Hill, Richard Schrader orchestrates a beehive of scholarship at the Southern Historical Collection with quiet aplomb; and research director David Moltke-Hansen will emerge not only for coffee but also to decipher eighteenth- and nineteenth-century handwriting. At Southern Historical Association convention sites and in the Northwest, Mart Stewart and I have spent countless hours talking agronomy, forestry, and the weather—I more often the learner, I suspect, than he. Stewart also provided the press a learned, conscientious, and sympathetic report on the manuscript for this book. I am also grateful for the constructive evaluation of another, anonymous, reviewer.

Michael O'Brien, dear friend and colleague-next-door, has been an intellectual partner throughout my work on this project. His enormous nineteenth-century research files, perfectly ordered and accessible on hard computer disk, enriched my own, harder-to-reach files, and answered at least one large question that arose during writing. O'Brien also read the entire manuscript with his steady, baleful eye, and remarkably—for O'Brien's disapproval of nearly everything is legendary—pronounced it pretty good. My boonest companion, La Constancia, a writer of elegant fiction and poetry as well as of piercing cultural criticism, read the manuscript twice, with profound effect upon my sensibilities both historical and literary. Her relentless, free-ranging curiosity, her encouragement of an experimental (for an historian, anyway) narrative style, and her infallible perception of logical structure were gifts beyond any author's just expectation.

Paul Betz, formerly social science editor at the University of North Carolina Press, recruited me as series editor, then as author. His amiable disposition and deep cross-disciplinary learning are cherished, his professional association sorely missed. Lewis Bateman, executive editor at the press, has meanwhile been a wry, wise, and generous impresario. And like many other authors, I am indebted to editor Christi Stanforth, who expertly saw this work through production in Chapel Hill.

Lastly my sister, Susan, to whom the book is dedicated. Hers is a character so sweet and loyal I would have her canonized. But her contribution to my attempt at a deconstruction of a particular modern landscape—her landscape—was crucial. A school librarian in Southampton County, Susan directed me to several of those local history collections at public libraries. She mailed press clippings and her own photos of peanut fields and the revived cotton culture of southeastern Virginia. She also shared my compulsion to find specific places so important a century and more ago, but now by-passed, defunct, and/or invisible to outsiders, even most locals. It was her persistence one day that led us, finally, to the ruined lock at the junction of Shingle Creek and Jericho Ditch in Suffolk, at the edge of the Great Dismal Swamp. I was already aware of the huge significance of that lock; now I could touch it. Such is Susan's benevolent way.

POQUOSIN

PROLOGUE

NATURE'S AGENCY

AND HUNGRY RIVERS

Nature was here something savage and awful, though beautiful. I looked with awe at the ground I trod on, to see what the Powers had made there, the form and fashion and material of their work. This was that Earth of which we have heard, made out of Chaos and Old Night. — Henry David Thoreau, The Maine Woods

In the beginning there was a river. The river became a road and the road branched out to the whole world. And because the road was once a river it was always hungry. — Ben Okri, The Famished Road

That man is, in fact, only a member of a biotic team is shown by an ecological interpretation of history. Many historical events, hitherto explained solely in terms of human enterprise, were actually biotic interactions between people and land. The characteristics of the land determined the facts quite as potently as the characteristics of the men who lived on it. — Aldo Leopold, A Sand County Almanac

Once upon a time, nature's personalities and powers were not questioned subjects. Humans shared a common spirituality and conversation with other animals, plants, living soil and inanimate rocks. The visible and tactile coexisted with the superreal and divine, the vulgar with the sublime. The truth of this unity, like all faith, was and remains profoundly complex and manifestly simple.

So-called Westerners—the Mosaic Hebrews, then Arabs, finally Europeans—began to divide the visible from the invisible, horizontally. Horizontal division specified hierarchy. Humanity became separate from and master of all that lay below. Cultural symbols from the lower natural world would persist only in complex ambiguity, as humans' distance from the rest of nature lengthened. Jehovah, the one great invisible god, ordained things so. For humans alone had souls, minds, consciousness, sentience—all to recognize Jehovah and to implement his mandate to subdue all other things on the earth.[1]

At the end of the twentieth century, scientific discourse persists in this Western tradition. Agency resides with humanity alone, because agency necessitates mind—or consciousness and sentience, vaguely overlapping descriptors. Except that computers or robots might exhibit "strong AI" (artificial intelligence), a phenomenon troubling to philosophers and scientists alike. A philosopher finessed the conundrum of mind/consciousness versus AI by fencing it with language: Computers and robots have syntax but not semantics and thus lack (human) consciousness. A few scientists, however, suggested (in 1992) the need for a radical new theory of consciousness, but they knew not where to turn.[2]

Curiously, neurobiological research ongoing throughout the AI debate pointed, however remotely, toward a new theory of mind that might ultimately legitimate "primitive" notions of a communicative circle encompassing humans and the rest of nature: Humans cannot reason, dream, or perform motor functions without neurotransmitters, the chemical-electric signals between the brain and other parts of the body. During the early 1980s neurobiologists discovered that glutamate, an ordinary amino acid, and nitric oxide, a poison—both of them found in lower animals and in plants—carried "information" along nervous systems. More important was confirmation (during the 1990s) of the neurotransmitting role of the chemical adenosine triphosphate (ATP). ATP is a molecule present in the cells of virtually every living thing. In humans it is a primary transmitter within the brain itself as well. Some researchers declared that ATP and other neurotransmitters are "intricate languages." Might these "languages," undeciphered, proceed past syntax to semantics? If they do, then trees (for instance) might be said to possess mind, even though they lack brains—an intriguing possibility and a perplexing joke on philosophers who maintain that consciousness is brain. On the other hand, Henry David Thoreau, who mourned humans' loss of the ability and will to talk with trees, would have been delighted. But the neurobiologists pursue only human medical diagnostic and prophylactic applications of this new knowledge. (Such are more likely to yield research grants.)[3]

For now, then, and perhaps forever, skeptical Western sensibilities dismiss the radical and transcendental as flaky. A Westerner myself, and a mere pedestrian reader of science, I demur but prudently hasten onto an evener, more conventionally Western avenue toward acknowledging nature's agency. This is geologic morphology, the science of landscapes' shapes and contents—a discipline so elemental to the subject of agency that humanists usually overlook it.

Long, long before demography, morphology—especially drainage—was destiny. The earth heaved and collapsed, creating mountains, ridges, hills, and drainage paths. Oceans rose and receded several times, leaving scarps and other divides on post-Miocene landscapes. Glaciers plowed southward and melted, remaking river valleys, estuaries, and lakes. Eons of explosions, winds, floods, deep freezes and warmings, friction violently sudden and voluptuously slow, shaped the landscapes of geology's yesterday. Resultant strata of rocks, clays, gravels, sand, and fossilized pollen, with plants and animals in each layer, reveal the process and chronology. (Stratigraphy is written history of the prehistoric sort.) The shape of it all—the morphology of, say, ten millennia ago—and especially the drainage system of each landscape would invite or limit or prohibit human agency when history began. For no matter if human settlers were few and subsisted in relative harmony with the rest of nature, or were many and obliged to harvest extensively, no matter if they were animistic or Judeo-Christian, passive or entrepreneurial, technologically primitive or sophisticated—morphology and climate, and drainage most of all, would direct them.

When rivers teem with fish and are relatively safe to enter, they feed higher, more resourceful animals. Silted banks and deltas invite agriculture, villages, trade, and every other sort of human intercourse. They spawn narratives of creation, religion, architecture—all that we term civilization. When rivers lead to oceans, and when technology permits extended travel, rivers become great roads, too. When they lead to culs-de-sac, commercially marginal and dark at their hearts, rivers will become lesser roads, but roads nonetheless. Humans will move. And for a very long time, until technology at last overcame landscape (albeit never completely), rivers virtually defined human linearity.

So much is obvious—or used to be. For most of us, I suspect, stratigraphy is not science but stunning art, most commonly revealed in the gigantic cuts in mountainsides which permit us to speed over highways. Here the foundations of landscape become vivid moving pictures. Only as we approach well-signed "great divides" along such human-made roads might we recollect the historical determinism of geology. (Indeed, the Colorado and the Kanawha flow westerly, the Rio Grande and the James easterly.) In landscapes of very low profile, such as the swampy patch in this study, stratigraphy is usually buried beneath dense vegetation, and the ages-long dictation of morphology is subtle, much more easily ignored. Motorists between Portsmouth and Suffolk, Virginia, for instance, pass over the Suffolk Scarp without notice. (I am a Portsmouth native but learned of the divide's existence and name only in the 1980s, while reading local geology.) Fifty miles west of the present Atlantic shore, the scarp was once the ocean shore itself; now it is a narrow ridge,

averaging perhaps twenty feet higher than the low plain to the east. In combination with a series of lesser scarps and ridges just below the James River,
along with the slope of the Piedmont from the Blue Ridge, the Suffolk Scarp
directed that the landscape to its west and south—most of southeastern Virginia and adjacent northeastern North Carolina—would be, in the seventeenth, eighteenth, and much of the nineteenth centuries, a remote hinterland rather than part of the cosmopolitan Chesapeake world. Slope, scarps,
and ridges forced the rivers west of the scarp to flow not eastward but southward, into Albemarle Sound, a lovely and expansive cul-de-sac with difficult,
dangerous access to the Atlantic. So close—agonizingly close to European
hinterland settlers—the deep and mighty James became a superhighway to
the Chesapeake and the rest of the world almost as soon as the English arrived. So did the Nansemond, the Elizabeth, and lesser deepwater rivers and
creeks to the east of Suffolk Scarp. Together they joined the linear universe
of the emergent world market system. The hinterland would long remain a
place of slow, mostly local travel via the Nottoway-Blackwater-Chowan system and the Roanoke, Little, Perquimans, and Pasquotank Rivers. People and
their productive surpluses would move only with difficulty and inconvenient
expense to the broader world. This was so until railroads and paved roads for
wagons and stages, then autos, finally overcame the scarps' and rivers' inconveniences and created an artificial east-west linearity through the hinterland.
Only then would the Suffolk Scarp become unnoticed, save by geologists.[4]

Today's low-profile landscape between the James and Albemarle Sound,
from the Atlantic to the fall line, is rather young. Toward the end of the last
glacial period, about twelve to eleven thousand years ago, the countryside
resembled parts of present-day Manitoba. The climate was cold, and along
freshwater streams the forests grew a boreal assemblage of pine and spruce.
Much land was open marsh—ancestor of what Woodland Indians would later
call *poquosins*. Small bands of Paleo-Indians roamed this landscape, occupied campsites for short times, and hunted. Their prey may have included
enormous (and now extinct) herbivores. Later, during the so-called Archaic
period (about nine to four thousand years ago), Indians brought down waterfowl with bolas. Twentieth-century hunters and archeologists have found
stone bola weights, many of them notched, from the Suffolk Scarp just west
of the present city of Suffolk, to near Virginia Beach, and down toward Albemarle Sound. As in many other parts of the world, the Indians knotted at
least two cords of equal length to bola weights and, twirling the contraptions (also called compound slings) above their heads, hurled them at prey.[5]

Meanwhile, as the last glacier began to melt, the sea level rose and the cli-

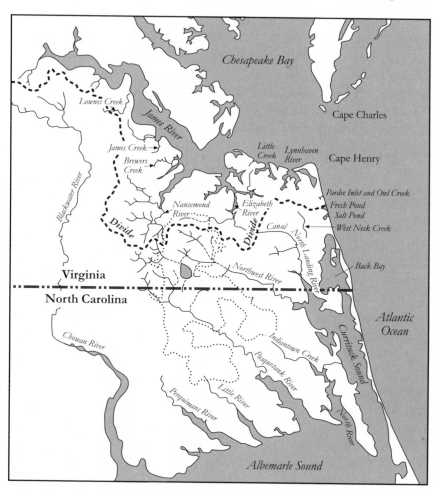

Map 1. Drainage in southeastern Virginia and northeastern North Carolina (Adapted from Paul W. Kirk, Jr., ed., The Great Dismal Swamp, *courtesy of the Virginia Division of Mineral Resources)*

mate began to warm. Just to the north, ice dredged out the Chesapeake Bay for nearly two hundred miles, along the primeval path of the Susquehannah River. As warming continued, the bay's shallowness on either side of the old river channel permitted sunlight to penetrate to the bottom, establishing subaquatic vegetation and promoting the production of phytoplankton and the development of a food chain that would render the great estuary the future United States' third-ranking fishery—following the Atlantic and Pacific. The great warming and melting also pushed up inland freshwater tables, and the creation of the Great Dismal Swamp and many lesser wetlands was under way. In the Dismal-to-be, peat deposits atop near-impermeable older formations with poor drainage indicated the ultimate structure of the swamp. Along stream banks, boreal forests gave way to the equivalent of present-day northern hardwoods by about nine thousand years ago. A mere millennium later, the now-dominant assemblage of gum, cypress, oak, and southern pines appeared. By six thousand years ago, probably a thousand square miles of the future Dismal was thoroughly mantled with peat deposits. In another two millennia the great swamp had probably extended to its greatest size— more than two thousand square miles, from the fringes of the future Suffolk, Portsmouth, and Norfolk, southward virtually to the Albemarle Sound. At last Lake Drummond appeared too, in the north-center of the swamp. This large pond (roughly a three-by-five-mile oval), its geologic origins still mysterious and romantic as its later history, was and remains the jewel of this most daunting of middle Atlantic wildernesses. Early freshwater ponding to the west of Suffolk Scarp also made the countless lesser swamps and pocosins that appeared on maps made by white men many centuries later.

So a regional landscape more or less familiar to us came into being not much more than three thousand years ago. With it appeared also the Woodland human culture, essentially the same one the English first encountered in 1607. Most important—both to the landscape and to the English—the Woodland people established agriculture. Along the Suffolk Scarp, geologists have collected fossilized maize pollen fully three millennia old. (Maize pollen is so large and heavy that it does not blow or drift very far, so the fossil locations are probably true to the original sites of this North American Neolithic Revolution.) These first farmers, founders of a food culture that Europeans and Africans adopted with few significant changes, organized themselves into political-familial groups, founded villages, developed pottery, refined stone and shell implements, and adopted the bow and arrow for their supplemental food-gathering. In addition to maize, beans, and other vegetables, they grew tobacco—a portentous commodity—and smoked it in clay pipes of their own fashion.

Creating civilization, the Woodland people altered their natural environment. Agriculture is the most elemental of human disturbances of landscape, and like other eastern North American aborigines, the Woodland folk practiced maize culture aggressively. Lacking iron or steel tools or other forest-clearing implements, they made their crop fields with fire. They selected promising land, then deadened trees by girdling (or slashing) their trunks, then burned and reburned the wood. This is virtually the same swidden or "slash and burn" culture known to other peoples (including Europeans) throughout the world. And, like others, the Indians did not remove stumps but made little hills with primitive hoes and planted their maize, beans, squashes, and tobacco on old forest floors, disorderly-looking to the modern eye. Thin humus and wood ashes provided sufficient nutrients for several years' crops. Swiddens were then abandoned to return to the natural succession of grasses, shrubs, conifers, and finally deciduous trees (except in localities where pines were climax plants)—a process that took perhaps twenty to thirty years. Woodland folk turned to new-burned swiddens and ultimately might return to ground used earlier within their commuting territory.[6]

Indians also employed fire in hunting. In the woodlands of the East, fire opened forested places to sunlight, creating grassy meadows that attracted browsing deer; these deer might be harvested in bulk, so to speak, from meadows' perimeters. The method seems to anticipate the industrial, as do Indian harvests of river and bay fishes with woven seines. Such skills must have rendered the indigenes susceptible to European market temptations later, however. Indian fire practice no doubt occasionally got out of control, too, destroying more forest than needed for agriculture or hunting. Yet seldom did Indian fire cause permanent change in the environment.

Agriculture and systematic hunting and fishing sustained larger Indian populations than could have subsisted upon hunting and gathering alone. Still, indigenous populations and their cultural practices must have caused minimal environmental degradation, especially in comparison with modern commercial cultures. For notwithstanding their harvests of maize, meat, and fish, the Woodland peoples remained few in relation to the land and water they used. Swidden culture would seem unaesthetic to those of us accustomed to industrialized farming's symmetry, but lightly hoed hills on relatively flat ground eroded hardly at all; and the incinerated forests were soon abandoned to nature's healing succession. Indian hunting and fishing methods, too, for all their potential to satisfy a large market, seemed to the English hardly to have diminished the natural fecundity of a second Eden.

The English brought plows, harness, and European small grains to Jamestown. They intended to lay permanently bare the old forests, exposing soil to constant disturbance, permanent exploitation, and the certain hazards of wind and water erosion. The permanent implementation of European practice was very long in coming, however, as we shall see later. Immigrant populations remained too small for the giant labor of re-creating Europe. The wisdom of necessity instead dictated the adoption of Indian fire culture and swiddens until the numbers of British and African settlers mounted to an instrument capable of subduing the wilderness. This would take a century and a half. In the meantime, however, the English were easily able to turn rivers into roads.

The broad mouth of the three-branched Elizabeth tilts toward the west, almost facing the expansive mouths of the Nansemond and the James. The English named the ensemble of blue-gray thoroughfares Hampton Roads. The worldly men who have passed there have been hungry for what might be found along the rivers' banks and in the secrecies of the roads' remote sources.

Below its mouth the Elizabeth itself is a vast crooked cross. Eastern and western arms (called branches) extend deep into low, marshy plains. Their tributary creeks are deeper and often wider than ordinary rivers in the Middle West, such as the Great Miami in Ohio. The Elizabeth's main course (the Southern Branch), with its own many tributaries, penetrates the northeastern Dismal Swamp, draining, clarifying, then salinating its cola-colored waters. The Southern Branch, especially, is an emblem for the region, both as road and as metaphor: Its broad mouth was safe, inviting, cosmopolitan, the future site of rich clustered farms, cities, factories, depots, wharves, and shipyards; its Dismal (yet not so distant) sources were a jungle too dark for civilization.

In 1699 young Thomas Story seemed daunted by neither the Elizabeth nor its swampy extremities. But then he was a Quaker missionary, a type that deserves more respect than Jesuits in Brazil, for Quakers were more respectful of heathens. Story was a determined operative of the Society of Friends' remarkable wave of conversion and influence in North America toward the end of the seventeenth century. Discovering Virginia first at Chuckatuck, by the Nansemond, he traveled eastward to the Western Branch, then the entire length of the Southern Branch. Story took little notice of the city of Norfolk, chartered nineteen years before and platted beside the river at the mouth of the Eastern Branch. This prompts little wonder: The seat of Norfolk County contained only thirty-odd lot-holders then; the courthouse was hardly five years old. The would-be city languished, despite the English king's design, for the same reason that urban development failed throughout the Chesapeake world: Tobacco—in the transatlantic economy, the region's reason for being—was accessible to ocean-going traders at hundreds of planters' private wharves along every river to its fall line. So until the rural population

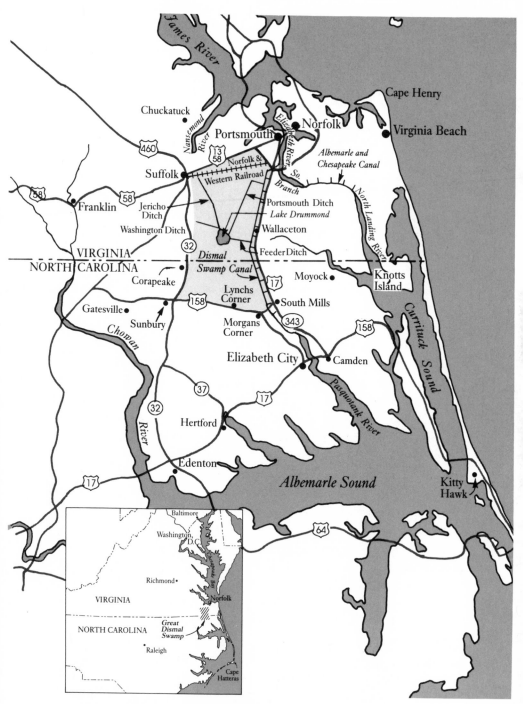

Map 2. *The James-Albemarle subregion (From Bland Simpson,* The Great Dismal
*[Chapel Hill: University of North Carolina Press, 1990], courtesy of the University of North
Carolina Press)*

massed sufficiently, especially west of the falls, to require town services, even the deepwater country would remain but a backwater to Philadelphia, New York, Boston, and especially the English ports.[7]

The scattered Anglo-Americans of southeastern Virginia—more than half a century after the Puritans came to Massachusetts Bay—seemed to Thomas Story "wholly ignorant of the Testimony of Truth, and little acquainted with Holy Scripture; and when the Truth was declared among them, some were amazed, others surprised; some afraid, and some a little affected with the invisible Power of Truth." Story's testimony was surely tinged with denominational partisanship. Yet the firestorm of Baptist and Methodist revivalism was still in the future; his rustic Elizabethan auditors were likely lapsed or unserved Anglicans, folks distant from churches and priests, perhaps unable to read the Bible.[8]

Curiously, as Story penetrated the Dismal Swamp, then entered northeastern North Carolina, crossing and recrossing Albemarle Sound, he encountered not only Indians, free blacks, and the plainest of white folks, but also many more Friends than northward. A Quaker smith near the Dismal in Virginia interpreted for Story an Indian spiritual life already deeply imbued with Christian language—and touched by an animal the English had introduced nearly a century before: The "divine Being," the smith explained, was "one that made all Things, and that he [*sic*] always beholds all the Indians as if they were comprehended together in a small circle." Bad Indians after death "go to a cold Country, where they are always hungry, cold, and in all Manner of Distress they can imagine." Good ones, on the other hand, "go to a warm Country, where they had fat Boar and Roasting Ears all the Year long; these being the most excellent Food they can imagine."[9]

Below the Dismal, Story met many Friends by "Piquimon's Creek" and the Little River. At meetings he noticed blacks and later engaged them in conversation. When Story queried one man as to how long he had attended such meetings, the response was "Always." So firmly were the Friends established in and around the great swamp and into North Carolina that while Story traveled, he spent but one night outside and alone, while crossing the Dismal itself.[10]

That Quakerism flourished not on the upper Elizabeth but at the foot of the cross, in the remote swamps, may be more than coincidence. For in the cosmopolitan Chesapeake world of Story's time and later, slavery was established by law and growing, along with social distance among whites. In England and in Philadelphia, Quakers numbered among the elite; but in other places, the Friends' theology had already led them to attack slavery and other class distinctions. Their tendency and culture were profoundly democratic; and so was the potential of nature in the Elizabeth's hinterland. Here was a countercultural place, where people removed themselves from disagreeable institutions economic and social and where enslavement was visible but relatively unimportant. By the end of the eighteenth century, Baptists and Methodists had eclipsed the Friends, but Quakers—and arguably the landscape itself, half-wild and remote from markets—had already influenced widespread private emancipations of slaves. By late-antebellum times, free black populations in some localities were nearly as large, sometimes larger, than slave populations. Some of these free blacks were nurtured spiritually in Friends institutions as late as 1850. That year in Virginia, Nansemond and Southampton Counties each had a meetinghouse, seating 250 and 200, respectively. In North Carolina, Northampton County's meetinghouse could accommodate 600, Pasquotank County's 800; and in Perquimans—where Thomas Story had found so many Friends—there were four meetinghouses with combined seating for 1,250.[11]

By 1850 the upper Elizabeth had largely achieved its cosmopolitan potential as urban and shipping center. Norfolk city's population passed 14,000. Portsmouth, across the river, had finally come into being during the 1750s. (Before then, it was marshes, farms, and a sporting place beyond Norfolk's law, a place sailors called Cock Island.) A century after William Crawford dedicated part of his farm to the city, Portsmouth had 8,122 white and black souls, with an additional 504 in the suburb of Gosport, where the federal government had established a naval shipyard that would later (and most curiously) be known as the Norfolk Naval Shipyard.

On both banks of the Elizabeth, business hummed: sawmills, brick kilns, gristmills, a ropewalk, factories making boots and shoes, clothing and hats, firearms, wagons and carriages, chemicals and drugs, books, and cigars. Wharves and warehouses took in fish from the river and bay as well as tons of produce from truck farmers, who, beginning during the 1840s, had lined the banks of the Eastern and especially the Western Branches of the Elizabeth. The "father of truckers" was Richard Cox of New Jersey, who had understood the feasibility of rapid, intensive cropping for northeastern urban markets. So in spring and early summer, the Elizabeth teemed with Yankee packets, laden with kale, lettuce, onions, strawberries, beans, cabbage, cucumbers, potatoes, and watermelon, bound for Baltimore, Philadelphia, and New York.[12]

Virginian packets and ocean-going ships plied these waters, too. Lighters (shallow-draft river vessels) brought up shingles and lumber from the swamps. Larger ships, often made in local yards, collected the swamps' axed and sawn resources from the lighters, then sailed off for American and European metropolises and to the Caribbean. Vessels engaged in the "West Indian trade" carried more grain—corn and wheat—than lumber, however. For since late colonial times, when tobacco culture moved west of the fall line, farmers from the Chesapeake, "Southside" (that is, south of the James), and nearby Carolina had devoted themselves to grain; and Norfolk thus became a regional export center.[13]

The Blow family—notably Richard, the progenitor (1746–1833)—were major architects of the upper Elizabeth's cosmopolitan development. Richard Blow maintained a country estate, Tower Hill, in still-remote Sussex County, to the west, but he and his son George focused their considerable energies and ingenuity upon Portsmouth and Norfolk. Richard built ships by the Elizabeth and sold grain, lumber, and other things in the West Indian trade. To further business Richard also became a founder, major stockholder, and president of the Dismal Swamp Canal Company, whose object was to connect the Elizabeth's Southern Branch with the Pasquotank River in North Carolina. Albemarle Sound's vast corn production might then pass quickly north, to Blow's ships; and the Canal Company would collect tolls on the traffic for its trouble. The canal itself would proceed directly through the Dismal Swamp—twenty-six miles of it, along a north-south route about three miles east of Lake Drummond. Black men, mostly slaves hired by the company, confronted the spongy peat, the morasses of vines, mosquitoes, and canebrake rattlesnakes, and the vast gum-cypress wilderness. In 1805, Virginia's state clerk at last announced that "a junction has been affected betwixt the waters of Elizabeth River and Pasquotank."[14]

The canal bed was not perfectly level, and there were no locks. Nor was the canal adequately supplied with water, for there was at first no "feeder ditch" from Lake Drummond to assure flotation. So the great would-be conduit was sometimes nearly dry, and the company collected but a few tolls, from shingle lightermen. Finally, following the War of 1812, locks and the feeder ditch to Drummond were constructed. As early as 1814 the first recorded substantial vessel was guided the length of the excavation. During the 1820s Congress bought into the project, Virginia guaranteed company bonds, and the canal was widened (to thirty-two feet) and deepened (to six and a half). In 1828 a steamer propelled itself from Norfolk to Elizabeth City. The following year President Andrew Jackson came to visit. A "collation" was held for him six miles south of Deep Creek (the canal's northern terminus); there the celebrants ate Virginia ham off cedar shingles.[15]

Dismal Swamp Canal: northern terminus at Deep Creek, Virginia (Photo by the author)

Thus was the Great Dismal opened—to comfortable travel and efficient trade, and to hotels, tourism, dueling, and trysting. A few steps beyond Drummond's shores and the banks of the canal and feeder ditch, however, the Dismal remained wild, a place fit only for rough shingle-getters, escaped slaves, white criminals, and desperate lovers. Nonetheless, the canal ultimately implied a near–death sentence upon the swamp; for, once opened, the Dismal became crisscrossed by other canals (or ditches, as they are more often called) and subject to more and more external market pressures. More immediately, geologists believe that shell spoil from digging the original canal route largely blocked swamp drainage toward the east. So sections of the swamp east of the canal slowly dried, and pioneers established large farms, especially opposite the feeder ditch at a place called Wallaceton. Ditching and drying—so-called reclamation—would ultimately reduce the swamp, by the mid-twentieth century, to barely a third its original size.[16]

George succeeded Richard as Blow patriarch a quarter century before the Civil War. At Tower Hill he built (with slave labor) an Edenic refuge for his family and friends, and a model of scientific agronomy. One August he advised a relative to come and "enjoy yourself up here. We can give you as fine Biscuits as you ever ate, and Honey. a Plenty of poultry & ... all the best

Dismal Swamp Canal: southern terminus at South Mills, North Carolina (Photo by the author)

fruit ... as good as I ever saw in my life[:] Peaches, Garden Grapes in abundance, Water & Musk Melons very fine and in profusion." George Blow was also an early correspondent and follower of Edmund Ruffin, who experimented with soil improvement in nearby Prince George County by the James. George and his sons were among the select few Virginia farmers who tried, then persisted with, Ruffin's prescription of marling for soil restoration.[17]

Perhaps logically, then, during 1860 and 1861, the Blows should have followed Ruffin to the triumph of secession and southern independence. But not so. For sentiment aside, it seems obvious that the family's cosmopolitan and commercial attachments to the Elizabeth were stronger than those to the plantation and slavery. Early in 1861, George Blow (who held the rank of general in Virginia's militia) was elected Norfolk's unionist delegate to the state secession convention. (James G. Holladay, another unionist, represented Portsmouth.) After Ruffin (reputedly, anyway) fired the first gun against Fort Sumter and Lincoln demanded volunteers to suppress the rebellion, the Elizabeth's urban citizens changed their minds and demanded that their delegates vote for secession.[18]

Soon the Confederates set about converting the USS *Merrimack* into an ironclad in Portsmouth's Gosport Naval Shipyard; rechristening it the *Virginia*, they used it to challenge the Union presence on Hampton Roads. The

Richard Blow monument, Cedar Grove Cemetery, Portsmouth (Photo by the author)

Virginia was checkmated by the *Monitor*, of course, and the rebels scuttled their dreadnought off Craney Island when their strategic situation became untenable. Early in the next year, 1862, George Blow's wisdom was brutally demonstrated. The Yankees came to the Elizabeth and did not leave. Local Confederate troops away at the front could not return to their families even if they survived battle. The occupying army, meanwhile, requisitioned public and private property, intimidated whites of suspicious loyalty, and finally liberated the slaves, arming the younger freedmen. At the end of 1863, the Yankees undertook to conclude a revolution begun by their presence on the Elizabeth and in Albemarle Sound.[19]

Between Norfolk/Portsmouth and Elizabeth City, and west to the Chowan and Roanoke, the war had begun to dissolve old institutions and social glue long before the Confederates' final capitulation. Black folks had long fled masters for camps in the swamps, sometimes making guerrilla war from these bases. Now the numbers of swamp maroons grew; and every time a Yankee gunboat appeared on a North Carolina river, slaves became free and the Union army swelled with local freedmen. Many whites of the lower and middling classes resisted the Confederacy, too—especially passively, by avoiding taxes and conscription when the Yankees were near. Following their loss of Roanoke Island early in 1862, the Confederates forfeited all the great sounds and northeastern North Carolina. Thereafter the government of the rest of the state sought to harass Yankees and unionists and to discipline remaining slaves in the region, with irregular military force. These troops, who seemed as dedicated to settling old scores with neighbors as to pursuing superior Yankee forces, were themselves soon reduced to swamp maroon status. But they were occasionally effective at potshotting gunboats and terrorizing detachments of Union troops they happened to catch, especially black soldiers.[20]

Then at the end of 1863, Benjamin Butler, the regional union commander, called forth a young brigadier named Edward Augustus Wild. The Massachusetts officer was aptly named, for to Confederates he shortly became a scourge more infamous than Butler himself—the Butler they later called Beast. Heading two regiments of U.S. Colored troops, Wild marched south along the Dismal Swamp Canal, laying waste to the property of southern sympathizers, taking white women hostages against the safety of black soldiers held by Confederate guerrillas, burning guerrilla camps and supplies, liberating slaves and recruiting more blacks into his ranks, and appropriating forage and other useful commodities, which he shipped to Roanoke Island and Norfolk. Three days after Christmas, Wild ordered the hanging of Daniel Bright, a native of Pasquotank County and Confederate guerrilla, in reprisal for the earlier hanging of an Ohio soldier. Bright's body was left on a tree, with a notice pinned to his back: "This Guerrilla Hanged by order of Brig. Gen. Wild."[21]

In the aftermath of the war, violence subsided—somewhat; but social divisions exacerbated by the conflict were cemented by the freedmen's acquisition of the vote. Black power came to the Elizabeth and to northeastern North Carolina, and it withstood the most determined opposition for longer than Republican government endured in either state capital.[22]

THE NANSEMOND

The western parallel to the Elizabeth is a much simpler river. Originating in the northwestern Dismal, particularly via a large creek the Anglo-Americans called Shingleyard (now simply Shingle), the Nansemond widens rapidly and drains magnificently into Hampton Roads. The Suffolk Scarp parallels the river near its western bank. Along the scarp, so rich in fossil shells, the aboriginals, an Algonquian-speaking people called the Nansemonds, established farms and their principal town, which lay on the site of present-day Suffolk. In 1611, when the English confronted the Nansemonds, their numbers included only (by English estimation) about two hundred warriors. The native men resisted, but their arrows would not pierce the Englishmen's armor. Recognizing that the invaders' guns used fire, the Indians called upon their priest to make rain. The English watched the priest dance about the riverbank with his "mad crew," shaking his rattle, throwing fire into the air, and shouting incantations. Rain indeed came—but some miles away, and the Nansemonds began to disappear. The English ate them, anthropologically speaking, by naming the river, and the new county around it, after the vanquished.[23]

Nansemond County, along with neighboring Gates County in North Carolina, had the densest swamps in the region. The river called Nansemond became a road that carried to the world the Great Dismal's trees, usually in the form of cedar shingles, so long as shingles remained North America's and northern Europe's common roofing material. River traffic in the agricultural commodities extracted from rich scarp farms would be only incidental, compared with wood from the swamp. But the swamp was for so long impenetrable. Shingle Creek was as mysterious as a tributary of the Orinoco or the Congo. So the Nansemond frustrated early settlers. Was the Dismal passable through its western side? Where did Virginia end, North Carolina begin?

A century after the English first explored, conquered, and named the Nansemond, William Byrd II appeared—in the winter of 1728—with his fellow commissioners, surveying crew, and baggage-carriers. Setting out from the Atlantic in Princess Anne County, the gentlemen and their entourage began to establish a "dividing line betwixt Virginia and North Carolina." Byrd wrote a clever, often erroneous, outrageously bigoted, and thoroughly engrossing secret history of the expedition. Allowing for his bias and irresistible wit, one still finds in Byrd's observations invaluable codas for aspects of swamp country culture.

From Princess Anne westward, for example, Byrd spotted "Booth Cattle and Hogs rambl[ing] in the Neighbouring Marshes and Swamps, where they maintain themselves the whole winter long, and are not fetch'd home till the Spring." Byrd thought this "ill Management," because settlers (those "Indolent Wretches") lost the meat from steers and swine that were never recovered during roundups. Also, cows set free part of the year yielded no milk part of the year. Below the dividing line, Byrd declared, "The only Business here is raising of Hogs, which is manag'd with the least Trouble, and afford the Diet they are most fond of. The Truth of it is the Inhabitants of N Carolina devour so much Swine's flesh, that it fills them full of gross Humours. For want too of a constant Supply of Salt, they are commonly obliged to eat it Fresh, and that begets the highest taint of Scurvy." Byrd thought that scurvy, when "Vitiated," became yaws and corrupted Carolinians' noses. Thus a pioneering Carolina joke—"after three good Pork years, a Motion had like to have been made in the [North Carolina] House of Burgesses, that a Man with a Nose shou'd be incapable of holding any Place of Profit in the Province."[24]

In fact, the open ranging of animals, especially swine, and a diet based on pork, along with the Indian staples of corn and beans, prevailed on the Virginia peninsula, Byrd's home ground, as well as in the Southside and Carolina. Both the open range and the pork-corn-beans diet persisted, too, for a very long while. During the Civil War soldiers ate up much of both the razorback and penned hog population, and many southerners (of both races) never quite recovered the independence that relied so heavily upon the open range. The range was finally closed, by law, only in the early twentieth century, and thereafter, more than coincidentally, ordinary people's diet, health, and physical appearance deteriorated to the point of international notoriety. Still, hardly anyone after Byrd noticed noselessness among the southern plain folk. Perhaps this was because range pork is lean, high in protein, and because beans provide the niacin and aminos to balance corn in a fundamentally healthy fare.[25]

Not unrelated to his perception of their poor diet was Byrd's portrait of ordinary people at work on both sides of the colonial border. From his comfortable lodging above the Dismal in Nansemond—Byrd kept his distance from hardship and rattlesnakes—the seigneur praised an exceptional white family he had met in the northern swamp: They showed "the happy Effects of Industry... the chearful Marks of Plenty." Yet "too Common, alas, in that Part of the World," Byrd continued, was "the Distemper of Laziness," which "seizes the Men oftener much than the Women. These last Spin, weave and knit, all with their own Hands, while their Husbands, depending on the Bounty of the Climate, are Sloathful in every thing but getting of Children, and in that only Instance make themselves useful Members of an Infant-Colony." After procreation, men slept late, lit their pipes and yawned, and leaned against their cornfield fences, in order "gravely [to] consider whether they had best go and take a Small Heat at the Hough: but generally [they] find reasons to put it off till another time." And so "they loiter away their Lives ... and at the Winding up of the Year Scarcely have Bread to Eat." Byrd concluded that white Virginians with "a thorough Aversion to Labor" were naturally drawn "to N Carolina, where Plenty and a Warm Sun confirm them in their Disposition to Laziness for their whole Lives."[26] So was born—or at least encouraged — the persistent legend of southern white laziness, which is virtually the same as the stigma of sloth attached to African Americans and to Indians, whose men also permitted women to perform the work most visible to travelers blinded by class prejudice.

Byrd's encounter with a family of mulatto herdsmen east of Nansemond, near the Northwest River, produced commentary hard of tone but loaded with verisimilitude. The group "call'd themselves free," he wrote, "tho' by the Shyness of the Master of the House, who took care to keep least in Sight, their Freedom seem'd a little Doubtful." Byrd understood that swamp country was refuge to the oppressed but that the refuge contained its own, more subtle, oppression for such families: "many Slaves Shelter themselves in this Obscure Part of the World, nor will any of their righteous [i.e., free white] Neighbours discover [i.e., betray] them. On the Contrary, they find their Account in Settling such Fugutives on some out-of-the-way-corner of their Land, to raise Stocks for a mean and inconsiderable Share, well knowing their Condition makes it necessary for them to Submit to any Terms."[27]

Free people of color (whether called mulatto or black) were ever so vulnerable and dependent, even in such obscure parts with friendly white Quakers about. In 1850 Nansemond's 12,283 souls included 2,144 "free colored" — almost half the number of slaves held in the county. Among the hundreds of households reported in the census that year were many modest property owners of seeming independent status: Jack Douglass, a fifty-year-old mulatto, was identified as a "laborer," but he owned $900 in property and supported a large family. Jim Bouzer, a forty-year-old black man, was a farmer with land and equipment worth $1,200. Temple Skeeter, a middle-aged mulatto woman, had $201. Henry White, a young black farmer, owned $800. And Jacob Holland, a middle-aged black carpenter, had $270. Other heads of households with tiny property values were identified as farmers, laborers, and sailors. Enumerators did not list the occupations of female heads of households, of which there were many in Nansemond. The grand total of propertied free-colored households was only 46, however, and in these presumably secure homes lived only 260 people, a small fraction of the county's total. So the great preponderance of such folks were without property. The poor majority were usually called laborers, and they lived as nuclear or extended families on someone else's property; or they lived singly or with a child or sibling in a white household, as farm laborers and domestic servants. A number of Nansemond's free people of color — some with modest property, some without, men surnamed Lassiter, Read, Riddick, Skeeter — appear also as shingle-getters in the records of the Dismal Swamp Land Company, which was the corporate giant of the great swamp and a source of cash for people with very little.[28]

In William Byrd's history one discovers again the coincidence of swampland, free people of color, and Quakers. Of the last Byrd wrote disdainfully: "We passt by no less than two Quaker Meeting Houses, one of which had an Awkward Ornament on the West End of it, that seem'd to Ape a Steeple. I must own I expected no such Piece of Foppery from a Sect of so much outside Simplicity." Byrd mourned the "want of Ministers [i.e., Anglican] to Pilot the People a decenter way to Heaven." Meanwhile, according to Byrd—who deserves to be punned—a friendlier "persuasion prevail[ed] much in the lower end of Nansimond county."[29]

Byrd's misunderstanding and hostility toward the Dismal itself, in this lower end of the county, was yet more profound. He could concede "one Beauty," that being the swamp's "continual Verdure," which was owing to "the Moisture of the Soil." Yet "at the same time the foul Damps ascend without ceasing, corrupt[ing] the Air, and render[ing] it unfit for Respiration. Not even a Turkey-Buzzard will venture to fly over it, no more than the Italian Vultures will over the filthy Lake Avernus." Byrd thought it "remarkable that towards the middle of the Dismal no Beast or Bird or even Reptile can live, not only because of the softness of the Ground, but likewise because it is so overgrown with Thickets, that the Genial Beams of the Sun can never penetrate them." This was the same Dismal thought fit for resorts in the next century, and whose waters were eagerly sought for their purity, taste, and portability by ships' captains. Byrd's solution to the swamp's pestilential menace, meanwhile, was reclamation. "It woul'd require a great Sum of Money to drain it," Byrd allowed, "but the Publick Treasure cou'd not be better bestow'd than to preserve the Lives of his Magesty's Liege People, and at the same time render so great a Tract of Swamp very Profitable, besides the advantage of making a Channel to transport by water-carriage goods from Albemarle Sound into Nansimond and Elizabeth Rivers, in Virginia."[30]

The channel from the Elizabeth to the sound appeared a century later, and Byrd would hardly be the last to propose draining the Great Dismal. Edmund Ruffin was among the notables who followed him, not for reason of public health and profit but for Ruffin's own peculiar reasons, which we shall assay later. In the meantime, the civilization of Nansemond proceeded apace. A quarter-century after Byrd passed by, the county paid bounties for the killing of twenty-nine wolves. A sharpshooter named William Butt claimed seven of them, alone. Seventy-five years later, Edmund Ruffin recorded a clamor south of Suffolk, where citizens hunted a lone male—the first seen in many

Jericho Ditch, facing north toward Suffolk, 1991 (Photo by the author)

Ruin of lock connecting Shingleyard Creek (left) with Jericho Ditch (right), Suffolk, 1991 (Photo by the author)

years and, as it turned out, the Dismal's last wolf. Farmers finally enticed the hapless creature to his demise with the aid of a large estrous dog.[31]

By the time of this event, Hampton Roads led directly to the heart of the swamp. Jericho Ditch, straight as an arrow, fed water from Lake Drummond north to Shingleyard Creek at Suffolk, and thence to the Nansemond River. Jericho lighters were fed by shingle carts — usually those of the Dismal Swamp Land Company; the lighters brought the bounty to the functionally named creek, and the world soon had its roofing and siding.[32] Suffolk thus became important enough to be fought over, as it was during the spring of 1862, when Yankees laid siege, forced the Confederates away, and ultimately wrecked the Dismal Swamp Land Company's assets and future.[33] Other enterprises would supply the Dismal's wood to the world for almost another century, but the world discovered an alternate roofing material just after the Civil War, and the age of shingles was over. Suffolk would never be the same.

THE PERQUIMANS

Seeping, merging swamp waters in Gates County, North Carolina, just east of the Suffolk Scarp, become a stream, then a broad river as lovely as its

Shingle Creek (formerly Shingleyard), meandering southward toward Nansemond River
(Photo by the author)

name, Perquimans. By the time the river reaches the town of Hertford (the seat of Perquimans County), its span is more than half a mile; below Hertford the Perquimans's cypress-stained waters exceed two miles before they merge with Albemarle Sound.

Just above Hertford, from U.S. Route 17, beside the river, one notices Spanish moss draped from twisted gray branches of cypresses standing in the water. Here is approximately the northern limit of this romantic emblem of the South. One may be reminded by the moss that this odd subregion between the James in Virginia and the Albemarle in Carolina is the northern limit also of the longleaf pine—a few stands remain in southern Isle of Wight County, Virginia—and the northern limit of the canebrake rattlesnake, the largest viper in North America. The subregion is, measurably, the top of the Southeast, the beginning of what is called "southern"—separated from the Chesapeake and the Middle Atlantic not only by scarps and drainage but also by climate and variations in flora and fauna.[34]

Once the people of the Albemarle were not so separate from the rest of the world, however. Settlers, most of them from Virginia and England, planted great crops of corn, then wheat as well, along the mouths of the North, Pasquotank, Little, Perquimans, Chowan, and Roanoke Rivers, and on the south side of the sound by Bull Bay and the wide Alligator River.

Cypresses with Spanish moss on bank of Perquimans River, near Hertford, North Carolina, 1990 (Photo by the author)

Gathered and packed in barrels, huge grain surpluses were shipped—albeit with risk—through an inlet connecting Currituck Sound and the Atlantic. Then, in 1728, a hurricane closed the inlet. Thereafter, ships' captains were obliged to sail eastward from Albemarle to Pamlico Sound, then south past Manteo and Roanoke Island to Oregon Inlet; or safer yet, farther south to Ocracoke Island and its inlet. Yet such was the wealth to be had in shipping grain to the West Indies that the ditching and draining of plantations continued, and the fringes of the Albemarle, at least, remained firmly in the grip of the world market and of the institution of slavery.[35] The valley and county of Perquimans, then, present curiously contrasting worlds through the colonial era and much of the nineteenth century: Near the river's mouth a heterogeneous population was preoccupied with the market; a few miles inland lay a hinterland of subsisting or semisubsisting farmers, woodsfolk (including free blacks), and Quakers.

Thomas Nicholson (1715–80) presents a certain intersection of the two worlds. A prominent Quaker minister and writer—and a plantation owner—he traveled and reported much that is revealing of the Albemarle country. As a young Friends leader during the 1740s, for example, Nicholson set out for Cape Fear (at the southeastern corner of the colony) with his wife and others to attend a quarterly meeting. This round-trip "journey of seven hundred and thirty-five miles" was accomplished overland, in forty days. Nicholson and his party spent nights in the homes of brother and sister Quakers every night but one, when they "lay in the woods." A quarter century later (in 1771) Nicholson attended another quarterly meeting, this one in Hyde County; the trip involved a boat-crossing of Albemarle Sound, then a clockwise, over-land return to Perquimans through present-day Northampton, Bertie, and Chowan Counties. Along the way Nicholson was received cordially by the colonial governor, his council, and legislators; and from his journal it ap-pears that his party lodged with Friends every night.[36]

Nicholson's missionary perambulations in the region were grander than Thomas Story's, but one is struck by the similarities in the Quaker network over the course of three-quarters of a century. Story and Nicholson shared a concern for Africans in America, too. Nicholson condemned the institution of slavery as an immoral infringement on the spirituality and the bodies of blacks, who had not been consulted about their enslavement. Toward the end of his life Nicholson coped with a slave trader whom he suspected of selling freed blacks. The trader had in fact admired Nicholson's own "many young Negros," but in 1779—amid the American Revolution—the Quaker was at last busy manumitting his human chattels.[37]

Freed of British rule, grain traders of the Chesapeake and Albemarle alike were also disconnected from their lucrative links with the West Indies. Some of these and other Latin American partners were recovered, however, by 1808, when yet another missionary appeared on the sound. John Early was a Methodist divine from the Virginia upcountry. Unfamiliar with this peculiar maritime world, Early found "the most corrupted place I ever saw in town or country." It was a place of "seafaring men and I have thought that (with a few exceptions) from the consequences that attend them and their manner of life, when men engaged in the seafaring business that they set themselves to work wickedness, as bad or worse than Ahab of old did." Early must have been reminded of Norfolk and Portsmouth, where he discovered twin dens of iniquity—"so much wickedness in public"—and where he was nearly drowned by a drunken Elizabeth River ferryman. But Albemarle was also a diseased sinkhole. From mid-August to November 1808, Early was quite "un-well" with agues and fever and was reduced to being transported about in a chair. He sought relief on a Currituck beach, but finally retreated to a physi-cian near Norfolk, who cured him—so Early thought—with medicines and a restorative diet.[38] Early was almost certainly suffering from malaria, whose symptoms usually subside by November anyway.

Faith and business have ever kept vulnerable outsiders in unhealthy locales. Eleven years after Early's retreat from Albemarle Sound, a young New England merchant and teacher reported from Hertford to his family in Bridgewater, Massachusetts, that "The country is filled with yankees[.] There are no less than four vessels in this river with goods, or potatoes ... rum Sugar mol[lasse]s Butter & Cheese, which the Inhabitants call a yankee cargo. There are two shoe makers from Barnstable at work here." [39] Clearly, Albemarle folks remained colonials in the economic sense. From their land and waters they extracted and exported grain, fish, shingles, and lumber. Yet their climate discouraged dairying and prohibited sugar culture; they had no local salt, and few manufactures of any sort. So Hertford, Elizabeth City, Edenton, Plymouth, and other Albemarle ports consumed mountains of imports, most of them with value added by manufacturing.

William S. Leonard was the Yankee who reported on other Yankees on the Perquimans. In 1819 he arrived in Hertford to participate in trade and to inculcate literacy at the local schoolhouse. At first he did well, at least in the former endeavor. Leonard reported to his parents in April that he had taken goods worth "about three hundred dollars" in a boat up the Alligator (across the sound) and sold them "at a profit of 100%." He also contracted with Hertford neighborhood parents to teach for a salary of $100 per quarter. The pay was good, but the job problematic. Leonard had forty-two students, some of them "Large schollars from different parts of the county." A twenty-one-year-old six-footer he finally ejected as hopelessly disorderly. Leonard also concluded that Carolina parents were unrealistic in their expectations: "People here have a very strange notion of education. They no nothing about grammar themselves and are very anxious their children should studdy it and every thing else at once"—that is, all in one quarter. "The fact is they never had much education themselves and want their children should have what they got in one quarter[.]" Whites' everyday conversation reflected Perquimans County's lowly cultural level as well: Society was dull. "When ever I happen to meet with any of the young people," Leonard complained, "their principal talk is the price of corn and wh[e]at[,] and some times the old brethren as they are called here begin as soon as the Blessing's given to enquire how the markets are, of one another whether wheat is like to rise[.]" [40]

Hertford's black folks, on the other hand, entertained the Yankee. During his first Christmas season in Perquimans, Leonard observed (without recognizing its cultural antecedents or significance) an exotic African–West Indian ritual, transplanted to Albemarle: "It is high times with the Negroes[:] for twelve days they keep Christmas or have liberty to play & visit. There is an old man they call John Canoe dressed in rags going about the streets and a great company following him and halloeing Caperring etc in order to get money to buy Rum[.] He appears every year at Christmas & goes through with the manouvers of jumping or stepping while two negroes bat one on a tin pail and the other on a jaw bone."[41]

A year later young Leonard sold Albemarle corn to Boston and imported small amounts of salt, cheese, nails, powder, and shot. These he sold in Hertford from a little store he operated with his brother, Isam. But a depression followed the national economic panic of 1819, and the Leonards feared the corn might not "fetch as much as it cost." They had reason to fear, too, that their neighbors' impoverishment would ruin the store. Two years later the brothers gave up and moved to Windsor, a town on the Roanoke in Bertie County; but times remained hard. Then, during the summer of 1825, Isam fell ill. William took him to Hertford to recover, but returned to Windsor ill himself. A business acquaintance reported to New England the "painful intelligence" of what followed: William "was attacked very violently with Bilious fever which lasted nine days." Thus weakened, he succumbed to "the Typ[h]us fever," which "set in and he was reduced very fast." So hardly six and a half years after his arrival upon the Albemarle, poor Leonard's body was interred in remote Carolina, another little monument to New England, to the market, and to the dangers of swamp country.[42]

In St. Paul's churchyard in Edenton stands another monument, over the grave of an Albemarle native, Tristrim Lowther Skinner (1820–62). This memorial might be said to commemorate a dangerous market as well: in this case the plantation economy, in whose cause Major Skinner fell at Mechanicsville, near Richmond, at the age of forty-two. Skinner's sudden and premature demise was so tragic—he left an adoring wife and young children —but in a sense so logical, too. For Skinner, as much as any dead Confederate, represented uncomplicated defense of class and country. The Skinners were Episcopalian, well-educated and -traveled, and powerful—perfect representatives of the Albemarle country's antebellum beautiful people. Based in Edenton, the Skinners owned plantations and businesses on both sides of the western sound. And as the family grew, the Skinners expanded their holdings. Perquimans County, just to the east of their Edenton headquarters, was the frontier on which the family placed surplus slaves and young Skinner men.[43]

Joseph B. Skinner, Tristrim's father, had established a satellite plantation in Perquimans by 1821—when William and Isam Leonard still operated their

store in Hertford, and when Alabama and Mississippi were still raw frontiers. Perquimans-away-from-the-river in fact resembled low sections of the
old Southwest. The elder Skinner's slaves cultivated some cotton in Perquimans, but his main crops were the prevalent grains. Twenty years later, as
Tristrim came of age, he and his father cut yet another new plantation from
the Perquimans forests, thirteen miles from Hertford. Tristrim recorded the
adventure for his future wife, who lived in Williamsburg, Virginia: They had
"moved to Perquimans county where we have established ourselves in the
midst of the wild woods. When we first came to it (we call it Mansion house)
it was the most dreary looking place you ever heard of, but even now it looks
much better, and begins to show what it will be in time. In a few years, with
proper improvements we will have one of the prettiest situations in the country." Tristrim, who had attended school in New Haven, Philadelphia, and
Williamsburg, allowed that Mansion House was rather isolated for him: He
wished he "could only see a little more of the world"; yet he declared "that a
farming life suits me very well." [44] So it would seem.

The 1850 census of Perquimans County reveals no fewer than eight slaveholding white men named Skinner. Most are grouped in the manuscript returns, indicating that they were neighbors. Together they held 230 people in
bondage. Tristrim alone had 79 slaves, but agriculture was not all. Joseph
Skinner owned a large fishery on the Chowan. Fisheries consisted of stations
on opposite riverbanks, boats, seines and supporting stanchions, packing-
houses, and a great deal of labor. In Perquimans, Joseph's relatives Charles W.
Skinner and Charles, Jr., owned two fisheries: Together they were capitalized
at $14,000, employed ninety-five men and twenty-four women, and produced
nearly 2,800 barrels of herring and 380 barrels of shad. Tristrim Skinner
also operated a stave business in Perquimans (which was not reported in the
census): In 1848 he estimated that 100,000 were "hauled to the landings on
Yeopin Creek & Perquimans river." [45]

Grain surpluses and fish alike moved on boats and ships, in barrels made
of staves. Before the Civil War the Skinner clan had not only settled themselves in the Perquimans frontier but had also moved into every extrac-
tive business known to generate profit. They were eastern counterparts—
although hardly ever recognized as such—to the men who made a cotton
kingdom of the contemporary Southwest.

THE CHOWAN

This beautiful Carolina river drains much of Southside Virginia into Albemarle Sound. Viewed from a simple map, south to north, the Chowan is a gently winding expanse, ever narrowing above Edenton until it ends at the border between Hertford and Gates Counties in North Carolina and Southampton County in Virginia. There the Chowan bifurcates and changes names: The Blackwater twists northerly and northeasterly, past Franklin, then Zuni, up in Isle of Wight County, where the river is tiny most of the year. The Nottoway arches and coils away northwesterly, past Monroe—birthplace of William Mahone, the railroad engineer and Confederate general—and past Courtland (once called Jerusalem), seat of Southampton and the scene of North America's most notorious slave uprising, that of Nat Turner in 1831.

That Southampton and Sussex Counties (to the northwest) were not organized until the mid-eighteenth century testifies to the Nottoway's unnavigability and the countryside's remoteness from markets. During the nineteenth century, steamboats occasionally reached Monroe, only a few miles north of the Chowan. Today, after the Army Corps of Engineers' ministrations, the Nottoway is navigable only a few more miles above Monroe—to Delaware, where a railroad bridge's supports obstruct traffic. The Blackwater was and remains little better for navigation. During the eighteenth and early nineteenth centuries, boats ascended but only about seven miles, to South Quay, where a customshouse and warehouses had been established for colonial tobacco exchange. Dredging extended navigation a little more than five miles, to Franklin, which became the pivot for travel from western Albemarle to Suffolk and Portsmouth. The Virginia overland trip was eased enormously, at last, in 1835, when a segment of the Portsmouth & Roanoke Railroad reached Franklin.[46] This was the earliest step in the lengthy process of defeating drainage and establishing human east-west linearity across the bottom of southeastern Virginia. In the meantime folks struggled with nature's inconvenient designs.

As late as the spring of 1806, Edenton was still the last outpost of civility before a raw hinterland to the north. To William Lay Smith, a young physician from Connecticut, rawness equaled opportunity, just as it did to his fellow New Englanders, the Leonards, who would follow him down shortly. Smith's three-week ship passage from New York was more difficult than usual owing to fierce winds off the Virginia Capes, among other man- and nature-made troubles. Once in Edenton, Smith explored prospects within a fifty-mile radius. He decided finally upon a place called Pitch Landing, up the Chowan. "The people here are far more hospitable and obliging than at the Northward," he informed his parents, "but not so inteligent [*sic*]." There would not be another doctor within twenty miles; and "within a few months ... I shall charge some hundreds of dollars. This I am encouraged to expect. The medical harvest is in August — Oct. & Sept[.]" — that is, the malarial season of agues and fever.[47]

Smith did harvest. He received, in "The customary mode," a rate of "forty cents a mile for travel, Fifty cents for a purge or puke & a dollar for bleeding or extracting a tooth etc etc." Smith discovered a land virtually without commercial drugs, however. The locals "expect a physician here to keep as much medicine as an apothecary," so he probably earned more money selling drugs sent from New York. Yet except for the malarial season, Smith found that Chowan valley "inhabitants are so healthy that they [doctors] must take a greater circuit" in order to earn a living.[48] So Smith rode his horse much about Hertford County, and he learned a landscape and rural culture strikingly different from Connecticut's. To his credit, Smith (so unlike other Yankee newcomers) did not interpret differentness as primitive or slothful.

Smith observed, for example, that the Chowan valley was fertile but problematic. It might "produce most luxuriant crops of corn, cotton, rice etc etc if it could be drained." The land was too low and the Chowan so high in spring and at other, unpredictable times, however, that most farmers demurred. Reclamation seemed an unwise investment. Cultivated land, then, consisted in the main of parcels of "low lands as are not likely to be flooded" and "the best of their pine lands." Pinelands are thin, sandy, and relatively unproductive, so farmers planted their corn hills far apart in order to supply sufficient nutrients from marginal soil. Disturbance of so much soil, however, invited heavy grass infestations in corn. Farmers responded with a technique later called cross-plowing — or as Smith wrote, "They plow their corn both ways." This practice efficiently lessened both weedy competition with corn and labor-heavy hoeing. Corn production by the Chowan was not so great as in the Roanoke valley a short distance to the west, where "they have no pines." Still, "The generality of the farmers ... think no more of raising a hundred barrels (5 bushel to the barrel) than you [of Connecticut] do of raising a hundred bushels." For corn was central, not only to the market but to the local culture as well. "They rely altogether upon their crops of corn," Smith noted, "for bread, for fattening their hogs and keeping their horses. They strip off the leaves of the corn for fodder as they cut no hay."[49]

Corn land wore out, and farmers were forever clearing new fields; this modified swidden system adopted both the Indians' principal method and their principal crop. Smith also observed, however, that hinterland people valued their trees for Yankee-sensible economic reasons: Trees fed "a great many hogs and some cattle, all of which run at large in the woods during summer and keep fat." Likewise, farmers raised turpentine and tar directly from the longleaf pines. This was wintertime work for white men and their slaves, and the business kept "Six or eight vessels ... constantly employed" at Pitch Landing in 1806. Finally, Smith himself entered the naval stores enterprise; it was irresistible to him, and ill health in Hertford was not earning him an adequate livelihood. Bad luck plagued Smith and his partner from the start, though: President Jefferson embargoed trade with the British, a major client for piney products; then came the War of 1812, which virtually ruined the business.[50] Smith's surviving papers do not reveal his ultimate fate on the Chowan. That of the river and its pines and pinelands unfolded more certainly.

Conceivably, in December 1806 the young Dr. Smith might have attended the birth of William D. Valentine at Oaklawn (also rendered Oak Lawn), a plantation near Bethel and Winton, in Hertford County. Or a little later, perhaps Smith attempted to ameliorate the childhood illness that left William lame for life. Poor fellow: William hoped so desperately for love but lived alone, a mockery of his surname; and he yearned for economic security and public acclaim, but lived near penury, receiving pity and disdain from white men of his class. Read in the law but finding no suitable place, William moved to Windsor in 1837 to teach school. This was not successful, so he went home, then to a most humble law office in Winton, but again with little success. Maintaining his little base in Hertford's seat, William commuted to courts in Bertie, Northampton, Gates, and Chowan Counties, searching for business. He found little, and often retreated, profoundly depressed, to Oak Lawn, where he gradually recovered, after his fashion, through comfortable solitude, walking, riding, and hunting. Little wonder that William kept a diary, one that grew large with expressions of bright expectation, delight with small pleasures, yearning happy and painful, dead boredom, disappointment, anger, whining complaint, humiliation, self-righteousness, and at last, as he approached fifty, the comfort of God's grace.[51] A century and a half after William quit writing, one reads with impatience and a pity he would certainly have loathed, but also with deepening appreciation—both for Valentine as a fellow human and for Valentine as a keen eyewitness. For while William's oeuvre was often distorted by frustration and depression, it was nearly always vivid; and through his Chowan countrywide perambulations one may see again, almost as on film, not only personalities but also landscape and culture.

Valentine's generation, for example, was the first to enjoy speeded connection with urban southeastern Virginia. From Oak Lawn he and his family drove or rode a few miles to Winton, where they could board a steamboat bound for Franklin, then via "the steam cars" to Portsmouth, and a quick ferry ride over the Elizabeth to Norfolk. Winton may have become, by 1853, "a dilapidated, antiquated partially deserted looking place," in William's view; but it was "not [a] secluded place from the great travelling world. A noble river rolls by its banks floating argosy by sail and steam." [52]

The Chowan's enhanced function as floater of trade in no way diminished its role as commercial fishery. Valentine cherished the annual runs of herring and shad not only because they heralded spring but also because the opening of fisheries occasioned an outdoor society that could not exclude him. At the Mount Pleasant fishery in April 1839, William "rambled about the banks viewing the scenery which was fine. I ensconced myself on the cliffs of a bank where I had a view of three counties, namely, Hertfort, Gates and Chowan." Four years later he opined that "people living remote from the great fishing rivers might with pleasure read a chapter on the Chowan fishing Spring. At this season of the year, fishing is the most intensely exciting business here of any. The whole country around are engaged ... back[ing] ... their carts and waggons to the beautiful river." And much later, while in Bertie County (at Colerain) trying to conduct business, William went "to the Pick Nick on the River" at a fishery situated atop what was "supposed to be an Indian burial" ground. "Perhaps the bowels of that hill might unfold wonders," he thought. Mostly William delighted in "the broad river ... and valley, variegated blossom and green leaf, and the green grass on which the girls walk and sit right down on." It was a party primarily for the young, with but "a few *old fogies*"; later there was "music and dancing." [53]

Valentine's observation of the exploitation of Chowan region's longleaf pines was both without delight and without Dr. Smith's unreflective greed. In 1843 a contemporary of Valentine's, the New York City editor and poet William Cullen Bryant, had remarked upon deadened stands in the region while journeying southward from Richmond: "We passed through extensive forests of pine," Bryant wrote, "which had been boxed, as it is called, for the collection of turpentine." Woodsmen had made large chevron-shaped cuts in longleaf trunks and attached collecting boxes below each. Too many boxes per tree overdrained the pines, or simply girdled them, as Bryant saw it. "This is a work of destruction; it strips acre after acre of these noble trees, and, if it goes on, the time is not far distant when the long-leaved pine will become nearly extinct in this region."[54] Valentine need not have been aware of Bryant's doleful (and quite accurate) assessment. He lived on this ground. Both an aesthete and a would-be creature of business, Valentine prescribed what would later be called conservationist forestry.

"[T]urpentine now being a good price," he wrote at the end of 1845, "the labor you bestow on it is now richly compensated. ... The question [is] how to cultivate your pines to best advantage." Valentine thought that boxing "the same crop of pines" year after year "is wrong. You should tend one year, then let them rest one year, and so on alternately as long as you choose. But if you think proper to let them rest [for] three years, the pines will be decidedly benefitted; they recover from the drains of its fluid which is its blood." Valentine was positive that resting pines would pay in the long run, but there seems more than a glimmer of doubt in his diary that woodsmen would resist killing longleafs for quick profit. Valentine probably persisted in public, as he did privately, with his sensible advice, however. He was that sort of fellow. He argued that over-boxing, too, was unwise: "The first egregious error committed heretofore over and often and which you should guard against—is the chopping of too many boxes in a pine. Frequently in a common sized pine there are three or four boxes cut. This, besides exhausting the pine faster than it can supply the oil, deprives the tree of so much bark at once that the tree soon dies." Valentine thought "The largest pines should rarely have more than three boxes—most of them not more than two." He was absolutely right; and while Valentine never used the word "extinct," as Bryant had, his prescription echoed the counterpoint.[55]

All in vain. For up the Nottoway and Blackwater, and down through the Carolina counties by the Chowan, men boxed and collected and distilled in the woods. Franklin, South Quay, Monroe, Winton, Colerain, and Edenton were entrepôts for the thousands of barrels of turpentine that, by the beginning of the twentieth century, brought Bryant's prediction to fruition. Ninety years after the poet, another Yankee traveler—the botanist M. L. Fernald—passed along approximately the same southeasterly route from Richmond to North Carolina. Fernald assumed that the longleaf was utterly extinct in Virginia, when he spotted a few survivors in southern Isle of Wight County, by the Blackwater near Franklin. These seem to have been harvested by the

Camp Manufacturing Company (now Union Camp) shortly afterward. However, a few of their offspring, now about seventy years old, rise splendidly in the Blackwater Ecologic Preserve.[56] An outdoor museum surrounded by corporate loblolly pine plantations, the preserve encompasses often-burnt stumps of old longleafs that still reveal the tell-tale signs of boxing, the remains of a turpentine still, and, delightful to the eye and touch, very young longleafs. Better than most, this museum signifies dramatic centuries in humans' long and ambiguous relationship with the rest of nature.

PART ONE

The Cosmopolitans

I THE MARINERS

The merchants [of Suffolk]... were in the habit of making semi-annual trips to lay in their supplies for the Spring and Fall trade. Some went to Philadelphia and others to New York.... Sometimes several merchants would get aboard of a shingle vessel and take a sea voyage around the coast and enjoy themselves hugely. — James Andrew Riddick, *on the 1830s and 1840s*

"A farm is another name for a chemical laboratory. It is only another way of manufacturing." — copied into the diary of Richard Eppes, 1859

The cosmopolitan elites of the James-Albemarle subregion—whether merchants or planters—were in a real sense all mariners. They shipped out with their shingles, like James Riddick's Suffolk contemporaries; or, like Richard and George Blow of Portsmouth-Norfolk—planters, merchants, canal-builders—they actually constructed and sailed ships. Owners of great farms by the banks of Albemarle Sound as well as the deep Virginia rivers sailed, too. They were often saltwater travelers, but at home they owned skiffs, lighters, and larger vessels; some carried compasses for navigating in rain, dark, and fog. For all of the cosmopolitans, whether they lived in towns or estates beside the great watercourses, a huge world of commodities and culture lay at their door, and they partook. They were a linear class, well-traveled of necessity but also seekers of sights and pleasures, sometimes of learning as well. Most were formally educated, some quite well, a few abroad. Some spoke Continental languages, mostly French. Most were comfortable in Baltimore, Philadelphia, and New York. Some were familiar with Europe, a few knew points beyond. They were recognizable by their good dress and confident carriage. They were the beautiful people of their time. Eighteenth-century examples included William Byrd II and the merchant-planter magnates of the Albemarle. Their nineteenth-century descendants were hardly less worldly.

The Skinners of Edenton and Perquimans County, for instance, seem not to have toured Europe, as did many of their equals and contemporaries; but they were never home-locked provincials. Tristrim Lowther Skinner's father and uncle conducted business in Norfolk, Philadelphia, and New York; and with their wives and children they vacationed at Nag's Head on the Carolina Outer Banks, at the Virginia springs, and in Saratoga Springs, New York, and Newport, Rhode Island. By the time young Tristrim—the family called him Trim—was seven (in 1827), he was lodged in a school in New Haven, Connecticut, along with his older sister Penelope, and was writing clear letters to his parents in Edenton. Seven years later, at fourteen, Trim boarded in a Philadelphia school and began his New Year's greetings to his father, "Mon cher Papa."[1]

Trim's educational exile from the Albemarle ended in 1840, when he took his baccalaureate degree at the College of William and Mary. As we saw earlier, the next year began his initiation into frontier planting and stave-getting in Perquimans's "wild woods." For a twenty-one-year-old used to the linearity of steamers and the new railroads, this was an exile of another sort. Trim did his duty in the swamps, but his restlessness was transparent. What made it worse was that before he left Williamsburg, he had fallen in love with Eliza Harwood, who remained in the Virginia town and was the object, it would seem, of continual local male attention.[2]

So poor Trim spent many evenings and rainy days at his writing desk, trying from long distance to charm, persuade, lure. Eliza was interested but hesitant, almost charmed but noncommittal—for nearly *six years*. The persistent Trim's despondency must have been visible, for a kind uncle finally offered (early in 1847) not only solace but timeless advice as well: E. L. Skinner was "truly sorry for your disappointment" because he "always believed that your heart was really interested." Yet "my dear Trim," he went on, "it is human nature to love only those who love in return and if you really believe the lady when she says she does not love you, you must soon cease to love her. I hope for *your sake* as much as for your fathers, that you will before very long turn your attention to some other lady." Readers of the Trim-Eliza correspondence cannot be certain why Eliza hesitated so long, then refused Trim. Chemistry and electricity ever govern us mortals. But perhaps morphology and linearity, too: Perquimans's remoteness may have figured large.[3]

But Trim and Eliza resumed their letter-writing in 1848 and married, at long last, in 1849. Eliza's prospects in the little Virginia crossroads may have diminished; or, one must conclude from later, very affectionate, correspondence, that Trim's persistence sparked something sweeter than resignation in Eliza. The married couple corresponded often during the 1850s because Trim succeeded his father as business traveler. He was off to Norfolk, Baltimore, Philadelphia, and so on, buying and selling; and to nearer places, representing St. Paul's Church at diocesan conventions. In Trim's letters to his wife, one watches the coastal world shrink, linearity become more streamlined, as steamers and railroads expand and improve. The same is true, on a smaller geographical scale, in the 1861–62 correspondence. Trim had organized the Albemarle Guards (afterward Company "A" of the First Regiment of North Carolina Volunteers) and become their captain. He was off to Virginia, the war, rapid promotion, and an early demise. Mail between Edenton and Richmond took no more than five days, more often three, sometimes but two. Eliza learned of Trim's death on 26 June 1862 only two days later, via a Western Union telegram from Raleigh: "Maj. Skinner is dead. Shot through breast. Body on way."[4]

Four months later, Edmund Ruffin drove out from Richmond and "passed through part of the battleground of the Mechanicsville engagement." There he witnessed a ghoulish spectacle that reminded him of reports from the Manassas battlefield the previous year. Participants from more southerly parts — "where buzzards are so plenty that any dead body left exposed for a few hours will bring them in numbers sufficient to soon devour it" — had remarked "that not one of these birds was visible, though thousands of carcas[s]es of men & horses were exposed over miles, & for days together, & many for weeks." Ruffin offered the consensus explanation: that "all the buzzards within reach of the sound were frightened & driven far off by the noise of the artillery." Now he observed "The same remarkable absence of buzzards" at Mechanicsville, where "probably 20,000 dead bodies of men & horses were scattered" immediately after the battle, and where in late October "many bodies, either left unburied, or not entirely covered by the slight burying, were exposed to both the senses of sight & smell, for weeks, or until nothing was left except the bones."[5] Such is nature's way, sometimes, when landscapes are blasted. Such was the fate of animals and poor men in war, too. The remains of the unlucky cosmopolitan elite, however, were respectfully collected, embalmed, and sent home, Trim Skinner's to St. Paul's churchyard. He was a traveler even in death. Eliza remarried; but two decades later, when she died, her body was buried next to Trim's. A nice story.

Nearly every eastern American place must have its startling personal tragedy from the Civil War. The best-known usually concern the young and the beautiful; and in the western Albemarle country, Trim Skinner's is forgotten in the shadow of Colonel Henry King Burgwyn, Jr., who was only half Skinner's age when he was blown out of his saddle on the first day at Gettysburg. It was a scene almost immediately legendary — the "Boy Colonel" at the head of his troops, taking up the colors when their bearer fell, and carrying them into the enemy's teeth. David Wark Griffith had his "Little Colonel" perform the act in *Birth of a Nation*, but the fictional model of cavalier fearlessness lived to hear his own legend. Harry King, not yet twenty-two years old, did not. A friend and a slave buried him under a tree by the Chambersburg Road, carefully mapping the spot. The slave (Harry's personal servant) decamped for Carolina with Burgwyn's horses and other property. Four years later Harry's family found the spot, had his remains exhumed, and reinterred them beneath an appropriate monument in Raleigh.[6] He too was linear, post mortem as in life.

The Boy Colonel's brief earthly sojourn is as exemplary of the nineteenth-century beautiful people as the romantic circumstances of his death. Harry led Carolina troops and considered himself a creature of Thornbury plantation in Northampton County, North Carolina. He was born in New York, however, of a Massachusetts-born mother, and spent approximately half his short life outside Carolina—another mariner. The Burgwyns escaped their Roanoke River estate—its oppressive heat and malaria—every late summer and fall. They were off to springs and spas, and to northern kin. Harry's mother, especially, insisted upon staying with her family in Massachusetts and New York, usually for half of each year. She sought her relatives especially when her children were to be born. So like the Skinners, the Burgwyns were often aship, in "the cars," or in coaches. Harry, like Trim Skinner, was sent off to northern boarding schools while still a small boy. In his teens he spent a year at West Point, New York, taking more lessons and hoping for an appointment to the U.S. Military Academy. When that plan failed—despite his father's considerable influence—Harry returned to North Carolina for a while, to the university at Chapel Hill, but then departed for Lexington, Virginia, where he was an accomplished cadet at the Virginia Military Institute when his home state seceded from the United States. Harry's use of French seems less certain than Trim's, but the younger man was (for his time and age) something of a mathematician and an engineer; and in late August 1861, at nineteen, he was no less than a Lieutenant Colonel of North Carolina Volunteers.[7] *Sic transit.*

Young Harry's cosmopolitanism rested upon a revealing nexus. His mother's distinguished family, the Greenoughs, were rich from trade. Henry King Burgwyn, Sr., was a merchant, too—he met Harry's mother in New York City, during a business trip; but he was also a great planter in a most propitious place on the western border of the James-Albemarle subregion. This was a flood-prone but rich alluvial expanse called Occoneechee Neck, defined by a giant loop of the Roanoke just south of Weldon, terminus of an early railroad to Virginia. The Roanoke was navigable to Occoneechee Neck, so producers of grain and cotton might ship commodities by water or rail. This riverine part of Northampton, then, was not hinterland but part of the cosmopolitan sector. The senior Burgwyn, with his brothers, inherited the Neck from their uncle Thomas Pollok during the 1830s, and they established their respective seats on the peninsula.[8]

In real senses Occoneechee Neck had always been valuable and cosmopolitan. Indigenous folk had long farmed along the Roanoke—and wisely, in all likelihood, shifting fields to take advantage of postflood deposits, foregoing the follies of ditching and permanence. The Neck had long seen human and commodity traffic, too, for it lay near the course of the old Occaneechi Path, a seventeenth- and early-eighteenth-century Indian/English trading route that connected the Carolina Piedmont with southeastern Virginia.[9] The Weldon Railroad replaced the Occaneechi Path, in effect establishing commercial continuity from premodern to modern times. The sort of farming that Polloks and Burgwyns conducted on the Neck, however, was most discontinuous with local tradition.

In the best European tradition, they confronted the river, aiming to control its silty wealth and its periodic indiscipline and to produce gigantic commercial profit. Permanent fields, permanent profit, and permanent protection from flooding necessitated enormous capital investment—in labor, machinery, work animals, fertilizers, and pest control. In 1844, at Occoneechee Wigwam, estate of Thomas Pollok Burgwyn (Harry's uncle), there were more than 140 slaves. Thomas was less the extended traveler than Henry, Sr., and maintained the most comfortable mansion, apparently, of the brothers. Eight of his enslaved workforce—four of each sex—were devoted to his household. Both before and after the war, other laborers—always men— specialized in controlling water on the place. At least one was called Ditcher in everyday address. Notwithstanding, the Roanoke's indiscipline was never entirely restrained. That business would wait until the middle of the twentieth century, when the river was dammed upstream, above Roanoke Rapids, and dangerous water from Virginia was thereby safely impounded in human creations named Roanoke Rapids Lake and Lake Gaston. Meanwhile, however, despite all natural hazards, the Burgwyns extracted enough wealth from the Neck to engage pleasantly in the larger world. The naming of mules (of the 1840s) at Wigwam reveals, perhaps as much as travel diaries would, the Burgwyn's immersion in international (and popular) culture. For in addition to Nelly, Jenny, Crossey, Kentuck, Gentle, Bobbin, Doctor, Jack, Rhonda,

Sherriff, and Dancy, there were Zip Coon, Pope Leo, Jim Crow, Jim Crack Corn, and Blue Tail Fly.[10]

Harry's post-mortem travel was postponed, it seems, because his father (who had suffered a stroke) fled the country to France just after the Confederate surrender. His mother holed up with relatives in Boston. Upon his return (after a year), Henry, Sr., tried without success to sell his Thornbury on the Neck; he was too weakened to cope with the new order. Ultimately he and Harry's mother settled into a house on Main Street in Richmond. Henry died in 1873, but Anna Burgwyn stayed on for many more years, maintaining her annual vacation ritual and close ties with family, especially her younger son, Alveston, who had been born in 1850. Alveston was rather sickly as a child, and he quit schooling prematurely in favor of dabbling at business and frequent company with his mother.[11] His postbellum wanderings reveal much of the continuity the cosmopolitans enjoyed, despite the ravages of a lost war.

Alveston became twenty-one years old on 8 July 1871. At the time he still lived with his mother on Main in Richmond and was employed as a bookkeeper with Messrs. Lee Sedden in the city. But a birthday occasioned a three-week vacation; so Alveston took a train to Norfolk, a steamer to New York City, then another train up to Boston, to see aunts, uncles, cousins. Then on to Cohasset, White Plains, and back to Boston. In October of the same year he was off again, this time on a sort of educational tour that began in New York. Alveston examined Central Park carefully, complimenting Frederick Law Olmsted's design. He inspected Wall Street, then riverfront wharfs and warehouses. And he attended plays and operas, enjoying *Lucia di Lammermoor* in particular.[12]

Then on 26 October young Burgwyn began a voyage to South America aboard the bark *Lord Clarendon*, commanded by a Captain Lavender (no less). The *Clarendon* was bound for the "River Plate" without a stop in Rio, and it arrived in Montevideo at the end of the year. There Captain Lavender introduced Alveston to modes of business in foreign ports; but young Burgwyn also went touring, saw sights (including a corrida), and took a steamer to Buenos Aires. The *Clarendon* returned to New York late in March 1872. Alveston took trains directly to Richmond. Having had quite enough of salt water, it would appear, he took employment in a Richmond tobacco factory. This work "at first made me very ill," Alveston wrote in his diary, but he endured for a while—until his mother asked him to accompany her north. So he was off to Cohasset once more, visiting his cousin Sarah, reading to his mother, and sailing his days away on placid waters.[13]

The mid-1880s found Alveston on Occoneechee Neck in the profession of his Carolina ancestors. At The Elms and Potecasi Wigwam he supervised the operations of tenants and hired laborers, who planted grain, cotton, and peanuts—and continued the Burgwyns' struggle with the Roanoke. Alveston fretted over the maintenance of ditches, canals, and dams and, in late June 1885, the serious crop damage and soil erosion occasioned by "the recent very heavy showers." Late in November that year he nearly ruined a team of mules in an attempt to plow under reeds on marshy low ground near a ditchbank. Steers—much less valuable than mules—could not pull the turning plows, either; so Alveston set men to work with grubbing hoes. Twenty years after emancipation, free labor still performed work too difficult for workstock; and landowners still disturbed rich but nearly intractable soil that might otherwise have lessened the damage of washing showers and floods. The following January he "Walked around the farm with 'Ditcher' Reed." Reed agreed to grub out drainage paths in return for specified supplies and the right to cultivate a plot of Alveston's land.[14] The quest for permanence went on and on.

So did the Burgwyn ritual of leisure. Alveston's mother descended from Richmond and was driven about, to Carolina relatives and to fairs in Weldon, other events in Jackson and Rich Square. When Alveston's cotton was laid by—that is, tall enough to shade out weed growth and no longer require cultivation, about the first of July—he departed northward for a "summer vacation" that lasted until late September. Christmases he spent in Richmond. In 1887 Alveston sold out to his brother, George, and "left ... for Seaboard [a town along the Weldon rail route] to begone for the summer." Following this vacation he settled for a while in Jackson; but soon Alveston bought 150 acres back from George and returned, without joy it seems, to the struggle with the Roanoke. Burgwyns persist on Occoneechee Neck at the end of the twentieth century.[15]

Richard Eppes (1824–96) took care to survive the Civil War. No romantic dead hero would he be, despite a stake in slave-made commodities at least the equivalent of the Skinners and Burgwyns. In July 1860 Eppes estimated his worth at $180,000. This included more than one hundred slaves, reaping and winnowing machines for his wheat crops, many hand tools, horses, mules, oxen, cattle, hogs, sheep, four plantations, and a rambling mansion called Appomattox Manor. The last stood at City Point, a high bluff overlooking the confluence of the Appomattox and the James—the northwestern corner of our low-country subregion—in Prince George County. South

Appomattox Manor, 1990 (Photo by the author)

of the mansion were two adjoining cultivated units: Appomattox, closest to the residence; and across convenient railroad tracks, a place called Hopewell. Directly across the broad James, in Charles City County, was Eppes Island (often simply "the Island"), separated by a tidal creek from Shirley, seat of the Carters—the redoubtable Hill Carter during most of Richard Eppes's time. Directly across the Appomattox River was Bermuda Hundred, in Chesterfield County.[16] The setting was (and remains) majestic, a model of mid-nineteenth-century grandeur and the basis of cosmopolitan advantage. Richard Eppes understood too well, however, following Abraham Lincoln's election, that if war came, his property's wonderful access would make it a very dangerous one.

Eppes voted for John C. Breckenbridge, the southern rights Democratic candidate—but without the enthusiasm of a secessionist, as he explained to a friend soon after Lincoln became president-elect. Eppes's position was, as he summarized, "viz: Equality of the States and Protection of Slave property in the territories, that I was opposed to a dissolution of the Union before an overt act had been committed by the Black Republican Government, that as we had gone into the election with the B Republican party, it was but fair that we should submit being vanquished until some act was committed against our institutions." A month later Eppes debated political philosophy again with another friend (unfortunately unnamed in the diary). The visitor shared with Eppes notions of the primacy of Virginia citizenship over the national, and the belief that universal male suffrage in the North had led to "mob Law Legalized." But Eppes disagreed with his guest's contention "that order can only be restored by a strong monarchial government. ... I believe," Eppes declared, "that with a slave basis such as we have in the South, the slaves occupying the place of the Northern free laborers, we can still retain our republican institutions and be a permanent government." [17]

Early the following February, Virginians voted for delegates to a "Convention to be held in Richmond to decide upon the future position of Virginia in the new or old Confederacy," as Eppes put it in his diary. Prince George County offered a classic confrontation between "Edmund Ruffin jr[,] who advocates immediate secession and prefers a Confederacy of the Southern States to the old Union under almost every circumstance" and "Timothy Rives[,] a regular politician and most extreme advocate for the Union." Eppes shrank from the extremes, "Being myself a moderate man in my views, preferring the old Confederacy to a new if the South can have her rights guaranteed but if not[,] feeling that our only hope must be in another union as a last resort." So he "could not vote conscientiously for either candidate and cast my vote simply to have the acts of the Convention referred back to the people." [18]

By mid-April the war had begun and Virginia verged upon secession. Eppes went to nearby Petersburg to do business—in vain, for "such intense excitement" prevailed, there was "no business[,] nothing but soldiers & ammunition in wagon[s] on the streets, excited crowds at every corner, truly altogether such a scene as I have never witnessed in Va before[,] reminding me of the revolution in Paris [in 1848] which I witnessed." Eppes at last had to face the inevitable, yet he resisted, still irresolute: "I suppose I shall have to fit myself out and become an active," he wrote, "having been heretofore a silent member[,] anything but agreeable for a man with a wife and three little children besides the constant vigilance required to superintend my own affairs, and the prospect of my wife being confined in childbed before the expiration of the summer[,] moreover I shall have to break up my household as she is unwilling to remain at City Point if I go off to the wars[.] I indeed hardly know how to act[:] all my feelings say go[,] my duty to my family say stay, how I shall act I do not know." [19]

Eppes's unhappy solution was to fit himself out for war—after a prudent fashion. Trim Skinner and many other men of wealth organized, equipped, and led their own military units. Other physicians went to war in their professions. Richard Eppes enlisted for a term in a Virginia militia unit, then decamped as soon as his enlistment expired. In 1864 he sent his family to Philadelphia while he labored for the Confederates as a contract surgeon. Eppes was captured, then released, by General Benjamin Butler's forces at the end of the war. In the meantime Yankee troops and gunboats raided up the James several times, sacking the Prince George homes of the Edmunds Ruffin, *père et fils*. In 1864 Appomattox Manor and City Point became virtually the center of the conflict in Virginia. General Grant's huge army crossed the Chickahominy, then the James just below Eppes's downriver neighbors at Flowerdew Hundred, and took the southern bank of the James. City Point became Grant's headquarters for the lengthy investiture of Petersburg. His staff occupied Appomattox Manor; Grant slept in a log cabin on the Jameside lawn. Rows of new wharfs and railroad tracks lined the beaches below. Most of Richard Eppes's slaves had already "ran off to the Yankees," as he recorded, between May and August 1862, when gunboats had first appeared. All productivity ceased, save slaughter.[20]

When that was at last over, Eppes returned to find his estate in ruins. All his animals were gone except two milk cows, retained, perhaps, for Yankee convenience. Virtually all his farming equipment had disappeared, too. Barns and outbuildings had been stripped of their boarding, and timber removed from his woodlands, especially at Bermuda Hundred. On City Point, fruit and other trees—all except the oldest shade trees—were gone or badly damaged. Appomattox Manor was not inhabitable. Yet Eppes seems not to have seriously considered quitting his place and practicing medicine full-time. Instead he borrowed $3,600—most of it from his wife, who remained in Philadelphia—and began to reestablish himself. Hill Carter, his neighbor, had somehow managed to harbor at Shirley nine of Eppes's mules and thirty-one head of cattle. Eppes bought another pair of mules, harness, and a wagon, brought in a cousin to manage Bermuda Hundred, and offered cash wages to black men and women to plant late crops. Eppes himself took up residence in an old overseer's house on the Island while his mansion underwent restoration. Early in January 1866 Eppes and brother James River planters— Carter, John Seldon of Westover, and other notables—convened on Turkey Island, upriver in Henrico County, and mapped their return to hegemony in this great eastern grain belt. The "James River Farmers" devoted nearly all their collusion to labor—a cash wage rate according to "classes" of men and women workers, and detailed conditions of employment—in particular a host of rules on duty and obedience which, if violated, would result in specific deductions from pay. About the same time, Eppes purchased from the federal government a number of cabins the army had built at City Point. Instead of using or selling the 100,000-odd board feet of lumber in the cabins, Eppes let them stand and rented them to freedmen and women, who became dependent upon him and secure laborers. So within a few years Eppes lived more or less as he always had, an elegant gentleman, practical student of agronomy, patriarch to his family and his labor force, and cosmopolite.[21]

Richard Eppes was first Richard Eppes Cocke, son of Benjamin Cocke of Bonaccord. The father died insolvent in 1836 (when Richard was twelve), a disgrace to one of Virginia's long-tailed First Families. But the boy soon inherited slaves and extensive lands from Archibald Eppes, his mother's brother; and at sixteen, still under his mother's guidance, he became, legally, Richard Eppes. This curious matrilinear scion briefly managed his properties, in 1847 (when he was twenty-three). But except for this early experiment he would not reside at Appomattox Manor or directly control its appendages for several more years. First he would be a scholar and a mariner, then later a proper Eppes and owner of a valuable island that bore his name. His formal education carried him, fortuitously, to medical school in Philadelphia. Gentlemen planters often had fall-back professions, but through his studies Eppes also found a wife: the daughter of his principal professor. Before the war Elizabeth Horner Eppes inherited $17,000—most of it in bank and railroad stocks—from her father; and this money helped restore Appomattox Manor in 1865–66.[22]

Meanwhile Richard took at least one, probably two, extended trips abroad. He was in Paris (we know from his April 1861 diary) when revolutions broke out over much of western and central Europe. If a creature of the James gentry had somehow been inclined toward bourgeois liberalism—an unlikely reading, I think—certainly Richard was cured by the revolutions of 1848. Disorder was his waking nightmare. Conceivably this same tour took Eppes to Venice, where he had his portrait painted. One may stare at a photograph of this creation today, searching for insight into a man who, beginning in 1851, started a diary that ultimately filled more than twenty volumes, but who revealed so little that was intimate. The Venetian artist did not disguise a hairline already much receded, although Eppes was only in his mid-twenties. The high forehead is instead ennobled. Well-formed dark brows, too, set off large, steady, dark eyes. A large full beard and mustache conceal the line of the young man's jaw and chin—but not his lips, which are symmetrical, the lower a luminous counterpoint to the noble brow. It is the long nose, however, that is simply magnificent: Eppes in Venice was a Renaissance saint,

Richard Eppes, ca. 1848
(Photo of oil portrait, courtesy of the Virginia Historical Society, Richmond)

or a clever *condottiere*, or perhaps the Doge himself. A daguerreotype taken during his trip to the Holy Land in 1849 seems to confirm the impression of the Venetian portraitist: A wealthy tourist captured in romantic costume by an unknown pioneer photographer-entrepreneur, Eppes is convincing as Byron redux, utterly comfortable in outrageous robes. The tall forehead is concealed beneath a fine turban; but that same striking leftward gaze lives

Richard Eppes in "Turkish" costume, ca. 1849
(Courtesy of the Virginia Historical Society, Richmond)

on photographic paper as on canvas, and that wonderful nose still demands deference.

Two years later Richard Eppes began his long serious life, taking his place on the James at twenty-eight. He was determined to excel not at medicine, which seems to have interested him little, but as a modern farmer. This he clearly announced on the inside cover of his first journal, in September 1851: "It is my intention," he began, "to keep a series of journals taking note, besides my daily transactions, of every important event occuring on my estate. ... As I am engaged probably more extensively than any man in the State in improving my land, should I meet with success, it may be interesting to those who come after me, to see what means I succeeded and what way I erred[,] profiting by my success [and] guarding against my errors."[23] No small ambition, for Richard Eppes began this enterprise in a valley almost continually in European-style cultivation for more than a century, where resourceful innovation was already the mode, and where his neighbors included Harrisons at the Brandons just downriver; Hill Carter of Shirley, already a famous and much-published practitioner; and Edmund Ruffin, the greatest American agronomist of the nineteenth century, arguably the father of what is called modern agriculture. Eppes's farming operations, then—documented so generously in his journals—are an important opportunity to understand again, this time agroecologically, the cosmopolitans' relationship with landscape.

The plow and seed wheat had come to Jamestown with the first English settlers. European immigrants intended to introduce the culture of their primary grain in this "new" world, and in the European style, on permanent fields. The intention was very long in implementation, however. For the forests were so dense and labor so scarce that the English forewent the plow and adopted Indians' fire and hoe culture. They girdled and burned trees to create crop fields, then hoed to grow corn, beans, squash, and tobacco in hills rather than rows. When the land "wore out" in a few years, like the Indians they slashed and burned again, shifted to new land. The English subsisted, then, on American grain cultivated the American way. They differed from the indigenes mainly in the extent of tobacco culture, which the English grew principally for the Atlantic market. Yet the *method* of tobacco culture, too, was native: a shifting hill-and-hoe cycle, with little or no soil erosion and, in the long run, little or no degradation of landscapes.[24]

Change began to set in throughout the Chesapeake world about a century before Richard Eppes's birth. Imported labor, especially from Africa, had accumulated to the point where forests were vulnerable to permanent, European-style crop fields. Population pressures in Tidewater counties pushed surpluses into new Piedmont lands. By the middle of the eighteenth century, tobacco culture was shifting westward, and the great Tidewater planters—George Washington was among them—abandoned tobacco in favor of an almost exclusive grain culture. Corn remained important both for domestic use and for the great West Indian trade. Wheat, however, could not be grown commercially without clean, stump-free, permanent fields, plowed, harrowed, and rolled smooth.[25] So the plow came to America a generation before political independence, and one is at a loss to rank the two in importance.

Paradoxically, as American provincials gradually discovered and defined their differentness from the English, the greatest farmers among them repudiated native agricultural practice in favor of the new English agronomy. The epochal land-use revolution—ca. 1730–70—chiefly aped the "Norfolk System" of East Anglia. There reformers had created productive, permanent fields through crop rotation, cultivation of grasses (for soil restoration), and especially through the maintenance of large herds of cattle, primarily for their dung. So Americans, from southern New England down into the Carolinas, took to plows, wheat — even turnips, because the English placed them in rotation — and cattle, and to British manuals that showed them the way. In the Chesapeake and Albemarle, great fortunes and still-standing plantation manses were erected upon wheat and manure. The central portion of Richard Eppes's Appomattox Manor was constructed in 1751, testimony to the boom. Through the 1750s, 1760s, and 1770s, Colonel Landon Carter (an ancestor of the master of Shirley in Eppes's time) kept track of progress in his own famous diary. During the mid-1750s Carter's slaves "drove [cattle] Gently" onto clover fields to distribute droppings before pastureland was rotated into wheat or tobacco. In 1757 he began to build portable, thatch-covered cowstalls, from which manure might be carted to fields and applied in prescribed amounts. The Colonel took delight that a visitor to his estate, Sabine Hall, was "surprized by my quantitys of Manure." Even the tragic death of Carter's young daughter Sukey on 25 April 1758 was subsumed by cow dung in his diary: Carter spent the day counting carts of manure, wrote an apostrophe to Sukey, then noted triumphantly within the same paragraph, "56 load Carryed out this day."[26] Such were the preoccupations of many of the men who also made the political revolution.

The introduction of European-style agriculture had profound environmental results, noticeable before the end of the eighteenth century. The plow, especially in hilly country, exposed soils to wind and water erosion. Streams silted to such an extent that some old tobacco port towns by the upper Chesapeake became isolated from river channels. Periodic siltation — usually during spring rains and freshets following plowing — clouds waters and deprives subaquatic vegetation of necessary sunlight. Since subaquatic vegetation produces phytoplankton, the origin of the food chain, all rivers, and certainly Chesapeake Bay itself, suffered losses (as they still do) when upstream lands go under the plow. Extensive grain culture also multiplied pest populations. Rust, Hessian fly, and other plagues (especially in wheat) frustrated and occasionally bankrupted farmers. Europeans had inadvertently introduced rats into the Americas earlier — they had consumed grain stores at Jamestown in 1609. The eighteenth-century resort to wheat undoubtedly multiplied these creatures, too, along with populations of native crows and other birds prone to feast opportunistically. So the land-use revolution also intensified Americans' war on pests. Colonial governments placed bounties on the scalps of crows. (Wolves, too, were bounty targets, but Americans seem early to have accepted the rat's immortal destiny.) In the nineteenth century, arsenic became the weapon of choice against both insects and crows; and before the end of Richard Eppes's time there were relatively sophisticated spray pumps for arsenic-based insecticides.[27]

Richard Eppes was a worthy scion to the eighteenth-century land-use revolutionaries, as well as to his mother's family. Studying his diaries, one is struck by the continuity of East Anglian crop rotations in American variations, by the plow and its problematic side effects, and also by the profitable pride such men took in harvests well made. During the fall of 1851 Eppes laid out his crop fields according to "the five shift or Pamunky system." (The Pamunkey River lies to the north of the James, dividing Hanover County and separating New Kent and King William Counties.) The rotation automatically became a five-year plan as well: "*1852* No's 1 & 2 [fields] in wheat, *No 3* in corn, *No 4* in clover, No *5* in pasture[.] *1853* No *1* in pasture, No 2 in clover, No *3 & 4* in wheat No *5 in corn*[.] 1854. No 1 in corn, nos 2 & 5 in wheat, No 3 in clover, No 4 in pasture[.] 1855. No 1 in wheat, No 2 pasture, No 3 wheat, No 4 corn, No 5 clover[.] 1856 No 1, clover, No 2 corn, No 3 pasture, No 4 & 5 wheat[.] 1857 No 1 & 2 in wheat, No 3 in corn, No 4 clover No 5 pasture thus the 1st and last are the same." Eppes understood (from Edmund Ruffin's agricultural chemistry) that rotation alone was not sufficient to maintain permanent fertility, however; so he also bought tons of lime for application to his fields. Lime unlocked nitrogen from his plowed-under clover and animal manures. Phosphate additives—commercial bone meal and especially guano—increased yields, and during the 1850s Eppes purchased and applied these, too.[28]

Sometimes science, investment, and discipline worked almost to perfection. Eppes's hands harvested his huge 1859 wheat crop early in July, and he reported with justifiable pride his preparations for shipment the following month: "Commenced this morning delivering the crop of wheat from the Bermuda estate aboard the lighter Henry Brown[,] Capt. W. H. Wiggins," he wrote, "and owing to the very great care taken by my overseer Mr Conway in cleaning the wheat[,] passing it five times through Montgomery's Van Sweeten's fanmills, three days being occupied in cleaning 1890 Bu's, we did not deliver more than 1170 Bu's the first day. The wheat was white wheat, dry cracking with a fracture under the teeth, very solid weighing within a fraction of 61½ lbs to the bushel, which is one of the best tests of its being well cleaned." Eppes found only a little spelt and a little cockle[.] I saw no onions or garlic and very seldom a grain of partridge pea. The wheat having been threshed and cleaned in the same barn had, as we often have it, when delivered almost immediately after threshing without lying in bulk any time, a slight smell of dust, which it loses after remaining [in the] barn a short time, this odor to one experienced is often mistaken for funk produced by the heating of wheat when threshed damp, but as our criterion is never to thresh wheat unless it cracks beneath the teeth & then to keep it in small bulks or scattered over the barn floor with the doors & windows open[,] we rarely have any wheat injured by heating and none I know of this year. The almost total absence of sprouted grains in the wheat delivered today after the very wet season was a little remarkable.[29]

Twenty years later, in the arid western plains and California's Central Valley, wheat culture would be simpler, for late spring and summer were nearly always hot and dry. Shipping wheat that "cracked beneath the teeth" from humid Tidewater Virginia was no small accomplishment. Eppes's knowledge and managerial skills, like those of Landon Carter before him, made it work.

Such men, with the capital and labor to bring forth the European grain in difficult places, were prone to perform any number of other environmental manipulations as well. Low-country cosmopolitans were particularly concerned with drainage on fields and the reclamation of rich swamps for grain production. Richard Eppes's Prince George and Chesterfield properties were high and apparently unproblematical. Eppes's Island, however, was nearly surrounded by swamps and was subject to washes and standing water, especially in the spring and fall. From a map of this plantation included in his diary, it appears that Eppes reclaimed about twenty acres of swamp near the James at the west end of the island, leaving a "margin of 30 or 40 yards near river to break the force of the tides and winds." And he struggled—without complete success it seems—to reclaim low "slash" land near the middle of the arable center of crop field number 3. A long east-west ditch extended from both ends of the slash, but this part of field 3 appears to have been too low completely to eliminate the slash. Eppes was more preoccupied with the maintenance of established fields. In November 1851, for example, he

Rode down to inspect the wheat, found it coming up badly, particularly on the flat lying between the river ditch and the old barn ditch along the sides of the ditches. . . . also on the small piece of land near the river. Upon observing several moist spots was lead [led] to examine the water furrows, found that not one in fifty would draw[,] particularly near the ditches where the water ought to pass off[,] being almost universally shallower than any where else. Called the overseers attention to the subject & told him to open a deep cross furrow along the ditch bank into which the furrow should empty & then cut two or three openings from it into the ditches[,] also to have the furrows cleaned out where needed[,] that I was very desirous to establish a reputation in this particular department of farming[.][30]

So from the first year of his permanent stewardship, Eppes was attentive to detail—a hallmark of the cosmopolitan agriculturist. His system of open ditches and shallower drainage furrows was not, however, state-of-the-art for the time. Edmund Ruffin had read of "permanent" stone underground drains in Europe and as early as 1822 had begun to construct covered drains at Coggins Point, his first Prince George farm. Lacking stone, Ruffin ultimately devised a scheme of sawn boards, constructed as long boxes ("pipe," he called them) and filled with rocks and straw, then covered with earth. Ruffin's experiments were not concluded until the 1840s, however, at Marlbourne, his new plantation in Hanover County, north of Richmond. And one gathers from his writings that construction of covered drains was labor-intensive—so egregiously labor-intensive that one does not wonder why few of his neighbors, even the wealthiest, followed Ruffin's example.[31] Well-maintained open ditches were sufficient for most, including Richard Eppes.

Reclamation was the most draconian of landscape manipulations among the cosmopolitans. Eppes did a little, Ruffin somewhat more. Their friend and neighbor Hill Carter, however, was more ambitious, honestly reported his efforts, and left a cautionary tale that was too little heeded.

In 1825 (when Eppes was a mere babe), Carter set hired Irish workers to clearing and draining eighty-five acres of swampland. Eight years later Edmund Ruffin invited Carter's report—"Account of the Embankment and Cultivation of the Shirley Swamp"—in Ruffin's excellent new journal, the *Farmers' Register*. Carter was sanguine: The "beauty of this land is," he wrote, "that it will last for ever without manure, provided you keep the water off; and if ever it sinks to low water mark . . . after a long while, why we can but use the pump as they do in Holland." Always the European references! Yet here was a vulgar sort of utopian dream, too—of permanent (i.e., European-style) crop fields without the problem of restoring fertility. Carter was already awaking, however, in 1833. Shirley Swamp had already sunk "about eighteen inches," he admitted. And only four years later, when he again reported to the *Farmers' Register*, all but ten acres of the original eighty-five had been abandoned. Dutch pumps were too expensive, mud dikes had failed, and Carter had consigned the land to forest swamp.[32] Ruffin was hardly constrained in his own thinking about reclamation, however, as we shall see in the following chapter.

Replication of an idealized European pastoral landscape, meanwhile, involved many more efforts, some of them very ambitious. The cosmopolitans believed, for instance, that the open ranging of livestock must be ended so that crop fields might go unfenced. Containment of cattle and especially hogs would not only protect crops from damage but would also permit farmers to husband virtually all manure, guard against livestock diseases, and develop heavier "purebred" stock. These and other cosmopolitan reforms are so closely associated with Edmund Ruffin that they will be pursued in the next chapter also. But cosmopolitans' cultural relationship with animals, especially birds, and their eagerness to introduce exotic plants, are well enough represented by Richard Eppes that they can be suggested here.

Although Eppes labored long in his study at Appomattox Manor and graced many a sitting room and ballroom, his place, like that of all men of all classes, was outdoors. (Most black women, who were field hands, and most ordinary white women, who also took a hand at crops, at least in season, also labored in the sun—but with little freedom to design and direct any manipulation of the landscape.) Outdoors, in nature, virtually all men worked and played intrusively, confrontationally, manipulatively, and with hostility, whether casual or purposeful. At work, nature was a challenge to overcome —all those trees, troublesome water, worrisome pests. At play, nature offered masculine ritual, respite, delight. Hunting might be termed both work and play. The aborigines, as we have seen, harvested deer and other animals, including fish, of necessity. Poor white and black men hunted this way, too, although hunting for them as for the Indians served other purposes, such as the socialization of boys with men. Firearms made hunting-as-harvest easier and at the same time invited boys and men to kill gratuitously, for sport and for the honing of marksmanship, a virtue among males. American adoption of European agricultural models multiplied pest and varmint populations, further justifying shooting, this time as social and economic duty.[33]

Eppes represented his class and time in no extraordinary manner. He rode and hunted with apparent pleasure, although in his diaries shooting is not much mentioned. Unlike poor William Valentine, whose depression required resort to the country and therapeutic tramping and shooting, Eppes led a full, gratifying life; for him, hunting seems to have been more a tradition to perpetuate, another dividend to his consuming and successful agronomic preoccupations. Therefore, when the twenty-eight-year-old Eppes reports the casual shooting of bats one day, then a hawk the next, one takes notice. One also takes notice when, with blunt delight, the thirty-five-year-old records that he "Killed 5 larks with one shot."[34]

By the time the good doctor's single shotgun blast did in the exaltation of larks, Americans' relationship with birds approached a confrontational junction. A few voices—all of them apparently elite—began to condemn the killing both of songbirds and so-called pests, such as crows. But at this moment—the 1850s—commercial harvests of both songbirds and waterfowl were well underway, and of course farmers continued their determined warfare on crows. The market for wild ducks shipped north from Norfolk, especially, complemented the already-developed Elizabeth River truck-farming business. Farmers and watermen in nearby Princess Anne County—particularly around Back Bay (south of Virginia Beach)—moved beyond sport and local supply to the great market. By the mid-1850s the duck trade was well organized, with steamers departing for New York loaded with barrels of canvasbacks, redheads, and mallards. One farmer employed twenty men as shooters each season. In 1857 this single enterprise "consumed ... twenty-three kegs of gunpowder, with shot in proportion."[35]

The songbird market, meanwhile, served the milliners of New York. Ladies had already taken to adorning their heads with the feathers of exotic avions. Now milliners began to place on hats the entire bodies of colorful songbirds. Supplies came not from the ladies' consorts—gentlemen such as Richard Eppes—but from little boys in the hinterlands, such as H. B. Ansell of Knotts Island, in Currituck County, North Carolina (just below Back Bay). In his old age Ansell recollected that "Every boy had his myrtle 'birding club,' cross-bow and arrows, his ... traps for birds, in every briery branch and fence-lock. By this means hundreds of strings of dead birds, even sparrows, were shipped to market." The boys carried their prey to remote country stores, whose proprietors sent all manner of country commodities on to towns such as Norfolk. In return the boys "obtained ginger-cakes, tops and chords, and other trinkets."[36]

The outcry against both casual and commercial slaughter of birds arose slowly. As early as 1838 Edmund Ruffin reprinted in his agricultural magazine a long article from another journal, protesting "Injury from Destroying Birds." The anonymous author advocated "the ultimate doctrine of Christianity, that every thing, however diminutive it may be, is formed for some end."[37] However, in the upper South, protest was seldom heard until the eve of the Civil War. The *Southern Planter*, published in Richmond, offered a veritable treatise on the question "What has become of our Birds?" in April 1860—shortly after Eppes blasted the larks. The author, who signed himself "C," described himself as a very old man and a hunter. He lived in Cumberland—a Piedmont county and town west of Richmond—but seemed comfortably familiar with the broader region. "C" recollected school days in Richmond during the 1790s, when skies were blackened with martins. By the 1830s, he averred, the martin population had declined precipitously, along with those of killdeers, catbirds, woodpeckers, and others. Why? "C" enumerated four reasons: climatic change—cold weather had decimated insects upon which many birds feed; habitat reduction—"We have cut down the greater part of our forestlands"; idle slaughter by boys and men, for sport; and purposeful slaughter by farmers of supposed pest-birds. "C's" first reason seems dubious, although the preceding winter had been especially frigid in central Virginia. (Richard Eppes recorded a Carter boy's skating across the frozen James and Appomattox.) The second explanation was probably correct, although exaggerated. The last two were certainly correct, and "C" devoted much of his epistle to defenses of woodpeckers, bats, and crows. Woodpeckers had a wonderfully symbiotic relationship with conifers, he observed: "I have known a large community of them actually to arrest the progress of destruction, from the pine-borer." Bats were incorrectly thought to breed chinches, so people killed them. In actuality, "C" argued, they live "entirely on insects," including mosquitoes, so he welcomed them. Crows, too, he insisted, should be protected. "The late John Randolph [of Roanoke] would not suffer one of them to be shot on his farm. Indeed, he fed them liberally when his young corn could be injured by them," because most of the year, crows' diets consisted of harmful grubs and insects.[38]

After the war, cosmopolitan naturalists North and South gradually coalesced into what might be termed a movement to arrest indiscriminate and misguided bird-killing. In 1869 the *Atlantic Monthly* published a testimonial to crows' propensity to consume far more grubs and bugs than corn, citing John James Audubon and other authorities. A Richmond farm journal reprinted the article. Less than a year later the same Virginia paper printed a letter from an Amelia County farmer, entitled "Spare the Crow." "[N]umerous examinations of his [the crow's] stomach, after death," he argued, "prove incontestably that his food is mainly of insects well known to be troublesome and injurious to crops."[39] At this point every defender of birds was a conservationist of the instrumentalist sort: Farm production—not crows' intrinsic value—called for different human behavior toward birds.

By the mid-1870s such instrumentalism had merged with elite aesthetics to produce a somewhat broader analysis of birds' value and the need for conservation. During the summer of 1876 tobacco crops were under attack from "flies," and few birds descended to help farmers fight the swarms. A writer for the *Richmond State* offered a novel explanation of birds' seeming demise: "With the end of the war began, and ever since has continued, an indiscriminate pot-hunt for birds—robin, blue-bird, fly-catcher (called sapsucker), lark, black-bird, thrush, wren, and swamp-sparrow; not one of them escapes the musket of the idle negro or the old shot-gun of the [white] urchin. Fall, and spring, and summer sees our fields and woods, sees every ditch-bank and shaded rivulet searched as with a drag-net and swept of the birds."[40]

Antebellum classless pot-hunting—such as Richard Eppes's—was thus conveniently ignored as southern urban and plantation elites moved toward alliance with northeastern conservationists. By 1886 the *Southern Planter*, always the voice of cosmopolitan policy and sensibility, endorsed the American Ornithologists' Union's condemnation of the "startling decrease in the number of many of our birds ... for the sake of fashion." Thus did a few southerners join the new Audubon Society of America. In another decade, representatives of the Virginia-Carolina sport-hunting elite would join northeastern colleagues in Ducks Unlimited in order to limit, if not actually extinguish, the commercial harvesting of waterfowl.[41]

Another characteristic of the cosmopolitans was an eagerness to introduce foreign plant species, both for profit and for beauty. Richard Eppes, Hill Carter, the Burgwyns, and the Skinners all followed eighteenth-century ancestors who created wheat culture, planted turnips and clover, then designed around their mansions formal gardens of grasses, flowers, trees, and shrubs from Britain, France, Latin America, even Asia. To this day some of these gardens—for example at Lower Brandon, long home to Harrisons, on the James just downriver from Appomattox Manor—survive more or less intact. Eppes's ornamental plantings were wrecked during the Petersburg campaign, restored, but then abandoned by his heir. During the 1850s, however, Richard Eppes was exemplary of his sort and time, sowing "Hungarian grass" in his pastures and, in his lawn, planting not only white lilacs, pear, cherry, apricot, and plum trees, weeping birches, and pairs of magnolias and ashes, but two "Japan gold leaf" trees as well.[42]

Beautiful people arranged beautiful environments, defined in the main by European standards of what was old, distinguished, exotic. In such settings beautiful social events might take place. Eppes described a James River instance early in 1859—a sort of human counterpart to gardens. About eight P.M. (in the dark), with his wife and the local minister, Eppes was rowed across the river to Shirley to attend the wedding of "Miss Georgianna Wickham granddaughter of Mr Williams Carter" to Lieutenant William Lee, son of Colonel Robert E. Lee, both of the United States Army. The Wickhams, of Hickory Hill in Hanover County, just outside Richmond, were related to the Carters of Shirley. The Eppes's crossing took half an hour, and they arrived just "in time to see the wedding. Marriage striking from all the groomsmen being in full uniform of the U.S. Army. Col Lee son of Gen'l Harry Lee of revolutionary fame & himself a distinguished officer of the U.S. engineering Corps was decidedly the most striking person in the room, (father of the groom)." Eppes, himself a member of a not inconsequential tribe, was pleased to meet not only the elder Lee but also a gaggle of Wickhams and Carters from afar. The doctor's pleasure seems palpably as aesthetic as social. The "Wedding passed off quite pleasantly & we returned home about 12½ oc.PM" (he probably intended to write "AM").[43]

Richard Eppes's early enthusiasm for a vaunted practical plant illustrates better than aesthetics the propensity of cosmopolitans to manipulate. The plant in question is the Osage orange, a native of the Ohio Valley. Permitted to grow naturally, the Osage orange becomes a mature tree of perhaps fifty feet with a pleasantly rounded crown. It is sex-differentiated: Females produce hard, heavy, green, softball-sized fruit. (These are the "oranges," but midwesterners more typically call them "hedgeapples" for a reason shortly to become clear.) Males fertilize females with spring flower-sperm and then grow menacing thorns. At least as early as the 1830s, midwestern farmers began to employ the Osage orange as permanent boundary fencing. When the trees were planted close together and kept pruned to five or six feet, their tough thorny branches wove together to form a nearly impenetrable hedge. By the mid-1840s nurserymen in Cincinnati and Dayton were promoting the tree throughout the United States. The editor of the *Southern Planter* had a "fine specimen" in his Richmond office—"quite a curiosity to several of our visitors"—during the fall of 1846; and in his December issue that year, he reprinted an instructive article from the *Ohio Cultivator*.[44]

One of Richard Eppes's first preoccupations, as he took up management of his estate in the fall of 1851, was to "*Estimate*...the number and cost of Osage orange trees" to fence part of his properties. The following January he ordered seven thousand plants from Ohio, to be set one foot apart.[45] I find no further mention of this particular exotic introduction in the doctor's diaries. Considering the local enthusiasm for relief from annual repair and replacement of rotting fences, one imagines keen interest in Eppes's initiative. Those of us jaded by actual experience with the trees *in situ*, however—the sore backs from gathering and removing hundreds of oranges, the hands and feet aching from thorn punctures—leap to comparisons with science-fiction horror, of exotic demons who never go away.

Indeed, as early as 1857 a writer for the *Boston Cultivator* debunked the Osage orange's use as a hedge, and a new editor of the *Southern Planter* agreed: "The trouble of trimming, the draft upon the land and crops of each side of the hedge, and the generally indifferent growth of such things forbid their use, economically considered." The editor had himself experimented with the plant and concluded he "cannot recommend it. On poor land it won't grow; on rich land it inclines to become a tree, and wants severe pruning just when you can't spare the labor."[46]

But the Ohio promoters and their collaborators seem to have won the day. The *Southern Planter*'s own horticultural correspondent endorsed the Osage orange in 1858. Appealing (I suspect) to eastern farmers' envy of westerners, E. G. Eggeling declared that endless miles of hedges stretched across the West, from the Ohio Valley to Mississippi.[47] Luckily, the sandy soils to the south and east of Richard Eppes's plantations did not accommodate the Osage orange. Even along the upper James the plant never quite became the scourge midwesterners know. Yet in the late twentieth century, the American "record" Osage orange was measured not in Ohio or Indiana but in central Virginia—a monument to the cupidity of Ohio salesmen and to the eager manipulativeness of our cosmopolitans.

2 THE WIZARD OF SHELLBANKS

Now, the first requisite to the civilization of any people, is to make them stationary.
— *William Gilmore Simms, 1842*

*[We] should be rejoiced to yield to ... arguments [against] our present unwilling
conviction of the truth of the heart-benumbing, hope-stifling doctrine of Malthus.*
— *Edmund Ruffin, 1836*

Photographic portraits of Edmund Ruffin might legitimately provoke debate over whether he was a "beautiful" person. Of medium height (five feet eight inches) and always thin, he had a stern, almost hawkish face. He remained shaven late in his life, well into the age of beards; and perhaps more eccentric, Ruffin wore his straight hair shoulder-length. In a picture taken with four of his children about 1851 (when he was about fifty-seven), Ruffin held an open book and had pushed his eyeglasses high up on his broad forehead—in the manner of Patrick Henry in the orator's best-known portrait. Henry had assumed the pose of nonconformity in his own formal day. Ruffin seems self-consciously to have offered himself—one cannot imagine him taking orders from a photographer—as the encircled family man, as scholar, and as a creature indifferent to, probably scornful of, conventions of public self-presentation. Ruffin's image was striking, to be sure, but determinedly unnoble and unbeautiful.

Nor was Ruffin beautiful in the larger sense of the previous chapter. Born in 1794 to a family long resident on Virginia's Tidewater rivers, he remained at least one rank below his neighbors named Eppes, Harrison, Carter, Seldon, Braxton, and Wickham. Ruffin was a "planter" by the arbitrary conventional measurement of ownership of twenty or more slaves. Between 1820 and 1860 he owned variously 41 to 66, and altogether his family held a total of 216 in 1860. Yet Ruffin called his properties "farms" and himself a "farmer." The plainness of the words convey his disdain for the conspicuous consumption and preoccupation with display of his wealthier neighbors and the parvenues of the cotton and sugar belts to the south. Nor was Ruffin a traveler. In 1827 he toured the northeastern states with a half-sister, and he delivered one of his sons to a New Haven school in 1828. Mostly he was stationary, well into middle age. Even then, his occasional perambulations carried him mainly to Petersburg and Richmond, rarely to Washington or Baltimore. When he became an editor (in 1833) he began to ride out, or take the railway

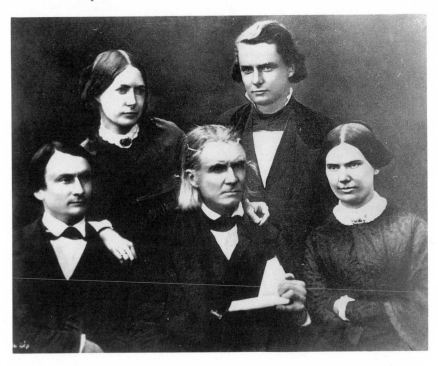

*Edmund Ruffin with four of his children: (*left to right*) Julian, Ella, Charles, and Mildred, ca. 1851 (Courtesy of the Virginia Historical Society, Richmond)*

cars, to inspect the eastern Virginia, then the Carolina countrysides. He was a local, businesslike creature until he was old. Only then—and then mainly to foment his secessionist mischief—did Ruffin become a regular and long-distance traveler. He remained a stranger to New York and Boston, and never went abroad. Nor was Edmund Ruffin a vacationer. In an autobiographical essay composed during his fifties, Ruffin described an exception: "The health of one of my daughters, Mildred," he explained, "required her going to the Springs in the mountain region in 1848, & she could not go without my being her companion. Accordingly I left home with her & another daughter, Jane, for companionship & the pleasure of both, the beginning of August, & did not return until the last of September." Both the destination and duration of the trip resemble the Burgwyns' flights from the Roanoke, but the context bears no resemblance to the lifestyles of the rich and famous. The Ruffins left the farm of necessity, and Edmund felt constrained to explain himself: "This absence would have been a serious disadvantage to my farming operations, & care of the farm, at any time." He had no overseer, but Jem Sykes, his slave foreman, was reliable; and Edmund's son Julian would stop by and check late wheat shipments (since Jem could not read), and so on.[1]

Circumstances largely deprived Ruffin of the beautiful people's carefree self-assurance, which was always nurtured by family and formal education. Edmund's mother died when he was a small child. His paternal grandfather died when Edmund was thirteen. His father, George, meanwhile, remarried and fathered six half-siblings (four of whom survived infancy); but then George, himself also an only child, died (in 1810), when Edmund was sixteen. So the teenaged Edmund was not only orphaned but also left without grandparents, uncles, or aunts. For two years he was the guest (in effect) of a stepmother who, while kind, had her own interests, which did not correspond to her stepson's. George's death had brought Edmund home from Williamsburg, where he had spent most of one dilatory academic year at the College of William and Mary. He had roomed in town, ignored many classes, read what he wanted—he seems to have favored geometry but little else—and indulged in liquor. This was the extent of his formal schooling. He had made no lasting friends and felt isolated. Back at Evergreen, now his stepmother's house, he remained apart from his young half-sisters and infant half-brother, reading desultorily in the mansion library. He had never gone to the fields with his father or grandfather, nor did he now. In August 1812, shortly after the United States went to war with Britain again, Edmund became a private in the Prince George militia. His company went off to Norfolk for a time, and he returned in February 1813, shortly after his nineteenth birthday.[2] Then began a difficult—but altogether stunning—transformation of the fortunes of Edmund Ruffin, his family and, potentially at least, the entire South Atlantic region.

Edmund had returned from the war determined to marry and to take charge of the nearby farm called Coggins Point, left to him by his grandfather. Realization of Edmund's wishes, however, depended upon a neighbor, Thomas Cocke, whom George Ruffin had designated Edmund's guardian. Cocke was amenable, and Edmund got both his patrimony and his bride. Cocke's connection to Edmund continued, nonetheless, until the older man's death (by suicide) in 1840. Despite the difference in their ages, Thomas became (in Edmund's words) his "most valued friend. . . . a man of uncommon mental power, pure principles, great liberality & kindness which he carried to the extent of imprudence." This "intimate & warm friendship" derived from more than propinquity, for Cocke was eerily like the younger man. His branch of the Cocke clan also stood a rank or so below the James River elite.

(Thomas was the older brother of Richard Eppes's ne'er-do-well father.) And Thomas was also isolated and bookish. "In his youth," Ruffin wrote in 1851, Cocke "had lived almost a recluse, with scarcely any associations but his books. After some subsequent years of social intercourse with his elder neighbors, their deaths had again left him almost alone. During his early and middle life he had never had a companion of equal mind & similar literary tastes—& his partiality for me was in some degree owing to my making some approach to that position." Cocke married late, became a father, then was widowed and isolated again. Young Edmund became pupil and soulmate, his own premature misanthropy reinforced by Cocke's. They were a weird and wonderful pair, eccentric oracles of the James's piney woods. "Before our intimacy," Ruffin wrote, "he had conversed but little with men, & very rarely with any but inferior minds. His information, his views, & even his ordinary language, were all derived from books, & very little from conversation."[3] Together, slowly, they would develop a bold scheme—Ruffin the wizard, Cocke the dour critic—permanently to Europeanize the South Atlantic landscape, to halt American restlessness, to make their countrymen stay put and be civilized.

Thomas Cocke's careless traditional farming practices and his bookish skepticism tested and finally confirmed young Edmund Ruffin's new agronomy, which derived from his utter lack of experience and dependence upon bookish intelligence. But there was something more immediate to propel Edmund's experimentation and ultimate boldness. During the fall of 1813 (a few months after Cocke released Coggins Point to him), Edmund married Susan Travis, a twenty-year-old orphan from Williamsburg. The following August, Edmund, Jr., was born; and before the end of 1832, Susan (poor Susan) gave birth to no fewer than ten more children: George (1815, died in infancy), Agnes (1817), Jane (1819, also died), Julian Calx (1821), Rebecca (1823), Elizabeth (1824), Mildred (1827), another Jane (1829), and finally Ella and Charles (twins, 1832). Edmund the isolated, Edmund the orphan and his orphan bride, produced an enormous household—a "Malthusian revolution," in the words of Ruffin's most recent biographer. And all these Ruffins were complemented by half a hundred slaves, all to be fed and otherwise supported on Coggins Point's 1,500-odd acres of marsh, ravines, pine woods, and worn-out crop fields. Ruffin seriously considered the common American solution—migration to the West. But no buyers could be found for such impoverished farms, and he had not the cash simply to abandon his patrimony.[4] So the dutiful young father resolved to stay by the James, consult his books, and submit to the skeptical mind of his "first friend." The next decade and a half witnessed a legend of American agronomy deserving summary here, notwithstanding its litanous familiarity to some readers.

In 1839 Ruffin reflectively recapitulated his stumbling early attempts at farming, his revelations, doubts, and ultimate success, in his agricultural journal, the *Farmers' Register*.[5] By this time Ruffin had put himself in historical context: His own ancestors demonstrated the general course of agricultural history in the East, gradually exhausting their lands to the brink of permanent ruination, leaving people with no recourse but migration to fresh western lands. It is likely that such historical understanding confronted Ruffin early and cruelly, when he was still a teenager. For in 1839 he recalled vividly Thomas Cocke's summary of the opinion of "experienced practical cultivators of his neighborhood"—"that our land which was naturally poor could not 'hold manure,'" and that "the whole country, was doomed to hopeless sterility." Young Ruffin resisted at first: This was "a monstrous agricultural heresy" and a "treason" to every "author on agriculture whom I had read or heard of. But at last," he conceded, "I was compelled, most reluctantly, to concur in this opinion." Local memory compounded his frustration; experience defied published authorities. Exhausted and despairing, Ruffin asked, "What was then to be done?"[6]

Before his father's death Edmund had read Thomas Hale's four-volume *A Compleat Body of Husbandry*, published in London in 1758–59. Hale, he recollected, was merely compendious, "and of little value or authority; but it gave me a fondness for agricultural studies, and filled my head with notions which were, even if proper in England, totally unsuitable to this country." Next he "greedily devoured" the American John Beale Bordley's *Essays and Notes on Husbandry and Rural Affairs* (Philadelphia, 1799), but discovered that Bordley also "drew almost all his notions from English writers ... [and] foreign materials." As Ruffin groped his way into a farming career, however—likely in his second crop-year—he found the work of a living American agronomist, a work that directed his life for half a decade and earned his everlasting admiration. This was the first edition (1813) of *Arator*, by John Taylor of Caroline.

Ruffin was only the second historian-reformer of agrarian decline. John Taylor was the first. Taylor had been born near the falls of the Rappahannock in 1753—about when the first stage of the Europeanization of eastern agriculture (i.e., institution of the plow, permanent fields, and wheat culture) was taking place. A fourth-generation American heir to a distinguished and well-connected family, Taylor received good preparation for public life in a private academy, at the College of William and Mary, and in the law office of his famous uncle, Edmund Pendleton. In early adulthood, however, Taylor was first a soldier. He served several years with George Washington's Continental Army, rising to the rank of major. Toward the end of the war he was briefly a member of Virginia's House of Delegates before reentering the army, now as lieutenant colonel, to defend his state against Hessian invaders in the campaign that led to Yorktown. Taylor received generous grants of western lands in reward for his military service—an ironic curiosity, considering his later hostility to immigration—but as he rose to prominence in the legal profession after the war, he invested much of his wealth in Caroline County lands. Taylor married in 1783; six years later he retired from the law and took up planting in earnest on several estates near his birthplace. Hazelwood, his residence, became legendary for the Taylors' unpretentious hospitality and especially for the colonel's agricultural experiments.[7]

Caroline County straddles the Virginia Tidewater and Piedmont, lying south of the falls of the Rappahannock, southeast of the town of Fredericksburg. North of the river is the Northern Neck, home to the seventeenth- and eighteenth-century estates of the Fitzhughs and Lees, Landon Carter, and George Washington. To the east and south lie Essex, King and Queen, King William, and other counties organized and planted in tobacco and corn at least a century before John Taylor's birth. By American standards, the country was old, and Taylor was hardly the first Virginian to acknowledge age and act in compensation. By the time John Taylor came into this world, his elders had discarded the hoe and Indian-style fire culture in favor of the plow and other European implements of farming on what were intended to be permanent fields.[8]

In little more than a generation—that is, toward the end of the eighteenth century, when Taylor began planting—European-style farming in America had begun to fail. Vast herds of cattle and mountains of manure were not maintaining fertility after all; crop fields were almost as impermanent as Indians' and early English settlers'. So Taylor set about reassessing American agriculture with a view not to abandoning the European model, but to finding means to make it work. Briefly, the view that culminated in publication of *Arator* began with Taylor's belief that fully three-fourths of the Chesapeake region's vegetative cover had been removed, impoverishing the chemical interactions between soil and atmosphere. Dung was ameliorative, but Taylor argued that vegetation—"green manure"—was essential to recovery. In a memorable letter to Thomas Jefferson, Taylor wrote that "Manure can only come of great offals, and great offals, only of great crops. These great crops, and great offals then are the desiderium." Cultivated vegetation must be returned, undiminished, directly to the soil. This necessitated what he called "inclosure," that is, the exclusion of animals from fields, preventing their consumption of clovers, grasses, hays, or corn. Since farmers must produce staples for money while restoring fertility, Taylor recommended corn culture. Actually, corn is a great nitrogen-depleter. Taylor understood little of soil chemistry; he assumed that the return of stalks, shucks, and cobbs to corn land, along with a regime of crop rotation, was more than sufficiently replenishing. He also championed the culture of clover and peas (nitrogen producers), as well as deep-plowing for the blending of manures and soils and interchange with the magical atmosphere.⁹ John Taylor was both correct and utterly wrong in his agricultural program, which seems significant now only as an awkward episode in the childhood of American agronomy. Edmund Ruffin discovered this, awkwardly and painfully, for himself. What remains important about Taylor, I think, are his motivation and the timing and manner of his reformism, most of which bear telling resemblances to Ruffin's.

During the 1790s, as Taylor segregated his animals from his crops and plowed deeply, he joined Jefferson in defending agrarian interests against the Hamiltonian Federalists. Taylor was elected to the U.S. Senate in 1792, and his first political tracts appeared in 1794, just as a Yorkshireman named William Strickland arrived in America to inspect New World farming. In 1801 Strickland published in London his *Observations on the Agriculture of the United States*. Taylor apparently read the pamphlet soon after. Strickland's "terrible facts" of American husbandry may have offended the Virginia colonel's patriotism at first, but Taylor discovered a concert of observation and belief with this "disinterested foreigner": American farming was exhaustive and ruinous. "Land in New-York," as Taylor quoted Strickland, "formerly producing twenty bushels [of wheat] to the acre, now produces only ten." The farther south the Englishman traveled, the poorer were the land and people: "Virginia is the southern limit of my inquiries," Strickland explained, "because agriculture had there already arrived to its lowest state of degradation." The authority of the "impartial stranger" emboldened John Taylor thereafter to link his agrarian politics with agricultural reform. In 1803 he published anonymously in a Georgetown newspaper the earliest collection of the essays that, in 1813, were to become a substantial volume, his famous *Arator*.¹⁰

Arator remains in print today—in an excellent paperbound edition—because its political views are beloved of American conservatives. Taylor asserted a localist republicanism that resonates with some yet, almost two centuries later. *Arator* is the foundation, too, for later Taylor political tracts that attack "usurpation" and "coercion" in central government—*An Inquiry into the Principles and Policy of the Government of the United States* (1814), *Construction Construed, and Constitutions Vindicated* (1820), *Tyranny Unmasked* (1822), and *New Views of the Constitution of the United States* (1823). Louis Hartz and other scholars have legitimately emphasized Taylor's anticipation of the southern "Reactionary Enlightenment" of John C. Calhoun, George Fitzhugh, N. Beverly Tucker, James Henry Hammond, Edmund Ruffin, and others—intellectuals who defended slavery in the abstract and attacked bourgeois values, especially "wage slavery." In his own time, ironically, Taylor was a Jeffersonian "liberal" whose style and sensibilities arched backward (not forward to Calhoun and Ruffin), to the Roman Republic, which he admired and upon which he thought Americans had made ingenious improvement. M. E. Bradford, the reactionary intellectual responsible for the fine paperback *Arator* (1977), understood this well and properly placed Taylor's best work in the "hard pastoral" tradition of Cato the Censor's *De Agri Cultura*. "Hard" pastoralism is political economy, of course, but first it is practical agronomy. So was *Arator*, and young Edmund Ruffin read it thus. Taylor was, to Bradford, "A Virginia Cato."[11] Ruffin was his worthy successor, a country practitioner who, while ultimately the political economist *in extremis*, was always the agronomist.

John Taylor, meanwhile, labored nobly against a profound contradiction that mocked his science, logic, and historical self-consciousness. One will recall that the Caroline planter was also a Kentucky landlord. As such, and as a knowledgeable public man, Taylor could not have escaped understanding that western lands were not only "new" but also intrinsically superior to the soils of the South Atlantic Tidewater. During the second half of his life, migration to the West surged, and the territory between the Appalachians and the Mississippi was filled with new states. Enormous surpluses of corn, wheat, and cotton floated down western rivers; and shortly after Taylor's death, the Erie Canal dramatically shortened the path of western competition with coastal grain farmers. The eastern states would supply grain to American cities and to Latin American markets for several decades more—but at increasing disadvantage. By the end of the nineteenth century, Maryland, Virginia, and eastern North Carolina farmers effectively gave up; their long age of grain ended (as we shall see). The whole agrarian East—not merely Chesapeake and northeastern North Carolina planters—had long been doomed, by Nature herself and by a world market system.[12]

This cruel destiny was becoming apparent by the beginning of the nineteenth century, but nowhere in *Arator* did Taylor directly acknowledge the West. It is instead a specter above his text, haunting the East, necessitating desperate but futile reformism. Only once, and then merely in passing, did

Taylor intimate his beloved region's physical disadvantage: In essay 15, devoted to overseers, Taylor admitted that "The Soil of the United States upon the Atlantic Ocean is naturally thin, and exceedingly impoverished." His next sentence insisted that this soil "produces, however, good crops, when made rich, almost under any species of cultivation." [13]

But making South Atlantic soils as rich as western lands was and remains quite impossible. Had every eastern farmer devoted himself to enclosures, deep plowing, "great offals," and then to Ruffin's later, corrective methods, westerners' advantages would have remained relatively the same. In fact, eastern farmers—often following Taylor and Ruffin—improved their lands and grain productivity until the Civil War, all the while slipping in productivity relative to new northwestern states. Virginia's corn crops fell from third largest in 1839 to sixth in 1849 to eighth in 1859, while production improved by more than three million bushels. The Old Dominion's rank among wheat states was fourth in 1849, fifth in 1859. (Illinois and Ohio were first and second.) Still, Virginia's 1859 wheat crop exceeded Pennsylvania's; and not only Baltimore but also Richmond, Petersburg and, to a lesser extent, Norfolk persisted as grain mill and shipping cities. The waters of the Chesapeake and Albemarle and of their great tributary rivers churned, as they had since the 1730s, with the great commerce in grain. [14] The continuity of land-use and production in the region—this long age of grain—is striking. Decline was relative only, but paramount in the minds of Taylor and his contemporaries, then Edmund Ruffin and his.

Young Edmund's crisis at Coggins Point was, in the meantime, quite real. Either in 1813 or 1814 he adopted *Arator* as his manual and persisted with Taylor's green manuring and "inclosures" for (as he later recalled) "four or five years." Yet nothing worked. Manuring "produced very little of the expected effect in the first course of crops, and was scarcely to be perceived on the second. Clover could not be made to live on land of this kind." Furthermore, "The general non-grazing of the fields under grass, or rather under weeds, produced no visible enriching effect, and the ploughing of hill land ... caused the most destructive washing away of the soil by heavy rains." [15] It was at this point that Ruffin came to agree with Thomas Cocke that their lands were effectively dead.

But another farm book had come to Ruffin by then. This was Humphry Davy's *Elements of Agricultural Chemistry, in a Course of Lectures for the Board of Agriculture*, first published in London in 1812, then in Fredericksburg, Virginia, in 1815. Ruffin probably had his copy by early in 1817. He "read it with delight," Ruffin declared, "notwithstanding my then total ignorance of chemical science, and even of chemical names, except as learned by its perusal." Davy was problematical also because his discussion and experiments were all of England. Ruffin had complained already about European texts and their inapplicability to American soils. However, this irritation masks both Taylor's and Ruffin's essential commitment to replicating—so far as American conditions permitted—an idealized European pastoral landscape. In the case of the Davy text, Ruffin stumbled again, but early on noticed something that, after adjustment for local circumstances, proved to be an American revelation: "There was one pasage in this author," he wrote, "which seemed to promise to afford both light and hope on the point in which disappointment had led me to despair." In illustrating "defects in the chemical constitution of soils, and remedies which proper investigation might point out," Davy had "adduced the fact of a soil 'of good apparent texture,' which was steril, and seemed incapable of being enriched." Davy's illustration (in the fourth "Lecture") electrified young Edmund: "If on washing [for analysis] a steril soil," Ruffin read, "it is found to contain the salt of iron, or any acid matter, it may be ameliorated by the application of quicklime." Ruffin's property—indeed "all the lands of lower [i.e., Tidewater] Virginia"—were both of good texture and sterile. So Ruffin conducted with samples from his own farm the simple test for salt of iron ("copperas"), which Davy had found in a sample of Lincolnshire soil. The test failed, and Ruffin began to despair again. Then he began to reason: "But though not a salt, of which one of the component parts was an acid, might not the poisonous quality be a *pure* or *uncombined acid*?"

This was the question. Once Ruffin considered unadulterated acidity, he all but confirmed an answer to his dilemma in the most superficial observations. For example, he wrote, "certain plants known to contain acid, as sheep-sorrel and pine, preferred these soils, and indeed were almost confined to them, and grew there with luxuriance and vigor proportioned to the unfitness of the land for producing cultivated crops." Then Ruffin assembled or contrived instruments for testing acidity in soils and worked about his property. He discovered that "of all the soils supposed to be acid which I examined by chemical tests, not one contained any calcareous earth." And further, "the small proportion of my land, and of all within the range of my observation, which was *shelly*, and of course calcareous, was entirely free from pine and sorrel, and moreover was as remarkable for great and lasting fertility, as the lands supposed to be acid, for the reverse qualities." Therefore "Shells, or lime, would necessarily combine with, and destroy all the previous properties of any acid placed in contact." Ruffin did not yet quite understand that calcium—in fossil shells (called marl or calcareous manure) and in lime—had the effect of fixing nitrogen in manured soils and that, thus fixed, nitrogen could be released into rich crops instead of the atmosphere. Gradually, however, he came to comprehend virtually all of it, and committed his learning to a scholarly paper that appeared in the *American Farmer* (in Baltimore) in 1821. By 1826 Ruffin had produced a book-length treatise; but Thomas Cocke's persisting doubts undermined Ruffin's confidence, and he retained the manuscript for years. Finally, in 1832, when Cocke had at last become an eager supporter, Ruffin published his epochal *Essay on Calcareous Manures*. In the meantime, he had located accessible deposits of shells and ordered his slaves to dig, load wagons, and haul the marl to his worn-out fields, beginning in January 1818. He made mistakes at first—especially in overapplication—but kept careful records, adjusted his methods, and during the 1820s enormously improved his farm's productivity.[16] The father would support his huge family in Virginia, after all.

Still, Coggins Point life and labor made Ruffin restless, anxious. He suspended his highly detailed farm journal in 1827. In hardly a dozen years he had exposed *Arator*'s fallacies and discovered Davy, acidity, marl, and then the correct application of marl. He had already written the first version of *Calcareous Manures*. So Ruffin, grown successful at last, now grew bored with the detailed tedium of a farm routine of his own invention. "The operation of the farm had ceased to be enough interesting or attractive to engage my continued attention," he later confessed. "The business therefore was ill managed, & altogether had become disagreeable to me." Too, Coggins Point's advantageous commercial location by the James, he convinced himself, was disadvantageous to his family's physical well-being. Nearby marshes bred malaria and "bilious fevers," and two of his and Susan's early children had died. In the sickly summer season of 1828 he moved his family somewhat inland, about three miles to the southwest, to a recently acquired property he called Shellbanks. By the end of 1829 Ruffin had convinced himself that Shellbanks was a healthy spot, and in 1831 he and his family departed Coggins Point for the new farm. It was here that Edmund briefly revived his enthusiasm for farming: The new place needed marling and ditching. But Shellbanks is more important as the site of his emergence as full-time scholarly reformer-editor-writer.[17]

Edmund named the new farm for marl, of course. (He did the same for his next and last place—Marlbourne, just above Richmond. His second son received the odd middle name of Calx, also honoring calcium.) Marl was the foundation of his and his family's security, and his fame. Marl is shells—fossil accretions in banks on ancient shores. The earth's rotation and lunar cycles of tides and waves brought them forth from the sea, to be abandoned, compacted with silicon and clay, and covered with silt and vegetation when the ocean receded. Indians knew shellbanks and exploited them agriculturally, in a modest way, as we have already seen. In all likelihood they had observed relationships between shelly and nonshelly lands and their vegetative covers and deduced accurate, practical conclusions, much as Edmund Ruffin did during the late 1810s. Indians also treasured shells aesthetically. Shells were decor and sometimes a medium of exchange. Like other so-called primitive peoples, Indians seem to have recognized shells metaphorically: They are elementally feminine, regenerative, magic—a wondrous distillate of Mother Earth herself.[18]

Europeans created and cherished shell-lore long after their own primitive origins. Like the Chinese, they regarded shells as emblems of good fortune. Shells' association with water implied fertility. Venus was delivered upon a shell in ancient myth, and Botticelli's huge Renaissance canvas perpetuates the association. The city of Rome is crowded with symbolic shells, from the floors of the forums to the Spanish Steps to the Vatican. Europeans also thought shells the symbol of regeneration—of the prosperity of a new generation arising from the death of its predecessors. (Infant oysters, for instance, must attach themselves to banks of lifeless oyster shells in order to survive.) Shells' feminine regenerative power was replicated in North American woodland peoples' corn goddess, who flew over the land, spreading her fecundity, then dying, so that crops might grow the following year. European elites, meanwhile, developed shelly decorative arts—first in loggia, grottoes, and baths, then within their houses—during the seventeenth and eighteenth centuries. Alexander Pope loved to meditate in his gloomy shell- and mirror-decorated grotto. Inside homes, however, shell rooms were cheerful places for women, often of feminine design.[19]

Europeans turned temperate North America into a neo-Europe during the same period that they developed decorative shell art to its most elaborate expression. Yet shells as art and symbol are difficult to locate in Euro-America. Some tombstones in Puritan and early eighteenth-century New England include carvings of the shell as well as the deathly skull. Shells denote pilgrimage and resurrection—important to place in triumph above the skull. But this custom seems not to have survived the eighteenth century. Countless Euro-Americans may have brought home from Atlantic beaches and elsewhere a beautiful shell or two and kept them at home, as we still do. But there were no shell rooms, loggia, grottoes, or baths that we know of, until well into the twentieth century—and these very few are the creations of artist-eccentrics. In the main, it seems, Americans were too poor—and much too busy struggling *against* nature's fecundity—to nurture shell-lore and ancient myth. Edmund Ruffin never pondered shells metaphorically either in his private or published writing. In 1843, when he conducted an agricultural/geological survey of South Carolina, his private diary—almost three hundred pages long in a recent (and condensed) printing—was crowded with observations of marl and other fossil shells. In every case Ruffin's interest was scientific and industrial. Once, exploring a cavern cut through marl, he admired the *absence* of recognizable shells. The river-made passage was "a beautiful fine grained marl, moderately soft, & without a shell remaining." In fact, this observation is unremarkable; for through Ruffin's entire lifetime, shell symbolism is utterly missing from written discourse.[20]

One might *imagine* Ruffin and Thomas Cocke, in spoken discourse by a marl pit, pondering the beauty and the feminine regenerative power of shells, as sweating slaves exhumed and carted marl for crop fields. Or perhaps they joked, salaciously—like twentieth-century men—of intact shells' resemblance to labia. Both scenarios seem unlikely, particularly the latter. One marl pit scene we do have, however, comes through the eyes of Edmund's affectionate half-sister, Elizabeth, from her diary sometime in 1827: "By B[rother]'s solicitation," Elizabeth wrote, she "went to see his newly discovered Marl-banks, and whilst his interested tongue spared not words of commendation, his ears open to every thing like a foretelling future beneficial results, and his very eyes appeared *charmed* and *dazzled* with the *transcendant beauty* and *lustre* of the sight; I for want of science, and experience could form not the least conception of its *invaluable nature*, and saw nothing at all but a mixture of pulverized shell and sand, which would never have attracted notice or attention from me."[21]

Beauty was to be discovered in science, then, and pulverized shells. And Edmund Ruffin is revealed as the essential eighteenth-century man—the rationalist and instrumental scientist. He was a man of charming enthusiasm, to be sure, but still the exemplar of Romanticism's opposite. Compare Ruffin with his younger contemporary, Thoreau—whose eyes dazzled when he squatted low in a rainy meadow, assuming the perspective of a muskrat: here was a genuine Romantic. The two men represent an elemental bifurcation of American notions of Nature, a split not yet resolved.[22]

In this century—while some Americans have rediscovered Thoreauvian wilderness-as-refuge and others collect decorative shells for profit—shell symbolism has largely been reduced to the salacious. In eastern North Carolina and other coastal places, labia with pubic hair are "bearded clams." In Manhattan during the 1980s, a Forty-Second Street marquee advertised "*The Pink Clam*." Beyond this there seems only—but importantly, I suspect— the ubiquitous commercial sign of the Royal Dutch/Shell Group, which appeared in the United States in 1912, when the European conglomerate battled with Rockefeller's Standard Oil for world market domination. Here the shell seems completely masculinized—industrial, perhaps even warlike, only vaguely geological, with slight reference, perhaps, to the old Chinese token of good fortune. The shell in the logo and name of the European petroleum combine actually derives from the British component: In 1830 Marcus Samuel had established in East End, London, a modest enterprise in the Asian trade. Among the many things he imported were polished seashells. Some were processed into mother-of-pearl for button and knife-handle manufacture. Others were purchased by women as domestic decoration (as in times past). Eventually Samuel's business became known as the "Shell" Transport and Trading Company, which grew large in international shipping under the leadership of his son, the first Viscount Bearsted. At the turn of the century Bearsted created the British-Netherlands conglomerate with Hendrik Deterding of Royal Dutch, a younger company that had developed oil wells and refineries in Sumatra.[23]

So the shell's ancient feminine power was lost to Europeans, it would appear, sometime in the nineteenth century, between the climax of shell art and the creation of Royal Dutch/Shell, perhaps about the time the projectiles of firearms and artillery became "shells." Euro-Americans had been determined to subdue nature from the start, and resisted shells' undisciplined fecundity. The ancient myths were still-born, so to speak, on the Atlantic shore. Then, by Ruffin's time—by coincidence and by what seems destiny—American men put the shell to work for their own ends. The shell became industrial in Ruffin's new agronomy long before the British and Dutch founded an oil company.

Even as Ruffin's slaves marled Shellbanks, Edmund sent out prospectuses for an agronomic journal he would call the *Farmers' Register*. Shellbanks itself was hardly forgotten: It was a family home, Ruffin's printing and editorial base, and the point from which he began his agricultural-geological expeditions. As a farm Shellbanks occupied only marginal space in his mind, however. Others managed this business—and rather badly, he later wrote. Ruffin would have preferred living in a city, a more appropriate place for a thinker and publicist. Meanwhile, satisfied with responses to his prospectuses, Ruffin established his farm paper at Shellbanks and contracted with a Richmond jobber to print and mail it. The jobber often deferred work on the *Farmers' Register* in favor of more lucrative printing contracts, however; so after a year Ruffin bought his own press, hired printers, and set up shop on his farm. This was 1833, the year following the first edition of his *Essay on Calcareous Manures*. Ruffin kept to Shellbanks for two more years; then he moved his press and family to town at last — to Petersburg. (There, Ruffin says in his autobiography, his younger children might be better educated; but one clearly senses as well his own yearning for the intellectual advantages of town.) Ruffin wrote later that he was naive about business. His journal did not fare well in competition with papers subsidized by state governments elsewhere. His subscription rate was too high. He did not collect enough owed to him. Ruffin also angered subscribers with intemperate (although well-justified) attacks on banks, especially in another (unprofitable) publication. Finally he closed the *Farmers' Register* in 1842, having completed ten volumes published at Shellbanks and in Petersburg. He mourned the costs of his education in the publishing business. But he had become famous; his circle of admiring acquaintances had widened far beyond those disaffected by his assault upon banks. He accepted the invitation of the governor and legislature of South Carolina to conduct a learned survey of their state's landscape. Agricultural societies and magazines noticed him. In 1851 *De Bow's Review* of New Orleans published a lengthy sketch of his career.[24]

Ruffin's fame was well deserved. The *Essay on Calcareous Manures* is the founding work of soil science in the United States. And the *Farmers' Register* is widely acknowledged as the best American agricultural journal of the nineteenth century. (In that nineteenth-century farm papers were more cosmopolitan and more openly concerned with political economy and their writing more original than that of their twentieth-century counterparts, one might say that Ruffin's journal is simply the best ever produced in this country.)[25] Like other editors, Ruffin reprinted articles from other papers, but always with critical prudence rather than desperation to fill space. He taught himself to read French, primarily, it seems, so that he might peruse agronomic journals from Paris and Brussels, then translate and print meretorious research reports and commentary in his own paper. Ruffin constantly sought original contributions from American scientists and practical farmers, too. They frequently failed him, so Ruffin supplied copy himself, often anonymously. His own pieces usually derived from systematic visits to representative counties in

Virginia and northeastern North Carolina—places rich in marl; places where agricultural reform was well underway; places utterly backward; places dark and murky, inviting vast reclamation and institution of scientific agronomy at rebirth.[26] In all, two interrelated projects appear: Ruffin's program to halt or slow western migration through reform of eastern farming, and an interpretation of history that would illustrate the necessity of reform and stable civilization.

Ruffin's paramount reform was of course the resuscitation of cropland with marl. He undertook discursive augmentations of the *Essay on Calcareous Manures*, publishing them (in 1835 and 1842) as new editions of his masterwork. In 1840 he reprinted Taylor's *Arator* in the *Farmers' Register* with a critical yet admiring introduction. Throughout his journal's decade, Ruffin never tired of educating his readers in the elements of modern agronomy, Tidewater geology, the appearance and grades of marl, and appropriate application of calcareous manures to various soils. But this was hardly all.

Ruffin anticipated by half a century the southern rural elite's notorious war on traditional fencing laws. During colonial times, when forests and marshes were vast and cultivated areas relatively small and isolated (like the human population), legislatures had required the fencing of crops to protect them against cattle and especially swine, which ranged at large. The system suited frontier conditions: The wealthy found ample resupplies of hardwood trees to extend and replace fencing, and the poor and landless supported themselves through enormous numbers of animals that fed on de facto commons—meadow- and marsh-grasses and bountiful mast (nuts and tender roots) in the woods. As the Tidewater and then the Piedmont became settled, however—especially after Americans resorted to the plow and permanent fields—tensions arose. Hardwood timber, already depleted by the making of tobacco hogsheads and myriad other uses, became harder to find, and planters resorted to pines, which rotted faster. Free-ranging animals broke down fences or grubbed beneath them and damaged crops, and farmers could seldom identify positively the owners of offending cattle and hogs so that they might collect damage claims under provision of fencing laws. During the early nineteenth century, northeastern states, then newer states of the Old Northwest, one after another adopted fencing laws that reversed colonial practice: Animals must be contained, not crops. Denser populations, a more thorough commitment to the market (as opposed to subsistence), and a European-inspired desire to breed larger, healthier farm stock seem to have propelled the Yankee reformers. In Virginia, a few larger farmers, including

Edmund Ruffin, took notice and, in the first two volumes of Ruffin's farm journal, began to air their discontent with the open range.[27]

Ruffin permitted some of his peers to express his opposition to the open range, yet he welcomed defenses of the old law in his columns. The latter saw reform as the scheme of the rich to deprive the poor of their livelihoods: Elimination of "the right of common upon every man's land, who does not choose to enclose it with a fence fully five feet high" would impoverish smallholders and the landless, declared petitioners to the General Assembly late in 1834. The yeomanry and the poor had insufficient cropland to devote acres to the production of fodder.[28] Ruffin's own response, published during the spring of 1835, corresponded to and doubtlessly confirmed in his mind an emerging historiography that informed all his reforms. The open range, he conceded, had served Virginia well during the settlement stages of the Tidewater and Piedmont. That historical period was now past, and the traditional law had become anachronistic and mischievous. "[I]n some parts of the northern states," he argued, "hogs are not permitted to range at large — and the fences may therefore be made at half the cost." Enclosing animals consumed fewer resources, in other words, than enclosing crop fields. Ruffin's response to the issue of class benefit strains credulity, however: "It is as much the operation of the fence law to accumulate many small tracts in few hands, as it is of the law of descents (however beneficial this may be in general,) to divide these accumulations." It would seem that huge and would-be huge planters would be more restrained by a law requiring the fencing of crops, than by a so-called reform requiring the penning of beasts. In fact, Ruffin cared nothing for the smallholder or the poor stockman, and he attributed the defeat of his fence reform bill in the legislature in 1835 to "the now demagogue-governed people."[29]

The best Ruffin could accomplish during the late 1830s was the General Assembly's declaration that Tidewater rivers and their tributaries were in themselves "'lawful fences.'" This relieved riverfront planters such as himself of the expense of maintaining miles of "perishable and useless fences" next to tidal watercourses. In 1840 Ruffin proposed statewide "ring fences" modeled after a voluntary Prince George County association he had initiated, apparently about 1830. The ring fence scheme, he explained, was "another imperfect yet very important means of reform ... by voluntary agreement of the proprietors of a number of contiguous farms to dispense with all fences, except a general enclosing fence of the whole neighborhood, and the separate enclosures for pasture, which each individual should have for his own stock, on his own ground." The individual stock fences within neighbor-hoods represented the reformers' ideal solution. The proposed rings, how-ever, look very much like a sort of apartheid, separating the rich, commer-cial, and progressive from the poor, subsisting, and traditional farmers of the Old Dominion. Almost two decades later (in 1858) the General Assembly finally created legislation permitting local option for ring fence associations. Ruffin exulted over "the commencement of a reform & revolution ... I have been laboring to produce, for 20 years."[30]

Ruffin's revolution would be very long in the realization, however. After his death the legislature (in 1866) invested county commissioners with the power to enforce the 1858 ring fence law, relieving the courts of that duty. Ruffin's first son, Edmund, Jr., was among those who protested that during Reconstruction, with poor men serving as commissioners—"either colored men or men of none or so little property and intelligence"—chaos reigned.[31] As late as the mid-1870s the editor of Richmond's *Southern Planter & Farmer* bemoaned the piecemeal, voluntary, and glacial progress of fencing reform. By the 1880s, however, cheap barbed wire had become available, and strenu-ous agitation for fence reform in other southern states seems to have reduced opposition to new legislation in Virginia. Even then, the General Assem-bly adopted a county-option system like Georgia's and North Carolina's, and it appears that the open range did not actually disappear throughout the Commonwealth until after the turn of the century, if then.[32]

To Edmund Ruffin, meanwhile, an open-ranged South Atlantic was emblem-atic of the ecological and social ruin his generation had inherited. People had attached themselves to the land and maintained communities only so long as they might exploit the soil without reinvestment. Planters aban-doned their places and moved on to a West where they would repeat their ruin. Poor folks remained, brutish and unambitious, because they could sus-tain themselves on livestock fed in a wild environment made wilder by the departure of migrants. Everyone lacked consciousness of social process, the preservationist ethic (usually associated with Europeans), and a love of place derived from historical self-consciousness. So during the 1830s Ruffin and a few like-minded men founded the Historical and Philosophical Society of Virginia. The society would rescue, preserve, and publicize the Common-wealth's documentary record. Written history might instill pride and induce Virginians to forego migration and learn to repair instead of abandon.

Ruffin himself interpreted the record in at least two historiographical ad-dresses. The first he delivered to the society, in Charlottesville, late in 1835—

"Sketch of the Progress of Agriculture in Virginia, and the Causes of its Decline, and Present Depression." With the addition of a lengthy appendix, the speech consumed nearly thirteen large pages when Ruffin published it the following year in the *Farmers' Register*.[33] Ruffin's title conveyed his thesis. It is his elaboration and especially his periodization that seem significant, for they anticipate a few twentieth-century professional historians' conception of the past in agroecological terms. Ignoring conventional political-military periodization, Ruffin divided Virginia's postaboriginal past into two eras. He did not name them, but "primitive" and "modern" would seem to suit well enough. In the former, white settlers adopted native swidden (slash and burn) culture of tobacco and corn, exploited the original fecundity of the soil for a few years, then abandoned worn-out land for new crop fields, also created by burning. The modern era began with the introduction of plows, grain culture (i.e., wheat added to corn), and permanent fields requiring perpetual refertilization. By the beginning of the nineteenth century, it had become evident that European refertilization and crop rotation systems were inadequate. Yields were reduced and the land itself seemed to have died. John Taylor offered a remedy, but it had failed. At last (during the early 1820s), modern soil chemistry revealed that neutralizing acidity would reverse decline. Marl (or lime) was the answer; old Virginia might be restored. But the survival of primitive laws—notably on fencing—and primitive attitudes frustrated modernity's potential.

Ruffin, meanwhile, became the most important publicist of Virginia's proud white past. From the late 1830s until he closed the *Farmers' Register* in 1842, he sought out and printed sundry documents that illustrated the necessity of his reforms. Often, too, in his agronomic essays and reports, Ruffin insinuated a historical perspective. He produced annotated copies of colonial legislation (from Henning's *Statutes at Large*), for example, on topics of interest to his readers—such as the colonial war upon the native wolf population. He researched and published the geological and human-proprietorship histories of famous plantations, such as the Harrison family's Brandons (Upper and Lower) on the James near his own place. Probably most important of all, Ruffin persuaded George E. and William B. Harrison, heirs of Benjamin Harrison and descendants of William Byrd II, to permit publication of Byrd's "History of the Dividing Line," "Journey to the Land of Eden," and "A Progress to the Mines."[34] Byrd—the quintessentially cosmopolitan Anglo-Virginian gentleman—was often on Ruffin's mind. Byrd was a reader and writer, a traveler and keen observer, a good farmer and astute businessman, the founder of Richmond and a river-based imperialist. He was (to someone unable to read the encoded "Secret Diary") altogether an inspiration for Ruffin's century.

Ruffin's ultimate historiographical essay came years later, in 1852, in Charleston—a place also obsessed with *recherche du temps perdu*. There he delivered "An Address on the Opposite Results of Exhaustive and Fertilizing Systems of Agriculture." The title and most details are didactic agronomy, a recapitulation of his aging discoveries and preachments. The work is more interesting for Ruffin's conflation of chronological and regional associations with the word *exhaustive*. Primitive frontier farming practices were exhaustive, of course. In the contemporary West, soil-mining was to be expected, for a time. In the East such farming was understandable in an earlier time, perhaps, but contemptible and socially suicidal in the nineteenth century. For the United States was becoming a mature nation (not unlike European states). The East must demonstrate maturity, nurture its history, landscape, and inhabitants. Continuity depended on the spatial stability and prosperity of people. Frontiers—which virtually defined the nation then and later—were actually the great enemy; for they invited social instability and the impoverishment, even the death, of the earth itself.[35]

Ruffin's historiography and reformism presented a logical dilemma with frightening implications for the future, however. He seems to have recognized at least part of the conundrum early. At the beginning of 1836—in the same *Farmers' Register* number in which his early historical essay appeared—Ruffin published a piece by another writer who refuted the demographic theories of Thomas Robert Malthus (1766–1834), author of *An Essay on the Principle of Population* (1798, with five subsequent editions through 1826). Ruffin disagreed with the article's thesis in a portentous editorial note: "We have not read Malthus for nearly twenty years," Ruffin admitted, "and now state his views, and our own inferences from recollection—but the lapse of time has not lessened our submission to his reasoning." Indeed, Ruffin "doubt[ed] the ability of our correspondent ... to show the theory of population to be false," although he "heartily wish[ed] him success" in alleviating Ruffin's own "unwilling conviction of the truth of the heart-benumbing, hope-stifling doctrine of Malthus."[36]

Actually, Ruffin recalled detail as well as "reasoning" from his remote reading. "The theory of Malthus of the laws of population and subsistence," he explained to his readers, "is, that population naturally increases in a geometrical ratio, while food can only be increased in an arithmetical ratio." When populations grow, so too will food supplies—"but however rapidly, it will not be geometrical, but in arithmetical proportion—not by doubling—but by regular additions of equal (or more often of decreasing) quantities. Thus food may increase at first, (and generally will, in new and fertile countries,) even faster than population—as in the ratio of 1 to 4, (or by additions of 3)—but then it will be only at the rate of 1, 4, 7, 10, 13, 16—and of course the increase of population will be rapidly overtaking, and then outstripping the means for its support." The inevitable geometric/arithmetic catastrophe might be averted only by other catastrophes—the so-called Malthusian checks, war and pestilence. (Later Malthusians promoted birth control, but Malthus himself opposed this strategy.)[37]

Malthus attempted to encompass the earth and all its human history in his theorizing, despite the paucity of reliable censuses in his time. In fact, there are so many exceptions to his "mathematical laws" in human experience as to render Malthusianism less a science than an elite intellectual movement. Nor did Malthus seriously consider the irrational *usage* of food and other resources by privileged minorities, leaving helpless majorities to starve. Still, in the nineteenth century and later, Malthus compelled. To Ruffin, he virtually defined political economy and prophesied all possible futures, with slight revision. Malthus understood, for instance, that slavery had been inadequate to swell the population of the Roman Republic. And "On the condition of slavery" in the Americas early in the nineteenth century, Malthus "observed that there cannot be a stronger proof of its unfavourableness to the propagation of the species, in the countries where it prevails, than the necessity of . . . continual influx" (i.e., from Africa via the slave trade).[38]

Whether Ruffin recalled this passage specifically is not known, but he certainly (and properly) took exception to Malthus's generalization in his 1836 editorial note. Ruffin's own slave force—and the African American slave population generally—grew at a healthy rate, he was well aware. So Ruffin opined that Malthusian checks *"have less influence on the slave population of most of the southern states, than on any other class in the world."*[39] Here, then, began the dilemma.

Despite Virginia's huge white and black families, the antebellum demographic growth curve was virtually flat. (A few Tidewater counties occasionally dipped slightly.) The Old Dominion's surpluses, like those of other South Atlantic states, decamped for the West, of course. So what was to happen, then, if Ruffin and other easterners succeeded in civilizing their fellow citizens, inducing them, in other words, to stay put? Ruffin, progenitor of eleven (nine surviving), seems a less likely candidate to become Margaret Sanger than was Malthus (father of merely three). His heart already benumbed by Malthus's "hope-stifling doctrine," how would Ruffin have fed the enormous human surpluses his reforms might have kept in the old country?

He could not, of course, and certainly knew it. Malthus's rule of normal growth doubled population every twenty-five years. In "back settlements," however, "where the sole employment was agriculture"—that is, places like the American South—Malthus found the population "to double itself in fifteen years."[40] So conceivably, Edmund Ruffin's grim expression in photographs was owing to more than the long exposure-times of camera shutters in his day. He was benumbed—but determined, too, to defeat Malthus, not by assertion but by some herculean remodeling of the low-country landscape.

By 1836, when he was reminded of Malthus, Ruffin was already long disgusted with the routine of farming and finished with original scientific experimentation. His chosen role now was to disseminate and implement modern agronomy generally, to civilize easterners, and—it now seems clear —to cope with Malthus. In this last and most daunting mission, Ruffin drew on his own and other farmers' experience with drainage—especially larger private reclamation projects—to develop the best scheme he could envision to increase food supplies adequate to projected population growth. African American slaves, whom he thought responsible for more than their share of the Malthusian nightmare to come, would bear a particular burden in realizing Ruffin's plan.

Final completion of the Dismal Swamp Canal—which was widened and deepened as Ruffin published his *Essay on Calcareous Manures* and founded the *Farmers' Register*—may have been a precedent and model of sorts. A water-highway, the canal (as we have already seen) dried the eastern swamp and aided establishment of huge corn farms opposite the feeder ditch to Lake Drummond. Ruffin had always been interested in improving the drainage of existing farms. During the 1830s, however, his interest turned more to what is curiously called reclamation, the drainage of "waste" land in order to increase croplands. He followed Hill Carter's ultimate failure to expand his holdings on the James. Then Ruffin took to the roads and railways, especially toward the south.

Ruffin finally entered the Great Dismal in 1836, as guest of a lumber and shingle company. Had he not been the beneficiary of the arduous labors of countless diggers, he probably never would have ventured into the morass, Ruffin averred. "[B]ut for the great highways now opened ... —the great canal, the road on its bank, from Norfolk to North Carolina, and the railway which dips into the northern extremity of the swamp," he might have at best taken William Byrd's option of circling fringes and awaiting others' reports. But these "highways"—plus many additional canals carved by his hosts and other timber-gatherers—made inspection relatively easy. The lumbermen and others had discovered already, too, what Ruffin reported to his readers in the *Farmers' Register*: that while one might assume "that the swamp was much lower than all the surrounding lands, and the general receptacle of the numerous streams flowing from them," in actuality "the swamp is higher than nearly all the firm and dry lands that encompass it, and the interior of the swamp is generally higher than the outer parts. The only exception... is found on the western side, where for some distance, say 12 to 15 miles, the streams flow from higher land into the swamp, and supply all its abundant and overflowing water." Lake Drummond supplied water to the Dismal Swamp Canal, still the possession of a private corporation. But the Dismal Swamp Land Company, engaged in shingle-getting, had dug additional, narrower canals (called ditches), also supplied with water from Drummond. In dry seasons (notably summer) some of the ditches had inadequate water even to float rafts, and Ruffin noted a periodic war for water among competing interests within one of the wettest places in the United States—a premonition of the vaster shrinkage of the swamp in later times, due to ditch-making.[41]

Ruffin was appalled by the jungly sponginess of the deeper swampland, where he occasionally alighted from a canal boat. He stood uncertainly on wet peat, rotted vegetation, and roots. Along the course of the Portsmouth and Roanoke railroad, however, he found that the "swamp soil ... was from 1½ to 2 feet thick, resting on a good dark colored clay." Elsewhere—especially along canal banks and by corduroy paths built for shingle carts—he was also encouraged by firm, obviously rich ground. Ruffin then put together his Malthusian nightmare with some Virginia history: "In comparison with the magnitude of the object, it would seem to be both a cheap and certain operation to drain this whole body of land," he decided. The old coastal South needed the food such land might yield. He would have dug two new canals on the western side of the swamp—one from Drummond northward to Shingleyard Creek (a tributary of the Nansemond) at Suffolk, another southward from Drummond to the Perquimans in North Carolina. (Ruffin apparently did not know of the Jericho Ditch, already completed from Drummond to Shingleyard Creek—or perhaps he thought it should be considerably expanded.) There Ruffin ended his travelogue and prospectus. But immediately after it he reprinted William Byrd's "Proposal to Drain the Dismal Swamp," suggesting a legitimating historical continuity.[42]

In 1839 Ruffin struck out for swamp country again, this time the delta of the Roanoke and the southwestern shore of Albemarle Sound. On the way down to Franklin to catch the train, he complained that "almost no use is made of" the Blackwater River, "this excellent navigable route, except by the small steamboat which runs regularly from the junction of the river [at Franklin] with the Portsmouth and Roanoke railway, to Edenton and Plymouth." The Nottoway and Meherrin, too—the other Virginia tributaries of the Chowan—Ruffin thought should be "transporting country produce" to markets.⁴³ In fact not one of the rivers was navigable very far from its confluence with the Chowan (either then or now). Ruffin seems to have been suggesting, then, that the rivers should be *made* navigable, like other watercourses manipulated for commerce. Navigation would bring the backcountry into the cosmopolitan world he knew by the James.

The Albemarle he saw as a giant cul-de-sac. "All the former *inlets* (as they are called) of the ocean, or rather *outlets* of the rivers and of Albemarle Sound, being now completely shut up by the sand, and the pent-up floods having to seek their difficult passage as far south as Ocraco[ke] inlet, the level of the waters has been raised above their former limit." So there was "scarcely any perceptible tide in the sound, and its water which formerly was salt, is now fresh." Sound waters were superb for navigation; yet owing to siltation from rivers that found insufficient outlet, the sound had become too shallow for vessels of more than five feet draft.⁴⁴ Ruffin did not specifically propose dredging, but his perceptive presentation must have left readers with a clear enough prospect.

Near Plymouth Ruffin visited a farm and observed that in this rich delta landscape, "very few persons have yet begun to drain their swamp lands." Instead they cropped less fertile higher land ("the firm knolls"), which was "now very much reduced by the unceasing cultivation of corn."⁴⁵ Proceeding westward through Washington County, Ruffin finally reached the enormous swamp plantations of the Collins and Pettigrew families near Lake Phelps. Josiah Collins and Charles Pettigrew welcomed Ruffin and showed him their canals, ditches, and giant cornfields—a model of what might be, perhaps, throughout the subregion. Ruffin marveled also at the huge cypress trees: "Very many are five feet through the body at 4 to 6 feet for 40 to 60 feet in circumference." Very many, too, were coming down, as the swamp planters' slaves continued the conversion of woodlands to drained crop fields.⁴⁶

In 1840 Ruffin descended the Blackwater and Chowan to Plymouth again, on his way to Wilmington via steamboat. This completed his observations of eastern North Carolina's lowlands. The next year he reprinted an essay by

Joel R. Poinsett on the subject of irrigation in such country, whereby "thousands of acres of barren land might thereby be rendered as productive as any in the United States."[47] In another year, as we have seen, he closed down the *Farmers' Register* and undertook his inspection of South Carolina's geological and agronomic prospects. All the while, and for at least another decade, too, Ruffin seems to have read widely (as always), but particularly on the subject of reclamation.

By 1852, when he delivered his summary address on historical necessity in Charleston, then, reclamation of giant proportions had become as important to civilizing the South Atlantic as marling was. Ruffin proposed nothing less than complete reconstruction of the low country—from Maryland, or at least from the Chickahominy, to the Savannah. The scale of his vision implied massive planning and public sponsorship. And Ruffin self-consciously invoked European precedent: The coastal South would become Holland, and he would obliterate "worthless and pestilential swamps" as had the Italians by "the celebrated borders of the Po." Rivers, too, would be dredged for navigation, dammed for flood protection (and perhaps for irrigation); and a canal system would connect rivers and render every farmer a commercial creature in tight contact with markets. Slaves would of course perform the amazing labors to effect the reconstruction.[48] So Ruffin emerged, by the early 1850s, as probably the United States' premier proponent of environmental manipulation, comparable to the most ambitious twentieth-century heads of the notorious Bureau of Reclamation or the Army Corps of Engineers.

Formulation of Ruffin's expanded scheme to thwart Malthus corresponded to the national crisis over slavery. I discover no more ecological ingenuity, no more schemes, in Ruffin's writings. He was no longer an editor, but for a while was a private farmer again, at Marlbourne, his new place in Hanover County near Richmond. Then he retired from farming for good, becoming a public man again, utterly (and quite logically) devoted to the defense of slavery and to the creation of a southern white republic based on slavery. As late as the summer of 1860, he worried again about Malthus, but the context was "free society" and "the competition of the indigent for food," not his own society.[49] In service to his beloved Confederacy Ruffin probably lost some of his hearing at Fort Sumter, where he theatrically yanked lanyards, loosing explosives on the Yankee outpost.[50]

There was much more for Ruffin to lose than his hearing. Yankee troops ascended the James in 1862, ransacking his and his sons' places, looting his library at Beechwood, and leaving the graffiti, "You did fire the first gun on

Edmund Ruffin in uniform of South Carolina militia, Charleston, ca. December 1860
(Courtesy of the Virginia Historical Society, Richmond)

Sumter, you traitor son of a bitch." Most Ruffin slaves who did not decamp with the Yankees in 1862 did so when the armies reappeared in 1864. Marlbourne too was damaged, animals and harvested crops appropriated, outbuilding boards and fencing burned for firewood. Such was the destruction everywhere of the built world of the cosmopolitans. There was worse, too. All three of Ruffin's sons, aged twenty-nine to forty-seven, and four grandsons went into the army. One of the latter, young Julian Beckwith, was killed at Seven Pines in 1862. Two years later, Ruffin's beloved second son, Julian Calx (by then forty-four years old), was also killed in action, at Drewry's Bluff. A year later, despondent with grief and despairing at the dependency his own physical infirmities had brought to him, Edmund Ruffin virtually replicated the suicide of his old friend and mentor, Thomas Cocke, a quarter century before: Placing the muzzle of his musket in his mouth, Ruffin pulled the trigger with his toe and blew off the top of his head.[51]

Malthus, meanwhile, was held off—by the calamity of war, but more by the vast expansion of grain culture in the West Ruffin had so despised. In his own country his reforms had small impact. His neighbors in Prince George, then in Hanover and down the Pamunkey River valley, adopted marling, along with others here and there in eastern Maryland and the Carolinas. Marling never became common, however. The digging and spreading was too labor-intensive in the age of slavery, unthinkable after emancipation. Instead, for those who were interested and who had cash or credit, there were commercial fertilizers high in phosphates—imported guano during the 1850s and after, then American-made bone and other concoctions. Older planters on the rivers who remembered Ruffin—Edmund, Jr., Richard Eppes, the indestructible Hill Carter—persisted with calcareous manures, especially lime. Such native survivors (and some new men) resurrected old grain farms after the war, paid free black labor cash wages and, as best they could, perpetuated the long age of grain in the Chesapeake-Albemarle country. Corn and wheat flourish still, in fact, on great James River estates (such as Brandon) that were first planted nearly three centuries ago. Generally, however, the age of grain was dying in the East. Farming itself had begun an irrevocable decline.[52]

The cumulative weight of ever-expanding western production, ruinous late-century prices, and world market convulsions gradually squeezed Ruffin's country into an agricultural periphery. Americans harvested 15.4 million acres of wheat in 1866, 52.3 million in 1899, while the average price per bushel fell from better than two dollars to about fifty-nine cents. As early as the mid-1870s, an anonymous correspondent to Virginia's principal farming journal asked, "Is it Wise, in View of Western Competition, to Counsel Virginia to

Grainfields of Brandon (southern view from the James River), July 1990 (Photo by the author)

Curtail Her Wheat Production?" His answer was positive; and in the following decade farmers throughout the South Atlantic not only curtailed grain
production but also gave up farming altogether.[53]

Many of those who quit were old enough to remember the Confederacy
that Edmund Ruffin had striven to create, and the war that nearly destroyed
everything men and women had created in the countryside. The accompanying graph suggests the volatility of agrarian fortunes in the second half of
the century. Farmers in only four counties of the James-Albemarle subregion
(and representative of that area) lost a quarter-million productive acres during
the 1860s. The following decade—their numbers augmented by newcomers,
especially black freedmen—they expanded acreage far beyond the peak of
the 1860s. But then Chicago became the center of American grain culture,
new foreign competition appeared, and disaster struck the East. During the
1890s a quarter-million more acres became productive, but the total of cropland and improved pastures for 1900 did not quite equal that for 1860. It
never again would.

Richard Eppes, cosmopolitan grain farmer from late antebellum times
until his death in 1896, observed the slow death of the age of grain with typical acuity. Toward the end of 1889 he complained in his diary that "there is
so little wheat shipped from James river, there are scarcely any vessels in the

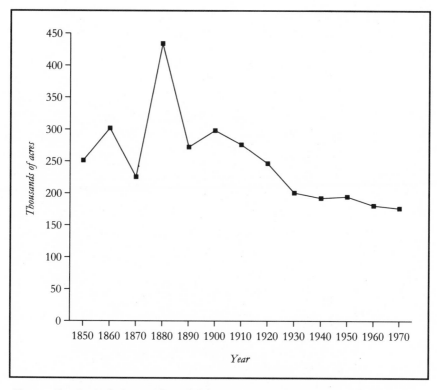

Figure 1. Farming in the James-Albemarle Subregion, 1850–1970: Acres Improved/Harvested, Prince George and Nansemond Counties, Virginia, and Bertie and Camden Counties, North Carolina (Source: *County tables, censuses of agriculture*)

trade." Railroads had supplanted river steamers, but their business was now long-distance, hauling westerners', not easterners', surpluses to market. "It strikes me," Eppes wrote, "that the great industry of growing wheat on the James river farms has pretty nearly gone up. There is now only one mill grinding wheat in Petersburg & only two or three in Richmond." Buffalo, Chicago, and Minneapolis were now the millers of North America, supplanting Philadelphia, Baltimore, and the eastern Virginia cities. Equally significant to eastern river planters were environmental and market revolutions in South America, which had been their principal market for generations. The pampas had been plowed, mills had been built in Argentina and Brazil, and a new empire of grain was thus established in the Southern Hemisphere. "The loss of trade in South America by the establishment of large mills in Reo Janiero Brazil," Eppes seemed almost to sigh, "supplied by wheat from the Argentine Republic is one cause[,] & the immense amount of flour ground

Richard Eppes at Appomattox Manor, ca. 1890, watching the age of grain die
(Courtesy of the Virginia Historical Society, Richmond)

in the West, flooding our whole country with cheap flour[,] makes the milling business hazardous & unprofitable both in Richmond & Petersburg."[54]

The long-lived Eppes represented the last generation of great wheat and corn exporters in the region. The age of grain, begun with the adoption of European plows late in the colonial period, was now done. John Taylor's and Edmund Ruffin's reformism had been for naught, insofar as each reformer had hoped most of all to preserve Tidewater civilization upon familiar grain culture. The West and neo-Europes elsewhere—in Canada, the pampas countries, and Australia—won the dubious prize of grain champion.

PART TWO

The Hinterlanders

I could remember hardly anything . . . except a continuation of pine trees, big, little, and medium in size, and hogs. . . .

Of living creatures for miles, not one was to be seen (not even a crow or a snow-bird), except hogs. These — long, lank, bony, snake-headed, hairy, wild beasts — would come dashing across our path, in packs of from three to a dozen, with short, hasty grunts, almost always at a gallop, and looking neither to right nor left, as if they were in pursuit of a fox.

— Frederick Law Olmsted, below the James, 1852

aniel William Cobb (born about 1812) started his life as a "1-horse farmer" in the Southampton County outback. The diary he began when he was thirty reveals much about the lives of small-scale property holders in the hinterland. In 1842–43 Cobb worked very hard to subsist. He raised corn, crowder peas, a lot of sweet potatoes and some Irish potatoes, wheat and oats. Cobb also kept chickens and a few sheep for his household use, and there were uncounted hogs that Cobb called his, roaming and rooting in the surrounding woods. In December he rounded up as many as he could find, penned and fattened them on corn for a couple weeks; then came the annual slaughter. The surplus bacon Cobb carried up to Petersburg may have been his principal source of cash during those years.[1] But things were changing, and Cobb was ambitious.

During the late 1830s, just before young Cobb began his diaries and his farming, the Portsmouth & Roanoke Railroad (later called the Seaboard & Roanoke) entered southern Southampton at Franklin and curved gracefully southward toward Weldon, North Carolina. The Petersburg & Weldon, too, extended north-south just to the west of Southampton, passing through Emporia on its way to the Roanoke. Then during the 1850s the Norfolk & Petersburg (later Norfolk & Western) was constructed through northeastern Southampton, and the Jerusalem Plank Road vastly improved transportation from Southampton's seat (the center of the county) to Petersburg. So finally, this backcountry place virtually without a navigable river achieved the beginnings, at least, of modern linearity, almost a century after the county's creation. Cobb was not so fortunate as to live next to a railhead, but he was encouraged to think beyond subsistence-plus-bacon money to production for markets. His marriage to the young daughter of a neighboring planter seems materially to have hastened the transition — despite the marriage's evolution into a nightmare of dissonance, and his in-laws' persistent treatment

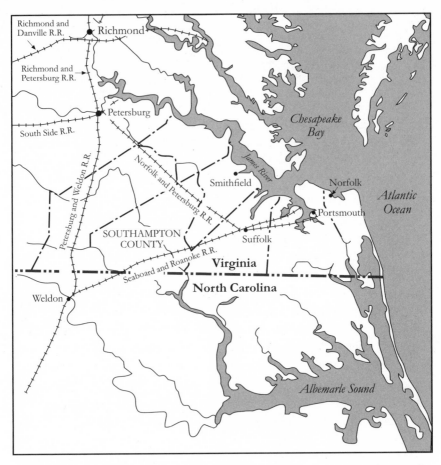

Map 3. Railroads, 1860 (Adapted from Daniel W. Crofts, Old Southampton: Politics and Society in a Virginia County, 1834–1869 *[Charlottesville: University Press of Virginia, 1992], who adapted from at least two other sources)*

of him as a poor relation. Yet however condescending, Cobb's father-in-law provided the benefit of his knowledge of markets, his credit, and sometimes his surplus labor. Gradually, Cobb purchased a few slaves of his own, hired other workers, and began to plant cotton and fertilize his new money crop with guano. His other money-maker was brandy, made at his distillery from his orchards of apples and peaches. Cobb was a strict Methodist sworn to abstinence from drink, but he reasoned that drunkards would get "Whiskey Rum & Jin" if his brandy were unavailable; and if any died from his drink, they would be "not much missed" anyway.[2]

Cobb's contemporary Southamptonite Elliott Lemuel Story (born in 1821) was another white hinterlander of middling social station whose experience survives with his diary. Both men were believing Methodists (although Story accepted doctrine much later in life). Both taught school in their youths (Story much longer than Cobb). Both were farmers, Cobb far the more successful, Story escaping twice to keep store in Franklin. Story sought to improve his mind as well as his income and property—he belonged to a young men's literary and debating society; and he was a Whig who consciously sought the cosmopolitan—in contrast with Cobb, who subscribed to biblical conservatism and a Democratic suspicion of the modern and technological. A complete analysis of the differences between contemporaries of similar status will ever evade the curious; but conceivably, geography may have been critical to Story's Whiggish cosmopolitan leanings. For Story was a creature of eastern Southampton, near the Blackwater and the town of Franklin. His father, like Daniel Cobb, had carried surplus bacon (along with a little cotton) to Petersburg, for cash. The coming of the Portsmouth and Roanoke to Franklin had an almost revolutionary effect on the Story family's orientation, however, by the late 1830s. Young Elliott, already in debt for store-bought supplies, could take a hundred pounds of pork with him on the train, stopping at Suffolk and Portsmouth, where he could sell farm surplus for cash— and pay his debts in Franklin upon his return. Story marveled at the speed and convenience of travel—an east-west linearity defying nature's inconvenient riverine routes. He welcomed more and better, and eagerly moved to Franklin to be in the center of a new world, where boats from the Chowan met "the cars" from the Elizabeth.[3]

Yet both texts and subtexts of these dissimilar men's diaries remind one that no new world appeared in whole. One is more struck, indeed, by the continuity of routine practice in farming—of the ancient cycles of human intercourse with the surrounding rural landscape. As farmers, both men (and their laborers) waged relentless war upon forests. Cobb was ever expanding his crop fields so he could make more corn, cotton, peanuts. So, monotonously, every winter, there were fellings of trees, heaping of logs and limbs, burning, reburning. Crop fields required fencing, so more trees became rails. In April 1843, when Cobb was still a one-horse farmer, he "malled 5600 rails" for his modest property. And well after the Civil War—into the age of barbed wire—Cobb and his workers "malled" rails still. Meanwhile the fires raged, usually every February: In 1843 Cobb "heaped my logs & burnt them in my oald land"—probably a long-abandoned crop field now reclaimed. Three years later a conflagration almost got out of hand: "I like to have had a tremendous fire from burning logs in new ground." In 1854 his hands were "burning logs to day and they burn fine." And on the virtual eve of Fort Sumter, Cobb was still "clearing up fresh land."[4]

On a smaller scale, Elliott Story's life of work was the same — the "tedious and heavy" annual task of clearing "new ground," of heaping, burning, reburning. Both men shadowed cosmopolitan agronomy somewhat: They ditched some, and both tried to maintain the fertility of existing fields. Cobb's hands hauled manure and river mud as well as guano to cotton. Ultimately Story bought fertilizers, too; but for a while he and his helpers gathered topsoil and leaf litter from the woods and spread them on fields. Mostly, however, these middling farmers seemed to depend on new ground and the ashes from the incinerated woods. Their work-lives seem little to resemble those of large-scale agronomic folk nearby, such as Edmund Ruffin and Richard Eppes, who did not practice fire culture. Yet, interestingly, the great river planters' neighbors — sometimes their own relatives (for example, Ruffin's son Julian) — attacked the forests with fire as well.[5] Such people — often younger men — had settled on old, overgrown farms with little "improved" land in relation to woods. So folkish fire practices survived in the midst of the cosmopolitan world as well as in the hinterland.

The other great constant is hogs at large. Despite Edmund Ruffin's best efforts, the open range survived the nineteenth century. This oldest of Anglo-American settled places remained sparsely populated and heavily forested. The forests were enemy to farmers in need of new fields, but they were also the great supplier of shelter, tool handles, and fence rails. The forests were equally important as harborers of swine, those self-reliant, omnivorous creatures Europeans loosed upon nearly the whole world in the sixteenth and seventeenth centuries. In 1705 Robert Beverley, Virginia's first self-conscious historian, observed that "Hogs swarm like Vermine upon the Earth, and are often accounted such, insomuch that when an Inventory of any considerable man's Estate is taken by the Executors, the Hogs are left out, and not listed in the Appraisement." Whether their ostensible owners lived or died, meanwhile, "The Hogs run where they list, and find their own Support in the Woods, without the Care of the Owner, and in many Plantations it is well, if the Proprietor can find and catch the Pigs, or any part of a Farrow, when they are young, to mark them; for if there be any markt [marked] in a Gang of Hogs, they determine the Property of the rest, because they seldom miss their Gangs; but as they are bred in Company, so they continue to the end." Swine, that is, were and remain companionable creatures.[6]

Today in the United States, hogs are bred and fed for slaughter entirely in confinement, often indoors, nearly always under conditions contrary to their construction and disposition. Swine are social (as Beverley observed) and naturally mobile, curious, foraging. And having no perspiration glands in their skin—they sweat through their nostrils—hogs crave cooling shade. They were born for the forested habitat. Hogs become "filthy" only when confined beneath the sun; in distress they wallow (preferably in mud) in order to cool their skin. Humans long sought to reconcile their own convenience and swinish distress: Hogs' undoubted happiness in the wild also freed people from the expense of feeding them, but feral hogs are hard to catch and prone to theft, injury, and disease.[7] Before the middle of the nineteenth century, cosmopolitan agronomists had arrived at something of a middle ground in the dilemma. Hinterlanders such as Cobb and Story approached the agronomic practice. Poorer folks, especially those living most remotely, probably went on with the laissez-faire arrangement Beverley described.

By 1770, for instance, the great Northern Neck planter and diarist Landon Carter tried to control his hogs as well as his cattle. Carter already penned and fattened swine each winter. Now he wished also to prevent his swine from damaging his own or his neighbors' crops, so he assigned a slave girl to herd them about, to feed and deposit manure in places Carter (not the hogs) desired. But she was too small, perhaps, to direct her charges—Carter thought her simply neglectful. So the hogs, he wrote angrily, "are now ranging over the Cornfields." A little later Carter, furious again, complained that his "hog wench is a very bitch, never to be seen and the hogs strolling about. I ordered her a whipping." A short time later, all his cornfield fences were down—probably hogs' mischief—and the hogs were happily foraging again.[8]

Richard Eppes's father, Benjamin Cocke, seems to have practiced a more satisfactory modification of the open range on his brother-in-law's convenient Eppes's Island plantation on the James. The island had woods and marshes about much of its perimeter, and there Cocke apparently permitted his swine to forage freely much of the year. From his reported slaughter weights, however, it seems clear that Cocke penned and fattened his hogs, too. An unfattened range hog weighed typically 60–80 pounds, depending upon available mast. In 1826 Cocke slaughtered hogs weighing 97, 100, 104, 110, 117, and 133 pounds. An early 1834 inventory reported thirty-odd hogs weighing between about 70 and 100 pounds. Later, Richard Eppes's diaries reveal the system more clearly. The island's perimeter was his principal hog range, and for a while apparently his only one. The island was hardly perfect, however. In April 1852 there were unusual floods on the James, and the

Eppes's Island overseer reported that his swamp hogs were "all swimming." This necessitated a roundup and the hogs' removal to a cowpen. The cowpen could not contain them, and the overseer was obliged to install extra planks.

After the war Eppes seems to have been unable for a time to fatten his hogs. But as his fortunes improved, Eppes enlarged his holdings and began to feed at least some of his hogs much of the year, both on the island and across the Appomattox on his Bermuda Hundred estate, which was well fenced. He kept separate accounts for "out hogs" and "Pork hogs." In December 1867, seven Bermuda hogs averaged about 180 pounds each at slaughter. In 1875 — a more typical year — thirty-one island hogs averaged 138 pounds, eleven Bermuda animals only 95. And so it went, inconsistently, as Eppes tried to make money selling pork to his hired workers the year round. In 1888, ten of the island's "smallest hogs" averaged 136 pounds. In 1890 a group of eighteen averaged only 87; thirteen more averaged 100. That same year, however, Eppes's son and namesake killed twenty-three island hogs weighing between 66 and 278 pounds (an average of 197). The largest approached, although hardly equaled, the fat national standard of the late nineteenth century, the enormous Poland-China hogs developed in southern Ohio.[9] Sagacious breeding for the market, year-round confinement, and feeding from farmers' own resources — the Middle Western corn-hog system — had rendered the best-governed southern plantation husbandry quaint.

In the meantime, the governance of swine on the most Europeanized cosmopolitan plantations was troublesome at best. Late antebellum agronomists usually had little more success than Landon Carter. One's own hogs escaped. Neighbors' were a plague. Richard Eppes was both victim and victimizer. Early in June, 1859, he was "much annoyed by a wild hog that infests ou[r] oat & corn fields" at Hopewell. Eppes set traps and, for good measure, armed a slave boy with Eppes's old gun in an attempt to kill the feral creature — both to no avail. Late in August his overseer reported that more "depredations had been committed by wild hogs, the same as injured us last spring." Riding out to inspect the scene, Eppes "was perfectly horrified to see the destruction done to the growing crop of corn by the wild hogs." He ordered the field fenced — indicating perhaps that Eppes already had a ring fence around his Prince George property. But this measure failed, too; and Eppes ordered his overseer to join the boy with the gun. Neighbors complained of firing at night, but the hogs were elusive. Finally and with great reluctance, Eppes had his overseer combine "some Strycnine with shelled corn" in order to poison the intruders and save what remained of his crop.[10]

Just after the war, when temporary poverty obliged him to range all his swine on the island, Eppes had the animals' snouts cut so they could not root up his evenly rolled wheat field. Unconfined island hogs escaped northward through a marsh and over a creek, however, to invade Hill Carter's Shirley, and Eppes sent a drover to herd them home. Ironically, almost exactly between the snout-cutting and the retrieval from Shirley, Eppes, as master of Bermuda Hundred, joined a ring fence association in Chesterfield County.[11]

Edmund Ruffin had exulted when the Virginia General Assembly finally sanctioned the ring associations. I find nothing in his papers about his own hogs, which he ever sought to contain. Son Julian, however, while a young man establishing his own farm at Coggins Point, slaughtered hogs averaging only about 76 pounds.[12] The weights would indicate swine of the nearly feral sort—fleet of foot and probably troublesome to young Ruffin and his neighbors. Farther from the deep rivers, ranging gangs were the norm. The city of Norfolk's common council finally forbade hogs' freedom in the streets in 1831. Franklin—a much smaller town, but an entrepôt to the Albemarle since colonial times and a railhead since the 1830s—did not ban swine until the 1870s.[13]

Daniel Cobb, who by 1861 had nearly achieved planter status, fenced his fields against hogs without complaint. That year he and his hands slaughtered sixty-two of them, averaging less than a hundred pounds each.[14] Elliott Story, the would-be cosmopolitan, labored to fill his cribs with corn-tops for the fattening of his at-large hogs; but in 1846 he mourned, "Our stock of hogs I think are too large for the best[,] for when one has more than he can feed[,] well I think he has too many." Two years later, Story spent most of a morning "in searching the woods for some hogs." And in 1853 he sent for a dog "to assist in catching" a boar. After a quarter-mile chase, Story, another man, and the dog brought the hog to heel.[15]

In addition to thousands of local range swine, Southampton County was also a thoroughfare for many thousands more, driven from the west and southwest toward markets in Suffolk, Smithfield, and Portsmouth. Enormous herds from the uplands of Virginia and North Carolina had passed through Southampton, then Isle of Wight and Nansemond Counties, since at least the early eighteenth century. In 1733, for instance, the governor of North Carolina declared that in good mast years, fifty thousand fat hogs were driven northeasterly to the Virginia port towns. More than a century later (in 1846), pork prices were miserable—only $4.25 per hundredweight, Elliott Story reported. Yet Story went on to remark that "There has already been more pork driven into this county from what I hear and have seen than almost ever was in a whole season before."[16]

The centrality of the open range and droving to Appalachian and upper Piedmont cultures throughout the antebellum era has long been understood.[17] The uplands were not yet utterly given over to market agriculture and remained frontierish as late as 1860. So, too, to a considerable extent, was the pocosin country between the James and Albemarle Sound. On the eve of the Civil War, in the seventeen counties east of the Roanoke there lived 186,652 human souls and 355,555 hogs. (Census enumerators—ever fallible—much more likely undercounted swine than people, relatively few of the latter taking refuge in the swampy woods.) If one subtracts Norfolk County (encompassing the cities of Norfolk and Portsmouth, with 36,227 folks and merely 16,038 swine), the dominance of hogs over people seems rather more considerable: 150,425 with two legs, 339,517 with four and snouts. Prince George, the relatively Europeanized river-county home of Richard Eppes (whose hogs lived in other counties) and of Ruffins and Harrisons, had an almost equal number of people and swine—8,411 and 8,680, respectively. But swampy Gates County—epitome of the hinterland—had 8,443 folks and 25,883 hogs.[18] Gates's demography and land-use systems invite further scrutiny.

This county's humankind were almost evenly divided between whites and black slaves. (The "free colored" population was only 361.) In 1850, 403 free households—approaching half the 880 total—included slaveholders; or (to express the statistic slightly differently), almost 46 percent of all free people belonged to slaveholding households. Only nine property owners in the county were worth so much as $10,000, however. Mills Roberts was the richest man in Gates: He owned $52,000 in various properties, including sixty-seven slaves. Timothy H. Lassiter, owner of fifty-six slaves, was worth $17,000. Corday Savage—Gates's census enumerator in 1850—was a "rich" yeoman comparable to, say, Daniel Cobb of Southampton County. Savage's $1,200 farm and sixteen slaves totaled $2,500 in estimated value. Most white Gates Countians were poor to middling-class folks. Among the latter, small slaveholders were prominent, and the two Jesse Hobbs—Senior and Junior—were typical. Jesse, Sr., owned a farm valued at $700; Jesse, Jr.'s adjacent farm was worth $300. The father owned three slaves, the son but one. Docton Riddick had no slaves but a farm worth $700. Mary Riddick, also slaveless, had a farm worth $5,000. But other Riddicks—the Dismal Swamp counties of both states crawled with folks of this surname—collectively owned quite a few slaves, and some may well have worked Mary's good farm.[19] Hogs suited such folks.

Gates's census data on hogs and on farmland *not* used for crops and pasture offer perspective on the landscape itself. Mills Roberts's plantation was unusual, for instance, because his "improved" acreage (i.e., that used for crops and pastures) exceeded the "unimproved" (woods and wetlands)— 1,200 acres to 800. Timothy Lassiter, the other planter, farmed 650 acres, while 717 acres of his estate were unimproved. Both of these wealthy citizens undoubtedly *used* their woodlands and marshes, however. Neither man appears in the manufacturing schedule among the many shingle- and stave-getting businesses. But unimproved acreage supplied wood for fences, construction, domestic heating, and meat-curing. And Roberts owned 200 hogs, Lassiter 150. Unimproved acreage probably fed all 350 most of each year. Corday Savage farmed 100 acres of his 302-acre property and counted sixty-seven swine. The Hobbs men together farmed 75 of their combined 230 acres and kept forty-three hogs. Docton Riddick's improved acreage was 60, his unimproved 175. He claimed no hogs, but one wonders if any living soul in Gates, free or slave, was actually without at least one. Mary Riddick farmed 250 of her 800 acres and ran 120 swine. The best-off among Gates's free blacks was a man called Willis Duck. His 100-acre farm—40 acres of it worked—was valued at $500, and Duck claimed a dozen hogs.[20] Such folks are representative of a culture closer to that of Appalachia than to, say, more tidily settled Ohio and Indiana. Gates's human population remained sparse; its towns were tiny, its farms more forest and wetlands than cultivated fields and managed pasture. Gates was a haven for modest slaveholders, but also for poor folks of any color who might live upon the wild and upon wild hogs.

Reconstructing past landscapes is easy to a point, then profoundly problematic. Climate and geologic morphology, including drainage, define much, as does natural cover. The latter consisted of mixed deciduous and coniferous forests, with conifers as climax trees in some localities that had particularly wet, sandy soils. The most important aspect of human impact upon landscape is population—expressed historically as reproduction over time. During the nineteenth century—with the exception of urbanizing Norfolk County—the population trend in this subregion is virtually flat. Counties susceptible to cotton plantations on the western side of the map—Bertie, Chowan, Hertford, and Northampton in North Carolina; Southampton and Sussex in Virginia—lost some population during the 1830s, then gradually recovered by 1860. Bertie, for instance, had 11,218 people in 1810, 12,851 in 1850. Southampton's population was 13,497 in 1810, 13,521 in 1850, 12,915 in 1860. Some swampy rural counties' demographic histories are numbingly uneventful. Currituck (at Carolina's northeastern corner) had 6,928 folks in

1800, 6,703 in 1840, 6,476 in 1880. Gates presents a lazy upward curve: 5,881 in 1800, 5,965 in 1810, to 8,161 in 1840; but then population growth stalled in the low 8,000s through the 1860s, fell to 7,724 in 1870, and passed 9,000 only during the 1890s. Prince George—a small territory long settled—resembles Gates: Between 1790 and 1870 the decennial totals bobbed about between 7,175 and 8,411. During the 1870s population momentarily shot past 10,000— only to decline and level off again in the 7,000s until World War I.[21] Humans were not crowding this subregion, then; despite some local volatility from time to time, population density remained almost constantly sparse.

Outside Norfolk County, too, human economic production remained rather constant. People farmed—mostly grain, but also cotton in the western counties, plus (after 1840) peanuts; and along the Nansemond River and especially the branches of the Elizabeth, beginning in the 1830s, farmers began to specialize in "truck" (i.e., vegetables and some fruits) produced intensively for northeastern urban markets. Cosmopolitan farmers—of large scale and near market transportation—sought to create a "European" landscape, as we have seen. Cosmopolitans were wealthy, politically influential, and articulate, dominating published discourse (and subsequent written history), but they were few and unrepresentative. The great bulk of the subregion's production was conducted with fire, by the shifting and abandoning of croplands, in cycles that suited the requirements and predilections of farming families over time. This production system was not European but American, a Euro-American version of aboriginal culture in which productive families did not commute about the landscape (like the Indians) but instead claimed farms large enough to shift fields within their borders. Most ordinary folk seem continually to have fired mature forests and created new cropland while old fields gradually returned to natural succession. At certain stages of their existences, some families were no doubt too large in relation to their farms' sizes to permit most of their lands to go unused (save for hog-running and the usual wood-gathering). Such families at such stages were obliged to emulate as best they could the permanent-field, European strategies of cosmopolitans. The subregion's sparse populations over the long duration indicate a norm of shifting fire culture, however. Abundant anecdotal evidence suggests all this, too. Then there are the great expanses of unimproved land within farms revealed in agricultural censuses, and the enormous populations of swine—most (if not quite all) of them free-ranged most of each year. What one needs, then, is synthesis—the integrated view, preferably from on high, or (that seeming impossible) at least from sources not blinded by the familiar, by class bias, or by a reformist agenda such as Edmund Ruffin's.

Then a landscape reconstruction might be as complete as possible without troves of photographs.

So, lacking the testimony of a literate historical vulture, we turn to the accounts of travelers from different landscapes—biased and agenda-laden to be sure, but keenly receptive to the unfamiliar, both in landscapes broadly and telescopically viewed and in human productive systems. David Hunter Strother—better known as "Porte Crayon"—was such a traveler. Born near Berkeley Springs, now in West Virginia, in 1816, Strother became one of the United States' most popular writers during the 1850s. His metier was the picturesque travelogue, with himself, as Crayon, figuring prominently in the narratives. Strother's light tone and humorous dialogue sometime strain credulity—he was, after all, a well-compensated entertainer of *New Harper's Weekly*'s subscribers. Yet Strother's details have verisimilitude. That he was also an outdoorsman and an artist renders Porte Crayon an outsider with a particularly valued eye. (Strother studied drawing, painting, and wood-cutting with Samuel F. B. Morse in New York City, then traveled and studied in Europe.) When he first saw France, for instance, Strother noticed that trees grew in symmetrical rows; the landscape was entirely arranged by humans, in jarring contrast with the American scene. Later, at the height of his popularity, Strother traveled in the South—particularly in the Valley of Virginia, then in the North Carolina Piedmont. One wishes Crayon had lavished more of his attention on the eastern low country. Of a brief (earlier) visit to Williamsburg and trip up the James, he left us but glimpses reinforcing many other outsiders' grim perspective: Williamsburg was a shabby mockery (Strother assumed) of its previous glory. Buildings rotted. Hogs and cattle roamed the streets. Ruffians harassed him. Strother was invited to dinner upriver at one of the Brandons—a treat; but he was more impressed by the sight of a barge on the James loaded with burned limestone from Maine. His host bought the barge's entire contents to fertilize Brandon's grain fields. Strother's offended reaction to the scene reveals much. A development-minded Whig from limestone-rich western Virginia, he hated the demonstration of his state's inability to get an essential commodity from its own mountains to its Tidewater. The romanticizer and maker of picaresques was at his heart bourgeois. Strother would become a Republican and a brigadier in the Union army. Later, however, Crayon did make one significant foray below the James—to the Great Dismal Swamp. So with care, we shall seek his services again.[22]

Another bourgeois outsider—Frederick Law Olmsted—devoted more of his time to the low country and wrote about his experiences with cold real-ism. Olmsted (1822–1903) was the fortunate son of a kindly, indulgent Connecticut merchant. The father provided an enlightened, book-filled home that probably influenced the youth more than his peripatetic and incomplete formal schooling. Young Fred did not care for business, so the father sanctioned his sea voyage (at eighteen) to China. Yale held him but a semester, when Fred decided he must become a farmer. The father blessed his apprenticeship with New York state's premier agronomist, George Geddes, then gave Fred a little farm of his own on the Connecticut coast. In less than two years he had moved to a larger one, on Staten Island. Young Olmsted loved nature. He also loved humanity and accepted the necessity of efficient markets, so he devoted himself not only to country living but also to making cabbages for Manhattanites.

Not for long, however. He fled the farm to accompany his brother and a friend to Britain, then the Continent, ostensibly to study European agronomy (with his father's subsidy once more). Fred seems to have spent more time enjoying the private gardens of the nobility, and new public parks on both sides of the Channel. The English garden-park, with its studied, asymmetrical arrangements, became his belle ideal—the inspiration informing much of his subsequent career as pioneer American landscape architect. The Staten Island farm declined from neglect, for this Yankee agronomist cared less for the routine of agriculture than the wizard of Shellbanks did. Olmsted became instead a literary man, the co-designer and construction superintendent of Manhattan's Central Park, secretary to the Union army's Sanitary Commission, then the architect of public parks and suburbs across North America. His early discomfort with business accounts notwithstanding, Olmsted made himself (well before 1861) a master of balance sheets, a time-clock keeper, a manager of hordes of free laborers, a technocrat. His friends hated slavery because it was immoral. Olmsted despised the institution for its inefficiency, and for its poisonous effect on the development of capital and social overhead capital. All these signature values of the mid-nineteenth-century liberal bourgeoisie were in place when Fred, passionate for literary fame, contracted with a New York newspaper to subsidize his plan to travel the slave states and submit detailed dispatches on his observations. The deal made, at the end of 1852 Olmsted began the first of his three great southern circuits—a "Journey in the Seaboard Slave States."[23]

The coastal sojourn began in Washington on 11 December. Olmsted took the train down to Richmond, then Petersburg. There he rented a horse and became lost in the hinterland, looking for a certain plantation in either Prince George or Sussex. Later he caught a boat at the City Point wharf (adjacent to Richard Eppes's home) and steamed down the James to Hampton Roads and Norfolk, where he stayed a spell before undertaking a jog into the Great Dismal. This last was a diversion he actually wished to avoid—"I would rather give $50 than go to Dismal Swamp," he wrote to a friend—but the Dismal seemed a landscape feature too important to avoid, and Olmsted may have felt obligated to report on the phenomenon to his friend Harriet Beecher Stowe, who was writing her swamp novel, *Dred*.[24] From the Dismal (on which he was unusually laconic) Olmsted went to Raleigh, then down to Wilmington, Charleston, and Savannah, then across Georgia to the Gulf Coast to New Orleans. After a brief foray up the Red River, he ascended the Mississippi to Memphis, and finally returned to New York on 6 April 1853. Much of the segment in the James-Albemarle subregion Olmsted spent in the cosmopolitan sector. His horseback ride in the piney woods, however, and certain other observations and hearsay he reported help to round out and confirm our perspective.

Reflecting on his dispatches three years later, as he wrote a preface to a revised and enlarged version of his "seaboard" trip, Olmsted termed himself "an honest growler." He wished to disarm southerners who might take offense at his impatience. Yet Olmsted decided he could never conceal his summary impression of "the notoriously careless, makeshift, impersistent people of the South."[25] Decline, neglect, gross inefficiency, and maddeningly premodern private and public behaviors greeted the perambulating litterateur even before he reached Richmond. It was as though Olmsted had been listening to Ruffin for years.

Between Washington and Fredericksburg he passed plantation mansions on elevated grounds, with groves about them and rows of slave quarters behind. Some were handsome, but "more commonly they are in a compact heavy style, not in particularly bad taste, but never elegant and usually failing in neatness and more or less needing repairs." Fredericksburg itself had busy streets but was "shabbily built ... show[ing] less signs of an active and prospering people, in the distance passed over, than any other I have ever journeyed through either in the old or new world." When "A coarse rough looking old man sat beside" him, Olmsted sought informative conversation: Was he "acquainted with the country"?, Olmsted asked. "No I ain't—don't look very fer*tile*, does it?," came the reply. "It does not indeed," agreed Fred. "I've heerd 'em say out West," reflected the older man, "that old Virginny was the mother of statesmen—reckon she must be about done, eh? This ere's about the *barrenest* look for a mother, ever I see."[26] Ruffin redeemed again.

The scenery along the James's "low and level" shores Olmsted found "uninteresting," but "frequent planters' mansions" there found more favor. They were "often of great size and of some elegance ... [with] pretty and well-kept grounds about them—finer than any other I have seen at the South—and the plantations surrounding them are cultivated with neatness and skill." The city of Norfolk was something else. Aside from its "safe and convenient harbor, forty feet in depth," the town had nothing to recommend it: It was "a dirty, low, ill-arranged town, nearly divided by a morass." Olmsted admired Norfolk's "single creditable public building"—presumably the neoclassical city hall (now the tomb of Douglas MacArthur), and he heard that an "agreeable, refined and cultivated" group of local families dwelled in "fine private residences." Mainly Norfolk had "all the immoral and disagreeable characteristics of a large seaport, with very few of the advantages that we should expect to find. ... No lyceum or public libraries, no public gardens, no galleries of art."[27]

A protracted scene at City Point, where Olmsted awaited the Norfolk steamer, provides a coda for the growling Yankee's confrontation with local carelessness and impersistence. He had taken a short train ride to the wharf from Petersburg. There, he and two carloads of other folks "were all discharged under a dirty shed, from which projected a wharf into the James River." They waited fully an hour, "sitting on a pile of baggage ... or, when it rained, walking up and down the dirty shed." At last Olmsted "ventured to ask what we were waiting for? For a steamboat to take us down the river" came the obvious reply. Well, then, "What is the cause of her detention?," inquired the traveler. "Oh, there was no detention—*no more than usual, yet*; it was *about time* for her to be along now, I was answered." Yet they waited almost another hour and a half before "the boat did come, and this [is] what they call a 'connection.' Nobody showed any surprise, or seemed to have any objection to the arrangement, though it must have been exceedingly disagreeable to the ladies, who had not even a chair or a clean bench to sit upon, and one would suppose might be a little provoking to the men of business."[28] No provocation at all, it would seem. Olmsted must have been the only person on the wharf with watch in hand. One wonders if Dr. Eppes, virtually next door, was consulting his own watch. He often did, but of course Eppes was little more at home in such a careless culture than Olmsted was.

One creature (at most) in Virginia that Olmsted truly loved was Jane, a filly he rented in Petersburg in order to reach the isolated plantation of Thomas W. Gee, who had issued an invitation. Jane was well trained but sprightly, a joy to ride and to talk to, as she and Olmsted—"gone woolgathering, and ... some miles out of our way"—pressed on along narrow lanes through endless pine forests. "'[N]ever mind,' said Jane, lifting her head ... 'I don't think it's any great matter if we are lost; such a fine day. ... [L]et's go on and see what we shall come to.'" A bit later, still more or less lost, Fred and Jane took a fork "into a dark evergreen forest; and though it was a mere bridle-path, it must have existed, I thought, before the trees began to grow, for it was free of stumps, and smooth and clean as a garden walk, and the pines grew thickly up, about four feet apart, on each side of it, their branches meeting, just clear of my head, and making a dense shade." Olmsted luxuriated in the "slightly balsamic odor in the air" and decided to ride hatless "and let the living pine leaves brush my hair." Only a good horse could make Fred Olmsted forget his watch. They found "a large plantation, though there was no cultivated land within sight of the road." Only the pines—"big, little, and medium in size"—and of course the straight-running gangs of feral hogs, as in a fox hunt.[29]

What Fred and Jane saw mostly was evidence of shifting agriculture, and Fred (at least) recognized this:

"Old fields"—a coarse, yellow, sandy soil, bearing scarce anything but pine trees and broom-sedge. In some places, for acres, the pines would not be above five feet high—that was land that had been in cultivation, used up and 'turned out,' not more than six or eight years before; then there were patches of every age; sometimes the trees were a hundred feet high. At long intervals, there were fields in which the pine was just beginning to spring in beautiful green plumes from the ground, and was yet hardly noticeable among the dead brown grass and sassafras bushes and blackberry-vines, which nature first sends to hide the nakedness of the impoverished earth.[30]

Olmsted was riding through a panoramic demonstration of natural botanical succession in the South Atlantic region; and while he did not employ this early-twentieth-century ecological term, he understood *nearly* all that he saw, about as well as we might.

"Used up" and "impoverished" imply censure in Olmsted's surmise, approximating the judgment of cosmopolitan reformers such as Edmund Ruffin, with the unspoken assumption that impoverishment was permanent. Nearby in Olmsted's text, however, are references to tall deciduous woods, usually in rough places, presumably never brought under cultivation. The traveler made no surmises here, but it seems appropriate for us, in trying to reconstruct the landscape, to be reminded that pines—even hundred-foot-tall pines—were not the "climax" plant in such country. Deciduous trees were and are. So in all probability, *all* the pinelands through which Fred and Jane traveled had been farmed, then abandoned. In most such places, without human interference, deciduous trees would ultimately top out the pines and become dominant. Shifting (or merely expanding) agriculture would not permit the ultimate, deciduous stage of succession to take place, however, except in places inconveniently rough; thus the patches of oak, gum, and so on that Olmsted noticed during his ride.[31]

Elsewhere, however, Olmsted made explicit what he neglected while atop the prancing Jane: that land abandoned to pines was reclaimed for cropland after suitable, lengthy resting. "As the oldest tilled land of the farm is thus dropped behind [i.e., abandoned]," he wrote to his New York readers, "every year a piece of the pine wood ('old field,' *of thirty years standing*, perhaps) is cleared, the wood burned mainly on the ground, and that in heaps, and the ashes seldom spread; and after some little grubbing of the smaller roots, during the winter, planted again with corn." He went on to decry the Virginia backwoods farmer's indifference to manure. "[L]ike the leach, [he] cries constantly give! give! give!" Olmsted declined (rather insincerely, I suspect) to generalize "that such is the *general* style of farming now in Virginia, but it certainly, even at this day, is not rare, and as far as my observation goes, is quite as common as any other."[32]

Confirmation of the persistence of American folkish agronomy from such a hostile, yet credible source as Fred Olmsted compels the next question: Did this synthetic European/aboriginal system actually impoverish the country? Were its practitioners so lazy, so careless, so unscientific? Olmsted (and the local reformers) thought so. Within their argument is the subject of the ashes from the incinerated woods—"burned mainly on the ground ... in heaps, and the ashes seldom spread." Edmund Ruffin was mostly uninterested in wood ashes, and only once approached a concession that fire culture might be beneficial. This came during his geologizing tour of South Carolina (in April 1843), when Ruffin observed the great open-range cattle business of Williamsburg District. He thought "leaving all the stock to starve in winter & spring" an "abominable system," of course; but Ruffin noticed that the "burnt wood-land" the graziers had created to attract feral cattle "already is covered with young grass, making it a perfect & continuous green, which is so beautiful as to greatly moderate my previous strong objections to this plan of burning the woods." Ruffin may have assumed that manure was largely responsible for the greened range, for he never moderated his opposition to woods-burning for crops, and acknowledged the possible value of ashes only in noting, like Olmsted, that folk agronomists did not spread the ashes. Exceptions included Edmund Ruffin, Jr., who spread 47 loads of ashes (about 165 pounds each load) on Beechwood (his father's boyhood home) in 1852—although he used much more animal manure, marl, and especially guano; and Daniel Cobb, who spread ashes on fields with care.[33]

It seems quite impossible to establish whether the fire culturists *generally* spread ashes after burning, heaping, and reburning. I shall assume that Ruffin and Olmsted were correct, but then inquire (first), did it make much difference if they did not? and (second), is this inquiry relevant, anyway? The incineration of forests releases ashes broadly, depending on wind speed and humidity. After heaping and reburning, however, heavy additional ash might accumulate in spots, perhaps to knee- or waist-high. Farmers without much labor at their disposal probably did not collect and carefully spread ashes. It seems equally likely, however, that human and animal traffic through new fields would have spread ashes considerably, albeit unevenly. So cosmopolitan agronomists were probably correct, but not entirely so: Fire culturists did not measure fertilizer applications and correlate with crop yields. I am convinced they did not *care*. Should we expect folks indifferent to the time of arrival of the "connection" steamer from City Point to Norfolk to measure, record, and adjust administrations of manures? They had neither the habits nor the material expectations of the Yankee bourgeoisie or of the local agronomists. Pressed with such habits and promises of greater wealth, they declined to change. Generations of experience taught them that burning the woods made fields producing as much as twenty-five bushels of corn per acre the first year, then less. This was good enough. Why should they tax themselves? So there was truth to Olmsted's lament that southerners were "notoriously careless, make-shift, impersistent," even though Olmsted was ultimately, fundamentally wrong-headed.

The fire culture folk did persist in woods-burning and makeshift, careless ash-spreading—because it was quite satisfactory to them and sustainable in the modern ecological sense. Neither Olmsted nor Ruffin ever seems seriously to have asked scientific questions about the qualities of wood ashes. Ruffin should have. Perhaps then the old culture would have seemed more satisfactory to him—but this seems unlikely, since the European model of permanent fields was central to his life and work.[34]

During the 1880s the work of R. C. Kedzie, professor of chemistry at the Agricultural College of Michigan, began to appear in farmers' journals, including the *Southern Planter* of Richmond. Before this time, wood ashes were perceived mainly as a source of very soluble potash with some soda and other minor ingredients. Kedzie demonstrated that by volume, most reduced wood contained more *calcium* (lime) than any other element. Hardwood ashes yielded 12 percent potash, but 70 percent salts of lime and magnesia. Softwood offered the same potash but less lime and magnesium—only 32 percent. A. B. Stevens, another chemist, separated lime and magnesium in an analysis of leached and unleached ashes. (Leached ashes are a significant by-product of soap-making.) In both instances lime was by far the more common element—21 percent in leached ashes (to 5 percent magnesia and only a trace of potash), 18 percent in unleached ashes (with 3.5 percent magnesia and 5 percent potash). Wood ashes were composed, then, of approximately one-fifth lime—the chemical most needed to neutralize the acidic soils of the South Atlantic region.[35]

Research conducted a century later—well into the Age of Ecology and recycling—confirms and elaborates. By 1990, American paper- and sawmills and wood-burning electrical generating plants were producing between one and a half and three million tons of ash annually. Plants in Maine alone yielded 300,000 tons. The great bulk of the ashes were dumped into landfills, or sludged with sewage or other industrial wastes. As landfills closed and costs of other means of waste disposal mounted, corporate "environmental engineers" (a new profession), agricultural chemists, and botanists rediscovered spreading ashes on cropland. Their searches of previous agronomic literature (beginning with a 1919 work) revealed only scattered evidence of an unexamined truism: that wood ashes contained calcium that neutralizes soil acidity. New tests with ashes from several sources—paper mills, power plants, domestic fireplaces—compared ashes with pure calcium carbonate, ground limestone (the predominant agricultural liming agent), and other sources, as well as the neutralizing effects of ash from several kinds of wood. None, however, considered ash from pines alone—strange, considering that many paper mills pulp primarily pines and feed pine chips and sawdust into boilers. Other experiments examined the effects of ash application on several crops. Researchers agreed that much more research must be performed.[36]

Nonetheless, several important generalizations and isolated chemical truths emerge: In terms of pH—the scale measuring acidity or alkalinity (seven being neutral, alkalinity being higher, and acidity being lower)—wood ashes' rating of 13 considerably bettered that of commercial limestone, 8.2. Just two cubic feet of hardwood ashes equaled a ton of "Grade A" ground limestone. (A textbook in soil science first published in 1965 reported that hardwood ashes were the exact equivalent of marl.) Ashes are very light and highly soluble, however. Lacking texture and weight, they perform none of the "mechanical" functions of ground limestone or marl in stiff clays. And leaching away rapidly in sandy, porous soils (including most of the ground in coastal plains), ashes' neutralizing effects probably are foreshortened. Researchers reported satisfactory pH levels after two years, but further tests will undoubtedly confirm the necessity of more frequent applications of ashes. Further, ashes from pine, spruce, apple, and a bit of scrap lumber of undetermined species (conceivably another conifer) offered 20.3 percent calcium (50.7 percent calcium carbonate), noticeably below white oak's 27.1 percent calcium (and 67.7 percent calcium carbonate). The late Professor Stevens's generalization of one-fifth calcium content in pine ash may thus have been confirmed. Ash composition is so various—depending not only on species but also on proportions (for example) of leaves, branches, and bark burned—that precise applications for crops would require not only conventional soil analysis but analysis of every ash pile. (Farmers demanding careful measurement and prediction of yield would be, in other words, at least as discommoded as adherents of Ruffin's marl reform, who were obliged to assay their marl.) Wood ash applications improved a hay crop but had no fertilizing effect on snap beans. Legumes (at least) require more fertilizer than ashes' offerings of potash and soda.[37]

Several applications of Age of Ecology research seem historically instructive, then. First, ashes from deciduous or mixed first-growth forests probably provided more neutralizing calcium than pine ashes from old fields. So since most first-growth timber on level land had probably already been removed by the middle of the nineteenth century, most woods-burning was pine-burning and of somewhat lower calcium yield. If the woods-burners indeed did not spread ashes deliberately, too, they certainly received uneven neutralizing effect. Still, on the whole, pine ash (however sloppily distributed) was essential to this sustainable agronomic system. Second, ashes' solubility *probably* (research is tentative on this matter) reduced the term of neutralizing, in comparison with marl and ground limestone. A recent experiment demonstrated a high pH count in formerly acidic soil two years after application of ash. If we speculate that pH declined below six (slightly acidic) after, say, *six* years—a plausible scenario—then most hinterland farmers would have been satisfied with perhaps one more crop before declaring the land "old field" and undertaking the process of creating a new field with fire.

But what about the necessary augmentation of ash's fertilizing elements? Hinterland farmers ran most of their cattle and hogs in the woods. Manure was unavailable for spreading most of the year, save that of a few milk cows, sheep, and hogs kept for interim family use. Corn litter—especially tops and leaves—farmers gathered for fodder rather than returning it to the soil (à la John Taylor) as "green" manure. However, while Fred Olmsted was correct that ordinary farmers (and some cosmopolitan planters) grew "corn, corn, corn," he neglected to mention what Edmund Ruffin and many other contemporaries observed: that among their rows of continuous corn, farmers had adopted something like Indian practice in planting peas of various names—field peas, cowpeas, black-eyed peas, and other legumes (sometimes beans). The legumes fed swine and cattle—both accidentally and by design; but much of these invaluable nitrogen-fixing secondary crops were returned to the soil.[38] Such were the workings of a system indefinitely sustainable—so long as population crowding did not take place—and of a system seemingly "careless" and only somewhat less orderly-looking than the Indians', to eyes trained by the European model.

The bias of written history belongs entirely in the European and cosmopolitan camp. European travelers crossed the Atlantic, beheld southerners' jumbled, irregular fields, and moaned. John Taylor wrote a well-preserved book, then Edmund Ruffin, who also left ten magnificent volumes of the *Farmers' Register* and, Yankee soldiers' trashing notwithstanding, a great trove of his personal papers. Archives, libraries, and historical societies, too, from College Park to Baton Rouge, veritably bulge with the ledgers, letters, and diaries of men like Taylor and Ruffin. When one at last finds written records from the lower social orders, they belong to literate, upwardly mobile white men such as Daniel Cobb and Elliott Story, connected by family and/or aspiration to the cosmopolitan world. Finally, when the modern profession of history was created toward the end of the nineteenth century (flourishing early in the twentieth), the young scholars who turned eagerly to subjects southern represented cosmopolitan upward mobility in their own fashion. The ambitious sons of solid commercial farmers, businessmen, preachers, or teachers, they owed their places of respect to academia's certification and returned respect most of all to modern education, including modern science applied for the benefit of the whole society.[39] They were bourgeois democrats and reformers, Olmsted rather than Ruffin, but they grasped the logical points of convergence between the two.

Both Taylor and Ruffin had been guided by acute historical consciousness: Their ancestors and contemporaries had mined the soil, leaving the coastal South exhausted, her people fleeing westward. If easterners could not reform agriculture, European-style, civilization would never take hold; ultimately Americans would mine and exhaust the entire continent. By the

1890s this vision was incorporated into the mission of the expanding cadres of the U.S. Department of Agriculture. These professionals—soil specialists, entomologists, horticulturists, agricultural economists, and agronomic generalists, trained in Europe and at the Cornell and University of Wisconsin colleges of agriculture—staffed the Department's Washington bureaus, the new experiment stations across the nation, and the faculties of newer agriculture schools affiliated with land-grant colleges and universities. Editors of the agricultural press were eager collaborators. Ordinary farmers resisted them and their "book farming," and the agronomists hungered for evangelistic conquest. The crusade would mean jobs for students in the farmers' colleges, professional legitimacy, and the conquest of science over ignorance. Nothing legitimates like history, so the professional agronomists adopted (among others) Edmund Ruffin as a "pioneer in agricultural science." In an 1895 essay for the Department of Agriculture *Yearbook*, W. P. Cutter, the department's librarian, asserted continuity from Ruffin's reformism to his colleagues' professionalism and good intentions. The *Essay on Calcareous Manures*, Cutter declared, was "the most thorough piece of work on a special agricultural subject ever published in the English language." Nine years later the editor of the *Southern Planter* paid homage to contemporary agronomists—educators such as Canadian-born Professor Andrew M. Soule, new head of Virginia's experiment station in Blacksburg; Professor C. W. Burkett, director of the Ohio State University's experimental farm; and freelance reformers such as Joseph E. ("Alfalfa Joe") Wing of eastern Ohio. The editor thought it appropriate, however, first "to remember that the South produced the first man (Edmund Ruffin) who, in this country, endeavored to apply science to the advancement of agriculture." Alongside the editorial he printed "a likeness of this gentlemen" sent by the wizard's grandson, Julian, of Marlbourne. Then came a reprinting of Cutter's essay from the 1895 *Yearbook of Agriculture*.[40]

Professional agronomists also inspired a curious reenactment of Ruffin's marl reform in Virginia during the Progressive era. Westmoreland Davis, a wealthy Loudoun County farmer, lawyer, and publisher of the *Southern Planter*, led a campaign (1909–14) to provide cheap lime to farmers. ("Lime, legumes, then anything you want to grow" was Davis's slogan.) That Davis and his allies were successful in gaining legislative and judicial approval of the project is remarkable, given Virginia's torpidity; but the inspiration for Davis's reformism is equally interesting: Wisconsin's college of agriculture (in the age of reformist governor Robert LaFollette) and the government of Illinois, where state-sponsored limestone grinding (with convict labor) was first demonstrated. The Middle West had emerged as the agronomists' showcase and reform export center. Davis, an intelligent and hyperactive modern creature, had instinctively looked to this great region of solid family farmers and progressive land-grant colleges. If he thought of the late wizard of Shell-banks at all, Davis minimized his efforts.[41] Ironically, it was a Middle Western ex-farmboy who would confirm the agronomists' connection to Ruffin while adopting Ruffin's own version of history. So even as the agronomists conspired with fate to destroy folkish farming, the historical profession adopted the cosmopolitan reformers' explanation of the past. Olmsted, whom the agronomists and historians resembled, was upheld. And Ruffin won his war after all.

Avery Odelle Craven (1886–1980) was the farmboy-cum-historian. He was born near Ackworth, Iowa, to a Quaker father who had fled North Carolina years before because of his disapproval of slavery. Accused of prowhite southern sympathies in his scholarship much later, Craven relished revealing his father's antislavery and anti-Confederate sentiments. Yet the Iowan became intimately associated with the South. This began serendipitously. After earning an A.B. degree in geology at Simpson College in Indianola, Iowa, Craven taught science in a local country school. A principal's request that he also teach American history led him to Harvard's graduate program. There his scientific and farming backgrounds influenced Craven to study the depletion of New England's soils. His seminar paper gained the notice of Professor Frederick Jackson Turner, who suggested that Craven explore the same phenomenon in Maryland and Virginia. Craven took his Harvard M.A. with Turner in 1914, and thereafter he was deemed "a Turner student" with good reason. For especially in his early books, Craven approached southern history via internal sections and stages of economic development. (And after Turner died, it was Craven who edited the master's last manuscript.)[42]

Turner advised Craven to continue his graduate studies at the University of Chicago, where he might work with William E. Dodd, who was both a southerner and a southernist. Dodd was already renowned not only as a regionalist but also as a reformer—that is, his history would inform the present of the necessity and the means of improvement. Certainly Craven was an eager student; and although Marcus W. Jernegen (another Progressive historian) ultimately directed Craven's dissertation, the young scholar's disposition remained in the William Dodd mold. The dissertation, meanwhile, was long a-borning, and Craven spent seven *Wanderjahren* at a series of Middle Western state colleges—Emporia (Kansas), Michigan State, and the University of Illinois—teaching while he finished *Soil Exhaustion as a Factor in the Agricultural History of Virginia and Maryland, 1606–1860*. During these years Craven cemented his connections both to Progressive history and to the agronomic cadres. He consulted with the latter—especially an Illinois soil scientist and a Chicago botanist—on the details of his Ruffinesque reconstruction of South Atlantic history.[43]

Soil Exhaustion was a novel work of agroecological history. While Turner and most of his other students focused on frontier landscapes, Craven ingeniously studied "old" land left behind. A few Europeanists had attempted similar projects, with poor results, Craven thought. Yet he was well advised—by his scientific consultants and his own good sense—that spotty sources and the many variables that make for poor crops rendered "soil exhaustion" a problematic concept. "[T]he term ... was used so loosely by the men of the past and applied to such a wide variety of conditions," he complained. So Craven decided that "'soil exhaustion' will be applied" in his book "as the men of the period applied it and no effort will be made at exactness."[44] In this disarmingly forthright fashion, then, Avery Craven adopted the perspective of his principal heroes, John Taylor and Edmund Ruffin.

Frederick Jackson Turner was never an uncritical celebrant of frontiers. His former student became, in *Soil Exhaustion* and his second book (a biography of Ruffin), a sort of antifrontier historian. For through Taylor and Ruffin, Craven exposed the shortsighted practices of frontier farmers, miners of the soil who, once their quick profits were made, moved on to the next-westward natural resources. Taylor and Ruffin stayed behind to restore, and to point the way to modern conservationist agronomy. Craven's Middle Western birth and long experience had taught him to adopt values that were modern. Folk practice was wrongheaded, and in the East, at least since the Revolution, it was historically hopeless. Such bias is evident in *Soil Exhaustion* and the Ruffin biography. Craven made it even clearer in an essay on John Taylor, published in 1938. He began with a meditation on farmers' nature: "The very character of his tasks renders him a rugged individualist," Craven averred. "Constant experience with the fixed ways of nature and the rule of thumb methods necessary to circumvent or co-operate with her make him both conservative and backward in his tendencies. He is, regardless of time and place and changing conditions, always more or less a frontiersman in his outlook." Such farmers might survive—on naturally rich ground, probably in the West. But history would eventually catch up with everyone. "When urban-industrial developments crowd the rural-agricultural order," he continued, "then co-operation, efficiency, and capacity for rapid readjustment are essential to dominance. The farmer lags behind. He loses social standing."[45]

Craven's condescension bears resemblance to a diatribe against backward

farmers more than half a century earlier, by "M," a pseudonymous correspondent of the *Southern Planter*. "The natural wants of man are really very
few," opined "M," "and hence even an ignorant, unaspiring man may manage to eke out a living at farming.... In most cases this man lives in a
shanty or miserable hut, and rears a family on a common level, so to speak,
with the animals on his farm. He is known as a farmer, but the name does
not correctly suit him. He is a botch at the business; a decided failure; the
very reverse of what would be called a first-rate farmer." "M," who equated
farming with business, bourgeois discipline with success, and success with
consumption, preferred a "farmer who really masters the situation, not only
accumulates money from year to year, but his farm grows better the longer it
is worked."[46] Craven merely updated.

Enter John Taylor of Caroline, who noticed William Strickland (the English traveler) and caused Craven to notice Strickland also. *Arator*'s appearance marked the dim dawn of progress. Then enter Ruffin and the triumphs
of *Calcareous Manures* and the *Farmers' Register*. "Exhaustion"—a term Craven questioned, then (like Taylor and Ruffin) adopted as actual—was negated
by science, discipline, and a hunger not only for "civilization" but also
for a bourgeois consumerism understandable in the twentieth century. And
the legitimating train of continuity rolled on. Craven's historical reformism, justifying the preprofessional reformers, has been repeated again and
again by succeeding generations of historians, whether reformers themselves
or not.[47]

The grand triumphs of agrichemistry and agribusiness in the United States
after World War II transcended the myth of reversing "exhaustion" to claim,
amid the so-called Green Revolution, the actual defeat of Malthus. Anyone
not aboard the train must be backward or, more likely, subversive. Only a
deepening public concern, then fright, following exposure of the side effects
of chemical pesticides and herbicides—inseparable companions of the Green
Revolution's engineered crop seeds—brought the agronomic paradigm itself
under suspicion. If scientific agriculture is dangerous late in the twentieth
century, might we not question its eighteenth- and nineteenth-century antecedents, too? Was there ever a sustainable agronomy in North America, after
the Europeans and Africans came? Was there not ultimate wisdom, perhaps,
in rustic carelessness and impersistence, and in a willingness to live close to
animals in shelters less than grand? Instrumentally, these last two queries
now seem moot. Where there is enough rain to farm, there are too many
people to re-create a world like that of the hinterland's hog-runners and
woods-burners. And the cash nexus—already crowding upon Daniel Cobb

and Elliott Story with the linearity of rails and roads—is so old that one can hardly dream of more than a few reclusive adventurers defying its dictates. Still, the intrinsic virtues of the hinterlanders are deserving of discovery; and we might yet find something in their ways instrumental to our own salvation.

By the time Avery Craven was born in Iowa, his Middle Western neighbors were doing their part, as we have seen, to doom the great grain growers of the East. (Richard Eppes made his global prophecy when Craven was three.) Hinterlanders, too, were grain farmers, and their world was doomed as well—because of the endless decline in staple prices, but also because of the gradual institution of fencing reform, the arrival of professional forestry and its dedication to stopping fires, and the oppressive intrusions of the agents of scientific agriculture. Dr. Eppes and many of the cosmopolitans, already accustomed to the cash nexus, survived the Civil War and rebuilt their cosmopolitan system upon wage labor, then machines. Most hinterlanders survived the war, too, but merely in the literal sense. Their way of life never quite recovered from its ravages, then was overwhelmed by wire fences, fire-watch towers, and county extension agents, with all the commercial mischief these cadres' presence implied.

The subregion's swine population may be as perfect an index to ruin as we might tease from all the censuses' banks of numbers. On the eve of the Civil War, the pocosin country was nearly overrun with 355,558 of them. Shortly, many hogs not already eagerly shipped to the Confederacy's burgeoning cities were requisitioned and devoured by troops regular and irregular, from both sides, who infested the landscape from Norfolk to Manteo to the Roanoke. The much-maligned 1870 census reported fewer than half that number, after half a decade of peace. I suspect that even if 1870s Republican enumerators did indeed undercount nearly everything, they did not err by far. For 1880's more respectable census revealed only 60,000-odd more than the 1870 count, still better than 120,000 below the 1860 population—and this while farming (numbers of operators and total farm acreage) expanded. The impoverished decade of the 1880s witnessed a hog decline, so the 1890 total approached the withered 1870 number; then during the 1890s the population expanded substantially and held through the 1910 census. The great 1920 count—316,573, reflecting World War I expansion and prosperity—still did not equal 1860's. The 1920s were more miserable than the 1880s, as reflected in the 1930 census; in the James-Albemarle, the 1920s represented the nadir of hogs and much more.[48]

During the late 1890s cosmopolitan correspondents of the *Southern Planter*

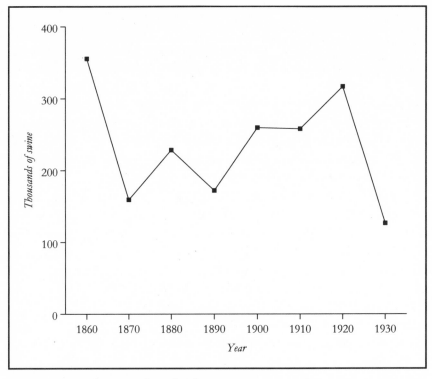

Figure 2. Swine in the James-Albemarle Subregion, 1860–1930
(Source: *County tables, censuses of agriculture*)

complained that Virginia's range remained entirely too open and that the legislature lacked the courage to close it once and for all. Nonetheless, fencing reform and the dispossession of the poor were making definite progress, which was revealed at least in part by an investigation of the business of curing hams at Smithfield. The study was conducted by the cadres of the U.S. Department of Agriculture's Bureau of Animal Industry—probably Yankees all. For they thought Smithfield hams were made from virtually feral hogs. The animals, they reported, were variously colored—black-and-white, sometimes gray or black or white, not uniform like hogs in the Middle West. And they seemed half-wild, with their long noses and legs and their "slab-sides" (i.e., they were thin). Close reading of the federal report, however, indicates that many of the swine of the Virginia counties of Nansemond, Isle of Wight, Southampton, and Surry were not free-ranged at all. Rather, they were often raised in the open on very large, fenced farms belonging to Smithfield packers such as J. O. Thomas. These men and other suppliers (not all, to be sure) ranged swine in fenced woods, herding them at appropriate times onto sweet potato and peanut fields, finally confining and feeding them some corn—but preferably peanuts—shortly before slaughter.[49] The bureau reporters faithfully recorded the curers' wonderful procedures, renowned the world over—the washing, salting and resalting, the black peppering, and the days-long smoking over hickory. They never quite understood that Smith-field hams could never be made from fat Middle Western hogs, or that odd-looking hogs could be anything but feral. What was more deeply significant locally was that the ham business was becoming somewhat vertically inte-grated. Despite agonizing delays in completing fence reform, hog-raising was becoming more a business, in fewer hands, than it ever had been before.

Farm tenancy rates comprise another index to the immiserization of the subregion's folks, white as well as black. In 1890 the seventeen counties aver-aged 34 percent tenants; in 1900, 43; 1930, 48. The averages masked huge divergencies, however. In swampy Camden and Gates Counties, 63 and 74 percent (respectively) of farmers owned their property in 1890. Western coun-ties within the subregion—resembling the Lower South, as ever, and now devoted to cotton as their first crops after corn—had much higher rates: Northampton produced 6,587 bales of cotton, and 44 percent of her farmers were tenants in 1890. By 1930, 72 percent of Northampton's farmers were nonowners. Southampton's cotton culture grew from 1,186 bales in 1890 to 8,633 in 1920, while her tenancy rate leaped from 31 to 59 percent. By 1890 the trucking (vegetable- and fruit-producing) counties of Nansemond and especially Norfolk had long been thoroughly market-connected, and they witnessed appropriate escalations of tenancy, too. Nansemond—part swamp and part cosmopolitan—remained a county of owners in 1890. Of the 22 per-cent tenants, only 8 percent worked on shares, 14 percent paying fixed rents. By 1920 Nansemond's tenancy rate was 35 percent; it was 45 percent in 1940. Norfolk County's rate was 49 percent already in 1890—29 percent on shares; and the rate persisted in the mid-40s until the 1930s, when it began to dip, probably owing to New Deal subsidy programs (which reduced tenancy else-where) and to the elimination of farmland through urban growth.[50]

In the black belts and deltas of the early-twentieth-century South, tenancy (including sharecropping) nearly always implied the *absence* of cash exchanges between landowner and tenant. So the impoverishment of small farmers in the James-Albemarle countryside would seem to have followed the pat-tern. Not so. In 1900 the census-takers began to list "labor expenditures" of cash on farms; and in our subregion, outlays were largest in the very coun-ties where tenancy rates were highest. In the cotton-growing western area,

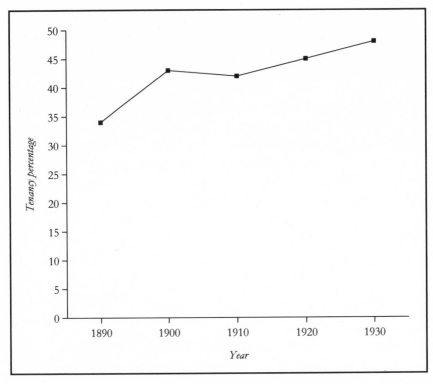

Figure 3. Tenancy among Farmers by Percentage, 1890–1930
(Source: *County tables, censuses of agriculture*)

planters' outlays ranged between $104,490 (in Bertie) to almost $200,000 (in Southampton). Nansemond's farmers spent $290,430, Norfolk's $398,850. Reports of expenditures for commercial fertilizers (another innovation of the 1900 census) reveal yet another instance of the cash-centeredness of farming. The trucking counties, once more, spent the most—Nansemond $210,510 and Norfolk $308,600. Corn/cotton counties spent about $50,000 or more. The swampiest counties spent the least—for instance, Camden only $6,980, Gates $19,039. Per-farm average expenditures for fertilizers, viewed comparatively, yield further perspective. Camden's average of $8.14 was lowest, Norfolk's $213.27 highest. Southampton farms averaged $32.73, Hertford farms $23.13. The United States average was $10.00, amounting to only 1.2 percent of the value of products grown with the fertilizer. Virginia's statewide average was $22.00 and 4.3 percent of value; North Carolina's was $20.00 and 5 percent. Farming in Georgia was considerably less cost-efficient in terms of fertilizer:

$26.00 per farm and 5.5 percent. Ohio almost exactly represented the national averages. But Minnesota farmers spent only twenty cents per farm on commercial fertilizers, or 0.2 percent of the value of their products.[51]

So the great disadvantages of farming in the East, compared with the West, lived on. Now the option of avoiding the market and cash withered away, and the most remote places within the old hinterland became themselves part and parcel of the cosmopolitan world. A nineteenth-century example was Wallaceton, domain of Major John Wallace, pioneer drainer of Dismal Swamp lands and the corn baron of the bottom of Norfolk County. Fred Olmsted visited Wallace early in 1853 and admired what he had accomplished. The pioneer, arriving during the 1840s, had established himself on the eastern bank of the Dismal Swamp Canal, which was already drying because (as geologists conjecture) spill from the canal's excavation slowed drainage in that direction. Then Wallace had, Olmsted declared, "with creditable spirit and skill, reclaimed four hundred acres. Having a sufficient outfall, he cuts wide drains parallel to each other, and about one hundred and twenty-five yards apart. These serve, at first, to float away, for market, all the timber of value left on the tract, as well as to draw the water from the surface. The ground is then grubbed, as much as it is thought necessary, and the stumps and worthless logs burnt." The reclaimed "soil is almost an impalpable powder, the foot sinks to the ancle in crossing it . . . when disturbed in a dry season." Wallace's slaves found such ground "easy of cultivation" and enormously productive (without manure) not only of corn, his first crop, but also of potatoes. Forty acres yielded a hundred barrels of these, which sold in Norfolk "at four dollars a barrel." (The potatoes were sold in New York, Wallace reported to Olmsted, "at from five to ten dollars a barrel.")[52]

The exemplary twentieth-century hinterland cosmopolitan was probably Dudley Warren Bagley (1889–1964) of Moyock in Currituck County, not far to the south of Wallaceton. Bagley grew up on Highland Farm—peculiarly named, given that Currituck is so low—a place of less than two hundred acres. His father sent him to Trinity College (later Duke University), but after two years Dudley transferred to the University of Virginia's engineering school. There tuberculosis was diagnosed, and Dudley was advised to seek health in the country; so he returned to Highland Farm to help his father in the hog and general farming business, which did not go well. By 1917 Dudley was strong enough to marry and to enter the army. Returning home once more after World War I, he determined to make a success of an inauspicious

place. In partnership with his wife—a smart woman trained as a nurse—
Bagley did just that.[53]

Highland Farm's 183 acres became a cornucopia, the Bagleys among
the most innovative and resourceful of American farmers. Before the war,
Dudley and his father, among other northeastern Carolinians, had numbered among the first soybean growers in the country. The value of the
Asian legume lay in soil-building and hog pasture. During the early 1920s the
family became producers of soybean seeds of several varieties, sold on contract to dealers in Portsmouth, Norfolk, and Baltimore. At the end of 1923
Dudley bought a "one-man" mechanical soybean harvesting machine from
the Scott Sales Company in Elizabeth City, which had developed and manufactured the machine before and during the war. Dudley himself built and
maintained intimate contact with the North Carolina experiment station's
soil men, botanists, and horticulturists, and he cultivated the state agricultural college's faculty as well, while he nurtured Highland Farm's fields. The
soybean seed business expanded to include seed corn (the "Norfolk Market"
strain), cowpeas, Abruzzi rye, then a wide assortment of nursery stock—
ornamental shrubs and trees and flowering bulbs, notably cannas. They added
sunflowers; and for a while, the Bagleys even hatched bobwhite quail for sale
to hunting clubs. Major Wallace (so Olmsted reported) had sold his potatoes
on previously arranged contract to Norfolk middlemen—a premonition of a
system common in the produce business late in the twentieth century. The
Bagleys raised and sold everything in this manner throughout the interwar
period. Dudley's business papers are voluminous—filled with contracts and
the correspondence of negotiations, sometimes with customers as far away
as Ohio. And there are lengthening payroll rosters and accounts. None bear
much resemblance to the farm records of earlier hinterlanders.[54]

The Bagleys' business was itself remarkable enough. Highland Farm enterprises also supported public lives. Ida Bagley chaired Currituck's Board
of Charities and Public Welfare, advised women's clubs on landscaping,
and brokered the local philanthropy of Joseph P. Knapp of New York,
who owned land on Knotts Island, where he loved to hunt ducks. Dudley
was president of the North Carolina State Farmers Convention, principal
founder of the Farmers Cooperative Exchange (a purchasing and marketing
network), and state committee chair of Ducks Unlimited (a conservationist
group in which Knapp was also interested). Dudley was also a Democratic
politician. Elected to a term in the state senate in 1932, he led the First District's party for years. In 1938 he was made chair of the state's Rural Electri-
fication Authority (a New Deal agency), and at the end of 1940 he moved

to Washington as second assistant comptroller general of the United States at the munificent annual salary of $6,500. After World War II the Bagleys returned to Moyock, but much of their business remained in the hands of managers. Retirement seems to have been altogether pleasant, for Currituck was both peaceful and close to the world.[55]

4 SWAMPERS

Away to the Dismal Swamp he speeds;
  His path was rugged and sore,
Through tangled juniper, beds of reeds,
And many a fen where the serpent feeds,
  And man never trod before.
— Thomas Moore, *1803*

Before I was aware of it I was in the Swamp. Lofty trees threw their arching limbs over
the canal, clothed to their tops with a gauze-like drapery of tangled vines.... The sky was
obscured with leaden colored clouds, and all nature was silent, monotonous, death-like.
— Porte Crayon, *1856*

The value of wetlands as water reservoirs, as links between surface and ground water,
and as modulators and filters in the downhill portion of the hydrologic cycle[,] has been
recognized for some time, but only recently have hydrologists begun to document in a
systematic manner these potential hydrologic values.... It was soon discovered [for instance]
that many wetlands were more productive than adjacent upland ecosystems. While there
are many factors, such as nutrients, climate, soil, or sediment conditions, which influence
productivity, a common denominator factor that seems to have a major and generally positive
effect is water flow. — Eugene P. Odum, *1979*

In the most humid of places there will be deep summer droughts, when water tables sink and dust rises with the least human exertion, or the slightest welcome breeze. Joy in life ebbs with water flow. Such moments were immortalized long ago in a flatland Virginia-Carolina ditty called "Summertime Blues," wherein the singer laments,

> Water in the well getting lower and lower
> Can't take a bath six months more
> Open the door, flies swarm in
> Shut the door, start sweating again.[1]

More often in this country, however, water seemed to stand forever above ground, and seep, gurgle, then flow broadly over pocosins and through swamps, creeks, and rivers sometimes frightful in their power. So folkish reference more often incorporates water into daily life's literal and figurative realities.

An antebellum cautionary tale for children, for instance, evokes the breadth of one of northeastern Carolina's great rivers. An elderly black tramp carrying a tow sack pauses by a plantation yard, threatening youthful whites at play: "How you chillen behavin' yourselves?," he demands. "I'm comin' back by here and if you been bad I'm gwine put you in my sack and tek you down to Pasquotank, where the bullfrogs jump from bank to bank." Another antebellum story—this from Gates County—enjoins lying. At a crossroads store, two men swapped tales about a famous footlog across Bennetts Creek. The first storyteller recalled that his father dropped a valuable lantern into the creek while hunting at night. Hours of attempts to hook the lantern's handle failed. Years later, however, while fishing from the same log, the father brought up the lantern (reported the son) *still burning*. The second storyteller then declared that *his* father, angling from the same log, caught a ninety-five-pound fish. The first man decided to preempt hyperbolic escalation: All right, he declared, "If you will take ninety pounds off that fish, I'll blow my lantern out."[2]

Hydraulic figures and contexts seem inexhaustible in such country. A urinating male is "making a branch." Jokes about preachers and fried chicken are expressed in terms of a set of false teeth lost in water, then retrieved by fishing with a drumstick. Water birds—especially white herons—join owls and vultures as harbingers of doom: A man spotted herons perched on his house. He shot them, and the next day lightning struck and killed his wife and daughter. "Swamp gas"—glowing eerily some nights—situates past tragedies in watery space. The Great Dismal has several such "lights," commemorating lost lovers of three races. But lights also abound in lesser swamps far away. "Ephriam's light," near Seaboard in Northampton County, immortalizes a local slave hanged for the murder of his master. Hertford County offers "Buffaloe's light," which supposedly began as a result of a Civil War tragedy: Confederates caught a local white man, a deserter, and shot him; but on discovering that the man was not yet dead from his wounds, they drowned him in a swamp spring. His ghost hovers above the spring. Other "lights" in this area—at Devil's Racetrack and Devil's Poquosin—seem to give substance to place-names.[3]

A contemporary ecological scientist (such as Eugene Odum) would conceive of the entire James-Albemarle subregion as a wonderfully efficient energy circuit based on moving water. Vast humidity rises from the Atlantic (or arrives overhead from the west) and, desalinated, falls as rain—sixty and more inches every year—soaking and resoaking the landscape. The water runs off

Porte Crayon, "The White Canoe" (Harper's New Monthly Magazine, September 1856)

higher, drier places into pocosins, marshes, swamps. Aquifers are more than recharged by rain. The wetlands hold some of the surplus in ponds. Most begins a slow voyage back to the ocean, slow because the wetlands (whatever local name is employed for them) are not stagnant, but the first vessels for this gradualist journey. Wetlands have three-dimensional shapes that ultimately channel surplus water into more perceptible vessels called runs, branches, creeks, finally rivers, which empty into bays, sounds, and at last the Atlantic. Throughout the circuit, water aground hastens decomposition of dead vegetative and animal matter and filters these and myriad people-made wastes. Water also distributes and nourishes seeds of grasses, reeds, shrubs, and trees that spread roots and hold the banks of watercourses.[4]

*Porte Crayon, "Lake Drummond" (*Harper's New Monthly Magazine, *September 1856)*

River-highways we have already observed here: The cosmopolitan culture of agronomists and merchants rested on the instrumentality of the James, Elizabeth, Nansemond, Roanoke, Chowan, Perquimans, Pasquotank. Much of the hinterland was (and remains) wetlands of the first stages of the return phase of water's great circuit, however; so here we must address a wet landscape that was not a convenient road, in order to discover what different sort of destiny humans found there. Maps—old ones and new—are the beginning.

During 1863 and 1864 cartographers of the Confederate Engineers' Corps constructed large, detailed maps of the western side of our lowland territory. (Yankees had already occupied Norfolk, Portsmouth, and Suffolk in Virginia, and Elizabeth City, Hertford, and other northeastern Albemarle towns; so there were to be no Confederate maps of the eastern side of the subregion.) The maps have wonderful detail for the practicalities both of waging war and of rediscovering landscape. Roads, railroads, and rivers appear, along with most creeks, as well as towns, depots, rural churches, and the residences of landowners both large and middling. The cartographers' work reveals first, however, that most of the landscape remained heavily forested. Farms and plantations are scattered white shapes amid vast speckled representations of woods. On some of the maps of lowland counties the artists imposed symbols of marsh grasses upon the forests to indicate wetlands. These usually correspond to networks of runs, branches, and creeks (as one might expect). Often, at the bottoms of such microdrainage systems, the mapmakers drew dammed millponds. Southampton County had dozens of these. Beale's Mill, for example, caught and used much of the drainage of the western side of the county. In the south-southwest, Joyner's Mill arrested drainage shortly before it entered the Nottoway River. On the eastern side of the county, Adkin's Mill interrupted Black Creek's passage to the Blackwater River; and downstream, Lawrence's Mill trapped Black Creek again. In approximately the center of Southampton, Ridley's Mill produced what appears to be the largest millpond of all, slowing drainage from the west into the Nottoway. Just to the south, Judkin's and Massenburg's Mills must have used most of the Jack's Creek system on its way to the Nottoway from the east. All the mills and ponds were surrounded by marshes and swamps. So was the large farm of our old acquaintance Daniel Cobb, whose place is marked north of Jerusalem, between the marshy banks of the Nottoway and a long stream known as Assamoosic Swamp.[5]

Sussex County, above Southampton, also remained a hinterland virtually covered in swampy forests. The next county north — Prince George — presents a rather different map. Forests still predominate, but less so, especially close to the James, where one easily finds Richard Eppes's farms, Julian Ruffin's, Edmund Ruffin, Jr.'s Evergreen, Coggins Point, Fleur de Hundred (now called Flowerdew Hundred), and the Brandons ("Upper" and "Lower"). Prince George was relatively crowded with railroads and roads, too; and remembering that the James and Appomattox were also excellent roads, one perceives in the Confederate draftsman's work a portrait of linearity both natural and built. The riverside portion of the county had its wetlands along the short runs and creeks that drain the line of ridges below the James's southern shore. Most of Prince George, however, belongs to the drainage system that heads south — through Sussex and Southampton via the Nottoway-Blackwater network to the Chowan and Albemarle. So most of the county map is marked with long north-south swamp/creeks — Blackwater Swamp, Warwick Swamp, Joseph Swamp, and Jones Hole Swamp. All of these, like the James's runs and creeks, were dammed and ponded.[6]

However detained, the swamp waters seeped southward, forming navigable rivers just north of Carolina, then the broad, beautiful Chowan. The Chowan River divides Hertford County from Gates, then Bertie County from Chowan. Confederate cartographers also worked this route, marking

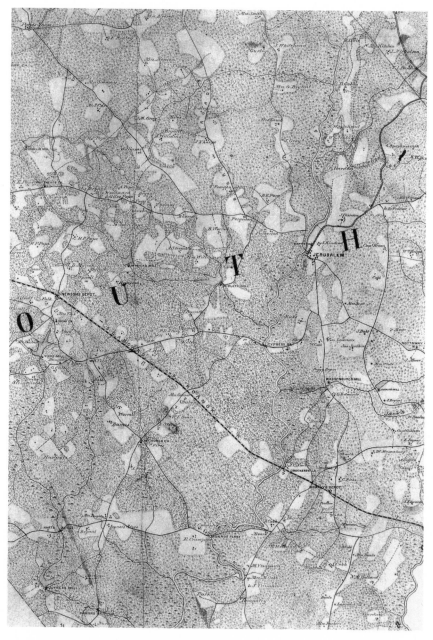

Map 4. Southampton County, Virginia, 1863 (detail identifying Daniel Cobb's farm, upper right, north of Jerusalem). (Source: *Confederate Engineers' Maps, Jeremy Francis Gilmer Collection, Virginia Historical Society*)

the fisheries that William Valentine so enjoyed each spring—Brennan's, Liberty Hill, Mount Pleasant. And the Valentine family estate appears, too, in a cluster of dots by the road southwest of Winton, on the way to California Crossroads. Most of the eastern Bertie landscape (like Southampton's) was wilderness, though, with widely separated clearings and a dot, or a dot plus a small cluster, representing other mansions and slave quarters. Meandering through it all are various swampy watercourses, draining toward the Chowan River. The Meherrin River, winding down from Virginia, conjoined dozens of swamps and creeks. Potecasi Creek—itself a large drainage system— joined the Meherrin just before it emptied into the big river. South and inland of Winton, Ahosky Swamp (now spelled Ahoskie) made a junction with Loosing Creek, which was fed by Quioquison Swamp; downstream they became Wickackon Creek, which joined Chinquapin Creek before entering the Chowan just upstream from the Liberty Hill fishery. Southern Chowan County was if anything more dominated by wetlands—the huge Will's Quarter Swamp, Roquest Swamp, Connaritsa Swamp, and other morasses associated with the Cashie and Roanoke river systems.[7]

Up the Roanoke, on Bertie and Northampton's western sides, one rediscovers sparsely settled plantation country, swampy and prone to floods. (Henry Burgwyn's place appears on the Confederate map, not far from Okoneechee Swamp, as the draftsman spelled it.) The little towns of Seaboard, Pleasant Grove, and Jackson sit on higher elevations, between the low swamp and creek systems. One is struck, once more, by the prevalence of dams and millponds. The largest was D. Deloatch's, which held back Potecasi Creek, Weekekany Swamp, and at least three other drainage systems. Taylor's Mill interrupted Corduroy Swamp's progress toward the Chowan; and downstream (to the east), DeBerry's caught the Corduroy and one of its tributaries. The unnamed swamp system near the Burgwyn plantation was stopped by no fewer than three large mills.[8]

Millponds appear on late-twentieth-century maps of the subregion, too. There are far fewer than before, however—appropriate to an age when using waterpower for local meal-grinding and timber-sawing is quaint. Still, Southampton County has seven substantial ponds, and others persist behind cataracts men built long before the Confederate engineers appeared. The largest of all lies near the center of Gates County—Merchants Millpond. Early in the nineteenth century (if not earlier), a consortium of Gates's merchants dammed Lassiter Swamp to create reliable power for their corn-grinding operations. Today the pond has shrunk to about seven hundred acres, from the original thousand, and the pond and its environs have be-

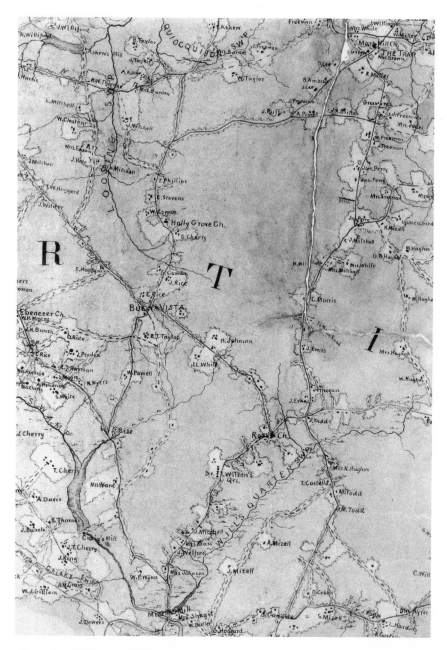

Map 5. Bertie County, North Carolina, 1863 (detail). (Source: Confederate Engineers' Maps, Jeremy Francis Gilmer Collection, Virginia Historical Society)

Merchants Millpond, Gates County, North Carolina, July 1991.
Tupelo gums stand in algae-covered water about three feet deep. (Photo by the author)

come a North Carolina state park. Other old millponds apparently also serve recreational purposes; and during droughts, they may be called into service for irrigating cropfields. The largest bodies of standing water on new maps —except Lake Drummond—are themselves new: Concentrated around the Nansemond River and Chuckatuck Creek, these are huge impoundments intended primarily as reservoirs for the urban populations of southern Hampton Roads.[9]

New maps exceed the Confederates' handiwork, both in topographical detail (which refines perception of drainage) and in representations of human reordering of landscapes. This is especially true of the U.S. Geological Survey's quadrangle maps (made during the 1960s and revised during the 1980s). On these, crop fields are larger, more concentrated—reflecting the capitalization of agriculture since World War II—but altogether, fields account for less space than the Confederates measured, reflecting the statistical abandonment of conventional farming in favor of forest plantations. And because the geologists (unlike the Confederate engineers) registered elevations on the quadrangles, students of recent maps may learn to distinguish swamps from pocosins. Swamps have definite contours and belong to active drainage systems. Pocosins have little contour and exist more as passive landscape, higher than swamps, less forested. They are marshy meadows or savannahs (although many have recently been planted with pines), the perfect middle ground of the subregion. The accompanying details from the Geological Survey's Runnymede quadrangle illustrate. (Runnymede lies mostly in Surry County, with a small portion in Isle of Wight.) Shrub, Tuckers, Cypress, and Willy Cox pocosins are all a bit higher than the interspersed waterways called swamps, such as Passenger and Moores. Elevations marked for Shrub Pocosin range only from 90 to 94 feet. Tuckers Pocosin shows only a 1-foot gradient on the accompanying detail, then another 3 feet (off this map) to the north. Cypress Pocosin appears utterly flat, at 90 feet; and Willy Cox—about a mile and a half long (north to south)—slopes only about 5 feet. Unpaved roads cross most pocosins, except for Cypress, which has state highways along three of its sides. Hardly any humans choose to reside on a pocosin—one spies few dots on the quadrangles, and these lie mainly next to good roads on pocosins' perimeters. Pocosins hold the stillest waters, and they are notoriously snaky; so presumably, one is well advised to live elsewhere. Residential dots are more numerous on the downslope gradients into swamps, such as Moores, which separates and drains Cypress and Willy Cox pocosins. The quadrangles' gradient marks for swamps—down to 80 feet, 70, 60, even 50 feet—demonstrate the three-dimensionality of these conductors of water, defying casual perceptions of swamplands as harborers of dank stillness and pestilence.[10]

Yet pestilence stalked the James-Albemarle country, like other low places around the globe. For a very long time, still waters were commonly associated with pestilence—yellow fever, typhoid, and especially malaria, that plague of agues and fevers which colored life so profoundly as to render wetlands, illness, and death inseparable.[11] William Byrd II was probably not the first Anglo-American to suggest the connection, but he may be said to be the first famous white man to do so. Only at the beginning of the twentieth century would the pathology of malaria at last be correctly understood: The bacillus breeds in stagnant freshwater, then a certain species of mosquito, the pestiferous vector, injects the disease into humans' bloodstreams. During virtually all the nineteenth century, physicians and informed laypeople *thought* they understood malaria's environment and transmission; but as we shall see, they failed to eliminate the disease environment and missed the vector.

In October 1825, Dr. Thomas O'Dwyer was subpoenaed to appear in Northampton Court. In a civil suit, a Major Sherrod charged that his neighbor's millpond "caused [his] family . . . to be so sick this fall" and several seasons

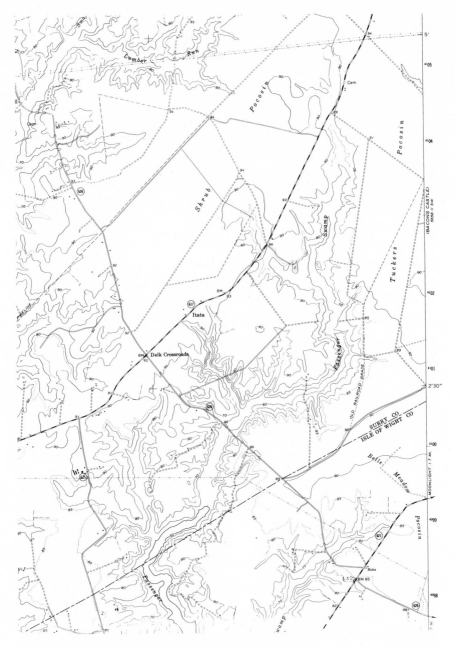

Map 6. Pocosins of Runnymede, Virginia quadrangle, 1966 (detail).
(Source: *U.S. Geological Survey)*

previous. Sherrod's attorney called O'Dwyer to affirm that the plaintiff's family had been similarly ill during 1819 and 1820. O'Dwyer could not supply admissible evidence. Still, the jury decided for Sherrod, but it awarded him only five dollars for three seasons of suffering and did not order the neighbor's mill dam removed.[12] The sanctity of private property was preserved; millponds would stand, harboring malaria and worse. Yet the jury's decision in principle for Major Sherrod also confirms public belief in the association between still water and illness. So what was to be done?

By this time Edmund and Susan Ruffin had already lost two infants at Coggins Point. Susan was herself subject to "billious fevers" (probably typhoid), and Edmund suffered often (as he later wrote) from "exposure to malaria — or marsh miasma." Convinced that their home was too low and unhealthy, they took the logical recourse of those with the means: They withdrew during the fall sickly season, then moved permanently to higher, drier ground, at Shellbanks. Ironically, after their departure, the old farm "had become much more healthy," and Ruffin felt obliged to admit a connection between illness and his enthusiasm for reclamation. "The former greater sickliness," he wrote, "was no doubt in part caused by the reclaiming & cultivating of the tide marsh." Ruffin's polder—like his friend Hill Carter's, across the James— "sunk very low" and must have held standing water. So he abandoned cultivation in favor of pasturing the land, finally permitting the tides to return.[13]

Later, Ruffin's geological survey of South Carolina was delayed by a recurrence of "marsh miasma," and when he moved to Marlbourne above Richmond, he was dismayed by the sight of "many shallow ponds of stagnant water"—the "worst sources of miasma." That dangerous first year, Ruffin, his family, and their overseer and slaves escaped serious illness by the Pamunkey; but Ruffin made drainage of stagnant water on Marlbourne a priority.[14] In the meantime, from Shellbanks and from his editorial office in Petersburg, Ruffin's war on malaria went public. Elimination of "marsh miasma" was an urgent requisite for a civilized South Atlantic. The cause of physical wellness assumed a place in Ruffin's reform agenda close behind marling and at least equal to fence reform.

Once upon a time, beavers had been the greatest cause of still water in all North America. Their industrious dam-building on streams flooded countless thousands of acres of land. European immigrants hated such industry, which inundated valuable crop fields and timberlands. Relentless trapping of the creatures to supply the transatlantic fur trade led to their extinction in the East before the end of the eighteenth century, however.[15] No wonder, then, at the excitement provoked by an 1838 *Richmond Enquirer* report of a *sus-*

pected beaver in Surry County. The local correspondent had not actually seen beaver in Surry but had "brought home several of the bits of wood nibbled by them."[16] Slim evidence, indeed; and I find no other reports of beaver in the subregion until very recently, when the government of Norfolk discovered a family of them imperiling a golf course near the airport.[17] By the 1830s, humans had effectively replaced beavers as dam-builders and makers of stagnant water. Edmund Ruffin understood this and had already begun to campaign against millponds.

Early in 1837 he declared in the *Farmers' Register* that "mill-ponds on all but rapid rivers and other large and constant streams, are enormous evils, throughout the whole country east of the mountains, in producing disease, still more than by covering much land of great value for cultivation."[18] Ruffin insinuated the Malthusian imperative here—croplands needed to feed human population increases were being lost to flooding from dams. But Ruffin ranked the threat to public health first, and more was to come. The July 1838 number of his paper devoted more than twelve large pages to Ruffin's exposition on malaria.

Like virtually all his contemporaries, Ruffin believed that malaria derived from "decaying and putrefying vegetable matter" under slow-moving or still freshwater. (Saltwater marshes seemed safe.) Southerly winds, especially during September and October, carried "effluvia rising from wet lands" into the lungs of human victims. Not content with wide reading in scientific literature, Ruffin had conducted investigations on his own of many suspected sources of malaria. These served to emphasize several aspects of current scientific understanding, especially that the stiller and fresher the water, and the more decaying vegetation, the higher the correlation with local and upwind illness. So he concluded, quite logically, that in the Virginia low country, millponds must be the most morbid of all wetlands. Ruffin warmed for the attack, reminding readers of the common knowledge that small mills were impractical, anyway. Most of them merely arrested the sluggish flows of swamps, seldom providing enough water to turn mills. Such mills seemed utterly indefensible, and Ruffin wondered rhetorically why they existed at all. His answers consisted of rustic frivolousness compounded by antique and mischievous legislation. Isolated farmers, searching "for amusement and excitement" but too poor to "raise race-horses," persuaded county boards to permit ponding (an easy matter), then they dammed swamps with flows inadequate to power the tiniest gristmill. "The law of Virginia in regard to the erection of mill-ponds, with perhaps the exception of the fence-law," Ruffin growled, "is one of the most stupid, and most regardless both of private rights and general interests, of all in our code"—all the worse because "the mill-law permits and encourages also the destruction of health and of life throughout the whole land." But to Ruffin there was more, intimately related to his broader reforms: Millponds, he declared, "are productive of little else than malaria and disease," while simultaneously they "indirectly, but effectually, [forbid] the drainage of extensive swamps." On reclaimed swamps progressive farmers would apply marl, fixing nitrogen from decaying vegetation and producing crops of grain to sustain a civilized country. A state board of health might supervise the millpond problem—i.e., forbid most of them—but Ruffin despaired that Virginians were capable of such enlightenment. His best hope for the moment was to educate the public about the menace of stagnant water.[19]

Early in 1840 Ruffin published an anonymous, urgent message from Washington County, North Carolina, on "Malaria and Millponds." The letter seems suspiciously set-up, considering Ruffin's passion on the subject and his recent travels along the southern shores of the Albemarle. In Washington County his hosts had been the Pettigrews, one of whom was probably author of the *Farmers' Register* piece. Whoever he was, the writer declared that six years before, he had literally moved his father's house in order to separate his family from stagnant water. His strongest language, however, supported Ruffin's campaign for governmental action against millponds: "If I know any thing that would induce me to accept the dictatorship of a country," he declared, "it would be that of having the power to constrain the inhabitants in the bilious fever region to remove all stagnant water from it, and to keep all arable land in the fall covered with vegetation, and thereby sheltered from the power and influence of the sun."[20]

Ruffin's own best hope of governmental action lay in Virginia's Board of Agriculture. In 1842 he reprised for the board his 1838 *Farmers' Register* exposition, which he republished early the following year. But the board was perhaps a greater disappointment to Ruffin than Virginia's curmudgeonly legislature. Nothing was to be done about millponds.[21] As ever, denizens of the low country were on their own: They might move, if they could, or take other precautions, as guided by wisdom folkish or professional. As late as 1897 the latter category included advice on safe drinking water. Dr. C. W. Dabney, Jr., recommended that people drink water only from deep (preferably artesian) wells, avoiding surface and ground-aquifer sources unless it was boiled first. Dabney's concern with imbibing (as opposed to breathing) seems new, but his explanation of the disease hardly differed from the antebellum understanding. "[M]alaria," he wrote, "is not peculiar to any section, but is caused by a specific germ or germs, which may occur wherever low, marshy lands contain large bodies of decaying vegetable matter."[22]

Shortly after Dabney published his advice, army researchers finally discovered that the vectors of malaria as well as yellow fever were mosquitoes. And soon Dr. Richard H. Lewis, secretary of the North Carolina State Board of Health—among many others—set about explaining malaria to his rural constituents. "By recent scientific investigations," Lewis announced, "the cause of the fever has been shown to be a microscopic animal known as the *plasmodium malariae* or *hem amoeba vivax*, which feeds upon the red corpuscles of the blood—hence the pallor of persons suffering from chronic malaria." The vector, too, was finally

> demonstrated beyond all question to be the sting of a certain variety of mosquito known as anopheles; the common mosquito, which while more abundant, is innocent as a carrier of disease, being known as culex. The latter species will breed in still water of any kind, no matter how pure[;] but the former, our enemy, will only breed in stagnant pools in which there is a certain amount of vegetable matter, especially if there are no fish, such as top minnows or sun-perch, which feed upon the larvae or wiggletails. This explains the fact that malaria is much more abundant after freshets, in the course of which the stream, getting out of its banks, washes holes in the ground, and speedily falling[,] leaves there stagnant pools with few or no fish in them.

Recommended prevention included "thorough drainage of all stagnant pools," of course, but also "keeping the surface of all such pools covered with petroleum," which "prevents the larvae from breathing and smothers them."[23]

To top-feeding fish as deterrents to anopheles, Lewis might have added dragonflies. The folk of our subregion called them "snake doctors" in my youth, but Mississippians have a more appropriate nickname for dragonflies —"skeeterhawks," meaning mosquito-hawks.[24] For dragonflies hover over still waters, devouring anopheles and culex alike. I observed the phenomenon myself during a visit to Merchants Millpond on a steamy summer afternoon. Expecting to confront swarms of mosquitoes, I was instead delighted to accompany squadrons of dragonflies, busy at their beneficial feasting.

Because dragonflies' appearance is not always guaranteed, however, people may have been well advised to spread oil upon still waters. During the 1910s and especially the 1920s, public health organizations in the South promoted this method; and by 1930, malaria seems to have been effectively eradicated in urban areas. Not so in the vast hinterland, however, where every remote (and perhaps abandoned) millpond, every empty posthole, and every depression left by strolling cattle and mules demanded, but did not receive, stifling petroleum treatments. A survey of the inhabitants of the Boykins neighborhood in Southampton County, early in the twentieth century, indicated a malarial infection rate of 45 percent. In 1919 a U.S. Public Health Service official estimated the annual costs of malaria in the South (especially in labor lost) at $100 million. And twenty years later another researcher announced that malaria's annual cost in "death, disability, and unproductiveness" was no less than $500 million. Conquest of the rural mosquito awaited DDT—a dubious victory if there ever was one. Elsewhere, in tropical latitudes around the globe, the disease thrived despite oceans of DDT. By the early 1990s, however, a Colombian physician had developed a malaria vaccine that promised relief to perhaps as many as two-thirds of sufferers in South America, Africa, and Asia.[25]

Malaria's dissipating effects sometimes rendered victims susceptible to other, and mortal, infections. But malaria itself was seldom fatal in North America. Instead, it profoundly affected the annual cycle of work and life of perhaps half the population, plus that portion of the uninfected who cared for the sick each autumn. Malaria weakened and dispirited, imposing limits on human effort and expectation. It seems reasonable to posit malaria, then, as a principal cause of hinterlanders' vaunted ambitionlessness, and their "carelessness" (as Olmsted put it). So still water, heat, a bacillus, and a mosquito, in other words, may have significantly retarded both modern agronomy and bourgeois behavior in the low country. Hinterlanders—folks of middling to poor circumstances—had no option of fleeing to mountain resorts in sickly seasons, so they suffered disproportionately. More than the cosmopolitans, they were obliged to accept a baneful aspect of nature's agency.[26]

Pathology alone, however, would be the most vulgar of explanations of hinterlanders' ways. Illness, and the near-absence of surviving written expression from these folks, do not mean that they lacked decisive will, that they did not rationally consider modern work discipline and decide to reject it. (Observing schedules, elevating work above leisure, and supervising others, or being supervised, with all the attendant negotiations and tensions, are, after all, quite awful; and many people still reject this mode today.) And in addition to rationality there is geography—the difficulty (or impossibility) of movement, especially transportation of the heavy surpluses that industriousness would produce.

Consider, for instance, Knotts Island and the experience of one of its natives, H. B. Ansell. Ansell was born on the island, near the northeastern-most point of North Carolina, in 1832, a century and four years after a hurricane closed a narrow inlet (or "outlet," as Edmund Ruffin preferred) from nearby Currituck Sound into the Atlantic. As an old man (during 1903–7), Ansell incorporated local history into his memoir, claiming that he remembered virtually everything since 1835. He cherished memories of a happy boyhood, which he spent roaming the local swamps, "birding"—it was Ansell who traded strings of songbirds for toys and candy—and listening to his elders' tales. Animals, unsurprisingly, preoccupied Ansell. He and his playmates found "many deep holes in the forest half fill[ed] up," he recalled. "The old people said these holes had been wolf-pits which their forefathers had made to entrap the wolves, and did so to their extermination." Ansell thought that dangerous snakes had become rare on the high center of Knotts Island by the beginning of the twentieth century, although "an abundance of moccasins and other snakes" infested the "swamp, knolls and marshes on the margin of this Island." Once upon a time, however—Ansell probably learned this from his elders, again—"A certain family had built a new log house with a clay fire-place, and unluckily this fire-place had been built over a den of snakes; the family went to bed leaving a hot fire in order to dry the clay; the next morning this family were found all dead and swollen to a puff, with snakes in the room a foot deep." Ansell never mentioned the Carolina parakeet. In his youth the colorful, foot-long bird was probably already extinct in those parts, like the wolf. The old people, however, might have told him how they saved their rich orchards of "apples, peaches, cherries and many other fruits" (which Ansell praised) by shooting and poisoning parakeets, which loved fruit, too.[27]

Ansell was a particularly valuable participant-observer of duck hunting. "The people of this Island," he wrote, "were, and are yet, born hunters." Knotts Island occupies a famous place (along with neighboring Back Bay, in Virginia) along the Atlantic flyway. Every fall enormous rafts of ducks rest and feed on the island's wetlands during their long southward migration. For a very long time, the men of Knotts Island supplemented their families' larders by hunting the migrants. During Ansell's antebellum youth, "The crawling practice was in vogue." That is, one would "Go into the marsh with noiseless care; look over the coves, creeks and ponds; see if any of the feathered tribe have ventured near enough to shore for a shot; if so, down on hands and knees, often in mud and water; crawl to the water's edge; peep through the marginal marsh or galls; see where the ducks were thick-

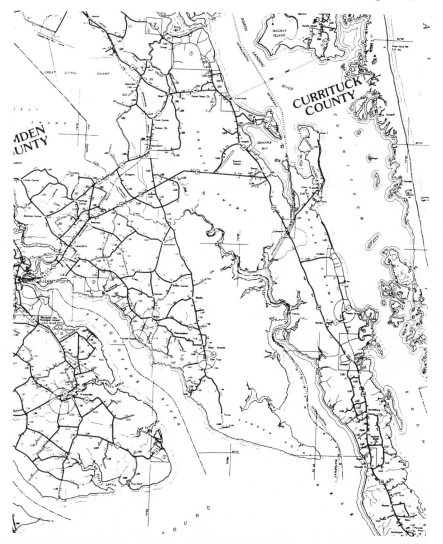

Map 7. Northeastern North Carolina, ca. 1990 (detail). Elizabeth City is left-center; Knotts Island is in the upper right, to the right of MacKay Island. (Reproduced from Camden-Currituck county map with local advertising, distributed everywhere in the territory)

est. Ready—aim—bang. Fuss and feathers, what clatter and scramble. There might be three or four or a score dead and crippled ducks." There were no blinds, and apparently no bird dogs, for "In went the hunter attending to cripples first, often chasing a wing-break a great distance." Two hunters, Ansell remembered, were more productive than one: "often one would shoot at the sitting, the other at the rise or flirt."[28]

Ansell bragged that "two persons would often kill a hundred [ducks or geese] in one day at the margin of the sand beach or on some conspicuous shoal near by it." Yet, inconsistently, by the early twentieth century he had become a conservationist, scoffing at others' declarations that "there are as many ducks frequenting our waters as ever in years past." He recalled a raft in "the old days" that settled "on the bay side up in Jones's Windmill," covering the water "for hundred[s] of yards, wedged so closely together that scarcely any water could be seen among them." He had actually seen "larger rafts ... in Knott's Island Bay and its adjacent shoals and Swan Island waters." Now, he estimated, "there cannot be over twenty-five per cent of the fowl that frequented our waters seventy years ago." Why? The "crawling fashion" of hunting was abandoned in favor of blinds and the use of retrieving dogs. There were more hunters, using much better guns. Human population had grown up around the flyway, so the demand for ducks and geese had grown. And hunting had become commercial, turning fowl into commodities carried away in new refrigerated railway cars to distant markets.[29]

Despite the great transition symbolized by the commercialization of duck shooting, Knotts Island remained a marginal place. It closely resembled the area about Moyock, to the west of Knotts Island, where a little after Ansell's time, Dudley Bagley and his Yankee patron promoted Ducks Unlimited. Conspicuous decreases in the fowl count reduced local consumption, in all probability; but the local culture remained remote from most markets, as it had been since the great hurricane of 1728. Of all this Ansell was himself well aware, even though his elders misled him by a century on the closing of the former Currituck Inlet.

From the old folks Ansell heard that "The old Inlet filled up in 1828." Before "that event, perhaps during a century or more," Ansell wrote, "there were many small vessels carrying staves, shingles, corn, wheat, etc., from Currituck and other North Carolina counties, through this inlet, to Norfolk, Baltimore, New York and other Northern markets; and bringing back sugar, molasses, cloths, calicoes, many other dry-goods and notions, and all kinds of liquors." Ansell suggested that the long age of the open inlet was golden; and he was essentially correct, despite the misdating. Men (not so much women) at that time made money in trade while simultaneously enjoying subsistence upon nature's bounty. (Women's lives, Ansell admitted—echoing William Byrd II's observation—were "not so easy as that of their lords; picking cotton and wool, carding, spinning, weaving, cutting, sewing and making clothes for the entire family, fell to their lot; besides there were other household duties.") "The men in those days" (on the other hand), "with fish and fowl in plenty at their doors, and chinkapins and acorns for hogs when taken from the marsh, could provide eatables for their families with but little labor; and so they had plenty of spare time." This, according to Ansell, they devoted mainly to sport, notably "fist cuffing, hair-pulling, eye-gouging." While the inlet remained open, "every [boat] crew and every neighborhood had a fighting champion"; so "After a few drinks of Jersey-lightning, balanced with cuss-words, these 'homers' [local fighters] and Northerners would wade in." And according to Ansell, the local historian, "The home champion always won; the other fellow went down." John Potter White—"a scientific boxer"—was the great hero of the early nineteenth century. In New York City White defeated the metropolis's "mulatto champion"; but after another bout in the big city, White died from a broken nose "driven in." Taylor Jones, who replaced White as the eastern Albemarle's chief manly artist, was especially esteemed for victories over rivals not from far away but from nearby Coinjock, which, according to Knotts Islanders, was an incubator of bullies. Specifically, Jones whipped a pair of Coinjock brothers improbably named Te and Shade Killum. This victory was accomplished, Ansell claimed, with a single blow that caused Shade to crumble and Te to decamp in haste.[30]

Violent sport among men doubtlessly outlasted the Currituck Inlet, but the cosmopolitan (even international) character of fighting seems to have subsided by the time Ansell was born. Ansell wrote that during the 1840s and 1850s, Currituck men fished for the Norfolk trade, and that middlemen appeared on Knotts Island to compete for business. Ansell also observed, however, that trading with Norfolk was never very important to Currituck folk. Knotts Island, especially, is closer to Princess Anne County (now a city called Virginia Beach), and the Virginians were already deeply engaged in fishing and fowling for the Norfolk market, which was more convenient to Princess Anne. Nor was the island much involved in the produce trade, either before or after the Civil War. "The soil of this Island," wrote Ansell, "is a light sandy loam, sand predominating; excellent trucking land, but even now [ca. 1907] little used for that purpose other than for home consumption." Why was "the whole place ... not a truck-garden"? Simple, replied Ansell: "the main reason ... is uncertain transportation."[31]

So until twentieth-century, hard-surface roads were in place, Knotts Island, Coinjock, and many other swampy places harbored hinterlanders who persisted in a culture close to subsistence. Even at South Mills, southern terminus of the Dismal Swamp Canal, this seems to have been so. There Walton and George Riggs (father and son) operated a general store for more than half a century, from the 1830s into the 1890s; and their business records demonstrate the persistence. From New York and Philadelphia, but especially Norfolk, the Riggses ordered guano, plow points, and other farming implements for (one supposes) the more substantial agriculturists who inhabited Camden County. The bulk of their imported trade goods, however, consisted of small consumable necessities, most of which could not be made at home: coffee, tea, medicines, cloth by the bolt (plus some ready-made clothing), snuff, candy, and whiskey. The Riggses must have been eager to handle large shipments of grain and lumber, but they had little business of such scale. The completion in 1859 of the Albemarle-Chesapeake Canal—connecting Currituck Sound via the North Landing River with the Elizabeth, at Great Bridge—sent the Dismal Swamp Canal into permanent decline as a shipping route. The older canal was too narrow for mid-nineteenth-century steamers. So the Riggses contented themselves with a large volume of small items. In return for the coffee, snuff, and candy, they accepted geese, chickens, eggs, ducks, rags (for papermaking), a little wool, some potatoes, peas, the occasional calf or hog, and the skins of many animals—mink, fox, raccoon.[32] It must have been at such a store that young H. B. Ansell exchanged his pretty birds for sweets and tops.

The Riggses' local customers were mostly plain swampers, modest in their commercial requirements, not yet "consumers" in the modern sense. Perhaps such folks were without consumerist ambition, trading what they found or made from nature only to acquire essentials that were unavailable locally. Coffee, for instance, the Riggses could provide, for a few coonskins. Ansell, a nostalgist, implied a sort of premodern virtue in the swampers. But there is additional testimony along this line from an unexpected source: Edmund Ruffin—the same man who hated woods-burning, the open range, and ordinary folks' amusing millponds, and who was obsessed with the disciplines and routines of agricultural productivity.

In 1836 Ruffin continued his "riding" visits to eastern Virginia counties, reporting his observations in the *Farmers' Register*. His visit to Nansemond County yielded lamentations extraordinary even for Ruffin. He was shocked that the "oldest settled and longest cultivated part of Virginia, and of the United States, should be now the least removed from the wild state of nature." Ruffin predicted mass migration from Nansemond and environs: "the time may come when the howling of wolves will be heard from the suburbs of Norfolk." Ruffin could not perceive that in 1836 the riverine sections of Nansemond and Norfolk Counties hovered on the brink of prosperity through truck farming for northeastern markets. His only relief from agronomic despair lay in "The farms on the banks of the Nansemond River"—

"most desirable as places ... for agricultural profit." Yet the lowlands were too prone to "autumnal fevers, the effects of malaria." Then came Ruffin's brief paean to the plain folks. I read it as more a scolding lecture to indolent river farmers than a genuine appreciation of hinterland culture, but his observations nonetheless repeat truths about "the people who cultivate the poor lands of the 'piney woods.'" "Deprived of all the comforts and luxuries furnished by the river," Ruffin wrote, "and compelled by the difficulties of their situation to be laborious and frugal, they have prospered in their estates, in spite of poor lands and a wretched system of agriculture"—the last meaning, one presumes, the open range and fire culture. "They live plainly, but comfortably," declared Ruffin, himself a relatively plain liver, and "have no fear of the sheriff before their eyes, nor anticipations of leaving their children in want, or dependence—and are able to exercise, and doubtless do exercise, true and kind hospitality, without ostentation, and without the waste of the entertainers' time and good habits, still more than of his victuals and drink, on idle loungers and dissipated companions and visiters."[33]

Perhaps Ruffin himself had had too much company. He obviously was not the guest of any of the "piney woods" folk, but chose to ennoble them from a certain distance. Ruffin was certainly wrong in generalizing that they resisted drink and other entertainments. H. B. Ansell (a genuine woodsman) and many others said otherwise. Nonetheless, Ruffin had a larger insight in Nansemond, which explained to his own satisfaction why even river farmers did not pursue marling and other agronomic reforms. All the folks of Nansemond County were beneficiaries of rich woodlands and the proximity of an excellent market—the federal government's shipyard in Portsmouth and Fortress Monroe (across Hampton Roads in Hampton). Elsewhere Ruffin acknowledged the additional market—enormous and international—for shingles from these same forests, especially within the Great Dismal Swamp. Farmers with woodlands and means of conveyance—usually a river or suitable creek—have ever devoted part of winter to the selective cutting of timber. In Nansemond and other swampy counties, too, cash was to be had this way; but woodcraft here more closely resembled modern business. Forest enterprises, Ruffin figured, demanded most of the labor that might otherwise have been devoted to modern agronomy.[34]

Early in 1834 Ruffin had attempted to solicit an article on the countryside south and west of Portsmouth from Charles Campbell, a young engineer who was at work surveying the route for the Portsmouth and Roanoke Railway. "The Dismal Swamp," Ruffin suggested, was "a perfect *Terra Incognita*."

Campbell was not responsive, probably owing to his hostility to the entire Southside Virginia landscape and its inhabitants. "The country here is miserably flat dull & destitute of [the] picturesque," he informed his family. "The population is meagre & devoid of intelligence. ... If you see one farm—one farmer & one farmhouse—you see all—[O]n the whole line—75 miles [i.e., from Portsmouth to Weldon]—there is nothing of interest."[35]

Ruffin finally wrote extensively about this landscape, including the Dismal, himself; and unlike Campbell, Ruffin found much of interest. The great swamp was not so *incognita*, he discovered, after all, but a place already much intruded upon via convenient thoroughfares. Indeed, the editor first cast his eyes upon the Dismal from a car moving over rails of Campbell's design. "I reached Suffolk," Ruffin wrote late in 1836, "by way of the railway, from Portsmouth, which passed through a few miles of the swamp at its northern extremity, and thus permitted a first slight glance." Ruffin meditated revealingly upon the jarring juxtaposition of darkest nature and modern linearity: "It seems unfortunate," he thought, "that the first approach to the swamp, of almost every person hereafter, will be the rapidly moving railway train. The savage gloom of the face of nature is altogether unsuited to the highly artificial facilities by means of which the traveller is flying past—and the discordance serves to lessen the high gratification which either the conveyance or the scene alone would cause, when new to the observer."[36] Much of the swamp remained inaccessible, of course, but the Dismal Swamp Canal, the good road alongside, and now the railroad all rendered the Great Dismal less mysterious. And there were more roads of other sorts, as well, for Ruffin to discover.

Lake Drummond being higher than most of the Dismal, the earliest entrepreneurs to enter the swamp calculated that Drummond water might float out valuable wood on canals—more often called ditches. Ditching began at least as early as the late eighteenth century; in the nineteenth it accelerated. There were short local waterways before the Dismal Swamp Canal was dug. Then came the Feeder Ditch and, a quarter century before Edmund Ruffin's arrival, the grand Jericho Ditch to Suffolk. (This was Ruffin's, Porte Crayon's, and countless others' avenue to the heart of the swamp). The Washington Ditch—honoring the most famous founding stockholder in the Dismal's largest wood-getting corporation—intersected the swamp's northwestern quadrant. And toward the end of the nineteenth century, the city of Portsmouth spent $90,000 digging the longest channel of all—the Portsmouth Ditch—in a futile attempt to make Drummond an urban reservoir.[37]

In Suffolk, Ruffin met Mills Riddick, Sr., master of "Riddick's Folly" on

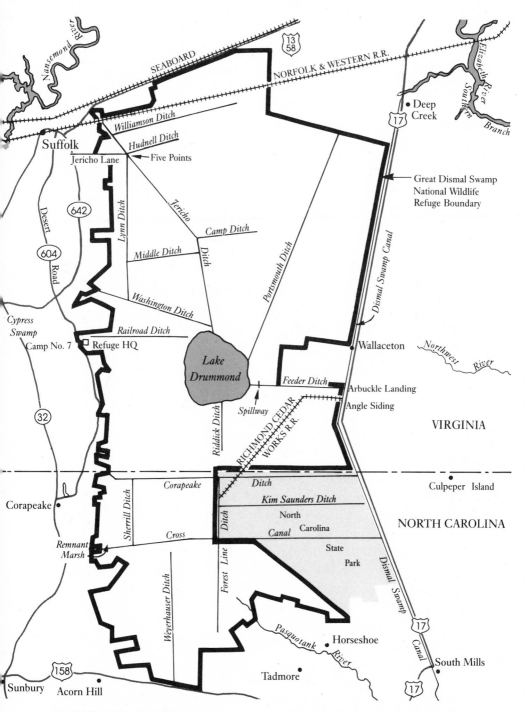

Map 8. Dismal Swamp ditch/canal system, ca. 1950s (From Bland Simpson, The Great Dismal *[Chapel Hill: University of North Carolina Press, 1990], courtesy of the University of North Carolina Press)*

Riddick's Folly, Main Street, Suffolk, 1990 (Photo by the author)

Main Street, his enormous brick residence, and dean of northern Dismal Swamp shingle-buyers and -shippers. Riddick told the editor that many years before, he had assisted Commodore James Barron—the killer of Stephen Decatur in a duel—in sounding the bottom of Lake Drummond. Ever since, Riddick and others had been busy lowering the lake into the ditches that gave Ruffin such easy access to the swamp. Ruffin seems to have descended to Drummond by way of Jericho Ditch, passing the junction with Washington Ditch just north of the lake, then taking the Feeder Ditch to the Dismal Swamp Canal. Ruffin thought this arrow-straight avenue represented a perfect conflation of human ingenuity and natural beauty. "The canal," he recorded, "with the trees on each side almost joining their branches across, presents a beautiful vista and perspective view—and with our singular boat and its equippage would have furnished a fine subject for a painter." Nighttime was magical in the swamp, "with the bright light of our fire partially displacing the general darkness." Altogether, Ruffin was charmed; his Byrd-like prejudice against the morass had been banished, at least temporarily. "A writer like [Washington] Irving," he opined, "might here find enough interesting matter for description and narrative, to fill a volume. The land and the water—the vegetables and the wild animals—the inhabitants in their habits and occupations—are all as different from the surrounding country, as if the traveller had suddenly passed into a far remote region."[38]

The charm of this particular remote place never attracted Irving. Harriet Beecher Stowe and Henry Wadsworth Longfellow, however, found the Dismal irresistible—without ever traveling the grand canal and ditches, and for a reason Ruffin doubtless disapproved (as we shall see in the following chapter). Porte Crayon also became Ruffin's enemy in 1861, but his swamp travelogue, published nearly a quarter century after Ruffin's visit, approached, at least, the lyricism Ruffin had wished for in Irving. Crayon more than fulfilled the promise of the painter.

By 1856 the Great Dismal was already old in romantic imaginations on both sides of the Atlantic. The popular Irish poet Thomas Moore had visited Norfolk in 1803 and—though whether he actually entered the swamp is in question—had become enthralled with the Edenic wetland below the city. The result was "The Lake of the Dismal Swamp," a long poem of incalculable sorrow. A young woman, a prospective bride, has died: "They made her a grave too cold and damp/For a soul so warm and true." Her spirit, however, has

> gone to the lake of the Dismal Swamp
> Where all night long, by a firefly lamp
> She paddles her white canoe.

Her lover, unable to accept the fact of her death, is determined that

> Long and loving our life shall be
> And I'll hide the maid in a cypress tree
> When the footstep of death is near!

So "Away to the Dismal Swamp he speeds/His path was rugged and sore." Calling and calling to the maid from the lake's shore, he finally gave up, made his own canoe of "birchen bark," shoved off, and "returned no more." Forever after, though,

> from the Indian hunter's camp
> This lover and maid so true
> Are seen at the hour of midnight damp
> To cross the lake by a firefly lamp
> And paddle their white canoe.

*Porte Crayon, "The Barge" (*Harper's New Monthly Magazine, *September 1856)*

Crayon—a creature of the western Virginia mountains—declared that Lake Drummond had "haunted" him "from my earliest recollection, owing, probably, to the fact that the exquisite ballad of Moore's was my lullaby in infancy, and even now, when in sad and dreamy mood, that old wailing melody invariably recurs to me as it was sung over my cradle, soothing the real with the wilder sorrow of the poet's fancy." At last in Suffolk, Crayon set out almost breathlessly, he wrote, down Jericho Ditch toward the lake, aboard a barge. The bargemen worked too slowly, and the swamp was utterly silent. Crayon, overcome with sentiment and impatience, involuntarily sought to imprint himself on the wilderness. He arose and began to sing Moore's "old mournful lullaby," which had arisen "to my lips unbidden." [39]

Crayon knew that his audience relished the exotic, and he obliged. "[A]ll nature was silent, monotonous, deathlike." Beneath reedy undergrowth he saw "extensive pools of black, slimy water, from which rose the broad-based cypress." On "a decayed log, lay coiled a dead snake, dragged untimely from his winter retreat by a hungry otter." And of course there is "a lazy, loathsome buzzard, scared from his perch and sailing away above the tree tops." Finally, "a broad sheet of water lay before us." Ely Reed and Jim Pierce, his barge-men, shouted in unison, "The lake! The lake!" "There it was—the dream of my childhood fulfilled ... the broad expanse of dusky water with its dim circling shores. ... It was complete at all points, a picture of desolation—Desolation," a winter scene appropriate to Crayon's imagination. Later, as a full moon appeared over Drummond, he heard a paddle and saw "a white object moving rapidly toward me, which soon took the well-defined form of a boat. I felt strangely. Can the old ballad be true, then? and do the phantom lovers still haunt the lonely lake?" At last a "white canoe shot up into the bay near our barge; paddled not by the death-cold maid, as I confidently expected, but by Joe Skeeters," who "holds the office of shingle-counter for the Dismal Swamp Land Company."[40]

Thereafter, Crayon's account includes several interesting observations on the swamp's physical characteristics—he saw a bald eagle over Drummond, and heard that the Dismal abounded with "bear, deer, otter, raccoons, possums, etc., pheasants, partridges, and wild ducks," as well as "fine fresh-water fish, the most esteemed of which are the speckled perch"; and he observed that the swamp's human inhabitants, most of them shingle-getters, seemed to enjoy good health, free of malaria.[41] For the most part, however, by the time Crayon had satisfied his dream of seeing Lake Drummond, he had become enthralled with the swamp men he met—with Ely Reed, Jim Pierce, Joe Skeeters, shingle-cart boys, and others.

Reed and Pierce were both "niggers," suggesting to Crayon the possibility of their "stealing" property, an association he wittily passed on to his readers. Reed was "a turkey-egg mulatto, well-formed, but with an unprepossessing face—with nothing about him sufficiently striking to justify either a description or a sketch." Later, Reed begged Crayon for a sketch that he might show his family; Crayon obliged, but made no copy to accompany his travelogue. Pierce—who was camp cook as well as bargeman—was more interesting to Crayon. "Jim was a tall wiry black, with his hair plaited into numerous pig-tails—a mode of dressing the wool common among the blacks at the South. He has goggle eyes and an intelligent countenance, talks better than negroes usually do, and cooks remarkably well." (Crayon had plain tastes, apparently, for Pierce had simply fried bacon and eggs. Later he fried speckled perch.) Crayon never identified either man's status as slave or free. Later he reported that the land company "owns a number of slaves, and hires others."[42]

*Porte Crayon, "Jim Pierce" (*Harper's New Monthly Magazine, *September 1856)*

The Dismal Swamp Land Company actually owned few slaves but hired many workers, both slaves and free people. At the beginning of 1861, the corporation owned a great many lighters (shallow-draft barges), carts, and mules, but only six slave men. The manager was committed to spending about $1,200 on the wages of hired hands that year, however. The numbers seem typical for the late-antebellum period of the company's history. Corporate slaves were often lightermen and laborers who maintained ditches; so Ely and Jim may have belonged to the company. The "free colored" list (with 2,411 names) within the 1850 manuscript census returns for Nansemond County, however, includes one "James Pierce," a thirty-year-old man described as "black" and as heading a household with Alicy Pierce (a twenty-eight-year-old black woman) and four children, aged eight to two. There is no Ely Reed; there are many free people named "Read," but still no Ely among them. During the summer of 1852, though, the Dismal Swamp Land Company's clerk listed an "Ely of Reade" among the "Hands employed in cleaning out and deepening the Co. Canal." This difficult work was compensated at the rate of $15 per month, but one cannot know whether Ely received the pay as a free man or whether, if he were a slave, his master negotiated and took most of the rate.[43]

Crayon well understood, nonetheless, that slaves hired out in the swamp, whether to the big company or to smaller operators, occupied privileged positions. "The hands," he wrote, "are tasked, furnished with provisions at a fixed rate, and paid for all work exceeding the required amount." Therefore an "industrious workman may gain a considerable sum for himself in the course of the year," and the distinction between free men and slaves could thus become blurred.[44]

Frederick Law Olmsted had noticed the same phenomenon early in 1853 — "slaves quasi freemen," he called the black swampers. An advocate of capitalism and wage labor, Olmsted was delighted with the apparent effect of cash initiatives upon bondsmen. Once a rude camp was established deep in the swamp, "The slave lumberman then lives measurably as a free man; hunts, fishes, eats, drinks, smokes and sleeps, plays and works, each when and as much as he pleases." All this so long as "he shall have made, after half a year has passed, such a quantity of shingles as shall be worth to his master so much money as is paid to his owner for his services, and shall refund the value of the clothing and provisions he has required." There was no "'driving' at this work. . . . No force is used to overcome the insolence peculiar to the negro. The [white] overseer merely takes a daily account of the number of shingles each man adds to the general stock, and employs another set of hands, with mules, to draw them to a point from which they can be shipped." The effect of the system upon "negroes working in the swamp" was remarkable, Olmsted almost exulted. They "were more sprightly and straight-forward in their manner and conversation than any field-hand plantation-negroes that I saw at the South; two or three of their employers with whom I conversed spoke well of them, as compared with other slaves, and made no complaints of 'rascality' or laziness."[45]

Edmund Ruffin, too, observed the swamp's "task" system, but rather more ambivalently, as one might expect. Ruffin examined shingle-getters' camps, where "houses, or shanties, are barely wide enough for five or six men to lie in, closely packed side by side—their heads to the back wall, and their feet stretched to the open front, close by a fire kept up through the night." The workers slept upon shavings made as shingles were cut from "juniper" (as nearly everyone called cypress). "Yet they live plentifully, and are pleased with their employment—and the main objection to it with their masters, (they being generally slaves,) and the community, is that the laborers have too much leisure time, and of course spend it improperly. Their heavy labors for the week [i.e., assigned tasks] are generally finished in five, and often in four days—and then the remainder of the week is spent out of the swamp, and given to idleness, and by many to drunkenness." Ruffin heard that "About 500 men are thus employed in the whole swamp, by the Land Company, and by numerous individual land owners." All those whom Ruffin saw he thought "remarkably healthy, and almost entirely free from the autumnal fevers that so severely scourge all the surrounding country."[46]

Joseph Skeeter (Crayon misnamed him Skeeters) counted many thousands of Dismal Swamp Land Company shingles brought up by such quasi-freemen. To Crayon, Skeeter was "a thoroughbred swamper" and "fair specimen of a Swamp gentleman." Since Joe was white and free, Crayon eagerly accepted his offer of "a drink of bald-face"—i.e., cheap whiskey—"which in these parts is the sacred pledge of hospitality, like the eating of salt among the Turks." Jim Pierce cooked perch caught by Joe's "lieutenant" (apparently a black man, who paddled Joe's canoe and snared fish in a gill net), while Joe regaled the stranger. Crayon said little more of him, but the Nansemond census of 1850 and records of the Land Company offer Joe Skeeter as almost typical of white swampers before the Civil War. During the 1840s Joe had been a shingle-getter himself—that is, a part-time entrepreneur who, during winters, took to the Dismal with strong sons, other relatives, and maybe a few slaves (Skeeter owned five), to earn cash. Joshua Skeeter, a relative, counted Joe's and his crew's shingles. Later, during the 1850s, Joe replaced Joshua as the company's counter. Joe's principal occupation, however, was farming. In 1850 his place was valued at $300; and besides his wife, Irene, Skeeter's household included four sons and a daughter. All the sons were teenagers and probably shingle-getters.[47]

Other getters in the company's records for the 1850s ranged in status from

*Porte Crayon, "Joe Skeeters" (*Harper's New Monthly Magazine, *September 1856)*

planters to propertyless free laborers. Elisha Norfleet, Sr., for instance, was a 51-year-old white farmer worth $10,000. Norfleet's household included no strapping sons, like Skeeter's, but Riddick Draper, a 30-year-old black freedman, lived on the place, along with twenty-four slaves. Norfleet apparently sent some of these to the swamp every winter. At the other end of the spectrum was Archy Miltear, a 22-year-old propertyless mulatto laborer. Miltear lived with Pheraby Skeeter, listed as 19 and also a mulatto, and three small children. So he probably made shingles either alone or with junior partners, since the company maintained an account in his name. Most getters fell between Norfleet and Miltear. Miles Lassiter (member of a large white clan) was in 1850 a 45-year-old farmer worth $2,500. William Saunders was a 24-year-old white farmer worth $300, Dempsey Lassiter a 25-year-old white propertyless laborer. A host of free mulattoes surnamed Read—perhaps relatives of

*Porte Crayon, "Carting Shingles" (*Harper's New Monthly Magazine, *September 1856)*

Crayon's Ely Reed—got shingles in the swamp: Jack (24 years old), Washington (40), and Jason (30) were regulars; all lacked property of their own. The company's shingle accounts also include the names of a few women, this in a world almost completely masculine. All the women's names that also appear in the Nansemond census for 1850 were those of white female heads of households in their forties and fifties, and each owned one or two slaves. Elizabeth Jenkins (48 and owner of two slaves), Sarah Rogers (40, with one slave), Hulda Knight (58, with two), and Sarah Saunders (58, two slaves) were widows or never-married women. Sons, nephews, or other able-bodied male relatives, along with the slaves, were part of their security.[48]

Work crews—whether free or quasi-free—might load shingles directly onto lighters bound for Suffolk or Portsmouth, if they happened to be splitting cypress next to a watercourse. More likely, by the 1850s, the crews labored far from ditches and canals, necessitating the carting of shingles over

*Porte Crayon, "Cart-Boy" (*Harper's New Monthly Magazine, *September 1856)*

corduroy paths. This was the labor of mules and black boys, as Crayon observed. "From the landing," he wrote, "a road, or causeway of logs, leads back into the Swamp." Resting and sketching at "Horse Camp," Crayon heard "a distant rumbling ... the approach of the shingle-carts. These presently passed, seven in number, loaded high with shingles, and each attended by a boy on foot." Once shingles were unloaded, "the boys mounted the carts and returned at a brisker pace." Crayon thought the "youthful drivers ... not particularly well dressed; but [the boys] did not appear to be ill-fed or overworked." The work seemed rather fun, indeed. Crayon admired the cart mules — "being the only animals proper for this particular service." They were "nimble-footed animals ... [that] get over the rough and unsteady causeway quite rapidly and, to all appearance, understand the negro lingo perfectly." In fact, the mules wore no reins and were "managed entirely by words and gestures, mostly consisting of oaths and kicks." Crayon could not resist a picturesque moment between black youth and recalcitrant mule, however — a nineteenth-century trope in dialect: A mule, its cart unloaded, wanders "into a puddle, to get a drink or cool his feet, perhaps." The boy driver "pranced and hallooed, 'Wha he done gwine now? Debbelish cuss — go on de road, da. I lam de har' off you wid a shingle! Hear me tell you get on de road? I beat your head wid a rail!'" The mule obliged.[49]

This scene, I suspect, signifies something beyond racist comedy — although I concede that such was no doubt Crayon's intention, given both his sensibility and the condescending white middle-class readers of *Harper's* at the time. Boy and mule had had a conversation without violence, the tone of the boy's rhetoric notwithstanding. The mule had cooled and rested itself a bit, but not so much as to challenge the boy's authority to a dangerous degree. The boy's prancing imprecations reasserted his control while simultaneously recognizing the mule's nature and its limited freedom. The two of them occupied statuses not dissimilar, after all, in a broad and perhaps vulgar sense: They were both property, productive and valuable, laboring in an environment conducive not only to limits but also to privileges and immunities seldom seen on upland plantations. They were, as Olmsted said so well, quasi-free, which is certainly better than unfree.

This same wetland environment rendered free humans freer to resist both bourgeois society and the agronomic reformers — just as Edmund Ruffin testified. In and near the Great Dismal, especially, woods-burning and hog-running country folk might live their "careless" lives — Olmsted's word again — and still raise cash at will, on the periphery of the world's market order. There is, of course, an obvious paradox here: The quasi-free and free alike maintained their independence from the enveloping order by extracting natural resources from its edge. The scheme's real force-relationship—its potential for violence—was not in boy versus mule but in humanity versus nature. The paradox ultimately becomes a Catch-22; for the work of independence diminished all the swamps, in turn diminishing independence.

But meanwhile, there was more in this wetland world. For while the swamps survived, they harbored people profoundly more subversive than cart boys, hirelings, mulatto freedmen, and poor-white swampers. In those thickets there were maroons and revolutionaries.

5 RENEGADES

I hope the sable coloured gentry in Jerusalem will not rise again while you are there at least—for I should not like to have your head taken off without my seeing it again. I dont see the use of making a rail road through such a country as that—for from all I can learn the whites are not much better than the blacks.
— *Lavinia McPheeters to Charles Campbell, 1834*

The slave, if he is indisposed to work, and especially if he is not treated well, or does not like the master who has hired him, will sham sickness—even make himself sick or lame—that he need not work. But a more serious loss frequently arises, when the slave, thinking he is worked too hard, or being angered by punishment or unkind treatment, "getting the sulks," takes to "the swamp," and comes back when he has a mind to. Often this will not be till the year is up for which he is engaged, when he will return to his owner, who, glad to find him property safe, and that he has not died in the swamp, or gone to Canada, forgets to punish him, and immediately sends him for another year to a new master.
— *Frederick Law Olmsted, 1856*

The Virginia Swamp has a historical memory clinging to it, sombre as its cypress and mosses. It was the hiding place of the Nat Turner insurrectionists after their first strike for liberty. For six weeks, to the whole south, it seemed that in those horrid recesses of nature the avenging genius of slavery crouched but for a moment before covering the land with desolation. — Cincinnati Commercial, *1869*

The legendary lake at the heart of the Great Dismal Swamp is aptly named for a rebel. Late in 1664 William Drummond, a Scots lawyer, descended from Virginia to the northern shore of Albemarle Sound to assume duties conferred by the company that owned Carolina, the Lords Proprietor. Drummond became the first governor of North Carolina; and at Halls Creek, in what is now southwestern Pasquotank County, under a leafy canopy, he convened the first Assembly of Albemarle in 1665. The colony's population consisted of hardly fifteen hundred white folks—rather few to govern and tax, and probably rougher than the Carolinians William Byrd would ridicule in 1728. The first assembly ruled that "the members should wear shoes, if not stockings, during the session and that they must not throw their chicken and other bones under the tree."[1]

A bit later the governor and some friends went hunting in the Dismal and —as the unsubstantiated story goes—became hopelessly lost. All the party perished except Drummond. When he finally emerged from the swamp, gaunt and deranged, Drummond raved about a huge lake he had encountered during his odyssey. His "discovery," however—whether or not it was the first sighting of the lake by a white person—seems less significant now than the Albemarle's rapid population growth and acrimonious colonial politics and Drummond's ouster by the Lords Proprietor in 1667. Drummond returned to Virginia, resettled his family in Jamestown, and began politicking anew—this time against William Berkeley, the imperious, mean-spirited governor of the Old Dominion. By the mid-1670s Drummond, as close adviser to Nathaniel Bacon, was literally at war—with frontier Indians and with Berkeley and his government. The Bacon rebels twice forced Berkeley to flee Jamestown; then, fearing they might not hold the place, they burned it down. Drummond torched his own family's home. By the fall of 1676 Bacon and his men controlled Virginia. But then Bacon died—apparently of malaria— and the rebellion dissolved. Berkeley's troops caught Drummond in Chickahominy Swamp and brought him to the triumphant governor, who bowed in malevolent greeting: "Mister Drummond, you are very welcome. ... [Y]ou shall be hanged in half an hour." Not quite; but the next day Drummond was marched, shackled and half-naked in the cold, to the site of Williamsburg, the future capital and the scene of his launching into eternity. Along the way, Drummond's guards let him rest and smoke; but when they offered him the ease of a horse, Drummond demurred: "I shall walk to my death," he reasoned, "soon enough."[2]

That William Drummond's name remains attached to the Great Dismal is nicely metaphoric: a fatally flamboyant renegade, immortal in the eerily beautiful recess of a great swamp. For deep swamps—like remote mountains—are traditionally the refuge of nonconformists, the dispossessed, bandits, runaways, sometimes revolutionaries. That Berkeley's men captured Drummond in a swamp—in this case the Chickahominy, north of the James, west of Jamestown—is nicely instructive. The Chickahominy was forbidding, another natural hiding place for rebels. The governor's soldiers must have been relentless to have found Drummond there, for many rebels have made swamps relatively comfortable alternatives to civilization and captivity. So were Ulysses Grant's legions relentless in the Chickahominy, nearly two centuries later. Circling Lee, they surprised the world by conquering the swamp, crossing its namesake river and then the James, headquartering at Richard Eppes's house, and laying siege to Petersburg. Grant had whipped the Chickahominy and doomed the Confederacy.[3]

More often swamps are not conquered at all. Rather, like mountains, they are gradually compromised. Yet even when canals and railways traversed such barriers to linearity as the Great Dismal, swamps retained for a long time their essential integrities as refuges. Like the mountains, too, swamps were a source of fascination to cosmopolitans. For refuges permit many versions of freedom disallowed in governed societies, including those calling themselves free. In the antebellum American South, arguably, swamps were more important (and more interesting) as refuges than mountains were,[4] simply because the culture of the southern mountains was less complex: It was overwhelmingly whiter, sometimes close to slaveless, with a much narrower social spectrum than the coastal wetlands; and while commerce was hardly unknown in Appalachia, the mountains' relatively sparse populations were much more devoted to subsistence and were thus more independent. Railroad penetration, natural resource extraction, dependency, impoverishment, and ruin awaited the Appalachians; but all this came later.[5] The historical misery of low coastal places is not more poignant, necessarily; rather, it is more layered, and longer.

Edmund Ruffin acutely perceived most of the paradoxical connections between swamp, market, and freedom—the last in the sense I have already suggested: freedom from both bourgeois discipline and from Ruffin's agronomy, with its own discipline, heavy capital requirements, and market dependency. "Piney woods" whites, propertyless (or nearly propertyless) free people of color, and slaves earned cash by extracting timber and shingles from the Dismal and other forested swamps. This particularly rewarding labor starved prospects for modernizing agriculture, Ruffin-style, in the cosmopolitan sector; and free workers used their wages—Ruffin may not have quite grasped this—to resist modernity and retain their relative independence. Most important—to Ruffin, Olmsted, and every other observer—slaves became quasi-free laborers in the swamps.

The hiring out of slaves was in fact a widespread practice throughout the South. Hiring rationalized uneconomic labor distributions among families and industries. It conferred upon many nonslaveholding white men direct experience with controlling the unfree—a stake in the system, as it were. For owners of surplus labor, it eased at least part of the burden of maintenance, while simultaneously producing cash income. For slaves themselves, hiring out probably divided families, temporarily, more often than sales did. The general effect of hiring out, however—on slaves and on the system—is problematic. Some temporary masters, especially those in agriculture, were harsh disciplinarians and microscopically close supervisors. Others—conceivably the great majority of slave hirers—were more interested in commodity production than the enforcement of slavery's discipline as conventionally perceived. This last may have been truest, and most destabilizing to the institution, in coastal turpentine forests and cypress swamps, where slave men (seldom women) labored with little or no supervision, bringing forth negotiated quotas of pine sap, staves, and shingles.[6]

Daniel Cobb of Southampton County—first a "1-horse" and finally a large farmer—hired neighbors' slaves almost every year, from at least as early as the 1840s until the peculiar institution collapsed. Cobb was a toughened and unhappy man who worked in the fields himself, in the faces of his own and hired laborers; and he tried to push them all to the limits of prudence. In all likelihood, neighborhood (often his in-laws') slave men and women found no relief, no blessed anonymity, nothing resembling freedom, when their masters sent them to Cobb's place.[7]

The great river plantations, however, presented a very fluid labor context that offered slaves at least a measure of anonymity. Down on Occoneechee Neck, by the Roanoke in Northampton, Henry Burgwyn, Sr., and his brother Thomas often put in wheat crops too large for their own slave forces to harvest. The Burgwyns' neighbors had their own bumper crops, so many planters entered a labor market that probably extended down to the Albemarle and far inland in all directions. The hired hands seem to have been unreliable and sometimes obstreperous strangers, too, skulking at night, disappearing, reappearing. Cosmopolitan farming was often lucrative, but it was a troublesome business.[8]

Other businesses undermined white paternalism and weakened supervision more subversively. Fishing was an important one in at least two manifestations. First was upriver seining each spring, especially on the Carolina streams flowing into the Albemarle. William Valentine, our hapless Winton lawyer, loved the shad and herring runs and the festivities accompanying the busy times at the Chowan fisheries. Valentine and other attorneys also benefited from the fisheries' heavy seasonal demand for labor: The lawyers prepared hiring contracts at regular "fisherman's courts"—that is, late January or early February county court days largely given over to labor exchanges for the shad and herring runs in April and May. The greatest of these, apparently, was held at Gates County's courthouse; and this may reveal much about the context of slave-hiring and the origin of many if not most hirelings. Gates was the exemplary hinterland county—remote, swampy, sandy-soiled, a place of relatively few planters and many "piney woods" folk who owned a few slaves. In 1850 Gates's population of 8,426 was almost half slave. Only

50 men owned 20 or more slaves, however; 353 other white men and women owned fewer, usually one to ten. It must have been the latter, primarily—along with hundreds of employers, agents, and lawyers—who flocked to Gates's fisherman's court on 1 February 1847. Valentine guessed that upward of two thousand attended. The huge "assemblage was made up of all grades and shades—wealthy fisherman, sturdy farmers, polished gentlemen, 'dusky white and sooty.' It was a fine mild day" and, despite the great size of the crowd, "the most orderly February court I have ever seen there." Everyone anticipated a fine run in the spring, so "Fishing hands hired high; No. 1 [workers] above [a] dollar per day."[9]

"No. 1" laborers were no doubt men sufficiently strong to set and haul great nets. Lesser-ranked workers probably included women; for the fisheries' main business was not supplying shad and herring for local subsistence but packing them in thousands of barrels for shipment to distant markets. Women and older children probably did such work; so on the Chowan and other rivers, slaves of both sexes labored away from home, under strangers' unpredictable supervision, and probably took care of themselves.

Other fishing took place from boats, year-round. John B. Chesson of Washington County, North Carolina, for instance, operated a fishing fleet on the Albemarle and up the Chowan. Chesson owned a number of slaves, but never enough to man his vessels. So he hired slaves (and perhaps free men of color as well), especially through the offices of a merchant in Winton. These men may have worked exclusively near home, on the upper Chowan; but many other slaves worked the decks of schooners far from their origins, throughout the sounds and on the ocean itself.[10]

The making of naval stores—pitch and tar—and the collection of resin for turpentine distilling was summer work for black men. This industry, too, involved much hiring of laborers, who went into deep woods and more or less took care of themselves. Naval stores, in turn, required countless barrels (as did shad and herring) for shipment. This meant huge demand for staves, the getting of which was winter work for slaves (many of them hired, as well). Staves were cut from local hardwoods and sent to coopers (some of whom, again, were hired slave men) for manufacture into barrels. (When one considers the impact of barrel-making on regional forests—barrels for wheat and corn, barrels for naval stores and turpentine, barrels for fish—it seems remarkable that any hardwoods survived the eighteenth and nineteenth centuries.) Most of all, these woodsmen and craftsmen escaped the discipline and supervision usually associated with plantation slavery.[11]

Dr. Thomas O'Dwyer of Murfreesboro, in Hertford County, was a supplier of hired-out slaves who probably worked in the woods much of the time. An immigrant from Ireland, a Roman Catholic, a single townsman, and a serious reader and thinker who belonged to the American Colonization Society and often attended Quaker meetings, O'Dwyer was surely an atypical white southerner. In some respects, however, he was typical of a large group of small slaveholders who seldom needed the labor of their human chattels. O'Dwyer held four in 1825, and seems (from his diary) to have required little: He had a small farm outside town, plus an office and house with garden in Murfreesboro. O'Dwyer conducted his practice (often on the road), studied, gossiped, and cared little for managing slaves. His two adult men, especially Bob, he usually hired out. O'Dwyer often simply sent Bob off "to look for work" on his own. Henry, the other man, was a pain to the doctor. One employer sent him back with complaint. (O'Dwyer lost $90 in Henry's wages.) Two other whites, in pursuit of a runaway girl, thought Henry had "inveigled" with her. Henry protested, and O'Dwyer decided not to whip him, although, he wrote, "I think he Deserves correction." [12]

We have already observed the Great Dismal's lumbermen and shingle-getters—Olmsted's quasi-freedmen who needed no "driving" and whose demeanors were "more sprightly and straight-forward ... than any field-hand plantation-negroes" he ever saw. The New Yorker attributed all this to the cash incentives offered to hired slaves. By way of illustration, Olmsted offered a typical statement of account from an overseer's book at the end of a five-month period of shingle-getting:

Sam Bo to John Doe, Dr,

Feb. 1.	To clothing (outfit)	$5.00
Mar. 10.	To clothing, as per overseer's account, ...	2.25
Feb. 1.	To bacon and meal (outfit)	19.00
July 1.	To stores down in swamp, as per overseer's account, ...	4.75
July 1.	To half-yearly hire, paid his owner	50.00
	[total]	$81.00

Per Contra, Cr.

July 1.	By 10,000 shingles, as per overseer's account, 10c	100.00
	Balance due Sambo	19.00 [13]

A white employer of such money-making slaves told Olmsted a remarkable story. A particular slave, "an old man," "was so trust-worthy," the informant said, "that he had once let him go to New York as cook on a lumber-schooner," where the hireling might "have easily escaped from slavery" but did not. Calculating that the slave "must have accumulated considerable money," the "employer suggested to him that he might *buy* his freedom, and he immediately determined to do so." His owner demanded $500, however—a very high price for "an elderly man." The slave hesitated, demurred, then finally changed his mind, reasoning "that if he did not live long, his money would not be of any use to him at any rate." But this was not all, the employer told Olmsted. The slave, in settling accounts with "white people in the vicinity" to whom he had made loans, discovered that he had "several hundred dollars more than was necessary" to purchase his freedom. "With the surplus, he paid for his passage to Liberia, and bought a handsome out-fit." Bidding his old boss farewell, the new freedman resolved to learn to read and write as soon as he reached Africa.[14]

The story illustrates a paradox of slavery and swamps. The latter were refuges to renegades and revolutionaries from near and far. But to those regularly engaged in industrial labor inside the swamps, the environment (and the relatively high value of all labor) guaranteed a life close enough to freedom to discourage renegadeism. The phenomena coexisted, in fact, as Porte Crayon demonstrated shortly after Olmsted's sojourn in the Dismal.

Having satisfied his yearning to see Lake Drummond, Crayon next hoped to catch sight of maroons, as long-escaped slaves were called throughout the Western Hemisphere. "The Swamp," he reported, "is said to be inhabited by a number of escaped slaves, who spend their lives, and even raise families, in its impenetrable fastnesses." Escapees "live by woodcraft, external depredation," Crayon heard, "and more frequently, it is probable, by working for the task shingle-makers at reduced wages"—an exploited subsistence that recalls William Byrd II's observation of suspicious people of color in the swamp a century and a quarter before.[15]

By the end of the antebellum era, in fact, swamp maroons were legendary in the United States. Even as Porte Crayon hoped against hope to spot one, Harriet Beecher Stowe was finishing her novel *Dred*, a Great Dismal escaped-slave saga that was inspired by the tradition and informed by Olmsted's journey. Many Americans were probably aware of John James Audubon's famous encounter in a Louisiana swamp about thirty years before. (Audubon's account appeared in the second volume of his *Ornithological Biography*, published in 1834.) Audubon collected specimens of birds he immortalized on canvas, it will be recalled, by shooting them. One day in the late 1820s, the ornithologist was struggling in bayou muck to transport his heavy gun and six dead wood ibises when his dog began to yelp, bug-eyed. Audubon then heard from a thicket the command to drop his gun. Out stepped "a tall firmly-built Negro" holding a rusty musket. Audubon did not drop his gun, which both men recognized as more likely to fire than the maroon's old musket, so the man pleaded with him: "I am a runaway. I might perhaps shoot you down; but God forbids it ... [so] I ask mercy at your hands." Audubon's curiosity got the better of him and, persuaded that he was too far from his base, anyway, to reach it before nightfall, he agreed to accompany the maroon to his camp. There Audubon was introduced to the runaway's wife, who, "though black" (in the maroon's words) "is as beautiful to me as the President's wife is to him"—and to his three children, whom he called "so many princes." They ate venison and potatoes, and Audubon heard their tale of separation through sale some eighteen months before. The man had escaped, gathered his family from four separate plantations, and re-created family life deep within a canebrake. Audubon promised to help them, and the next day sought the intercession of a wealthy planter of his acquaintance. This man gained the maroons' pardons and purchased them all himself. A happy ending, Audubon thought.[16]

Porte Crayon had no such adventure, but his maroon moment in the Dismal was vivid enough; and unlike the ornithologist/painter, Crayon left a portrait. At Horse Camp, a ditch-side shingle depository, Crayon watched and sketched cart boys and their mules, and mused about runaways. "I had long nurtured a wish to see one of those sable outlaws who dwell in the fastnesses of the Swamp," he began. Crayon had queried black shingle-getters about maroons, "but they evaded the questions, and changed the conversation immediately." So he "determined to visit the spot where the shingle-makers were at work, to see what I could." Making his way within earshot of the workers, Crayon "left the causeway, and made my way with the greatest difficulty through the tangled undergrowth." He "crawled and struggled on until ... nearly exhausted. At length my attention was arrested by the crackling sound of other footsteps than my own. I paused, held my breath, and sunk quietly among the reeds." Suddenly, "thirty paces" away, was revealed to Crayon "a gigantic negro, with a tattered blanket wrapped about his shoulders, and a gun in his hand. His head was bare, and he had little other clothing than a pair of ragged breeches and boots." The maroon's "hair and beard were tipped with gray, and his purely African features were cast in a mould betokening, in the highest degree, strength and energy." As the man "reached forward his iron hand to clear away the briery screen that half concealed him," Crayon thought the "expression of the face was of mingled

*Porte Crayon, "Osman" (*Harper's New Monthly Magazine, *September 1856)*

Porte Crayon, "Horse Camp" (Harper's New Monthly Magazine, *September 1856)*

fear and ferocity, and every movement betrayed a life of habitual caution and watchfulness." [17]

Crayon was vastly relieved the maroon did not spy him, "but presently turned and disappeared. When the sound of his retreating footsteps died away, I drew a long free breath, and got back to the causeway with all haste." There Crayon paused "to rest, and to make a hasty sketch of the remarkable figure I had just seen." Then back at his barge by Horse Camp, Crayon tried to entice from Jim Pierce and Ely Reed, his guides, more information by "intentionally le[aving] my drawing where the men could see it." When Jim saw it, "he uttered an exclamation, and beckoned to Ely. I fancied," Crayon recalled, "I heard the word Osman." But the men would not help: "'Do you know that, Jim?' 'No, Sir . . . dunno nothin' 'bout um.'" Instead Jim and Ely whispered together, while Crayon wondered. "I began to get nervous. I had been rash in showing the picture — yet how, and why? Who was Osman? Was I the possessor of a dangerous secret? In the Swamp a man might easily be murdered and concealed where the buzzards couldn't find him." Finally, Ely cleverly changed the subject by requesting a sketch of himself by the famous white traveler. Crayon heard no more of Osman, although he presented his astonishing portrait to the world, in the pages of *Harper's*. [18]

Assuming that Osman was indeed real—not a fiction of Porte Crayon's irresistible imagination—Jim and Ely probably knew him. Like other black swampers, they may have aided him materially from time to time, perhaps seeing to his surreptitious employment as a shingle-getter. Osman may not have depended on such work to survive, however. For like Audubon's maroon, he might have subsisted from the swamp itself. The Louisiana runaway had acquired his rusty hunting musket from a bear trap—along with the carcass of the victim. Swampside farmers often protected corn crops from foraging bears by setting such muskets to fire when bears (or other creatures) disturbed bait attached by wire or cords to triggers.[19] Osman, or anyone else interested in acquiring a gun, had excellent opportunity anywhere farmers intruded on swampy bear country.

Edmund Ruffin's observations on bears in and around the Dismal, however, might cast logical doubt on maroons' prospects, with or without firearms. Before his visit to the swamp late in 1836, the editor had assumed that few bears had survived humans' extermination campaigns, even in deep swamps; they had "long ago [been] driven from every other part of lower and middle Virginia." But he discovered instead that "they were so numerous, that there were but few men who resided near the margin of the swamp who had not killed one or more." Indeed, bears made it "difficult to raise many cattle or hogs on the adjacent farms ... owing to the slaughter committed on them by the bears. A bear," Ruffin heard, "will with ease kill a full grown cow, and has strength to drag away the carcass to a suitable hiding place. No dogs will hunt these animals to much purpose, and therefore it is not often attempted."[20]

Throughout the South, poor folks depended on feral swine and cattle for meat. Runaways and maroons stole hogs and other penned farm animals, but they must have especially relied on range animals caught in the wild. Ruffin's bear-infested Dismal, then, offered precious little pork and beef for anyone unable to purchase it from safer territory. Still, the swamp remained a cornucopia of native fish and meat. Crayon and countless other visitors testified as much. Osman's gun, then, was likely trained on deer, perhaps on bear, too—more difficult targets than cows, to be sure, and hardly less sporting than fleet razorbacks.

By depriving his master of his body and labor, a man like Osman broke the law and became an outlaw. As such he represented a tradition, already old in 1856, associated with deep swampy woods. Osman's fearsome appearance, great strength of physique and will, and especially his mysteriousness captured Crayon's imagination and, a century and a half later, commands our own. Who was he, indeed? We know less of Osman than of other outlaws during the three centuries of slavery in this countryside, and as with Osman, for those outlaws' stories we are so dependent on white sources — sources fearful and misinformed, ignorant, repressive yet often hyperbolic. Whites' insistence on their comfortable familiarity with safely enslaved Africans is unconvincing. Blacks, and the Indians before them, remained opaque, different, dangerous. The danger was potentially — sometimes actually — physical; but it was also a cultural and a profoundly spiritual danger. Folkloric sources that combine white and black traditions reveal much of this sense of threat.

Many whites knew that blacks resented enslavement. And white men's imaginations encompassed a notion of black men's prodigious sexual power. The latter comprises a legend larger than our subregion, but an old story from Hertford County illustrates. One William Barell Wise, a planter outside Murfreesboro, possessed a slave stud called Sam who had fathered a remarkably large and healthy young workforce for Wise, attracting the admiration of neighbors near and far. One day a visiting planter from Mississippi asked Wise for the loan of Sam, so he might comparably enrich his own estate. (The story's subject resembles that of Kyle Onstott's salacious 1957 best-selling novel, *Mandingo*.) Wise declared that it would be up to Sam; so the stud inquired of the Mississippian, "How many [women] in dere?" He answered, "Oh, I suppose five or six, take or give one or two." Sam, turning to Wise, decided quickly: "Boss, if it jes' as well wid you, I druther not go. Too fur a piece [to travel] for jes' a half-day's work."[21] The joke attempts to defuse white men's fear of black men, harnessing their potency to further the expansion of slavery. Fear lurks, nonetheless. And Crayon's Osman suggests, I think, among other things, a middle-aged virility both enviable and troublesome. He represented the swamp itself.

The positive-negative mystery of people of color was expressed especially (and for both sexes) in what seemed an unfathomable spiritual power. Within Ahoskie Swamp (also in Hertford County), for instance, there remained as late as 1920 a bare circle, about a hundred feet across, known as Witches' Dancing Grounds. Indian sorcerers' pounding feet had kept vegetation away, and the effect lasted long after the natives' demise. Not far away, near St. John's, is a site remembered for a Meherrin Indian woman who was burned at the stake there for witchcraft. And the Indian Woods area of western Bertie County — once the Tuscaroras' reservation, following their defeat in 1713 — was long known as a place of "intense" witchcraft, where pacts with Satan were made and people assumed other forms, such as that of snakes.[22]

Africans replaced the natives as witches and conjurers. The most notorious example I have discovered in the subregion lived relatively recently—Sally Ann Smallwood, who was born into slavery and died (probably) during the 1890s. After Emancipation, Sally gained a small plot in Bertie County next to Lorenza ("Renzy") Smallwood, who was not a relation but her enemy. Renzy added a little land to his plot, but Sally began to garden it. When Renzy ordered her to desist, Sally, a witch, began to "ride" Renzy every night, like a horse, leaving him exhausted every morning. Renzy resolved to catch her; so, pretending sleep one midnight, he watched for Sally's apparition above his bed, then fastened an iron grip on her. The battle continued until dawn, with Sally assuming one terrifying shape after another—a black cat, a snake, a bird with a razorlike beak. By the time Sally finally broke away, Renzy's tenacious grip had left her virtually skinned alive. Sally called in her sister, a famous herb doctor, but there was no use: Sally dried up and died. Renzy slept peacefully thereafter; and as late as 1900 he owned an awesome reputation in the neighborhood—especially among men, most likely—for his victory.[23] Women, their symbolic association with nature's power undone, may have slept less happily.

Whites took comfort when most African Americans, slave and free, converted to Christianity. Yet Sally and Renzy and those who remembered them were in all likelihood Christians, by their own lights. Poor people, especially slaves, have ever construed the Word for themselves, their betters' strenuous efforts to the contrary notwithstanding.[24] Religion is an opiate serving more causes than the masters'. It is intoxicating stuff. Consider the Book of Revelations, and tremble for order! And consider Nat Turner of Southampton, the United States' most famous slave rebel.

Turner (1800–1831) was a precocious reader, especially of the King James version of the Holy Bible, and a seer and prophet. He preached, baptized, healed with his hands; he described events that had occurred before his own birth, then told the future. During his twenties Turner received revelations from God, revelations that anointed him a minister, then a military man with an awful mission: to turn the region's watercourses red with the blood of whites. During the summer of 1831 there was an eclipse of the sun—another sign from God; and Nat began to gather his cadres, meeting with them at night. A last meeting occurred on the afternoon of 21 August, by a remote millpond. The slaughter of whites in west-central Southampton began shortly before midnight, continuing through the next day. In all, about sixty—men, women, and children, including infants—were shot, beheaded with axes, stabbed, bludgeoned to death. The rebellion faltered on

23 August: The militia appeared; Nat's forces, divided and weakened, were killed, captured, or fled, leaving Nat himself alone. He hid for two months before a dog and a man discovered him. Nat gave a remarkable "confession" to a white lawyer, but he pleaded "not guilty"—because (as he told the lawyer) "he did not feel guilty"—at the Southampton courthouse, in Jerusalem. Turner was hanged near the jail, from an oak tree that still stood, tall and vine-covered, at the turn of this century.[25]

Thomas R. Gray, the opportunistic local attorney who took Turner's "confession" during the first three days of November 1831, found Nat perplexing. Nat, he wrote, "was never known to have a dollar in his life; to swear an oath, or drink a drop of spirits." The slave "certainly never had the advantages of education, but he can read and write, (it was taught him by his parents,) and for natural intelligence and quickness of apprehension, is surpassed by few men I have ever seen." Gray was satisfied, too, that plunder had not been the object of the rebellion. (Nor was rape, incidentally, as a recent historian has declared.) Nat was no manipulative trickster, either: He expressed to Gray his contempt for conjuring and witchcraft. Rather—we must conclude, with Gray—Nat was a man possessed by God. Gray's summary impression is memorable: "The calm, deliberate composure with which he spoke of his late deeds and intentions, the expression of his fiend-like face when excited by enthusiasm, still bearing the stains of the blood of helpless innocence about him; clothed with rags and covered with chains; yet daring to raise his manacled hands to heaven, with a spirit soaring above the attributes of man; I looked on him and my blood curdled in my veins."[26]

Conjurers, especially in the role of healers, mediated, negotiated with nature.[27] Nat did more, as Gray reported. The "Spirit...appeared to me," Nat explained, and "reveal[ed] to me the knowledge of the elements, the revolution of the planets, the operation of tides, and changes of the seasons." Such understanding—"this revelation in the year 1825"—led to "true holiness" and "true knowledge of faith." Turner was "made perfect; and the Holy Ghost was with me." In this justified state, Nat shared with the deity the power to manipulate nature. (He told his followers he could move clouds.) So Nat became Jesus' surrogate—Jesus, he told Gray, had laid down the cross—and along with God and the Spirit, Nat shared the agency behind nature's agency.[28] Combined, such force became destiny beyond understanding, a fate both wonderful and awful. Nat's and his men's (and one woman's) blood lust, and finally Nat's own soaring spirit and resignation to martyrdom, become just that.

The God-possessed mercilessness that curdled Gray's blood was not en-

Nat Turner (Sketch by unknown artist used in 1831–32 newspaper accounts of the rebellion)

tirely unrestrained in Nat, however, either before or during the revolt. In 1827 Nat befriended — tradition has it — an ostracized and miserable white man named Etheldred T. Brantley. Preacher Turner prayed earnestly with Brantley; and when blood began to ooze from the poor white man's face, Nat fasted and prayed more, for nine days, until Brantley was healed. Then Nat, to the white community's outrage, baptized both Brantley and himself in Pearson's Mill Pond.[29] More important (and probably reliable) evidence of Nat's mercy for poor whites is contained in the Jerusalem court's trial record of Davy, another rebel, early in September 1831, two months before Nat's trial and execution. Instructed to recount the course of Nat's soldiers through the countryside, Davy testified that "Capt Nat in passing a house where some very poor people lived said he would not kill them because they thought no better of themselves than they did of the negroes."[30] This from a commander who did not hesitate to order the murders in their cribs of the infant children of slaveholders.

But Nat's class discrimination was not unique. In the year of his birth, slave conspirators in and around Richmond determined to arise and slaughter whites — sparing, however, the poor of evangelical persuasion. And only nine years before the bloody Turner war in Virginia, black conspirators in Charleston, South Carolina, were joined (so testimony at trials declared) by "white men of the lowest characters" — a condescending description, it would seem, of poor men.[31] Americans' understandable preoccupation with race, lamentably, diminishes appreciation of such interracial sympathy among the humble.

Meanwhile, Nat the avenger, Nat the preternatural force, never died in the memories of black folks. About a quarter century after the rebellion, according to oral tradition, there lived on the fringe of the Great Dismal near Suffolk an old man called Uncle Alick. Alick was the owner, it was said, of a mule that was once the property of Nat Turner himself. Uncle Alick's mule was locally famous for its association with Nat, but perhaps more so for its remarkable ability to climb trees to get bee honey.[32] More mystery transcendent. Alick was probably the same Uncle Alick whom Porte Crayon met after his brief encounter with Osman in the swamp. Crayon described him as "a reverend gentleman of color who resides on the border of the Swamp[:] . . . small in stature, like St. Paul, and bandy-legged, like the rest of his race, with an intellectual expression of face, in common phraseology, 'sharp as a steel-trap.'" Alick told Crayon he was converted to Christianity while serving as a drummer boy during the War of 1812, and he read — or recited — "a sermon on the scriptural use of the exclamation Behold!" Crayon was amused, but reported nothing of a mule or Nat Turner. Instead, he re-counted Alick's troubles, apparently during the 1830s, with Irish railroad con-struction workers who laid track through his sweet potato patch and used his fencing for firewood.[33] So much for cross-racial sympathy among the poor; but the Irish—helpless immigrants often employed in the South at work considered too dangerous for valuable slaves—were much-used, themselves, and everywhere they worked they were set against blacks, slave and free, by their employers.[34]

Much later, John Wesley Cromwell (1846–1927) claimed that Turner always lurked in his consciousness. A Portsmouth-born teacher, politician, editor, and lawyer, Cromwell wrote early in the twentieth century that "Nat Turner was a familiar name" in his boyhood home. Cromwell's father was an Eliza-beth River ferryman who purchased his own and his family's freedom, then moved with them to Philadelphia when John was five. After the Civil War, while still a very young man, Cromwell returned to Virginia to complete the work of liberation. He was selected to be a member of the federal jury empaneled to try Jefferson Davis, in Richmond. He politicked as a Radical Republican and for a while taught school in Southampton County, where he became acquainted with people who remembered Nat.[35]

As late as 1969, a seventy-year-old black man living in Southampton was able to outline for a white historian the principal details of the rebel-lion, citing his mother as his source: "My mother was telling me that Nat Turner... was God's man. He was a man for war, and for legal rights, and for freedom." Another Southamptonite, in his early fifties in 1969 and sur-named Turner, considered himself a descendant of Nat's. His father was his source. As late as 1970, black families in Norfolk and Portsmouth claimed they owned Nat's sword and Bible.[36] And in Portsmouth, about 1981, a man born in 1906 related how his Southampton-born grandmother perpetuated the memory of the great rebel. "All she would talk about would be Nat Turner," he recalled. "She grew up with him in a sense. That was still the... big story in Southampton County during her younger days." So when the grandson traveled back to the old county, he learned to associate places with Nat and the rebels. "When I passed Nat's Corner, I'd know it wouldn't be long then before Boykins, you know."[37]

Whites' initial reactions and memory have been different and various. At first the rebellion seemed almost a geographical phenomenon. According to early white reports, vengeful "Banditti" had swarmed from the Dismal like plague-crazed rats. The editor of the *Richmond Constitutional Whig* reported on 23 August 1831 (even as Nat's band collapsed), "We understand that the insur-

Porte Crayon, "Uncle Alick" (Harper's New Monthly Magazine, *September 1856)*

rection in Southampton is little more than the irruption of 150 or 200 runaway slaves from the Dismal Swamp, incited by a spirit of plunder and rapine." Such misapprehension nonetheless reveals whites' long-justified assumptions about dense swamps, maroons, and danger. Once the truth, more or less, became known—that Nat and his rebels were locals, not maroons—southern whites passed repressive legislation, then drew the shade of memory against the matter, which became a nonevent. More sympathetic whites persisted, however, in associating the rebellion with romantic wetlands. Such was the case thirty-eight years after the event, when a writer for the *Cincinnati Commercial* evoked the "historical memory" of "The Virginia Swamp[:] ... those horrid recesses of nature [where] the avenging genius of slavery crouched but for a moment before covering the land with desolation."[38]

In fact, instability and disorder plagued the subregion throughout the long era of slavery, and desolation was more than a brief nightmare of 1831. The American Revolution unglued and nearly destroyed the institution when, in 1775, Virginia's last imperial governor confronted white rebels by inviting their slaves to desert them and join royalist forces. Many did, and thereby won their freedom. In 1793 whites uncovered insurrectionary plots among slaves in Norfolk, Portsmouth, Petersburg, and Richmond. The next year, Hertford County whites were convinced that their slaves were poisoning them. In October 1799, Georgia-bound blacks in a coffle on the road from Broadwater to Jerusalem murdered the slave traders who escorted them. (Four or five of the slaves were hanged for the deed.) Panic again gripped the Virginia Southside and northeastern North Carolina following discovery of the Gabriel plot in Richmond in 1800. Two years later, two Southampton slaves killed their overseer, then Norfolk authorities uncovered a slave plot to burn the seaport. Simultaneously, "serious disturbances" (in the words of an amateur Hertford historian) broke out in the Albemarle region. Thirty or more blacks were executed as a result of the 1802 plots and white hysteria—eleven in Bertie County alone, one each in Hertford and Perquimans, two in Currituck, and four in Camden County. The tragedy is sometimes attributed to persisting white nervousness in the aftermath of the Gabriel affair. The Hertford historian—John Wheeler Moore, a former slaveholder and Confederate officer—thought the plots and local rebellions were not only substantial but were also a logical and predictable outgrowth of the successful revolution of slaves in the French colony of Saint Domingue (later Haiti): "It is more than probable," Moore concluded, "in the frequent intercourse with the West Indies[,] the spirit of San Domingo by some chance was recommended to them"—that is, to the Albemarle slave rebels.[39]

The subregion's emblematic renegade was not Osman or Nat Turner, but Bob Ricks. In 1824 Ricks freed himself, without bothering to pay his owner. Establishing a band of fugitives, Ricks led raids on plantations in Sussex, Southampton, Nansemond, and Gates Counties for months. Four men identified as his followers were caught in Petersburg with forged "free papers," attempting to sail north. But Bob Ricks was apparently never caught. Perhaps he succeeded in getting north. Perhaps he subsisted in the swamps. (Could young Bob have become Osman?) Meanwhile, also during the 1820s, Southampton whites worried much about another renegade, called Mr. Womble's Tom.[40] Like countless other runaways, Tom seems to have stayed out longer than usual, to have appeared at too many plantations at night, begging, stealing, conspiring—taking too much advantage of the peculiar institution's vulnerability, and of the landscape's opportunity.

The Civil War was a horribly fitting climax to the James-Albemarle country's tradition of renegadeism. Early on, Yankee legions grabbed most of the subregion's cosmopolitan sector; then gunboat-borne raiders, snaking further and further inland from Hampton Roads and Albemarle Sound, destroyed the old river plantation political economy and its society. Slaves rushed to the Yankees by the thousands. Many of these men joined Union troops and fought near home. Others, unable to join the Yankees, fled their owners and took to the swamps. Some of these men became de facto soldiers, defending themselves against local posses, militia, and Confederate troops.

Gilbert Holloman of Hertford County is one of the best-remembered wartime slave rebels. Holloman ran away from his master and became a maroon at China's Mash, a deep swamp about two miles west of Ahoskie. From this base Holloman seems to have raided his owner's and other plantations, collecting recruits (including his wife) and enlarging his encampment. Holloman was aided—so his enemies thought, anyway—by local white unionists. Hertford Confederates determined to eliminate the Holloman band. A posse of about fifty, accompanied by a "nigger dog," converged on China's Mash. Silently surrounding the camp, they surprised Holloman, his wife, and another woman. The dog leaped toward Holloman's cabin just as the posse's leader shouted the command to surrender. Holloman grabbed his gun but immediately fell dead, with the two women, in a hail of bullets. Simultaneously, the furious dog landed in quicksand and disappeared. The white men dumped Holloman's and the women's bodies there, too.[41] The Holloman band's demise was hardly the end of Confederate troubles, however.

Slaveholders' capacity to impose order upon the hinterland evaporated early. Divisions among whites—by class, politics, clan—that had often been bitter before the war now became deadly. Some natives were unrepentant Confederates; others were determined unionists. Many—most, perhaps, by 1863—were desperately neutral, harassed and impoverished by a terrifying and bewilderingly complex local civil war.[42]

In June 1861, seventeen-year-old Richard T. Barnes trained and played hard as a new volunteer with North Carolina's Hertford troops. The son of Jet T. Barnes—a planter, the inventor of a manure spreader, and a prominent Baptist layman—Richard had eagerly set out from his home near Buckhorn (now called Como), near the Virginia line, for camp at Murfreesboro. He expected to fight in Virginia, but now the governor ordered the Hertford soldiers to Ocracoke, on the Outer Banks, to protect the seaway to the sounds. Officers would rank the men and march them to the eastern edge of town, then onto wagons bound for the Chowan at Winton. From there they would steam down to Edenton and, transferred to schooners, set sail for Ocracoke. The Edenton-to-Ocracoke trip, Richard noted, would take "18 hours[,] or about 10 miles an hour."[43] Speedy travel to danger. For soon the Yankees would come to Hatteras in preponderant force, sweep away the thin line of defenders, and threaten all of eastern Carolina. (Young Barnes survived to farm in Virginia, just north of Como.) But first, in the last of Murfreesboro's white happy days, came a fine expression of white community spirit, history evocative of D. W. Griffith's fictional Confederate send-off in *The Birth of a Nation.*

"We soon made all necessary preparations" for departure, wrote Richard, "and on Tuesday the eleventh of June the citizens of Murfreesboro gave us a fine Dinner." He relished the "great number of Ladies . . . in attendance with their smiling faces radiating with beauty[,] giving life to the whole Scene; after we had taken sufficiently of the repasts the ladies then pas[sed] around and gave Each one of us a bouquet, after which we gave 'three cheers for the Ladies of Murfreesboro.'" As the men marched out to the wagons, their way was lined by students from the Murfreesboro Female Academy and other citizens, each of whom bowed to the soldiers as they passed. At last, wagons loaded, there were final speeches of thanks and farewell.[44]

Ten weeks later, as though the world were at peace, Richard Benbury Creecy took most of his family, as was his custom, to Nags Head for summer vacation. Creecy was master of Cloverdale, a slave-worked farm in Pasquotank County, an attorney practicing in nearby Elizabeth City, and (in the future) an author, the longtime editor of *The Economist* of Elizabeth City, and a trustee of the University of North Carolina. Missing at vacation time was Creecy's young daughter Betty (Elizabeth Brosher Creecy), who was in

Raleigh, a student at St. Mary's School. At the end of August, Creecy wrote to Betty, complaining of the long and uncomfortable boat trip to Nags Head, but assuring her that despite occasional recent appearances of "Yankee war ships," he did "not think there is any danger here." A well-intentioned but disingenuous father; for on the same day, Creecy wrote to St. Mary's headmaster, reporting the Confederate debacle at Hatteras and begging him to look out for Betty, in case her parents should "be cut off." The Creecy vacation was ruined, but as late as mid-March the following year, the father tried to console his daughter even as he began to yield to alarm. Who knew when things might return to normal? Creecy "had intended to invite" a friend of Betty's "to spend the fall with you at Nags Head," he wrote, "but alas! Nags Head is in the hands of the Yankees, & the future is uncertain to us."[45]

Indeed. By this date Elizabeth City itself was already in ruins. Early in February the Yankees had captured Roanoke Island (including Nags Head, Kill Devil Hills, and Kitty Hawk), opening the way for their advance into the eastern Albemarle country. Soon, as Creecy wrote to Betty, "The Federals ... [were] in their vessels near E. City. The town has been fired, I do not know by whom, and a considerable portion burned. It is expected that the remaining portion will be burned. Nearly all the inhabitants have fled." The Creecys had withdrawn to Cloverdale, thinking themselves not "in any danger in the country, and don't wish you to be alarmed about it. It is supposed their [the Yankees'] object is to attack Norfolk, and we are entirely out of that range." Creecy warned Betty that her mail might be interrupted or lost and suggested she route letters home via a friend in Norfolk.[46] This would not work for long, because Norfolk would soon fall, too.

Meanwhile, Betty had been reading in the Raleigh newspapers that back in Pasquotank County, whatever semblance of Confederate consensus had existed, now rapidly unraveled. "The report to which you allude," her father responded, "about the magistrates of this county determining not to resist, is true to some extent." Creecy had not attended the meeting and he did "not approve of their course. From what I have heard of it, it was not exactly an order not to resist, but I think it very probable they meant that, as I believe there are some, if not a majority, who are submissionists now." Growing bitter, now, Creecy advised his daughter: "But it's nothing for you to *cry* about. If you cry whenever you hear any thing to the discredit of this county—you may have a good deal of crying to do. So save your tears."[47]

By early April 1862, the countryside northeast of Albemarle Sound was no longer safe for slaveholders and Confederates. "We had an unexpected visit," Creecy reported, "from some 8 or 10 armed Yankees. They came up unexpectedly, but I had time to meet them at the door. They were coming into the house without ceremony." Assuming that guests, invited or not, should knock at front doors, Creecy demanded the attention of a gentleman — "the officer in command of them." After "representing" to the officer and his soldiers "the impropriety" of intrusion, much less theft, Creecy wrote, "they desisted." A remarkable early-war scene, not much repeated as the conflict grew older. Still, "as they went off," one of Creecy's unwanted visitors swiped a duck. The Creecys were lucky. For these same men, approaching the neighborhood from New Begun Creek "in search of vessels ... visited several houses ... committing depredations — killing hogs — poultry — taking bacon — guns & pistols etc, in fact any thing they happened to take a fancy to." [48]

At that moment Creecy took hope because the Federals had abandoned Elizabeth City and "a regiment of Southern troops" had taken their place. The "Yankees will be afraid to venture far on shore," he thought. But soon the Northern gunboats returned, shelling the town and landing troops on the opposite (Camden County) side of the river. The armies met on 19 April a few miles up the Pasquotank, near South Mills in Camden, southern terminus of the Dismal Swamp Canal. The Yankees had "marched up towards South Mills by way of Camden court house," Creecy wrote to Betty. There Georgia troops had engaged them before noon and fought "until nearly night, when the Yankees retreated & at the same time the Southerners fell back to some breast works which they had thrown up near South Mills." Creecy had heard that the enemy was "a good deal dispirited" by the defeat, and he assured his daughter that their government was capable of "resist[ing] any force which the Yankees may send." [49]

Futile hope. The Confederates' stand at South Mills was their last substantial demonstration north of Albemarle Sound. The government had already revealed its fatal incapacity — or incompetence — to defend the Carolina coastal region at Hatteras. Now, with the Yankees on the Pasquotank and Northwest Landing Rivers (entrances to two canals leading to Norfolk) and in control of Hampton Roads as well, the Confederates abandoned Norfolk, Portsmouth, and then Suffolk, too. The Great Dismal and its deep hinterland fringes were now almost encircled. Norfolk County Confederate troops, ordered out of Portsmouth on 10 May 1862, would ultimately be reduced by one-fourth through battle and disease — but in campaigns elsewhere. Among them, volunteers from Deep Creek called the Dismal Swamp Rangers (Company A, Third Virginia Regiment) fought at Malvern Hill, Frazier's Farm, Second Bull Run, Antietam, Fredericksburg, Gettysburg, and on and on, until they surrendered at Appomattox. But none of the survivors could come home until the war was over. Inside the swampy circle, war became more irregular, less predictable, meaner. Regular Confederate forces evaporated; and Zebulon Vance, North Carolina's enraged governor, sanctioned guerrilla units that ambushed Federal troops, assassinated local unionists, and terrorized the remaining slaves. White unionists—middling and poor men called Buffaloes or Buffs—lurked in the swamps, too, and retaliated. The Creecys, meanwhile, were visited again and again by Yankee troops, who requisitioned their corn and all the healthy animals they could find. Richard's young son Eddy hid the mules in the woods.[50]

Allegiance among the many white people who remained within the circle during the war was and will probably forever remain murky. There is evidence that some poor and aspiring men, resentful of planters and their allies before 1861, saw justice in the unionist cause and opportunity in the social revolution the war introduced. For others, however, family and neighborhood traditions diminished or overcame the logic of class and, as in so many other places across the South, led the poor to march in Confederate ranks. One wonders, for instance, about the rough subsistence farmers and woodsmen of Hall Township in Gates County, a place long known as Scratch Hall because of its frontierish fighting customs. *Scratch* referred to clawing and eye-gouging; and folks from Hertford and other, more civilized counties declared that a man could not pass through Hall and retain all his body parts. The exigencies of civil war might move such contentious spirits in unpredictable directions. And one wonders, too, about the loyalties of a legendarily malodorous old man—perhaps in northern Camden County—who, the story goes, bought a goat but had no pen. A neighbor inquired, where would the goat live? "I'm going to let him stay in the house with me," came the response. "Well, what are you going to do about that smell?" The man answered, "Well, that goat has just got to get used to it!"[51] Within this old joke, class condescension fairly seethes; and one wonders further: What did the war have to do with such white men, anyway?

The momentum of war acknowledged such questions hardly at all, and poor Camden and other Carolina communities were torn asunder. When hostilities first began, Peter T. Burgess (1835–1903) was elected an officer in Camden County's Confederate militia. Later, however, Burgess was demoted through the chicanery, he thought, of his company captain, who was the son-in-law of a wealthy planter who disliked the Burgess family. Offended pride—not class or discernible abstract principle—led Burgess to sign up with the Federals (as a first lieutenant) in August 1862 and thus become Camden's chief Buffalo.[52] By this date the Confederates had repulsed Yankee forces at South Mills but then had withdrawn, leaving the area to Burgess and his men, foraging Union cavalrymen, irregular Confederate bushwhackers, and dramatic punitive expeditions by black Federal soldiers.

Ten months later a Yankee army surgeon named Bradney surveyed this dangerous and doleful scene. Early in June 1863, eighty Confederate officers, prisoners of war, had overpowered their guards and escaped. U.S. troops expected them to cross the Pasquotank "below North West Landing" on their way south. The Federals dispatched four companies of mounted riflemen in pursuit; Bradney accompanied them. At the Camden courthouse Bradney admired "the largest and noblest oaks I ever saw" and encountered a sixteen-year-old white girl who averred that she "could say nothing against Yankees individually, [but] hated them as a mass." At "Indian Town, a town which has no existence beyond its name," the troopers camped on the property "of one Wright," reportedly an abettor of local Confederate guerrillas. Wright hid his horse in the woods while, in Bradney's words, "The men ransacked his barns and house," stealing the blankets and sheets from his bed.[53]

Galloping on to the Currituck courthouse, the Yankees were greeted by a white man who had bedecked his porch with American flags. He charged cash for "corncake and bacon," however. On the way back to Camden, they stopped at the "house of Mrs. Shaw[,] wife of Col. Shaw of the 9th North Carolina Vols. Ex United States Congressman. She received us with great civility," Bradney reported, "prepared, without being asked, a truly handsome supper, and refused, almost indignantly, pay for the same." Mrs. Shaw "was a true Southern woman most strictly Sesesh, and bitterly opposed to Abolitionism. She conversed pleasantly in all subjects from politics to crops. She had lost most of her negroes. They had not left voluntarily, she said, but were stolen"—a significant point with most slaveholders. "They were so afraid of the Yankees that one of them became crazy and has so remained."[54]

Her last detail may have been not only true but also justified, from poor black folks' perspective. For by mid-1863, slaves had been encountering Yankee troops for more than a year, and the encounters were often confusing if not profoundly disillusioning. During the previous summer (i.e., prior to Lincoln's preliminary Emancipation Proclamation), Union officers in the Albemarle region had welcomed, fed, and harbored runaways, in defiance of the provisional governor's policy of maintaining slavery under a new hegemony of unionist planters. White unionists abused blacks everywhere; and in the occupied town of Plymouth (at the mouth of the Roanoke), New York troops beat refugees. By 1863, however, Yankees became less perplexing, as they eagerly recruited black men throughout northeastern North Carolina to serve, especially in General Edward Wild's Virginia-based "African Brigade." [55]

However mysterious and inconsistent Yankees were, though, they were decidedly preferable to white southerners under virtually any circumstances. Dr. Bradney's assumption of this great fact was verified at least once, while he and the troops hastened to and fro in their futile pursuit of the escaped Confederates. One day, about "Five miles from Camden [Courthouse] an old negro stopped us," Bradney wrote, "with the information that half a mile on the guerillas were in ambush awaiting our coming." The ambush did not materialize, but Bradney seemed grateful for the warning. Black folks were ubiquitous Union spies, everywhere the war went. By late in 1864, over in Bertie County, the overseer at Scotch Hall, the estate of George W. Capehart, complained of his inability to protect Capehart's property—his harvested crops and hogs, especially—from the enemy. "The Yankees says if you carry a single thing from down here they will take the balance & destroy the place. They sent a boat to the creek last week to see if anything had been moved. You cant move anything secretly," the overseer declared, "for the negros will tell them every thing." [56]

Meanwhile, back in Indian Town—"the place that is not"—once more, Bradney and the troopers met a picturesque white man they considered emblematic of the Albemarle country. He was, Bradney observed, "an interesting specimen on horseback in his Sunday best—Henry Whitehouse, or as he pronounced it[,] White'us." The Yankees were strangers to the region and its spoken accent, so Whitehouse's "I reckon" and "right smart," among other peculiarities, provoked amusement. He was the male equivalent of many local women, who were "neither models of beauty nor elegance. Many of them smoke, some chew snuff, and a few are anything but ladies." This was a bizarre landscape indeed. There were guerrillas of either side everywhere in the swamps, often without proper uniforms. The troopers also saw many "Young and able bodied men" in the open, too. Bradney conjectured that Confederate conscription in this country was either "poorly managed" or "successfully evaded." If the latter were true (as he seemed to believe), then were these young whites loyal? In Elizabeth City, the doctor had been "called in to see a woman who had been brutally kicked and beaten by a fellow because her brother was in the Yankee service, and she unguardedly had expressed sympathy with the Union cause." Bradney finally concluded that most whites were emphatically "*neutral*." Mimicking the local patois, Bradney summarized: "They ain't got no interest (?) [*sic*] no how in the war. They don't assist no side, and only want to be let alone to take care of their farms."

Here again, "Henry White'us" became emblematic: "He didn't think he could stand" being in the Confederate army, Whitehouse told the doctor, "and he heard they were mighty careless in their fighting."[57]

Not very far to the north of this scene—at the center of our subregion's cosmopolitan sector—matters of loyalty, warfare, and social relations were less ambiguous. When the Confederates abandoned Norfolk, Portsmouth, and Suffolk, Yankees marched in with revolutionary as well as strategic intent. To be sure, during 1862 and at least part of the next year, the Federals often behaved badly toward black folks: Some were beaten, shanghaied, and in effect reenslaved to labor on fortifications. But soon Portsmouth and Norfolk became major garrisons for black troops. Their white commanders, especially General Wild, were of the abolitionist persuasion, as were at least a few of the Yankee enlisted soldiers. One of these was Private Charles C. Miller of the 148th Regiment, New York Volunteers, who declared in his wartime diary, "I will pour hot oil into anyone's bowels that upholds slavery." On 2 April 1863, Miller noticed, while passing the Portsmouth jailyard, "a whipping post—the relic of barbarism—and what a disgrace." Later, after attending a black Sunday school, Miller determined to rid the seaport of the odious jailyard post. A black woman had told him that she had herself been whipped at the post and that she had seen a white man "whipped 10 days in succession—the last time he fainted—and then was sent to prison for 10 years for helping a slave off." Miller's accomplice in the theft of the post was a "contraband"—"a courageous man" who had fled slavery to occupied Portsmouth. Together, by dark of night, they scaled the jailyard fence and, with considerable difficulty, removed the post to Miller's camp. There the compatriots disassembled the whipping post, crated it, and mailed it to Miller's brother in New York.[58]

By this date it was becoming unnecessary for militancy to wait for nightfall. Disloyalty to the United States and disrespect for members of its armed forces, whatever their color, were not to be tolerated. On 11 July 1863, Second Lieutenant Alanson C. Sanborn, a young New Hampshireman, led a column of armed black troops down Main Street in Norfolk. From a sidewalk came loud expressions of disgust made by David Minton Wright, a Nansemond-born physician who had practiced in Norfolk since the 1830s. Sanborn stopped his column and moved to arrest Wright. Wright drew his pistol and shot Sanborn dead, whereafter Wright was convicted of murder by military tribunal and hanged. Over in Portsmouth, black soldiers and white residents of Gosport (site of the naval shipyard) exchanged insults and blows throughout the fall of 1863. Then J. H. D. Wingfield, the young rector of Trinity (Episcopal) Church in Portsmouth, ran afoul of the new regime, although less fatally than Dr. Wright. Local unionists and Yankee occupiers had mingled with pro-Confederate parishioners at Trinity services, and tensions mounted. When the priest refused (early in 1864) to say a prayer for President Lincoln, General Wild had him arrested, placed Trinity and all other white churches in Portsmouth and Norfolk under the control of his provost marshal, and ordered the churches to accept black soldiers at services. Wingfield, languishing in jail, refused to swear an oath of loyalty to the union. Wild threatened to confiscate the rector's personal property, while Wingfield's friends appealed Wild's orders to the area Federal commander, General Benjamin Butler. Butler finally waived the proposed punishments when Wingfield submitted to the loyalty oath.[59]

Wild demonstrated his relentless abolitionism more spectacularly the next spring. On 10 May 1864, some of the brigadier's pickets, operating on the James's north shore west of Jamestown, brought in a white native named William H. Clopton. Wild reported that Clopton had "acquired a notoriety as the most cruel Slave Master in this region," although "in my presence he put on the character of a Snivelling Saint." Among black refugees from Clopton's farm, Wild had identified "half a dozen *women* . . . whom he had often whipped unmercifully, even baring their whole persons for the purpose in presence of *Whites* and *Blacks*." So Wild had Clopton himself "laid . . . bare and [put] the whip into the hands of the Women, three of Whom took turns in settling some old scores on their masters back. A black Man, whom he had [also] abused finished the administration of Poetical justice." Wild was not a little disappointed that the refugees exacted their justice with restraint—he wished that Clopton's "back had been as deeply scarred as those of the women, but I abstained and left it to them."[60]

By the time Private Miller's brother received his odd parcel from Portsmouth, the subregion's major formal military engagement—the Siege of Suffolk—was under way. Miller may have participated, along with other New York troops. Back in May 1862, Confederates had withdrawn to the Blackwater River, west of Suffolk, while New York cavalry moved into the Nansemond seat to begin defensive preparations. The main war raged above the James, on the Peninsula. The Confederate purpose below the James was to contain the Federals below Hampton Roads and, through occasional harassment, prevent substantial numbers of them from joining McClellan's hordes confronting Lee before Richmond. The following spring a larger Confederate force under General James Longstreet crossed the Blackwater, and the siege itself was under way. Longstreet aimed to forage in Isle of Wight and Nansemond Counties and, once more, to prevent Southside-based Federals from joining the Army of the Potomac, to the north. There were skirmishes at South Quay, and on Edenton, Providence Church, and Somerton Roads. Climactic battles occurred during the second half of April on the old Norfleet family farm by the north bank of the Nansemond River, and at Chuckatuck—probably on the same marly ground where the Nansemond shaman had summoned rain to quiet English muskets in 1611. Federal gunboats played a crucial part in the capture of a key Confederate battery on the Nansemond. Longstreet's purposes had been served, however, and he began to withdraw on 3 May; the siege was over.[61]

The Suffolk campaign was only a sidebar, perhaps, to the dramatic conflict above the James—yet within the campaign are details that reveal significant aspects of warfare in a particular landscape and political economy. Two private soldiers of the Sixth Massachusetts Volunteers, for instance, reported heavier labor against the Nansemond forests than the Confederates. Henry H. Ingalls, of Company K, was ever on fatigue duty at the various forts on the western side of Suffolk. On 10 October 1862, he recorded, "We logged timber" at Fort Halleck. Two weeks later he was busy "digging a place to put logs where the cannons are to be mounted" at Fort McClellan. Late in January Ingalls "Went with 40 others in front of Fort Nansemond to chop down trees. 1 man of Co. was killed by a tree falling upon him."[62] Solomon Augustus Lenfest, of Company G, reached Suffolk via the same railway that Edmund Ruffin took almost three decades before—"a ride ... on the cars ... through the Dismal Swamp ... away down in the heart of Secessia ... only 10 miles from the North Carolina line." Lenfest then found himself happily "camped in an orchard with plenty of apples." He participated in many of the Blackwater area feints and responses preceding the siege itself. Some of his comrades were killed. Mainly, however, Lenfest logged. There were shelters and breastworks to be constructed, fields of fire to be cleared, and log barriers to be laid "to obstruct the road by which the rebels are expected to come when they attack us."[63]

The most interesting testimony from the Suffolk campaign (to my mind) comes from a sailor. Frank B. Butts, a Rhode Islander, served on a Nansemond gunboat that helped capture the Confederate battery in the principal battle of the siege. Butts also witnessed the effects of Confederate foraging in the countryside between the Nansemond and Blackwater—a scene that was replicated throughout the South, sorely testing white loyalty. When Longstreet's Confederates came, Butts remembered, "Their business was to collect forage and animals from the plantations, which were well stocked, there not having been any soldiers of either army in that section previous to this time. There was no limit to the rebel pilaging; friend and foe suffered alike by their robberies." Butts saw the work of Confederate requisition when he was detailed from his gunboat to reconnoiter Longstreet's advance along the line of the Norfolk & Petersburg (later Norfolk & Western) Railroad. Traveling secretly, mostly at night, Butts moved far inland, all the way to Wakefield, in Sussex County. Near this little depot town, the sailor met slaves who took him to a plantation cabin. "I was surprised to find myself in the midst of a great number of colored people," Butts wrote. "A middle-aged man appeared to have charge of the meeting." A black sentinel outside signaled safety, and Butts "learned from these people that the confederate soldiers had been actively engaged in repairing the railroad, and the meeting was held by these slaves to consider the question of escaping to the Union lines." Butts gave assurances, and soon, he reported, "great numbers of them came into our lines" at Suffolk.[64]

By this time Portsmouth and Norfolk had become bases of military operations directed southward, into the swampy circle of murky loyalties. From these troubled little cities went forth relentless young officers in blue, at the head of legions of black southerners. Marching alongside the Dismal Swamp Canal to South Mills, Elizabeth City, Camden and Currituck courthouses, and the town of Hertford, they closed the circle and scourged what remained of the old order. Sadly, there seems to survive no testimony from black participants in these expeditions of December 1863 and January 1864. White accounts from both sides help us to encircle (if not capture) the experience, however.

On Wednesday, 9 December 1863, Elizabeth Curtis Wallace wrote in her journal, "A regiment of negro troops with their white skinned officers came through and went to Carolina today." Elizabeth lived at Glencoe plantation, Wallaceton, the great corn enterprise that Major John Wallace had claimed from the Dismal on the eastern side of the canal, almost opposite the Feeder Ditch to Lake Drummond. (Frederick Olmsted, it will be recalled, had visited the place during his seaboard journey a decade before.) "They, that is three black niggers and three white ones[,] came and carried off our dear Old Pete horse," she continued. "Bette who owned him used every argument to prevent the Captain from taking him but to no purpose. They [also] carried off all the negroes that would go with them and stole besides horses and mules from all the people that had them without 'protection papers' as they call the [Loyalty] Oath. Poor old Pete!" Elizabeth lamented, "His days are numbered now."[65] War was hard on horses, and others.

The Wallaces were atypical in their open allegiance to the Confederacy. Wild thought

> the majority of people along our track to be reasonably neutral — that is to say, although sympathizing with the South, they were tired of the war, or weary of their own distresses and privations, harassed by the frequent alternation of masters, being plundered by both sides, or despondent of the ultimate success of the South, or convinced of the doom of Slavery, or aware of the mischief arising from the presence of Guerrillas in their midst; or if really neutral, or sympathizing with the North, they were usually (and reasonably) afraid to speak their minds, on account of the Guerrillas etc etc.

The general thought his troops' presence nonetheless aided "the rapid development of loyal sentiment." He supervised public meetings of unionists in three counties, and determined to root out the last Confederate guerrillas.[66]

Poor Pete, meanwhile, had much company. Hardly three weeks after his departure from Glencoe, General Wild summarized his forces' confiscations — crops, animals, equipment, and other personal possessions — from Confederate sympathizers: "we sent by water 9 loads to Roanoke Island and two to Norfolk, besides 4 long trains overland." Wild estimated, too, that his men had liberated 2,500 slaves — "exact numbers ... [being] impossible to count, as they were constantly coming and going. ... But few recruits were gained, as the ablebodied negroes have had ample opportunities to escape heretofore, or have been run over into Dixie" (i.e., transported by their masters behind secure Confederate lines). At the end of 1863, the institution of slavery in the subregion was dying fast. Wild also "burned 4 Guerrilla camps, took over 50 guns, 1 drum together with equipments, ammunition etc etc — burned over a dozen households, two distilleries etc etc, — took a number of prisoners, including 6 Confederate soldiers, armed with furloughs." The Federals lost nineteen men — seven killed, one dead from poison, nine wounded, and two taken prisoner.[67]

The next numbers in Wild's report reveal more about the unhappiest side of unconventional warfare in the swamp country: "Also four hostages for our men taken prisoners," he wrote, "3 women and one old man, — hanged one Guerrilla."[68] The war had exacerbated and partially, at least, legitimated class, racial, and personal conflicts in northeastern North Carolina. Yankees had given uniforms to Jeff Burgess and other Buffaloes, sanctioning their expropriations and murders of Confederates and their sympathizers as well as more conventional military activities. Governor Vance, in turn, sanctioned Confederate irregulars—"guerrillas" beyond the laws of war, in Federal parlance—who responded in kind. The Carolina irregulars, their position inexorably deteriorating with Confederate fortunes, were now hounded from towns to farms to swamp fastnesses. Wild's Christmastime sweep destroyed several of these. And, failing to halt the disintegration of slavery, the irregulars turned their attentions to ex-slaves become Union soldiers. In the aftermath of the Battle of Plymouth (mid-April 1864), Confederate regulars executed every black man found in Union uniform. At the Roanoke waterfront they shot down in cold blood a number who had surrendered; others they chased into the woods, caught, and hanged. The irregulars set the local precedent and went further than the regulars; white Federals were not exempt from their hostage-taking and executions.[69]

At the beginning of January 1864, Carolina civilians buried the body of Samuel Jones, a soldier of the Fifth Ohio Regiment. A notice pinned to Jones's uniform announced that he had been hanged by guerrillas in retaliation for the 18 December 1863 hanging, on General Wild's orders, of a Georgia soldier. (No explanation for this execution, seemingly of a Confederate regular, is found in Wild's papers.) Wild, meanwhile, had also ordered the execution by hanging of Daniel Bright, a guerrilla from Pasquotank County. The sign pinned to Bright's back read, "This Guerrilla Hanged by order of Brig. Gen. Wild."[70] The commander was playing a dangerous game, for guerrillas still held several of his black soldiers captive. Wild's security was female civilian hostages, as he wrote to John T. Elliott, a "Captain of Guerrillas," in mid-December: "I still hold in body Mrs. Munden and Mrs. Weeks, as hostages," Wild warned, "for the colored soldier taken by you. As he is treated, so shall they be: even to hanging. By this time you know that I am in earnest. —Guerrillas are to be treated as pirates. You will never have rest until you renounce your present course, or join the regular Confederate Army." Wild penciled at the bottom of this message his directions to Elliott: "Any day that you will send your colored prisoner to Deep Creek Village at the terminus of Dismal Swamp Canal you will find these women returned there the next day. This on the faith of one who keeps his word."[71] Wild's word, indeed—like that of U. S. Grant, another conqueror of southern swamps—was relentlessness.

He was a match, in his way, for the black Carolina men he commanded. Most (if not all) of them former slaves, they faced not only a deadly, lurking enemy in the Confederate irregular bands, but also the terrifying prospect of reenslavement or execution if they were captured. But they, too, were relentless. One unit—the Second North Carolina Colored Volunteers, headquartered in Portsmouth—set out from Elizabeth City in mid-December 1863 (in the words of their white colonel) "to collect recruits and contrabands in the Counties of Camden and Currituck." They narrowly escaped an ambush by seventy guerrillas at Shiloh, then engaged their enemies the next day near Sandy Hook, by an "impenetrable swamp." Later, after marching through Currituck Court House, they proceeded to "Crab Island in the midst of a dense swamp, accessible only by means of a pathway of logs laid, lengthwise"; but they found and "burnt their [the guerrillas'] quarters, consisting of nine log buildings, [and] captured a small quantity of arms and equipments, some commissary stores, and a quantity of new uniform clothing." The Second North Carolina's commander reported that "In all the encounters in which they were engaged, the colored troops showed the utmost courage and determination, desiring nothing better than to be led into the presence of an enemy. Though lame from two weeks' incessant marching, they disputed for the privilege of going upon any expedition of danger." The colonel was "certain now," he concluded, "of what I always firmly believed, that the colored troops can be relied upon, in any situation of difficulty or danger."[72]

But for me, the straightforward military victory of these Carolinians—in this particular landscape—still resonates with irony; for *they* were the logical descendants of swamp renegade ancestors. Their Confederate enemies had been the scourgers of runaways and maroons. Now the roles were reversed, and ex-slaves won civil legitimacy by routing and suppressing the swamp renegadeism of their ancient oppressors. Their military conquest of the swamp, too, must be seen as another significant step toward the end of the swamp itself—the end of its mystery, of its romantic function as refuge.

PART THREE

The Woodsmen

6 THE ENTREPRENEURS

I say, let the Yankees come, provided they have the capital, and develop the immense natural resources with which Virginia abounds; since they have ruined us, let them now help us, and every dollar of northern capital invested in Old Virginia, will just be so much more to our interest. — An Isle of Wight schoolteacher, 1873

If the Camp Manufacturing Company has ever been a success, it was due to sticking together and talking over our affairs together and coming to a conclusion between ourselves. — Paul D. Camp, 1917

When the Yankees came to Suffolk in June 1862, they found the great shingle- and lumberyard of the Dismal Swamp Land Company at the junction of Jericho Ditch and Shingleyard Creek. The corporation's president, Tazewell Taylor of Norfolk, was in Confederate service; and Willis Riddick of Suffolk, the managing agent, had been doing business with the rebel government, selling mules and wooden rails (although not collecting payment). So the Yankees were hardly constrained, either from expropriation or from wanton destruction. At the beginning of July, Riddick reported bad news to Taylor: "A great deal of our lumber has been destroyed & our lighters sunk by the soldiers. The loss is considerable." Riddick had rather hoped to switch sides and continue business, as of old, with the North; but authority— permission from corporate directors and military occupiers—was so uncertain. Should he raise and repair the lighters? And if he could deliver orders, "what sort of money" should he accept?[1]

By the end of September Riddick had managed to broker two shingle sales within Virginia, but his buyers were unable to get their consignments. "If they [the shingles] remain during the winter," Riddick wrote, "not one ... will be left." Yankee soldiers "are hawling them off by wagon loads" while "daily destroying" other company property. Riddick had "repaired lighters, wheel barrows, run new roads & hawled some shingles"; but now his world lay in ruins and he felt "compelled to stop [business] altogether." "It is now impossible to employ hands at all. They are all free. Shall I continue to feed negros that will not work? We are in a terrible fix here." The harried agent finally managed to sell cordwood to the Yankee-run segment of the Norfolk & Petersburg Railroad early in 1863, but the Dismal Swamp Land

Company—the subregion's corporate giant for almost a century—was dying almost as fast as slavery.[2]

When the war was finally over, Riddick made doleful tallies and wrestled with persisting uncertainties. He calculated that approximately 978,000 shingles of various sizes had been "lost & destroyed" as a result of the occupation, along with thousands of staves, bolts, pailings, and rails. Riddick had "made out an acct against the U.S. Government about August 1862," he reported to the directors, which "was proved before the Provost Marshall and sent to" the Union area commander; but "nothing has been heard from it since." The agent claimed $10,648 in damages—shingles and lumber carried away or burned, lighters and skiffs expropriated or sunk, buildings and fixtures burned. If the directors could supply about $2,000, Riddick figured, he might "commence operations" again; $4,000—not $10,648, curiously— would be "the cost of putting every thing as it was before." The directors seemed uninterested, and Taylor moved (so Riddick heard) to Baltimore. A prominent stockholder, William Mahone, appeared for a short visit in September, and Riddick may have taken hope, briefly. For Mahone—Southampton's most famous white native, an ingenious engineer, the builder of the Norfolk & Petersburg, boyish Confederate brigadier, hero of the Battle of the Crater at Petersburg, and future U.S. senator—personified confidence and regeneration. But Riddick's hopes were not to be fulfilled. Mahone observed a company in ruins, an expensive free labor market, and a Dismal Swamp that was dangerously dry.[3]

The first holocaust began shortly after General Mahone's departure. The fire raged out of control for weeks. Riddick's free workers had gotten many shingles during the summer; now more than 200,000 of them were burned up, along with better than two miles of wooden cart roads. "The fire is still raging," the agent wrote, "but the probability is that it cannot burn much more for the Co., but may destroy [his kinsman] E. C. Riddick's lumber which we sold him." Much might "have been saved if there had been any water in the canal, to move them. But it is the dryest time we have ever seen." Highlands near the Dismal blazed as well, with "fences & farms ... burning all around."[4]

The second holocaust occurred the following August. This "great fire," Riddick declared, "is still raging in the swamp, and the prospects is that if it doesn't rain soon & put it out that it will almost entirely ruin the Swamp. It is destroying all the young growth of timber and leaving holes in the ground ten ft deep." In other words, peat dried in the preceding drought was now burning downward. This time the company lost no lumber, and Riddick claimed some credit—being by then sadly experienced—in setting backfires near canalside stockpiles. Riddick and stockholders were not so fortunate in the third holocaust, however, which came three years later. The conflagration of August 1869 "entirely consumed" the corporate railroad "and all the lumber on that road has been burned, not a rail or piece of lumber left." As before, water in the Dismal Swamp Canal and all the corporate ditches was too low to float anything to safety. A short time later, the company's officers dismissed Willis Riddick.[5]

Poor Riddick, Job of the woods, took umbrage, and properly so. For fourteen years, through some of the best and most definitely the worst of times, he had superintended the company's business with acumen and imagination (as well as frustration). A shingle-counter had impugned his managerial integrity, so Riddick heard, and he fretted and demanded vindication. Tazewell Taylor relented, at length, and offered Riddick another contract. But neither Riddick nor the Dismal Swamp Land Company worked the woods much longer. From late in 1869 through 1870, Riddick paid workers—many with familiar white, black, and mulatto surnames from antebellum rolls: Skeeter, Butt, Parker, Copeland, Daugherty, Pearce, Riddick. These men split few shingles, however—Riddick told directors toward the end of 1869 that he had "not sold a shingle this year." Other roofing materials—tin, slate, gravel compounds, and a predecessor of asphalt shingles—had seized the huge market. Sales persisted for staves, railroad ties, telegraph poles, sawn lumber; but the Great Dismal, farmed out, burned out, too worked over, was no longer a prime forest. Neighboring shingle companies—Albemarle Swamp Land Company, Pungo Swamp Company, and others—were going out of business. Taylor and his directors did, too. In March 1871 they announced the end of operations. The Dismal Swamp Land Company thus became a mere landlord, leasing its more than forty-one thousand acres to "interested parties."[6]

The corporation had outlived its long, often dramatic times. The Dismal Swamp Land Company was originally an emblem of eighteenth-century capitalism in the New World—a group of investor-adventurers sanctioned by the King of England. In 1763, at the triumphal conclusion of a colonial war with France, the Virginia Council had chartered the organization, which included as stockholders George Washington, William and Thomas Nelson, Robert Burwell, John Robinson, and other late-eighteenth-century luminaries. Washington himself, the experienced surveyor, entered the Dismal to measure and scheme on behalf of his compatriots. Before long the Washington Ditch was using Lake Drummond water to convey corporate goods toward the cosmopolitan world. Stockholders aimed especially to supply rice to the British Caribbean, to feed slaves too busy with sugar production to feed themselves. An early crop went to Antigua, supplementing wheat and corn from the Chesapeake and Albemarle. But rice culture proved too uncertain in so northerly a latitude. Shortly, too, the company lost much of its labor force—eighteen men and boys, at least, ran off to the royal governor or (later) to Lord Cornwallis's British forces during the Revolution; and with independence, the new United States lost the commercial advantages of the British Empire, including much of the business of feeding slaves in Antigua. But by the mid-1790s the getting of cedar (called "juniper") shingles had become far more important than the uncertain making of rice.[7]

The Dismal Swamp Land Company recovered, then, from the inconveniences of American nationhood and, grasping another commodity in demand at home and abroad, persisted more or less in the old corporate mode: A Suffolk-based manager/agent directed natural resource extraction on behalf of cosmopolitan stockholders, whose names remained familiar—Bushrod Washington and his heirs, various Harrisons, Cockes, Pages, Byrds, and the College of William and Mary. By the 1810s—when the Dismal Swamp Canal and Jericho Ditch were completed—the company had settled on a labor system, too. They would own but a few slaves, mainly to maintain and improve transportation (ditches and their locks, roads); most labor they would contract, through the hiring system still flourishing when Ruffin, then Olmsted, Crayon, and Yankee soldiers visited Nansemond and Norfolk Counties.[8] It was a quaint enterprise—capitalist, with capitalist and noncapitalist social relations; and it thrived in the long term, in a thoroughly capitalist market system. Had the Western world continued past 1870 to roof and side much of its housing with wooden shingles, the Dismal Swamp Land Company almost certainly would have continued, too. Agent Riddick was learning fast to cope with free (not just quasi-free) labor, when he lost his job.

The end of the era of shingles had a profound impact on the swamp, too. For from all available accounts, neither the Dismal Swamp Land Company nor other shingle-getters cut down many cedars (or cypress or other trees) to obtain their millions of shingles. Rather, laborers found downed trees—often by probing beneath peat with poles—and raised them if necessary, then sawed logs to two- or three-feet lengths and used axes to split shingles. Some standing trees fell, to be sure, to make lumber, telegraph poles, railroad ties, and staves. But if the company's records reflect activities of the broader industry, nonshingle business was incidental in the great swamp.[9] Certainly shingle-getting had not been without impact upon the landscape, and the number of fallen trees was hardly infinite, no matter how deeply the swampers probed. It was canal- and ditch-making, then railway construction and wildfires, that probably wrought far more permanent or long-term degradation to the Dismal. Finally, the great postbellum resort to lumber-getting from standing trees, underway ferociously by the 1870s, was a turning point in the swamp's and subregion's history.

The destruction of live trees was hardly novel, of course. Woodcraft and wanton destruction were both ancient phenomena in eastern North America when the postbellum entrepreneurs arrived. Indians fashioned parts or all of their homes, as well as dugout canoes, weapons, farming tool handles, and some housewares, from wood. Wood was also their principal cooking and heating fuel. And (as we have already seen) Indians purposefully burned forests to create crop fields and hunting parks. Europeans used more wood, both absolutely and relative to their greater ultimate numbers. In their wooden houses—most of which had wooden chimneys—they constructed huge fireplaces that consumed mountains of firewood, approaching perhaps the staggering figures one scholar has calculated for colonial New England. At Christmastime 1686, a visitor to William Fitzhugh's Eagle's Nest estate on Virginia's Northern Neck observed that "[i]t was very cold, yet no one ever thinks of going near the fire, for they never put less than a cartload of wood in the fireplace & the whole room is kept warm." The English and Africans also built wooden barns, tobacco houses, cow stalls, slave huts, boats, and implements agricultural and martial. They constructed miles of rail fences to protect crops from ranging animals. Manufacture of tobacco hogsheads may have strained supplies of white oak in parts of the lower Chesapeake, where the tree is less plentiful than in Maryland. Tobacco culture moved westward, into the Piedmont and new stands of white oak, while Tidewater farmers adopted grain culture—which also required staves for barrels.[10]

Landon Carter—himself a Northern Neck tobacco-cum-grain-farmer—worried about wood supplies in his diary, in April 1770, while snow lay on the ground outside. (Carter had been observing the gradual cooling of the late-eighteenth-century climate, the appearance of the so-called Little Ice Age.) "I must wonder," he wrote, "what succeeding years will do for firewood. We now have full ¾ of the year in which we are obliged to keep constant fires; we must fence our ground in with rails[,] build and repair our houses ... and every cooking room must have its fire the year through." With "the natural death of trees and the violence of gusts that blows them down," Carter mused, "I must think that in a few years the lower parts of this Country [i.e., the Tidewater] will be without firewood." The colonel hoped for the discovery of "mines of coal" not too distant, but feared that "we must find out a way of burning" pine, which seemed always to replace felled hardwoods.[11]

In another century, railroads would bring down from Appalachia more than enough cheap coal to heat domestic Tidewater. And Virginia women learned to cook quite satisfactorily on stoves fueled with pine. Landon Carter was a notorious worrier. For his own generation and for many to come, hardwoods and conifers alike were commodities or, more often, the great enemies to agriculture, obstacles to civilization and wealth. Through the seventeenth, eighteenth, and nineteenth centuries, the human denizens of the Chesapeake (and the rest of eastern America) hewed, split, sawed, built with, and shipped wood. More often they burned, piled, and burned again—wasting, we might say—what was to them not a resource but a perpetual nuisance. Winter journal entries of farmers large and small recount with metronomic monotony the ritual of felling, heaping, and burning, then reburning wood to clear land. Edmund Ruffin's sons followed this course; so did smaller farmers such as Daniel Cobb and Elliott Storey. The elder Ruffin also had slaves install wooden drains of his own design in the low fields of his Hanover County estate, and he recommended the devices to brother farmers. Following the Civil War, relatively inexpensive tile drainage became available, but Virginia's relatively few progressive farmers continued to drain with Ruffin-style plank boxes. Likewise, wooden fences prevailed here long after wire became common elsewhere. Incredibly, even wooden chimneys persisted well into the 1880s. As late as 1890, too, farmers seriously discussed the merits of open fireplaces—notoriously wasteful of fuel—versus stoves. A writer in the *Southern Planter* suggested a compromise: stoves for cooking, dining, and guest rooms, an open fire for "mother's chamber." Fireplaces, he opined, "have a more unitizing influence on a family ... [and provide] one of the ... greatest comforts of a country home in winter." (Mothers presumably craved company every evening.) Prosperous farmers near cities (such as Richard Eppes) began to burn coal for fuel during the late 1860s and 1870s, but more isolated rural houses were apparently heated by wood well into the twentieth century.[12]

Commercial wood-taking is not yet well researched or understood, historically, but the following developmental pattern is probably accurate. Individual farmers have always engaged in off-season lumbering, turpentining, and shingle-getting. This was often their principal means of acquiring cash—for taxes, for purchases of farm animals and real property, and for sugar, coffee, and other comestibles they could not produce at home. Part-time commercial lumbering probably had little impact on landscapes, however, for

Survivor: three-hundred-year-old red oak behind Bacon's Castle, Surry County, Virginia, 1990
(Photo by the author)

the selective cutting of prime trees and the difficult skidding of heavy trunks to watercourses was more dangerous and laborious—for men and for the animals employed in skidding trunks—than any seasonal farming operation, plowing included. A few such farmer-lumbermen perhaps hand-sawed logs into planks. Most probably floated them to small and middling-sized saw-millers who supplied lumber to large farmers, cities, and the export trade. Wrenns Mill on Pagan Creek in Isle of Wight County, apparently a very substantial enterprise, was established as early as 1646; and Wrenns Millpond, half a mile long, survives to this day, about a mile inland from Burwell Bay on the James. Wrenns and other sawmills, whatever their sizes, were likely only seasonal businesses. Agriculture remained the preeminent business of the countryside; and labor for the woods was available, for the most part, only during the winter off-season. The subregion's largest woods products corporation, the Dismal Swamp Land Company, seems only partly exceptional: Labor was available primarily during the first five months of each year. Some work went on the rest of each year, but water in ditches and canals was often too low in summer and fall to transport shingles out of the swamp. This company's and other operators' greediness—they cut more and more ditches dependent on poor Lake Drummond—also exacerbated this problem over time.[13]

Turpentining among the longleaf pine stands—a subject entertained previously—seems more the proper "industry" existing alongside (as opposed to within) the pursuit of agriculture. For this was summer work, mainly for slave men who cut chevron-shaped "boxes" in the trees, then walked miles every day collecting resin. William Valentine (you will recall) observed—but did not measure for us—what seemed to be a considerable turpentine business late in the antebellum period, along the Chowan. The censuses of manufactures for the period are more helpful: In 1840, Bertie County produced 22,439 barrels of naval stores—presumably tar, pitch, and turpentine; Northampton produced 2,000; Chowan and Gates produced only 624 and 633, respectively. The rest of northeastern Carolina made less or nothing at all that was reported. In southeastern Virginia, Nansemond, Southampton, Isle of Wight, and Sussex produced 2,253, 1,238, 934, and 547 barrels, the other counties little or nothing. Bertie's and Northampton's production were probably what grasped Valentine's concerned attention. For what had been in colonial times a very significant industry had obviously declined in importance. By 1860—according to the manufacturing censuses again—naval stores production had ceased to exist in the entire subregion, and there would be no revival sufficient to warrant reporting. Valentine's and others' prediction that

Mixed-pine forest, with longleafs, Blackwater Ecologic Preserve,
Isle of Wight County, Virginia, 1989 (Photo by the author)

overboxing would destroy the longleaf and the industry came true, more or
less. In fact, among the few surviving stands of these stately giants below
the James, turpentining persisted on a very small scale at least into the 1930s.
A forester showed me the remains of a tiny still—abandoned probably during the Great Depression and sufficient for hardly more than local supply—
in the Blackwater Ecologic Preserve, at the southern end of Isle of Wight
County, near Franklin.[14]

The longleaf's near-destruction in this country has another cause, however: that icon of the South and mainstay of folk culture, the hog. The poor
longleaf's vulnerability lay in its peculiar infancy, unique among conifers.
Longleaf seed fall to the earth packaged within huge cones. During fires,
usually, the seed are released in ash-fertilized earth. A few actually germi-
nate and begin to grow. Here begins the longleaf's odd infancy—the "grass
stage," which may last several years, depending on environmental conditions.
The tree stands about a foot or so high, already festooned with a fine skirt
of long needles, plus a loose, vertical crown of needles. This crown encompasses the tree's delectable finger-sized terminal bud—virtually pure protein
—from which the future giant will grow. But the terminal bud sits for several
seasons at eye level to the average hog. The crown needles conceal but cannot

Forester-ecologist Allen Plocher with grass-stage longleaf, Blackwater Ecologic Preserve, 1989
(Photo by the author)

protect terminal buds. Human fingers may part the crowns easily; relentless inquiring snouts doubtlessly discovered terminal buds by the thousands, and for this reason thousands of grass-stage longleafs never achieved maturity.[15]

Unknowable or little-known variables render estimation of hogs' role in the decline of longleaf pines difficult at best. If (for instance), about 1750, a square mile of forest in western Gates County, or southern Southampton or Isle of Wight — all paths of regular hog drives from the south and west — contained 5,000 mature longleafs and 15,000 infants, what effect would the passage (as a colonial governor of North Carolina once reported) of more than 50,000 swine have on the forest? If drovers moved the hogs toward Smithfield or Portsmouth at a leisurely pace, *and* if brush and most of the deciduous understory of the forest floor had been burned recently — making passage through the forest easy, and surviving grass-stage longleafs accessible — then it is hard to imagine the hogs missing a terminal bud within a hundred or more yards on either side of a trail. Consider, too, the huge numbers of local hogs, most of them free-ranged most of the year, a century later. Then the possibility of no longleaf regeneration whatsoever becomes probable.

Some infant trees did survive, nonetheless. The ruin of the Isle of Wight turpentine still in the Blackwater Ecologic Preserve, apparently in use until the 1930s, is evidence. So are the preserve's fire-scarred longleaf stumps. The stumps of trees cut for timber during the 1930s, after years of turpentine box-ing, show seventy or more rings, indicating that they shot up from the grass stage during the 1860s. (Were these trees beneficiaries of Civil War soldiers' carrying off so much of the swine population?) But there are not many such stumps. Turpentining, timbering, and hogs had accomplished a profound work of near-extermination.[16]

Big trees felled during the Great Depression had approached maturity at the end of the nineteenth century, when so many Virginia and Carolina farmers gradually gave up their farms and let croplands return to forest. The new entrepreneurs who descended on the subregion after the Civil War came to fair prospects, then. Centuries of land-clearing for agriculture, and cul-ture generally, had vastly reduced stands of hardwoods; but most of the landscape was still covered with pine of commercial potential. Europe, the urban East, and especially the "developing" American West had need for such wood. Southern lumbermen (whether native or newcomers) got their starts then, during the 1860s, 1870s, and 1880s, while other entrepreneurs cut out the forests of the Great Lakes states. By the end of the nineteenth cen-tury, when the exploitation of the northern woods was complete and when South Atlantic farmlands were becoming grown over again, the southern lumbermen would be positioned for vast expansion and profits.[17] During the interim, meanwhile, many entrepreneurs came and went. Some stayed to prepare the way for a reorganization of the countryside that amounted to a new epoch—an age of forest plantations, which replaced the age of grain and continues today.

The "interested parties" to whom the Dismal Swamp Land Company directors leased their woodlands were Francis R. Baird, John L. Roper, and Joseph W. Gaskell. The partners were all Pennsylvanians. Gaskell remained in Philadelphia, but Baird and Roper migrated to Norfolk in 1865 and estab-lished sawmills at the North Landing River in Princess Anne County and at Deep Creek. They shipped from Newton's Wharf on the Elizabeth. (Six other sawmillers occupied Norfolk's riverfront, too, in 1872; and there were two more across the Elizabeth, in Portsmouth. No one, apparently, sold shingles anymore; but, tellingly, before the end of the century Norfolk had a "Felt, Cement, and Gravel Roofing" firm called S. L. Foster & Son.) Baird and Roper became J. L. Roper & Company following Baird's death in 1876; and over the next quarter century, Roper virtually defined the industry's mode of operation. This meant not only aggressive marketing but also acquisition either by outright purchase or ownership "in fee" (i.e., by lease) of vast forest reserves. Roper moved southward, down the coast of Carolina, and by 1900 claimed more than 200,000 acres. New sawmills followed the southerly expansion—at Gilmerton in Virginia, the mill town of Roper near Albemarle Sound, and finally at Winthrop, North Carolina (on the Neuse River). Roper also helped define the lumber industry's success by pioneering corporate associational activities. A cofounder of the North Carolina Pine Association, Roper was its president in 1901.[18]

Roper & Company's imperium in coastal Carolina was hardly solitary, however. During the 1880s the brothers William and James Blades arrived in New Bern from Maryland; Calvin Conrad of Philadelphia and his partners established the Pamlico Lumber Company; and G. W. Kugler of New Jersey founded another sawmill, also in Beaufort County. Meanwhile, George T. Leach of Carbondale, Pennsylvania, brought his Eureka Lumber Company to Hyde County. Leach worked with a league of associates (from his native state and New York) who owned Appalachian coal mines; Leach supplied them with mine props and rollers while producing barrel staves and sawn lumber to other customers.[19]

Railroads—small, local ones, then interstate syndicates—snaked through the hinterland to carry out logs to multiplying sawmills. Up on the James, for instance, Major William Allen, master of Claremont Manor in Surry County, resumed logging on his property after Confederate service. About 1880 Allen's business was absorbed into the Surry Lumber Company, the enterprise of newcomers from Maryland, who built the Surry, Sussex, & Southampton Railroad. This was a narrow-gauge affair locals called "the Sick, Sad, and Sorry," but its purpose was more hauling company logs than serving the sarcastic public; and as such the SS&S ultimately became an important segment to an emergent system.[20]

In Surry and much of the rest of Southside Virginia, the new system was built around William Mahone's old railroad, the Norfolk & Petersburg, which eventually became the Norfolk & Western. With its expanding limits and multiplying spurs, the N&W became a giant of natural resource exploitation, depositing enormous loads of Appalachian coal and hinterland pine lumber at its huge Norfolk wharf. The Chesapeake & Ohio, N&W's rival, operated in parallel, sometimes the same territory, and had its own huge terminal in Norfolk. Allen Anderson McCullough, another Maryland-born lumber and coal seller, had built his shipping wharf on reclaimed land on the Elizabeth waterfront. In 1893 McCullough more than recovered his investment when he sold the property to the C&O for $500,000.[21]

Norfolk's domination of the hinterland to the south was further consolidated through the creation of the Norfolk-Southern Railroad, which consumed the old Portsmouth & Roanoke (Weldon) and other southerly routes. The fate of Chowan County's forests illustrates the railroading dynamic. During the 1870s, for instance, Nansemond sawmiller W. H. Gay undertook construction of the Suffolk & Carolina Railway. As this line slowly crept southward, Chowan forests—except those in old crop fields, according to the county's early-twentieth-century historian—were "virgin." (This seems an exaggeration, but it may be true of forests inconvenient to the Chowan and Perquimans Rivers.) During the 1880s, however, both Gay's railway and the Norfolk-Southern reached Chowan County. Agents bought timber rights for as little as twenty-five cents per thousand board feet, and within a dozen years the county's forests were virtually cut out. Small local lumbermen followed the railroaders and persisted on their leavings for some time, but the Chowan experience demonstrated with devastating emphasis the postbellum conquest of the formerly remote hinterland.[22]

In 1906 a syndicate including the Norfolk-Southern took over John Roper's great corporation. By this time Roper had expanded his holdings down to New Bern, with mills there as well as in Belhaven and Oriental. In 1911 the syndicate was the largest lumber manufacturer in North Carolina, with holdings of about 400,000 acres. This corporation (which had retained the name Roper) ceased operations after World War I, but the genius of enlarging scale knew no end. Norfolk-Southern/Roper holdings ultimately devolved upon the international wood products giant Weyerhaeuser, which in 1975 possessed about 650,000 acres in eastern Carolina alone and operated an enormous pulp/paper mill at Plymouth.[23]

In the meantime, lumber entrepreneurs both descended from the Northeast and emerged from the hinterland itself. Alfred L. Gray, of Sussex County, Delaware, migrated to Carolina, then to Nansemond County, Virginia, and finally to Waverly in Sussex County, Virginia, where he established the Gray Lumber Company, which has flourished to this day. Alfred's grandson Garland (born in 1901) became the emblematic enlightened southern lumberman. Educated entirely in the Old Dominion—he earned a master's degree in southern history at Washington and Lee University—Garland Gray assumed control of the family business; by midcentury, as a member of the Virginia senate, he had become the industry's model law-giver. In 1867 W. H. Parrish of Richmond established the Richmond Cedar Works, but the company's principal mill and stave factory was the "Norfolk Plant"— actually located at Great Bridge, at the edge of the Dismal Swamp. Rich-

Weyerhaeuser papermill, Plymouth, North Carolina, lighted for Christmas 1992
(Photo by the author)

mond Cedar ultimately owned 200,000 acres of "swamp hardwoods"—white cedar, cypress, and tupelo—and contended with rival corporations for Lake Drummond water. Pennsylvanians Edward Hedley and the brothers R. J. and William Neely founded sawmills in Southampton County on the Nottoway and by the Blackwater at Franklin, respectively, but they would not persist. Both firms were incorporated into a homegrown giant-to-be, the Camp Manufacturing Company of Franklin.[24]

Camp Manufacturing's emergence—it was founded about 1875, incorporated in 1887—is mysterious in several ways. The creature of three ambitious brothers, the company became a juggernaut, absorbing native- and Yankee-owned sawmills, raising Franklin as the industrial capital of the hinterland, building railroads, buying much of the Dismal Swamp in Virginia, then far exceeding John Roper and the Norfolk-Southern syndicate in a race through Carolina—then Georgia and Florida—for the pine forests. For only the barest facts are known of the Camp family before the late nineteenth century. They were Baptists, farmers, small slaveholders, pro-Confederate, and prolific—nothing remarkable, little to suggest a cradle for captains of industry. George Camp II (1793–1879), progenitor of the entrepreneurs, fathered fourteen children with his two wives. He owned two farms on the Black-water immediately above the village of Franklin; and like most rural men, he engaged in the timber business during the winter. So did some of his strong sons. Perhaps—as with Elliot Storey, who lived nearby—George Camp's proximity to a navigable river and a town with a railroad depot inclined him and his progeny toward education, disciplined work, the outer world. During the Siege of Suffolk, Longstreet's Confederates occupied the Camp farms and ate their hosts to the brink of poverty. Perhaps the vicissitudes of providing for themselves after the war encouraged enterprise. George maintained himself on part of one of his farms, but most of his property seems to have been subdivided—for productive purposes—among sharecroppers, some of them former Camp slaves. Sons needed to find other work, and the Camps perceived education as a path to success. So the boys went to academies in Southampton and Hertford, to the University of Virginia; one (Benjamin Franklin Camp) graduated from medical school in Baltimore.[25]

Paul Douglas Camp (1849–1924), sixth child of George's second family but first among the entrepreneurs, was exceptional. P. D. (as he was called) worked to support at least one sibling's schooling, but he seems to have had little interest in or time for schooling himself. He left home to become a hired hand for two older brothers, paddling four miles up the Nottoway River every day to reach their logging operations. He drove wheat harvesters in adjacent counties. He briefly ran someone else's sawmill near Boykins, then his own in Como, down in Hertford County. When brother James L. (called J. L.) finished his business schooling in Baltimore, P. D. took him into P. D. Camp and Company. Back in Franklin, finally, P. D. and J. L. bought out the Neelys and incorporated Camp Manufacturing Company. Their brother Robert J. (always R. J.) joined them, forming the triumvirate that P. D.'s son John described many years later: "P. D., a good far-seeing trader and with courage and confidence, was made president (he had the largest interest in the company). His foresight, optimism, and courage were largely responsible for the company's expansion. R. J., a natural salesman and diplomat, was secretary and treasurer. J. L., a natural operator, a detailed man, a pessimist, was a success at manufacturing. The three made a wonderful, well-balanced, successful team."[26]

P. D. Camp inspired awe. A large man fond of hunting in the Big Woods near Como, often from horseback, he was aggressive, imperious, and paternalistic, but fair-minded at business and indulgent with his enormous family. P. D. was widely known to be blunt-spoken and altogether rather rough-edged. John C. Parker, the company's longtime attorney and an admirer of P. D., observed in 1911 that "He is a most excellent man, in many respects and has done much good in this community, but he is not an English scholar and does not always mean just what his words would indicate." Camp illustrated both his qualities of wisdom and directness and his legendary rough edge a few years later, in a letter of advice to two of his sons, who were to be his executors: "I am getting along in years and so is Brother Jim," P. D. began, "and none of us have any lease on our lives and we may not be here long to advise with you, and therefore, I am giving you a little advice now." The sons must "Recognize that the other side has its right as well as your side," he declared, "and if any tangle questions should come up, talk them over and try to reason them out." Reasonableness and patience were the keys to a family corporation's success. Prudence, too: "Keep your affairs as near to yourself as you can. It don't hurt to get advice from other people, but there is no use to say anything about whether you are making or losing—it will do you no good."[27]

Meanwhile, this optimist and aggressive opportunist had acquired much for his doting sons. John Camp recalled that during "the 1890s, expansion was in the air. The company bought from John A. Arringdale his mill and two years' supply of timber at Arringdale, Virginia," then "bought timber and built a mill at Butterworth, Virginia, finally enlarging it to a two-band and resaw mill." Both operated until 1917 or 1918. In 1896 P. D., J. L., and R. J. bet that Republican William McKinley would defeat Democrat William Jennings Bryan, benefiting business. So "between July '96 and July '97 they bought all the timber they could by using cash, credit notes, etc. Their judgment was correct, and the company made lots of money by risking all."[28]

In 1899, William Nelson Camp acquired the old Dismal Swamp Land Company property—the "Washington Entry"—and a few years later distributed shares among his brothers. The huge tract's 400,000,000-odd board feet of mostly hardwood stumpage became Camp Manufacturing's most important asset. But the three Franklin brothers knew no rest. At the beginning of the twentieth century they bought the Marion Lumber Company in South Carolina, plus a controlling interest in three lumber companies in and near Wilmington, North Carolina. They also became partners with a New York wholesale dealer—Wiley, Harker, and Camp—that would sell their own and others' lumber. Camp Manufacturing continued operations in Hertford's Big Woods near Como but also logged by the Lynnhaven River near Norfolk, in Dinwiddie County beyond Petersburg, and in Giles County in southwestern Virginia. By 1903 P. D. and three brothers were cutting 4,311 acres of cypress in Liberty County, Georgia; and the family doctor, Benjamin Franklin (B. F., of course), was mining phosphates and cutting timber (often with R. J.'s and P. D.'s backing) in central Florida.[29]

Even the smallest lumber operations involved troubles as well as the possibility of profit; far-flung ones brought plagues of litigation that kept John C. Parker and other Camp attorneys busily engaged. Corporate railroad engines blew sparks onto others' property and set fires. Owners sued. When W. N. Camp purchased the Washington Entry in 1899, he immediately sued the Lake Drummond Canal and Water Company, whose drafts upon the lake had dried up Jericho Ditch. About 1907, a lumber operator in Brunswick County, Virginia, apparently bought from a black couple a fifteen-foot-wide strip of land in order to block Camp Manufacturing's access to a lease on adjoining land. Parker went to court again. The Camps' avid expansionism ran afoul of the business cycle about the same time. In the aftermath of the Panic of 1907 they fell far arrears in payments to many creditors. Parker negotiated. External auditors agreed that company assets and management were sound, and the Camps endured, catching up and restoring grace by the beginning of 1910.[30]

In the woods, meantime, the dangerous labors of felling trees and carrying timber to mills went on. In Georgia, workers rafted cypress down the Altamaha to Darien—the traditional method. But in the Dismal and elsewhere, lumbermen laid track and employed railroads: This was the new mode, which freed the industry from deep creeks and rivers and facilitated the clear-cuts of remote places that devastated postbellum landscapes from Wisconsin to the Gulf Coast. Logging with railroads was particularly dangerous for Camp workers in the Dismal. "The railroads were all put in there on matting," recalled John Camp's son, Jack, "or on pilings—and we had a lot of wrecks on them because the footing in the Swamp was so treacherous." Track beds "would change from day to day," and the company superintendent would "rare and pitch" as "a crew of men" with "a jury-rig crane" wrestled "to get a whole locomotive back on the track."[31]

Setting derailed trains aright was perhaps the least dangerous aspect of logging work, but on other hazards Jack Camp was silent. For example, beginning in the 1890s, southern lumbermen adopted steam skidders. These stationery contraptions rotated near rail sidings, drawing steel cables that were tied to downed trees and were sometimes a thousand or more feet long. As the skidders turned, cables tightened and pulled the logs toward the sidings, where men would use small cranes to load logs onto trains. Unwary workers were caught by cables and trees, but sometimes even the wary were maimed or killed when cables snapped and whipped into flesh. Crane rigging broke,

Small sawmill near Windsor, North Carolina, 1990 (Photo by the author)

and trains ran over men. The sawmills were hardly healthy, either. A woman described them as "a kind of topside coal mine — noisy, dangerous work with an inexorable tendency to destroy the worker."[32]

Jack Camp did allow that the men who cut company timber in the Dismal were generally huge. Early mornings, they would appear at the edge of the swamp, at the corporate rail line. By the 1920s, a Ford fitted with railroad wheels would convey workers back into the forest. Once at the worksite, the men would seek out the skidder, their tin lunch pails in hand. Another worker would have fired it hours before; so while work began, that most dangerous instrument of logging would heat the men's lunches of meat and rice. "[B]y noon," Jack Camp said, "they had beautiful seasoned rice, each grain was standing apart, and they had a hot lunch. And they'd take an hour for lunch and rest." At such sites — so long as cuttable timber remained — Camp Manufacturing maintained a machine shop, a store, and housing for workers. The housing usually consisted of portable eight-by-sixteen-feet boxes — better shelter, arguably, than the shingle-getters' lean-tos Edmund Ruffin and Porte Crayon described. Such company housing might have accommodated families, but Camp's camps were probably villages of men only.[33]

Some southern timber-getting and sawmill work crews were biracial. Most, however, consisted of African American men bossed by white men

Logging in Dismal Swamp (Pasquotank County, North Carolina), 1991 (Photo by the author)

like Camp's hot-tempered logging superintendent. The late nineteenth and early twentieth centuries' economic developments squeezed and stressed black families. Farming depended on family labor, but black people seldom enjoyed the relative independence of farm ownership. They were tenants, more likely sharecroppers, and afflicted (along with most other American farmers) by declining commodity prices. Women and children found domestic or other "public" work in cities or the multiplying railroad depot towns. Older boys and men, however, discovered their best opportunities in seasonal work, with the railroads, and the vastly expanding lumber industry—almost always far from home. Marriages were strained. Some men, oppressed by Jim Crow's relentless cruelties and by a short life expectancy, grasped chances for cash and freedom and never returned. Most did return, of course. Camp lumber-getters may have perpetuated a tradition begun by free shingle-getters for the old Dismal Swamp Land Company—commuting, as it were, between tiny family homes in Suffolk, or at the edge of the swamp, and the woods. But as early as 1915, across the urban South, a pattern of female-headed black households had begun to emerge.[34]

The huge black men who cut timber for the Camps probably preferred this rough work to sharecropping, but they saw no cash in return. For the Camps maintained company stores and, as Jack Camp related, "they didn't pay off in money, they paid off in store checks, fiat money, it had serrated edges. You'd come in, pay-day, they'd pay you off in company checks and you'd come back and spend them at the store." An alcoholic, black-sheep Camp brother kept such a store in Florida before his premature death. In Virginia, Norman Poarch (among others) stocked the Camp commissary with the over-sized overalls and boots the big timber-getters bought with their serrated "checks." Poarch was possessive of his little domain—another hot-tempered white man. Customers were not to lounge about, sitting on "his" counter. "[H]e'd rant at em and rant at em, and get em all off of there and five minutes later they'd be back." So Poarch strung wire across the counter and attached it to an electrical battery. This "put out a lot of volts that would just shock the bejabbers out of you," Jack Camp remembered.[35] More danger in the woods.

But for all the enormity of the industrialization of the deepest hinterland, there remained some aspects of life that recalled the times of Ruffin and Crayon, even those of William Byrd. During the 1950s, for instance, Camp Manufacturing and Richmond Cedar Works finally (after years of litigation) settled on an eastern boundary for the old Washington Entry. Before this was accomplished, however, a surveyor spent a night in a tree, surrounded by a herd of wild cattle. Then, attempting to consolidate the peace with Richmond Cedar and govern the entry according to modern forestry practice, the Camps—as Jack Camp put it—"tried to get the hunting established so that we would have everything organized in hunting clubs who in turn would be responsible for fire control." Company-sanctioned clubs apparently did not include many of the locals. The Washington Entry, he explained, "was ringed by people who were all pretty damn independent." One of them told a company lawyer (as Camp recalled), "'Look, don't bother me about hunting. I hunted here, and my father and my sons, and we're gon hunt here as long as we want to hunt here. You can forget trying to tell us what not to do.'" Jack Camp knew the company was flummoxed. "If people got upset with you, they'd set your woods on fire. That was their retaliation. . . . They had all kinds of devices that would allow them to be out of the woods be-fore the fire ever was detected." The Dismal remained outlaw country. "Boy, once they get something against you, they'll burn your woods, or shoot you, or something like that. Pretty tough crowd."[36] *Plus ça change . . .*

7 THE EXPERTS

One of the most important forestry problems ... is to secure a satisfactory natural regeneration of the loblolly pine after cutting.... [T]here is a hardwood undergrowth, which, when the pine is removed, springs up rapidly, often crowding out any young pines that may have started.... Since the pine is much more valuable than the hardwood from the timber growing standpoint, unless some artificial help is given ... the resulting forest ... will be much less valuable. — Maryland state forester, 1925

I feel that the greatest thing that has happened for forestry in the South is the grouping of many small tentatively held ownerships into larger ownerships held by strongly financed concerns which have the know-how.... Large ownerships can afford to employ skilled technicians and can afford to pay the taxes and carrying charges and wait for returns. — Retired U.S. Forest Service forester, 1959

We think we're doing what's right. But trees will grow in spite of foresters. — Paper corporation forester, 1991

During the late 1910s and 1920s, Dudley Bagley, the enterprising young farmer of Currituck County whom we encountered earlier, allied himself closely with Benjamin Wesley Kilgore. Kilgore, a Mississippi-born chemist, directed the North Carolina agricultural experiment station at Raleigh. Bagley was the ideal citizen-client, eager for the chemist's mastery of soil and seed. Kilgore was also the first director of the state's Cooperative Extension Service, a branch of the U.S. Department of Agriculture—the supervisor, that is, of pioneer county agents who brought twentieth-century agronomy to the grass roots. As such Benjamin Kilgore might be monumentalized as a father of what is called modern in a state that had been called backward.[1]

Kilgore was also, however, a man ambitious for personal wealth, perhaps excessively so. He had come to North Carolina in 1899 to assume the position of state chemist. Within four years Kilgore had also associated himself—as vice president—with the Standard Turpentine Company of New York City. In a brochure of the period, Standard claimed to be "the owners of the first process yet discovered by which pure white turpentine of standard grade is obtained direct from ... [longleaf pine] dead wood." Indeed, the company promised "MILLIONS in Dead Pine.... There is more money in the dead long leaf pine than in the virgin trees." Standard owned the key to wealth for countless woodlot owners down the South Atlantic Coast. So the company offered "partnerships" to all proprietors who agreed to construct distilleries on their properties. New York would send a chemist with the secret extraction process. Benjamin Kilgore's name on corporate literature conferred the illusion, at least, of authenticity.[2]

Standard Turpentine's process is not revealed in Kilgore's papers. For some time, however, wood chemists have known how to extract turpentine from longleaf stumps and deadwood: Both are chipped (rather like wood for pulp and paper manufacture), then cooked to separate components, including turpentine. The procedure is appropriate—even advised, today—when labor to collect resin from live trees is scarce and expensive. In Kilgore's time, labor remained relatively plentiful and cheap, so even if Standard's formula were legitimate, the venture would retain an odor of dubiousness.[3]

Kilgore, a credentialed scientist and public official, was useful to the New Yorkers in their targeted market. In their recruitment of a corporate president, however, Standard's investors scored a coup. He was Thomas Dixon, Jr., indubitably the most famous living Carolinian, probably the most famous southerner, of the time. Owners of pinelands would recognize and trust a native son, presumably, even though Dixon had left his home state. He had become a Baptist minister in the big city itself. But Dixon's name was already associated with literary bestsellerdom. His *Leopard's Spots* (1902) was a cruelly provocative, racist formula, and Dixon followed it with a sequel called *The Clansman* (1905). Dixon's work encoded and nationalized a violent neo-Confederate negrophobia. The filmmaker D. W. Griffith would create his 1915 masterpiece, *The Birth of a Nation*, largely from Dixon's material. In 1903, meanwhile, Dixon assured Kilgore that "All is well" with Standard Turpentine in New York. Less than a year later, however, Dixon grew impatient with the company's demands. "I am utterly disgusted with the details of the management of this business," he confessed, "and wish to give my entire time to my literary work." Dixon offered his 183 shares in Standard to Kilgore at par and disappeared from the scheme.[4]

Kilgore continued his association with Standard Turpentine at least until 1908. After that the company may itself have disappeared; but its existence, however brief, reflected more than aspects of the characters of Dixon and Kilgore. Standard Turpentine's New York alchemists simultaneously resembled Yankee entrepreneurs of the older sort and modern experts heralding a new age. Like the postbellum lumbermen, they would descend upon poor people occupying landscapes soon to be ruined. But like twentieth-century corporate experts, they offered shortsighted hope of better living through chemistry. Both meanings of Standard's historical place are, to me, filled with pathos. An additional, mythic, dimension disturbs more. For if, as in ancient belief, the cutting of live trees signified humans' own mortality, the floating of logs the transport of corpses, what are we to make of Standard's secret formula?[5] Resurrection? I think not. Other early-twentieth-century experts had less bizarre plans, perhaps, for southern forests.

There was good reason, by 1906, for Maryland to become a "progressive" state—to tax its citizens to hire experts to measure and manage its dwindling forests, with a view to conservation and sustainability. For Maryland was becoming (statistically) an urban state. Only 35 percent of its area—about two million acres—remained forested, providing hardly a third of the state's requirements in timber. Maryland had, in short, a wood deficit, rendering it dependent on Virginia and other timber-surplus states. What to do, then? No one seems seriously to have considered a willful reversal of historical trend: deurbanization and reforestation. Rather, Maryland's first state forester, Fred Wilson Besley (b. 1872), proposed to manipulate the surviving two million acres. With modern scientific management, he asserted, "the yield might eventually be increased three to four times as much per acre." European agronomy applied to forests—the German system associated with Theodore Roosevelt and especially with his chief forester, Gifford Pinchot—had come to the Middle Atlantic.[6]

Maryland's deficit was actually long known. Back in 1879 the federal Census Bureau had conducted a national tree count and had published its report in an unprecedented special volume of the decennial census the following year. The bureau estimated forest density in terms of potential fuel—cords per acre. Surviving woods in Maryland's upper Tidewater counties, on both sides of the Chesapeake, had very low densities—one to three cords per acre. The most heavily forested sections of the state—the southern Eastern and Western Shores, and the Appalachian highlands—had much higher densities: about five to ten and thirty-plus cords per acre, respectively. The state's cooperage industry (barrel stave–making), formerly so important, was nearly dead, except in western Maryland; but even in the highlands the cooperages bought logs from out of state. Twenty years later, the Maryland Geological Survey cooperated with a federal Forestry Bureau survey of Allegany County; then the survey itself studied several more counties in central and eastern Maryland. Predictably, the state's forests were less dense than in 1880. Now, however, public officials (and perhaps the public as well) were eager to intervene, to *do* something.[7]

In 1906 the legislature created a state Board of Forestry headed by a state forester. Besley began work in July, virtually alone. He was to be professor—to educate the public, especially owners of small woodlots, in scientific forestry. He would encourage the private planting of commercial trees. He was to cooperate with the Geological Survey in further studies. And he was to institute fire protection, the heart of his profession's catechism. To this end the state appointed about fifty part-time forest wardens. They watched for, reported, and helped suppress fires. But the state paid the whole group of wardens only $25.33 during the second half of 1907. (The legislature had aimed to force individuals and corporations responsible for starting fires to pay the costs of extinguishing them.)[8] A small yet significant start.

By 1908 and 1909 Maryland had 60 part-time forest wardens and provided about $200 a year to compensate them. In 1915 there were 135 wardens, and Besley completed a superb survey of the state's forests, county by county. By this year, too, Maryland had established a state nursery "primarily for the growing of forest planting stock which would be of the standard kinds for commercial planting." Citizens and corporations in Maryland might purchase seedlings by the thousands at below-market prices. Besley was particularly interested in serving the paper industry, which needed good, fast-growth pine. Much of eastern Maryland was covered with scrub ("jack") pines, which were commercially useless. The loblolly might be the perfect tree, but it was native only to the lower Eastern Shore and the southernmost Western Shore counties. Besley directed the state nursery to specialize in loblollies, then successfully experimented with the reseeding of northern coastal counties, on both state land and private farms.[9]

The climax of Besley's promotion of loblollies came in 1923, when the Board of Forestry published Joshua A. Cope's *Loblolly Pine in Maryland: A Handbook for Growers and Users*. There was a second substantial printing in 1925; another, with a supplement, appeared in 1926. The volume was well produced, with illustrations, tables, and maps. The tree's odd name, Cope explained, derived from the Gulf states, where moist depressions in the land were called loblollies. There the tree flourished, as well as along the South Atlantic coast, up to the Maryland counties southeast of Washington, D.C. Cope hoped to demonstrate, however, that loblollies might be introduced farther up the Chesapeake shorelines, approximately doubling the species' extent in the state. By the time the handbook entered its second printing, however, the state forester had identified the major obstacle tree farmers would encounter—the labor-intensive business of eliminating deciduous competition with pines where pines were not the natural climax tree. Pesky "hardwood undergrowth . . . springs up," he wrote, "crowding out any young pines that may have started." Decades would pass before chemical herbicides would appear, making monoculture sure in both agriculture and forestry. In the meantime, Maryland's program must be deemed a huge success, and a model for the lackadaisical commonwealths to the south. Besley's state never became self-sufficient in wood—an absurdly chauvinistic goal from the start. Yet despite continued urbanization, then runaway suburbanization, Maryland's forests in 1980 were almost exactly the same size as in 1910—somewhat more than two million acres. The loblolly was well established as an introduced species. And a large proportion of the state's woodlands was held by corporations, facilitating the wise management forestry professionals loved.[10]

At the beginning of the twentieth century, neither Virginia nor North Carolina had need to introduce loblollies, and there was as yet no pulp/paper industry in either state. Between the James and Albemarle Sound, the national tree census of 1880 had recorded a forest density exceeding southeastern Maryland's—about ten to twenty cords per acre. Virtually all of this woodland was a "second-growth" assemblage of pines and oaks. W. W. Ashe's excellent survey of eastern Carolina, published in 1894, provided much more detail. Ashe took note, for instance, of the extinction of the longleaf pine "over large tracts lying to the north of the Neuse river[,] which were formerly occupied either exclusively by this pine or by mixed forests of it and hardwoods and the loblolly pine." He blamed excessive turpentining, lumbering, and burning for pasture; open-range husbandry—especially of hogs; and the loblolly's opportunistic propensities—its lighter, easily dispersed seed and its quick growth. For the loblolly was becoming dominant everywhere, standing over the ruins of the old naval stores industry. "That [longleafs] ever occupied much of the land might be questioned," Ashe observed, "but for the tar-kiln mounds with which these counties are studded, the land having now a heavy growth of loblolly pine, and the mounds even bearing trees of this latter species two or three feet in diameter." The phenomenon repeated itself in the Dismal Swamp, a different environment. There, Ashe wrote, industrialists had largely mined out swamp hardwoods during the 1880s. Loblollies— gold to Marylanders but, for the moment, almost weeds to a Carolinian— invaded to take their place. The pines were so remarkably regenerative, Ashe figured, that although sawmilling in the Dismal was "not one-half of what it was ten years ago . . . there remains not less than 25,000 acres of merchantable pine" in the Carolina part of the great swamp.[11]

By 1910 North Carolina, too, was becoming progressive. The state Geological and Economic Survey (which had published Ashe's report) included the office of state forester. The occupant of that office, J. S. Holmes, wished especially to fight forest fires; but he had neither the authorization nor the funding. Holmes and other officers of the survey did have constituencies, however: the tiny corps of professional foresters, especially at the Biltmore estate near Asheville, where Gifford Pinchot had begun his career; organized lumber corporations — Roper & Company, Camp Manufacturing, and other members of the North Carolina Pine Association; and women's clubs interested in nature trails and forest preservation. So the survey initiated organization of the North Carolina Forestry Association (NCFA), which was formed in 1911. The NCFA lobbied the state legislature four years for a forest fire control act. In 1915 the General Assembly finally enacted a toothless law, without appropriation for enforcement. Eastern Carolina, where purposeful woods-burning accounted (according to the NCFA) for "nine-tenths of all the losses" to fire in the state, was the particular enemy of modern forestry.[12]

Yet it was the Albemarle country that produced the chief enemy of the woods-burners and, as it turned out, of the open-range husbandmen, too. This was Dr. E. J. Griffen, who represented Chowan County in the assembly's lower house. In 1917 Griffen urged upon the NCFA "the close relation of the free ranging of cattle to forest fire" — that is, men fired woods to open land to sun and promote grass for their cattle — and he pressed for support of his "statewide stock law bill" before the General Assembly. North Carolina finally closed the range by law the following year. The legislature also finally succumbed to its forester and the NCFA, too, and created the office of chief forest fire warden. W. Darrow Clark, who occupied that position during the 1920s, devoted himself to scourging the old culture of burning; he declared in one circular that incinerating woods actually destroyed soil fertility by consuming humus. Clark's hands were full, for by the time he assumed office, the boll weevil had reached the northeasternmost limit of cotton culture, and Carolinians — especially those in the east — were, like their Lower South brethren, firing woods next to their crop fields in the belief that weevils wintered there. Or so Clark was informed by the Department of Agriculture's county agents (more experts).[13] But despite such persisting struggles between forces of light and darkness, North Carolina had embraced the principles of forestry, and the old culture was in full retreat.

Virginia trailed. In 1879, while midwestern forests were being clear-cut, Virginia lumbermen harvested about 300,000,000 board feet. Thirty years later, when national production had shifted to the South and the West Coast, Virginia sent 2,100,000,000 board feet off to market — a historical peak for the state, never again equaled. Seventy percent was pine; hardwoods came from first-growth forests in Appalachian counties. Two years later (1911), Congress passed the Weeks Act, to protect watershed forests (especially in the East) through public purchase and cooperative fire control. Virginia still had no bureaucratic forestry and no political will to cooperate and thus did not respond to Weeks. In 1914, at last, Virginia's General Assembly created the Division of Forestry within the state Geological Commission. The "division" was to be another one-man bureau. Chapin Jones assumed the office of state forester early in 1915; and, typically, his task was to act as another virtually penniless antifire Jeremiah. The Weeks Act provided funds for a few fire patrolmen in the more vulnerable hardwood counties of the state's southwestern area. The assembly had given counties the option of matching meager state and federal support. Few did. Norfolk County was a rare exception in the low country. In 1916 corporate woodlands owners in southwestern Virginia cooperated with Jones in establishing more fire patrols. But as late as 1925, only 53 of Virginia's 100 counties had volunteered to join in the state-sponsored fire suppression program. Still, by that date the state's forester had been able to accomplish two goals that did not require counties' cooperation. Virginia planted its first tree nursery in 1917, recognizing that the enormous clear-cuts of the century's first decade needed human intervention to be remedied. And during the early 1920s the division sponsored publication of forest studies, including one of the white cedar in Dismal Swamp.[14] Neither success equaled the scope of Maryland's state forestry; but now Virginia, too, was slipping into the hands of experts.

It was the lumber industry (particularly the larger corporations)—not the public and state government—that had the greatest stake in fire control, reforestation, and the rest of the canon of modern forestry. So it was industrial associations that most encouraged the profession. Governments generally followed, usually at the urging of industry. In the South the ultimate trade group was the Southern Pine Association (SPA), organized early in the century by John Henry Kirby and other Gulf Coast lumbermen. During the 1920s the SPA undertook an eastward and northward expansion; it reached the Carolinas and Virginia about 1931–32. Largely owing to the initiative of the Camp Manufacturing Company, the old North Carolina Pine Association agreed to dissolve itself into the SPA. In return, SPA officers agreed to locate a regional office in Norfolk.[15]

The Camps and other large dealers were now well positioned to govern their industry. The big lumbermen hoped to limit production and raise prices —squeezing out small operators, who seldom supported forestry or joined trade groups. Their best opportunity came in 1933, when Congress passed the National Industrial Recovery Act (NIRA). The legislation aimed to achieve recovery from the Great Depression through government/industry planning. Each industry would have its "production code." The SPA became an official "administrative agency" within the Lumber Code Authority. J. L. Camp, Jr., served on Virginia's NIRA board and on the authority's Control Committee. Alas for big lumber, the Supreme Court invalidated Congress's enabling legislation, and the structure collapsed. Not the SPA, however, which continued to set standards and restrain trade rather effectively. The New Deal was hardly a failure, in the meantime. For through the Civilian Conservation Corps and other agencies, thoroughgoing fire protection came at last to forests throughout the country. Thousands of fire-watch towers went up, and thousands of miles of fire roads were created in private as well as public forests. States including Virginia and North Carolina eagerly adopted federal "Keep Green" public education programs.[16]

This happy victory for forestry happened to coincide with the dim origin of another momentous change (although one that would not be obvious until the 1960s)—the shift of the pulp and paper industry to the South. Before World War II virtually all newsprint in the United States was manufactured from Canadian spruce. Southern pine, it was thought, was much too resinous to make anything but yellow paper and kraft—that is (in Swedish and German), a "strong" material such as cardboard, for boxing. And newsprint as well as kraft were made outside the South. In 1913, for instance, an Ohio kraft manufacturer, Fox Paper of Lockland (near Cincinnati), established a pulp mill at West Point, Virginia. (West Point, north of Williamsburg, at the source of the York River, had excellent rail connections to the West.) Fox bought thousands of cords of pine from local farmers and lumbermen and hired a chemist named Elis Olsson—a veteran papermaker both in his native Sweden and in Canada—to oversee institution of the cheap (and malodorous) new sulfate process of pulping pine. Then West Point pulp was poured into railroad tankers, which transported the heavy, batterlike material to Fox's kraft machines in Lockland. Fox employed two hundred people in the new West Point mill, and local woodlands owners earned cash. Still, southern chauvinists—foresters and chemists among them—fumed over the region's persisting status as natural resource supplier. "They knew we were behind the rest of the country," said a forester, "and when you came right down to it, the reason was that we were a colony. We shipped all of our product out to be processed somewhere else and all we got out of it was stumpage and loading it on cars." Dr. Charles Herty, a Georgia chemist, did more than fume. During the 1930s Herty demonstrated in his laboratory that *young* southern pines were essentially resin-free and an excellent (and cheaper) material for the making of white paper. Herty predicted correctly, too, that papermaking of all sorts would come to the source of these undervalued trees.[17]

Fox Paper, in the meantime, put its West Point pulp mill up for sale in 1918. Elis Olsson joined a group of New York financiers to make the purchase, and seven difficult years of development were then under way. Olsson was determined to make the new organization, called Chesapeake Corporation, into a papermaker as well as pulper of southern pine; and he was equally determined to make Chesapeake the owner of its own forest supplies. In 1920 the New Yorkers withdrew, and Olsson found bankers and a partner in Richmond. Chesapeake would supply pulp to the Albemarle Paper Company, a confusingly named kraft enterprise in Virginia's capital city, only forty miles to the west, as it gradually acquired and installed its own "big machine" to manufacture kraft paper. Chesapeake thus became a "Virginia" corporation; and the Olsson family settled into Romancoke, near West Point, on the Pamunkey River. The estate once belonged to the Custis family, then to Robert E. Lee, Jr., and it lay not many miles downriver from Marlbourne, where Edmund Ruffin rested. Chesapeake began to make kraft and profits in 1925 and to build its forest reserve, which reached almost 24,000 acres by 1929. The onset of the national depression tried the pioneer papermaker, but by the end of 1934, Chesapeake paid dividends to its shareholders and Christmas bonuses to managers and hourly workers alike. Olsson was able and amenable, then, two years later, when J. L. Camp, Jr., came to West Point with a deal.[18]

The Camps had themselves accumulated enormous forest properties and the expertise to reseed them with fast-growing loblollies. Their huge Franklin sawmill, furthermore, produced enormous wastes of sawdust and chips. Might not both the reserves and especially the wastes be put to work—turned into pulp, then into kraft? Chesapeake had papermaking experience and access to Richmond creditors friendly to the industry. Olsson interceded with his bankers and partners at Albemarle Paper. Stocks were exchanged, and the limited partnership of Chesapeake-Camp Corporation came into being. Olsson family members trained in paper chemistry and engineering came to Franklin to oversee design, construction, and installation of the Camps' big machine by the Blackwater. Paper production was underway in 1938. Two years later Olsson pulled out; he and his partners were worried about corporate governance and especially about the market implications of new wars

Union Camp sawmill/pulpmill/papermill, Franklin, Virginia, 1990 (Photo by the author)

in Europe and Asia. Separately, both Chesapeake and Camp continued to innovate and expand, and both were well positioned to take advantage of national economic growth after World War II. It was Camp, however, that realized the Georgia chemist Herty's dream. During the 1950s Camp constructed a bleach plant alongside its new papermaking machines and went into the white paper business.[19]

During the war, meanwhile, Virginia's forest products tycoons further organized themselves. Virginia Forests, Inc., grew out of a 1943 conclave at Richmond's exclusive Commonwealth Club. Among the principals were Elis Olsson of Chesapeake Corporation, Garland Gray of Gray Lumber, H. C. Parrish of Richmond Cedar Works (Norfolk), Thomas B. Stanley (a future governor) of Stanley Furniture, and Hugh Camp and J. L. Camp, Jr. Virginia Forests would have a full-time executive director whose tasks were all promotional—publishing a quarterly magazine, *Virginia Forests*; urging expansion of Division of Forestry programs, especially the nursery; and conducting "forest safety" programs in schools (for example, "Keep Virginia Green"). Virginia Forests aimed to influence public policy, of course, with legislative agenda for both Richmond and Washington. They agreed to support a congressional lobby, but the trade group's main concern was state taxes and assessments. Senator Garland Gray was their great spokesman, the man singly most responsible for nurturing forest products, ultimately, as the state's most important rural industry.[20]

The North Carolina Forestry Association, a group rather broader of constituencies, nonetheless declared in 1944 that "state control" was essential to the well-being and prosperity of Carolina woodlands and human citizens alike. Government alone could impose safety and other standards upon so many interests, especially small woodlot owners. Garland Gray and Virginia Forests, Inc., agreed absolutely. In 1946 the Virginia General Assembly passed the Forestry Service to Landowners Act, authorizing state foresters to survey, evaluate, and mark private timber for marketing. Fees for such services would be used for Division of Forestry fire and reforestation programs. Then, in 1948, Gray introduced more important legislation, the Forest Products Tax Bill. Here the industry (through Gray) offered itself for taxation—albeit modest—in order to produce an additional $100,000 per year exclusively for the division's programs. (By such means the industry partly avoided taxation for the state's general fund.) Other Gray-sponsored laws toughened penalties on forest arsonists.[21]

Gray's legislation happened to appear at a moment two federal scientists perceived as a "crisis" in southeastern forestry. Thomas Lotti and R. D. McCulley, silviculturists at the Forest Service's experiment station in Asheville, North Carolina, periodized and detailed the region's forest history in a brief narrative that represented Forest Service understanding and remains useful. Between about 1600 and 1900, they wrote, settlers adopted and perpetuated Indian fire culture, burning forests to make crop fields, then abandoning them. Three centuries of this practice brought about pine dominance not only in the coastal plain but in much of the Piedmont as well. Then began, about 1900, the great cut-down of conifers, averaging ten million board feet annually. By midcentury the "crisis" was manifest: Hardwoods had returned—doubling their area in Mississippi, where clear-cutting had been most draconian. In coastal Virginia low-grade hardwoods already occupied 20 percent of what had been pine sites, and they were imperious. What had happened? Loggers left deciduous trees behind while taking down all the conifers, including those that might have reseeded cut-over lands. Agriculture had been either stabilized or abandoned. Fire, death to hardwoods, had been suppressed. What to do? Lotti and McCulley were committed monoculturists, and they offered the already-familiar formula: Loggers must leave seed loblollies; there should be more loblolly nurseries, public and private; foresters must persuade small woodlot owners to participate in replanting programs.[22]

Corporate loblolly nursery, New Kent County, Virginia, 1985 (Photo by the author)

Triumphant at last on the question of fire suppression, foresters and the industrialists were now free to focus on the crisis of southern pines. The Maryland model from the beginning of the century became Southwide policy at least as early as 1945. That is, replanting was monocultural—loblollies and more loblollies. The policy favored pulp- and papermakers, as opposed to lumbermen and furniture manufacturers. For as Chesapeake and Camp enlarged their forest reserves, both corporations also established their own loblolly nurseries for replanting—Chesapeake below the York in New Kent County, Camp at Capron in Southampton and down in Hertford County near Murfreesboro. From then on, government nursery seedlings were increasingly designed for smaller landowners' lots, which also served the pulpmakers. More state incentives strengthened all segments of the industry. In 1971 Virginia imposed a severance tax on trees cut—with yields matched from general revenues—to subsidize reforestation of private woodlots. The same year, the General Assembly protected industrial woodlands from "fair market value" local taxes; such property would be taxed according to use. Some counties and cities did not oblige, so in 1977 the assembly in effect overrode noncooperative localities. A principal sponsor of this legislation was state senator Elmon Gray, son and heir of Garland Gray. North Carolina and other wood industrial states had similar protective laws.[23]

The pursuit of loblolly monoculture throughout the South finally, inevitably, produced a revision of the U.S. Forest Service's canonical struggle against fire. It had been a Yankee canon, anyway; European and then Yale-trained foresters had sought to prevent holocausts in familiar deciduous forests. Gradually and with difficulty, within the profession, southerners (mostly) educated their brethren about pine. One of these southerners was Kenneth B. Pomeroy, who in 1949 worked for the Forest Service around Franklin, Virginia. A thoroughgoing monoculturist himself, Pomeroy asked an instrumental question: "Can Hardwoods Be Controlled?" The problem was deciduous plants' regenerative advantage over conifers: "Abundant pine seed crops do *not* occur every year," Pomeroy wrote, "but at intervals of three to five years. Hardwoods, on the other hand, sprout readily, and some produce seed prolifically." Pine monoculturists must garden, then. They must scarify land—the disturbances of logging were helpful; actual cultivation was yet more effective. They could kill hardwoods by grubbing, cutting, girdling, or poisoning. The best—and easily the cheapest—method, however, would be "prescribed burning." This expression referred to a purposeful, controlled burning of deciduous underbrush and understory, removing competitors and rendering pine forests neater and more accessible to harvesters at the appropriate time. Pines' bark is naturally resistant to fire, too; and foresters were reminded that some conifers—notably the longleaf pine—released seed only in fires.[24]

During the 1950s, then, the Forest Service, its state counterparts, and some woodlands corporations began prescribed burning in southern pinelands. (Fire prevention in deciduous forests remained canonical.) By this time, however, agrochemistry had been applied to forestry and become the primary means of practicing monoculture. Public and private foresters sprayed DDT from trucks and planes to kill insect pests. More important were the postemergent herbicides 2,4-D and 2,4,5-T. These not only killed deciduous competition in the coastal plains, natural home to pine- and mixed-pine forests; they also turned (or returned, if Lotti and McCulley were correct) vast acreages of the southern Piedmont, where hardwoods are naturally dominant, into loblolly plantations. By 1965, chemistry offered small woodlot owners, for only $35, a hand-held weapon called Tree-ject, with which one might inject "2,4-D amine undiluted" into nearly four thousand hardwoods per gallon. The manufacturer claimed that the tool "Reduces labor cost up to 1/3." During the 1970s the federal Environmental Protection Agency banned DDT, then the herbicides. Virginia Forests, Inc., protested both governmental intrusions into private business. Replacements were found, nonetheless.

Most important among these was an herbicide called Roundup, which the Virginia Division of Forestry began to spray in 1981. Although it was no match for 2,4-D and 2,4,5-T, foresters still thought Roundup "reasonably effective" in killing the loblolly's competitors.[25]

Thus did the hinterland of the old James-Albemarle subregion—along with vast stretches elsewhere in the world—become plantation country beyond the imagination of the looniest champion of the antebellum Cotton Kingdom. The geography and political economy of the pine plantations not only define rural culture today but also profoundly configure public life generally. For where the loblollies spread in rows for miles and miles, human populations remain low and, directly or indirectly, dependent upon corporate organizers and owners of the countryside. The social spectrum retains a less-than-ideal shape, with a weak middle class. In such places political office is more likely to be handed down, father to son, than vigorously contested for. The hinterland resembles much of Mississippi, and also Maine, Wyoming, Montana, and Alaska, other resource-extraction landscapes with skewed social spectrums and colonial politics.[26]

During the 1940s the populations of Norfolk and Portsmouth took off. Suburbanization overtook neighboring Princess Anne and Norfolk counties, which by the 1960s disappeared into the new and uncentered cities of Virginia Beach and Chesapeake. Suffolk did not mushroom; but out of ambition and perhaps fear of Chesapeake, it subsumed Nansemond County. Hopewell, an Eppes farm at the northwestern corner of our subregion until 1911, reached a population of 23,471 in 1970. Nowhere else, however, could one find a settlement much larger than sleepy town status. Elizabeth City sheltered 14,069 in 1970, almost exactly the same number as a decade before. Edenton's population remained under 5,000, Ahoskie's a little more than that; Hertford's was 2,023, Murfreesboro's 3,508, in 1970.[27]

Most hinterland counties had no cities—Isle of Wight (Smithfield hardly qualifies), Surry, Sussex, Currituck, Camden, Perquimans, Gates, Bertie, Northampton. Southampton's Franklin had only 6,880 people in 1970. Nearly all the hinterland counties—with or without cities—*lost* population, too, during the 1940s, 1950s, and 1960s. Bertie, for instance, always one of the most populous counties, lost almost 6,000 between 1940 and 1970; its population density (people per square mile) fell from 37.8 to 29.4. Camden, always one of the smallest, had exactly thirteen more citizens in 1970 than in 1940. Gates County had 10,060 souls in 1940, 8,524 in 1970; its population density declined from 29.3 to 25.3. Isle of Wight and Nansemond counties grew

Loblolly plantation by US 460, Sussex County, Virginia, 1990 (Photo by the author)

somewhat; Southampton's population remained flat for three decades. Surry and Sussex counties lost 5 and 8 percent, respectively; and since both were entirely rural, their population densities declined proportionately, as well.[28]

The loblolly's advance correlates with humans' withdrawal or stagnation. By 1957, for example, when a Virginia state agency conducted a county-by-county tree census, the forests of Sussex were already 51 percent loblolly; Surry's were 52 percent, Isle of Wight's 57 percent. A dozen years later, Virginia Forests, Inc., trumpeted the planting of 54,685,710 commercial tree seedlings in Virginia. They did not provide data by county, but reported that of the enormous total, 50,472,760 were loblollies. Unsurprisingly, 30,055,000 of the seedlings were "Industrial plantings on company lands"; and of these, 21,960,000 were set by pulp and paper corporations.[29] Some portion of the 24,630,710 seedlings not planted on corporate plantations may have gone into public land, but one must assume that most were planted on smaller woodlots belonging to families and individuals. If this is indeed the case, then foresters and wood products companies had made solid progress in directing the sector that had ever been so unresponsive to modern land management.

Or had they? During the 1980s, business was brisk throughout the southern pinelands. Foreign demand for lumber soared. American annual per capita paper consumption reached 650 pounds (compared with a world average of 93 pounds). But foresters and industry and government planners worried about future supplies. Between 1980 and 1985, the number of live pines in the South actually decreased. An American Forestry Association researcher was certain that small landowners—that is, those with one hundred acres or less—were not reforesting, despite a cornucopia of tax incentives and free management services. Why not? Conceivably, southern country folks persisted in their historic indifference to agronomy, with its attendant disciplines. The researcher assumed, however, that capital remained the principal obstacle, despite all the public subsidies: bulldozing and preparation of seedbed, $50 to $200 per acre; herbicide treatments, $25 to $100 per acre; loblolly seedlings, $224 for twenty acres. Such costs, not to mention the physical labor and paperwork, deterred small woods-owners, who collectively possessed 70 percent of the South's forests.[30]

The southern problem attributed to the small-private sector obtained in the James-Albemarle subregion, too, as Norfolk business writers worried in 1991. Of ten counties (plus two county-sized cities) in Virginia where more timber was cut than planted, four (plus both cities—Chesapeake and Suffolk) were in the low country south of the James. Only in Isle of Wight County and the city of Virginia Beach were there more seedlings growing than trees harvested.[31]

By this time, too, inevitable tensions between papermakers and lumbermen had erupted. Paper corporations cut out loblolly plantations about every twenty-five years. "One of the most unproductive situations you can have," said a Chesapeake forester, "is a mature stand of timber." He meant, of course, timber too large to be pulp bolts. Independent lumbermen, on the other hand, were hard-pressed to find suitable mature trees. "Our timber is getting smaller and smaller," complained Thomas Coxe, co-owner of Ashton-Lewis Lumber in Gatesville, North Carolina, early in 1991. "We feel as though the paper companies have tangled up the lumber. We feel like we're at odds." Coxe hoped for cooperation between sawmillers such as Ashton-Lewis and giant papermakers such as his neighbors, Union Camp of Franklin. They might "swap" timber to assure prosperity for both.[32]

Neighborly swapping might untangle somewhat the conflicting interests of papermakers and sawmillers. It will not undo the hinterland's fundamental organization into plantations and its dependence on chemically maintained monoculture. Nor, of course, would corporate neighboring disturb corporatism itself. For rural people between the James and Albemarle Sound (and beyond) rely excessively upon the wood products companies—especially the Franklin giant—for employment, support of public services, and leadership.

Yet so long as the companies are "good corporate citizens," it is argued, all is well. Paternalism, it is assumed, is inseparable from plantation economies.

The most enlightened paternalists, it is further suggested, are never absentee. The Camp family serves to illustrate. For almost three-quarters of a century, three of the original brothers, then their descendants, lived in Franklin and ran Camp Manufacturing Company. They were the largest contributors to church building funds and nearly every other charity. They built houses and neighborhoods. P. D. also built a hunting camp — Camp P. D. — in his woods near Como in North Carolina. But then on Sunday, 29 May 1956 — "Black Sunday," it was called in Franklin — old J. L., Jr., called supervisors in to inform them that he and Hugh Camp had negotiated a merger with the Union Bag and Paper Company of New York. The Camp family held 74 percent of the stock in the Franklin manufacturer. Camps would serve on Union Camp's board for many years, but the family had surrendered control in order to gain size, credit, and listing on the New York Stock Exchange. The merged corporate headquarters would be in New York City.[33]

A few Camps lingered, but by the 1980s no one with that name remained with the company. The James-Albemarle hinterland, then, might have become a counterpart of Maine, where five absentee wood products corporations control almost half the total land area and all the state's rivers, and where pulp and paper workers are often in rebellion against unsympathetic, far-away bosses. There was, in fact, a strike in Franklin after the merger. For the most part, however, Union Camp has nurtured its Franklin plant, which remains a significant division of the corporation. (Union Camp now has manufacturing facilities in twenty-two American states and operations of some sort in twenty-two other countries.) The merger permitted Camp to complete installation of a fourth papermaking machine in 1956 and add a fifth in 1966. Two years later the corporation spent nearly $60 million on new pulping facilities and other infrastructure; then came a sixth machine, this one the world's largest maker of fine paper, in 1970. By the 1980s the entire pulping and papermaking process was computer-directed, and the huge sawmill attached to the plant employed lasers to guide sawblades. All the Franklin operations provided work for about 2,600 men and women in 1987; their pay amounted to more than $70 million annually.[34]

Good corporate citizenship arguably begins with technological sophistication, profitability, and the maintenance and growth of local employment. In this sense Union Camp directors — now headquartered in Wayne, New Jersey — have shone. Managers and technicians at the Franklin division are, in the main, representative of the mobile cadres who run most corporations.

Union Camp encourages community service, however, so the Camp family's former role in civic order has been competently assumed by others. The company has also been eager to accommodate the sensibilities of the Age of Ecology. Although blessed with abundant water from the Blackwater River and wells, the Franklin pulp mill reuses water as many as twenty times, then aerates it in a relatively safe holding pond before releasing it into the Blackwater. (And fishing in the river south of Franklin is fine, I am informed.) Papermaking is sulfurous, and Union Camp has invested in electrostatic precipitators to abate odors. At least as important, in 1993 the papermaker substituted ozone (a form of oxygen) for chlorine in its bleaching towers and undertook to use 30 percent recycled paper. Eliminating chlorine cost Union Camp $108 million. This investment and the resort to recycled paper were, as an executive put it, "market-driven" decisions; but the Franklin plant still scored well with environmentalists. Twenty years earlier the corporation had crafted another public relations masterpiece when it donated to the Nature Conservancy its entire holdings in the Dismal Swamp—the old Washington Entry. It was the largest wildlife preserve ever given to the public. (The donation also gained the corporation a tax advantage worth more than $12 million.) Later Union Camp gave the Nature Conservancy a 318-acre tract in southern Isle of Wight County called the Zuni Pine Barrens. This land is site to the last known remnants of standing longleaf pines in Virginia, as well as to other rare plant species. The Nature Conservancy conveyed the tract to Old Dominion University of Norfolk, which renamed it the Blackwater Ecologic Preserve and established a research program there for faculty and students.[35]

At the end of the twentieth century, then—a century into the age of forestry—the genius of Union Camp at Franklin has been to foment change in order to avoid structural change. The prevailing structure indeed works, in its own fashion. It is a version of what is called civilization, in the James-Albemarle country and many other places.

EPILOGUE

NATURE'S MORBIDITY AND

HYDRAULIC CONFOUNDMENTS

Nature offers to art the plastic hand. — *William Valentine, 1853*

Nature is a temple where living pillars
Sometimes let out confused words.
Man passes there through forests of symbols
Which observe him with a familiar gaze.
— *Charles Baudelaire,* Les fleurs du mal

V alentine had been depressed again when he wrote this line late in winter. Approaching fifty, still unmarried and without a sustaining law practice, he had retreated to Oak Lawn once more. His elderly father, long a widower, had moved to the home of his new bride, leaving Oak Lawn to his three bachelor sons. Then William's youngest brother brought his own bride to the old place. The middle brother soon departed with apparent good grace, and William grew uncomfortable. Finally he left the couple alone, returning to nearby Winton and trying desperately, one sees in his diary, to accommodate himself to life in this "dilapidated, antiquated partially deserted looking place." Winton, he reasoned, was "convenient" to the work he hoped to gain in "the upper and lower parts of" Hertford County. The dark, peaceful waters of the Chowan flowed past. The landscape about the town was "skirted by ravines and pyramids [i.e., hills] romantic and scenic." If only Winton itself measured up! Valentine seemed to wish for a local di Medici to sponsor reconstruction of the town, creating a built landscape at least compatible with the "plastic" natural one surrounding it: "Capital enterprise and taste could render Winton a beautiful spot," he wrote. Winton might, in other words, regenerate, emulating nature. Remembering William's detailed attentiveness to and joy in the natural world, one must think he meant more than seasonableness in his use of "plastic," however. He implied, I think, subtle as well as obvious beauty ("taste"), to be observed in isolated moments as well as in the processes of seasonableness, in small as well as large perspectives.[1] "Plastic" may also have suggested nature's susceptibility to tasteful management, vigilantly pursued—that is, gardening.

But Winton's reality and dim prospects only worsened poor William's depression: "Winton lies neglected, important only as the county seat."[2] And so poor Winton would remain, without plasticity of the sort Valentine dreamed, but in a marathon stagnation that continues even now. Today Winton is almost isolated. Humans travel along paved highways (US 13 and US 158) *around*, not through, the town, over the Chowan bridge north of the bleached remains of Valentine's little world. Those who make the effort to enter Winton find not the antiquated—not the eighteenth- and nineteenth-century restored buildings one sees downriver in Edenton—but simply the dilapidated. Only a few well-shaded, well-kept houses border the river's bank. On a visit one sultry July day, I sought Winton's public wharf—this so I might stand where William once hobbled to greet river packets bearing his newspapers and other word from the cosmopolitan world. At last, and with no little difficulty, I found Winton's one surviving wharf, and reverie evaporated. (I should have known better.) For what remains of Winton has long looked westward, to the highways, not eastward, to the river. The Chowan's "argosy" (as Valentine once put it) is reduced to tugboats and barges. The river has become one of Union Camp's supply lines, Winton's wharf one of many marshaling points for loblolly pulp bolts gathered in the hinterland.

So much for nature's plasticity. William Valentine never begrudged human agency in nature; he was a conservationist at heart—a would-be wise user of resources—long before the word was invented. Valentine probably never imagined that his premise of intelligent management would lead, inevitably it seems, to massive manipulation. (His somewhat older contemporary, Edmund Ruffin, did, of course.) To Valentine, I feel certain, nature's plasticity implied nature's own agency at least as much as its susceptibility to human will and ingenuity. Now, what was nascent has long been manifest. The greater plasticity is human will—and, ironically, humans have become rigidly unimaginative. They cut pulp bolts from forest plantations in Hertford and across the river in Gates, feeding Franklin through an artery called the Chowan River; but who apostrophizes "ravines and pyramids romantic and scenic"? William is sorely missed.

Half a century after Valentine yearned for nature's influence on art, sailing vessels still plied the Chowan, and Winton still had three wharfs. By one of the wharfs, boatmen dumped oyster shells that had been dredged downriver. The "huge pile," wrote a local historian, "kept its size for years...despite

Winton wharf on the Chowan River, with stacks of pulp boats, July 1990 (Photo by the author)

the fact that farmers were regularly hauling from it all over the county to use for fertilizer."[3] The mechanized harvesting of oysters had gone on since the 1880s, when Yankee entrepreneurs first appeared on Chesapeake Bay with labor-saving dredging technology. Submarine banks of dead, empty oyster shells—upon which infant oysters ("spats") attach themselves and depend for maturation—were diminished and destroyed; and to this day, oyster production has not recovered from the carnage. By the 1960s dredgers were required to return some shells, while state oyster commissions supervised the maintenance and reconstruction of shell banks. But many shells were sold to chicken feed manufacturers and cement-makers. Both fowl and construction engineers have need of calcareous matter, too.[4]

Hertford County farmers' use of oyster shells as fertilizer at the beginning of the twentieth century, meanwhile, is a matter of interest. For oyster shells, broken and ground roughly, are not exactly fossilized, but they resemble marl and had beneficial effect in Hertford beyond their high calcium content. Much of the county's soils were what geologists then called the Coxville type—poor, crusty, and compacted; so oyster shells must have served to render it finer, more friable. Coxvilles may have been what early-nineteenth-century Hertfordians called frog levels. William Valentine observed (in 1841) that "Many perhaps do not believe that their 'frog levels' can be made rich," but it had not been farmers' "habit to contemplate much the excellence of good farming," anyway. "They are incredulous as to its success on their poor land." So Coxville soils were considered waste, at best suitable for pasture. Applications of oyster shells improved pasture or permitted the expansion of commercial cultivation. Norfolk-type soils (covering 37 percent of Hertford County)—the sandy loams that were long the mainstay of crop-making in the subregion—had been Edmund Ruffin's target of marling reform, and surely oyster shells fixed nitrogen and improved yield.[5] So had Ruffin won his war for agronomy, posthumously, after all?

No and yes. In 1890 Richard Eppes reported to an agricultural journal his successful use of green-sand marl, a fertilizer degraded with sand; this marl was then mined commercially in Virginia and Maryland. Curiously, Julian M. Ruffin, Edmund's grandson and heir to half of his Marlbourne estate in Hanover County, reported to the same journal that his and his cousin Edmund III's farm had not been marled since the Civil War. Their crop fields did not seem to require it. I doubt that the grandfather's marling had wrought a permanent agronomic miracle. Rather, Marlbourne's continued productivity was more likely owing to applications of other fertilizers from a multitude of commercial offerings—guano, mined phosphates, ground bone from the vast abattoirs of Baltimore, and so on. There were so many—and so many of them larded with rocks and other fillers—that by 1890 Virginia and other states had begun to regulate fertilizers. The poor lands of the East sucked them up disproportionately, as we have already seen, and as early as 1900 the federal census bureau reported a portentous trend in farmers' cash investments in fertilizers. Hertford farmers spent $41,350 in 1899, an average of $23.13 each. The county's historian implied that local farmers stole from the Winton wharf oyster-shell pile. Even if they did pay, shells were likely a small portion of their costs.[6]

But Ruffin won, so to speak, in that his disciplined money-mindedness in farming became compelling, most obviously after about 1900. Years of declining commodity prices and the gradual constriction of the open range and accessible forests, and of growing farm tenancy, conspired to sort out those operators who were not prepared to live and work in a world Ruffin envisioned. Then, early in the twentieth century, commodity prices mended, encouraging the survivors and the agronomy educators. E. W. Gaither, the pioneer Hertford County agent of the federal Cooperative Extension Service, witnessed and vigorously assisted the "revolution" (as he named it) in rural folks' ways. Gaither thought that "scientific" agriculture's first glimmerings appeared "by 1900." He became part-time county agent in 1911, full-time in 1917. Gaither specialized in animals and campaigned from the start for closing the range so that fat, healthy, pure-bred cattle and hogs might thrive. He supervised installation of a dip vat to eradicate ticks in cattle and promoted an anti–hog cholera program. A home demonstration agent joined him in 1918; she educated farm wives in canning vegetables and meat and improving poultry production. The same year Gaither undertook 4-H work with farm children and started boys' "corn clubs" to promote improved production techniques among the next generation (as well as among their fathers). North Carolina's statewide fencing reform law enormously aided Gaither's labors. Thus advantaged, he invited a crisis he knew he would survive. One day (about 1920 or so), Gaither later wrote, he "made the remark before a group of farmers that a hog, to be profitable, should weigh two hundred pounds at six months of age. The farmers all laughed at the idea and said it could not be done." Gaither figured his assertion "had to be proven or the county agent would have been run out of the county." So he found a "demonstration" farmer with a sow and seven piglets "which were fed out and exhibited at County Fair"—all under Gaither's supervision—"and at six months of age weighed an average of 225 pounds." Fair-goers, he claimed, loved the demonstration pigpen as much "as any side show," and he "was allowed to remain" in Hertford County.[7]

The county fair was a fitting scene for Gaither's triumph. An established institution approximating harvest festivals, fairs had been notorious for cruel, nature-mocking amusements—freaks in many manifestations and the display and abuse of large animals such as tigers and bears. In North Carolina and other states, Christian ministers and agronomists sought to reform fairs by banning liquor and purging midways of salacious and brutish distractions, all to promote wholesome and prosperous rural family life. Virginia below the James, however—the city of Norfolk being the sole exception—apparently had no fairs at all during the late nineteenth century. In November 1889, when the Tidewater Agricultural and Mechanical Society held one at Franklin, the reformers filled a vacuum very admirably. There were exhibits of crops and animals, tools and machines, and edifying examples of fine arts imported from Richmond and Norfolk. Horse races were apparently well regulated and decorous. Gradually, the reformers had their way with fairs almost everywhere. By Gaither's prime (about the 1920s), fairs emphasizing agronomic achievement and family entertainment had become the norm.[8] The preachers and county and home demonstration agents deserve appropriate credit. But encroaching historical and market forces conspired with them. Reformed fairs are an apt signpost to what had become obvious to all who wished to remain in farming during the hard 1920s: Discipline yourself to the gospel of the experts—to scientific praxis, especially labor-saving technology—or get out.

Cotton and tobacco culture would remain profoundly labor-intensive and folkish until after World War II; but early on, peanuts—next to corn, the subregion's great staple—became transparently a business for businessmen. Between 1899 and 1902, Jesse Thomas Benthall (b. 1856) and Finton Finley Ferguson (b. 1849) tinkered in Hertford County with a mechanism to be used in the field to separate peanuts from their vines. Winning a patent in 1905, they set about manufacturing the machine in Murfreesboro. Then the partners separated—Benthall to Suffolk (later to Norfolk), where he established the Benthall Manufacturing Company, and Ferguson to Suffolk with his Ferguson Manufacturing Company. Theirs was the first generation of labor-saving equipment in peanuts; the equipment permitted a huge expansion in production at a time when rural population growth slowed and began to shrink. Businessmen at the next level—processing and distribution—responded appropriately, integrating their enterprise horizontally. Pembroke Decatur Gwaltney, Sr.—the subregion's first (oxymoronic) "Peanut King"—opened a cleaning plant and warehouse on the James at Smithfield in 1880. Later he and Augustus Bunkley incorporated the Gwaltney-Bunkley Peanut Company in Norfolk, but they returned to Smithfield after a fire destroyed their city plant. The new Gwaltney-Bunkley building rose four stories (with two elevators) behind their great wharf. A larger merger occurred in 1911, when Gwaltney-Bunkley joined American Peanut of Norfolk and Bain Peanut of Wakefield to form the American Peanut Corporation.[9]

There would be other mergers and other "peanut kings"—Planters came later. And more generations of peanut-harvesting machines also came, supplanting the Benthall-Ferguson stationary separator, ultimately, with mobile, combined operations. Farmers who survived the postwar blitz of costly labor-saving to tell their tales cheered every innovation. For peanuts' enormous requirements of labor at harvest remain a living nightmare to older proprietors. A Nansemond County farmer recalled grimly (in 1986) his harvest seasons during the 1950s and 1960s, before he acquired a peanut combine. "I would go to Suffolk," he said, "and pick 'em [i.e., black laborers] up off the street corners, uptown. Sometimes you'd get some good ones," but just as often, after a few hours, hands would stop and declare, "'I want you to pay me off.'" They had labored "long enough to get some wine," he figured, "and they want[ed] to go back" to Suffolk. The farmer would refuse to take them until evening. Men and women less preoccupied with cheap wine had by this time long decamped for Portsmouth, Norfolk, or other places of opportunity. World War II, declared a Camden County peanut farmer, was "like a total division" in the history of farm labor. So he, like the others, welcomed the new Massey Ferguson peanut-digging plow, the combine, then— perhaps best of all—chemical herbicides that obviated weed-hoeing.[10]

The agronomic dynamic that Ruffin and others had given momentum early in the nineteenth century now roared into orbit grandly—or crazily out of control, depending on one's perspective. The vaunted Green Revolution of the 1950s, 1960s, and afterward rested on human-engineered high-yield grain seeds. But agricultural chemistry was the great vector for the revolution's worldwide implementation. The general pesticide DDT, families and generations of more specific pesticides and fungicides, and a burgeoning variety of pre- and postemergent herbicides enabled farmers to achieve near-perfect crops of one commercial plant. Farming became as capital-intensive as manufacturing. Labor requirements, meanwhile, were fractioned and re-fractioned, while machines and mechanical attachments grew in size, cost, and functional specificity. When commodity prices were high (as with corn during the 1970s), the high-investment system of store-bought seed, chemi-cals, and machines discouraged crop rotation and soil conservation in favor of the perpetual cropping of one plant on the same fields. ("Continuous corn" was both a practice and a maxim until grain prices collapsed in 1980.) A new commercial fertilizer, another chemical, made this possible—at least in the short run: Farmers leased great tanks of anhydrous ammonia and sprayed it into their furrows of corn, cotton, soybeans, and so forth, along with ex-pensive seed, pesticides, and preemergent herbicides.[11]

Such investment alone encouraged larger and larger scale in farm-ing. Government commodity-support payments, too, disproportionately re-warded the largest operators, magnifying the phenomenon. This amounted to a dramatic second act in the long-term decline of farming in the sub-region. Agriculture, you will recall—in terms of number of farms and acre-age harvested—began to stagnate, then shrink, after about 1900, as the age of commercial forestry got underway. Now, after World War II, crop acre-age receded at a slower pace, but the number of farms dropped precipitously and average farm sizes leaped. In Bertie County in 1940, for instance, there were 3,095 farms, with 80,922 acres harvested; in 1970 there were 1,477, with 75,927 acres. Hertford County had 2,023 farms, with 52,642 acres, in 1940, and only 773, with 39,933, in 1970. Prince George had 869 farms, with 24,945 acres, in 1940, and only 326, with 19,213 acres, in 1970. Like neighboring Hertford, Southampton—another place where loblollies became the most important crop—suffered the loss of more than half its farms in only thirty years: 2,175 in 1940 to 876 in 1970 (while acreage harvested shrank from 87,544 to 74,636).[12]

During the 1970s, the federal Environmental Protection Agency angered farmers at least as much as corporate and state foresters when it banned DDT and the herbicides 2,4-D and 2,4,5-T. Like the forest monoculturists, though, farmers made no structural changes and persisted with substitutes. During the late 1980s and in the 1990s, many of the remaining farmers in the subregion, worried about the future of tobacco, unpromising corn prices, and production problems with peanuts, resorted to another high-cost, chemically dependent crop: cotton, which had been an important staple in the western side of the subregion from the 1840s until about 1940, when the boll weevil and California competition made cotton cultivation unfeasible. The pesky boll weevil's immunity to postwar pesticides and the triumph of synthetic fibers made cotton's reemergence in the East as likely a possibility as the resurrection of the Confederacy. After 1980, however, consumers spurned polyester, and agrochemists at last conquered the boll weevil. So cotton came back, extending as far north and east as Isle of Wight County, virtually to the doors of Suffolk. In 1991, investors constructed the Southside Gin (in western Southampton County near Emporia), the first cotton gin in Virginia in many years. One of the investors, Sam Pope, Jr., was himself a Southampton cotton-grower and the descendant of antebellum Popes whose slaves had chopped and picked the staple. Sam's 1991 crop was picked by one man named Turner—but a white Turner, who drove a two-row mechanical harvester.[13]

The tragedy of a people no longer able to sustain themselves harmoniously on a rural landscape is inseparable from the tragedy of a landscape poisoned. Tragedy, whether protracted or a sudden event, seems so starkly two-dimensional, save perhaps to those effected. Tragedy that is also ironic acquires depth, and one can hardly imagine a deeper one than that of Hopewell. At first an English-Indian trading point at the confluence of the Appomattox and the James, Hopewell was for more than two centuries a grain farm supervised by Cockes and Eppeses. General Grant and his staff interrupted a while, camping there late in the Civil War to oversee the destruction of slavery. But Richard Eppes soon restored Hopewell to its traditional function. After another quarter century of farming this and his other properties, Eppes announced the end of the age of grain in the East. Then, in 1896, he died, passing the land to his son and namesake. In 1911 the junior Richard

Eppes sold Hopewell to the Du Pont de Nemours Company, the venerable Delaware chemical giant.[14]

Within two years, Du Pont had built a small dynamite plant on the property. The next year, with the outbreak of hostilities in Europe, the company added a gun-cotton factory that soon became the largest of its kind in the world; and Hopewell, the town, veritably exploded: Its population reached 30,000 in 1915 and passed 40,000 in 1918. The boom brought immigrants from near and far, and Hopewell became notorious for its high prices, open sin, and violence. In October 1918, two companies of state militia and two more of federal troops from nearby Camp Lee quelled a race riot in which several black Hopewellians were killed. Peace in the town was soon followed by peace in Europe, and Du Pont scaled back production abruptly, then (in 1919) dismantled the gun-cotton factory. Hopewell's population shriveled to 1,400, adjacent City Point's to 2,500. Du Pont settled a manufacturer of artificial silk on the place in 1920, however, and Hopewell began life anew as a chemical city of about 8,000.[15]

Another quarter century later, Hopewell joined the explosive new business of agricultural chemistry, facilitating the Green Revolution near and far. Then, in July 1975, the most disastrous environmental incident in the subregion's entire history occurred. Workers at the Life Science Products Company, makers of a lethal pesticide called Kepone (under exclusive contract with Allied Chemical Corporation), became ill. Some of them exhibited several alarming symptoms at once—anxiety, tremors, unfocused vision, low sperm counts. Physicians found Kepone in the workers' blood and the blood of their families as well. Then was discovered, too, an enormous spill of the chemical into the James. Investigators found Kepone in shellfish sixty-five miles downriver, and the governor closed all the lower James to fishing. The pesticide's "afterlife" in the river, biologists estimated, was a century.[16] So—pursuing the African novelist Ben Okri's metaphor again—the James, so long a road as well as a river, was at last no longer hungry but was now confounded. The James's rhythmic immortality, its ancient indifference to human-born *Sturm und Drang*, seemed suddenly to end, that summer. But was not the tragedy foretold, so long before, when Dr. Eppes copied firmly into his diary the cosmopolitan maxim, "A farm is another name for a chemical laboratory. It is only another way of manufacturing"?

Kepone was not exactly an agricultural agent but a chlorinated hydrocarbon designed to kill household roaches—one of the countless consumer products spun off from the new agrochemistry. Belatedly, Kepone went the way of DDT and the banned herbicides. Other pesticides and weed-killers came along, however, as we have observed. During the 1980s, Virginia farmers spread an average of more than five million pounds of poisonous chemicals on their crop fields annually. Pesticide runoff killed fish in creeks, the James, and every other river; and when washed into watercourses, fertilizers supercharged their nitrogen levels, producing enormous blooms of phytoplankton ("red tides") and of algae ("green" and "blue tides"). These not only smothered other aquatic life (compounding the work of pesticides) but also diminished sunlight, harming subaquatic vegetation, the basis of the food chain.[17]

Farmers' entrapment in chemistry is hardly the sole cause of hydraulic ailments. Urban sewage was long discharged directly into rivers. (Washington, D.C. sewer discharges fueled algae blooms on the upper Potomac at least as early as 1916.) Norfolk, Portsmouth, Suffolk, Elizabeth City, and other towns in the James-Albemarle subregion were late in building sewage treatment plants, too; the Nansemond, the Pasquotank, the Southern Branch of the Elizabeth, and other rivers were open sewers for two centuries. Urban industries—shipping, tanning, food processing, and so on—were polluters as well. The Elizabeth's long main segment between Norfolk and Portsmouth—dredged and widened far beyond its colonial dimensions—in the twentieth century became one of the great heavy metal–filled bodies of water in North America. Ship cleaning and repair spilled petroleum distillates and lead, mercury, nickel, copper, and cadmium, among other things, into the river. Downriver, toward the Dismal Swamp, plants manufacturing fertilizers and agricultural chemicals spilled PCBs, PCPs, and PAHs—all of them known carcinogens—into the Elizabeth. Mullet alone seem to thrive in such water; other fishes have rotted fins, lesions, and tumors, usually cancerous. About 1980 the state government banned the taking of oysters, clams, and mussels from the Southern Branch—but not fish and crabs. Researchers' samples offered conflicting, indefinite evidence of pollutants' effects on fish and crabs and on humans who eat them. A marine scientist in Norfolk could only lamely advise (in 1991), "I wouldn't make a steady diet of it."[18]

For very long the industrial stretch of the Elizabeth was virtually friendless. Unlike the Potomac and Chesapeake Bay, whose near-death provoked enormous popular and organizational responses during the 1970s, the Elizabeth was not accessible to the public, had never been a playground. The federal Clean Water Act of 1972, which mandated cleanups to render polluted watercourses "fishable and swimmable," had no discernible effect in southeastern Virginia. Then, during the 1980s, Norfolk and Portsmouth, both of which had abandoned their riverfronts, redeveloped them with an eye to tourism and marketing. Norfolk's Waterside, a retail complex made mostly of glass and located beside a new riverfront hotel, invited locals and visitors back to the water. Portsmouth followed with Portside, a smaller dock with food stands next to a regentrified part of the city's eighteenth-century neighborhood. Ferry service between the two downtowns was resumed for the first time in nearly thirty years. So at last the Elizabeth acquired concerned "friends" and corporate interests vested in cleanup rather than abuse. In 1988 the state Water Control Board finally created an Elizabeth River Initiative and hired a bureaucrat. She convinced private shipyards and other polluters "to turn off the valves." The old Norfolk Naval Shipyard in Portsmouth was slower to cooperate; officials could not map all its valves. Evidence of substantial abatement was forthcoming in a relatively short time, however, encouraging optimists. The Southern Branch's potential as a playground remained very remote, nonetheless. During Norfolk's Harborfest in June 1991, a boating participant (who happened also to be a marine researcher) scraped his knee and wet it in the Elizabeth. The next day the entire limb was infected and swollen.[19]

The gasoline engine drives (literally and figuratively) the greater Hampton Roads urban/suburban sprawl. Autos and trucks may be called another, larger sort of swollen infection, harming the subregion's air and hydraulic system more than farming and shipping and other industries. For farming, after all, is shrinking in area, while industrial valves are being shut and smokestacks equipped with scrubbers. But earth-movers and concrete trucks grind and rotate night and day, finishing a massive scheme to encircle and section an enormous area with superhighways and new bridges and tunnels. Ancient marshes and creeks disappear, filled to support housing projects and weighty mobile things. Commuters live where they may, assured of convenient private travel to work. Realtors remap the landscape with absurd abstraction, achieving a sort of cognitive symmetry evocative of the clean geometry already achieved by modern agriculture.

But there is nothing clean about the extensive ribbons of concrete and asphalt. Faster than machine-compacted crop fields, highways, streets, and parking lots speed runoffs of heavy metals and other pollutants into waterways when it rains. Airborne automotive emissions, too, are an important cause of the acid rain that sickens both trees and waters.[20] The allied realtors' map of Hampton Roads might be interpreted as evidence of profound human alienation from landscape. True, I suspect; but also untrue. For on

Urban Elizabeth riverfront, 1990: Portsmouth seawall (right), naval shipyard crane (center), and ships in Berkely drydock (left) (Photo by the author)

weekends and during summer vacation periods, many cars and pickup trucks pull fishing and pleasure boats on trailers—off to Chesapeake Bay, to the Elizabeth's branches, the Nansemond, the rivers draining into Albemarle Sound, and westward to Lake Gaston. These drivers and boaters—many of them hunters in winter, too—are hungry consumers, to be sure. Some must be oblivious to their paradoxical degrading of the beloved. (As Freud observed long ago, humans' tolerance for reality is of necessity limited; otherwise we would go insane.) Others are not oblivious, but what can they do? Water, after all, like forests, is magnetic, a spiritual necessity.

Water is also a practical necessity. Cities and suburbs crave and demand, tapping aquifers, great empoundments, and distant rivers, channeling water upward and eastward in an engineered copy of the hydraulic cycle's own directional flow. In a place so riparian, with such huge average rainfalls, one might assume that supplies of water could never become problematic. But they did, both in metropolitan Hampton Roads and in other parts of the East, during the 1970s and especially the 1980s. Surging population growth, as we have seen, consumed old rural counties, and new, centerless, southern California–style cities appeared. The Reagan administration's massive military buildup suffused Virginia Beach, especially, with money and newcomers.

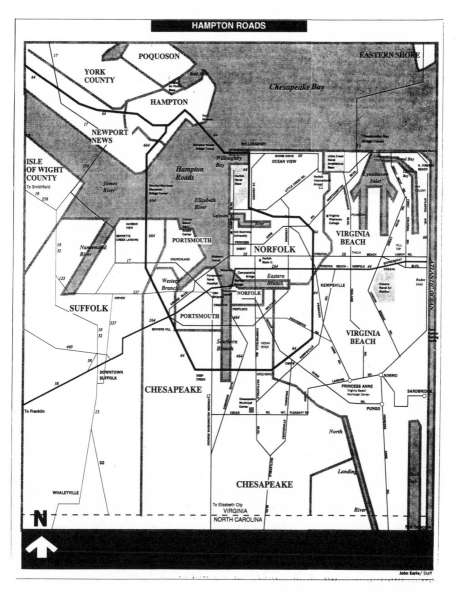

*Map 9. Realtors' map of Hampton Roads, 1993
(Courtesy of the* Virginian Pilot/Ledger-Star)

"The Beach" encompassed farmlands and swamps to become, remarkably, the largest city in Virginia. Then a series of droughts challenged the sprawling behemoth's very legitimacy and propelled its leaders into the role first created in Los Angeles early in the century—that of William Mulholland and his powerful confederates, who brought water from afar and saved their city.[21]

The fathers of modern Los Angeles—to put it bluntly—stole water from the Owens Valley, 250 miles distant; it was a remarkable achievement on several levels. Even then, they were privileged beneficiaries of the West's long experience with the problem of aridity, which had produced the legal doctrine called prior appropriation, permitting distant parties to claim water, establishing priority over local residents who had failed to claim the water first. Easterners were stuck with the riparian legal tradition that gave those closest to sources first right to water. Mulholland himself would have been frustrated in Virginia Beach, which had grown like Topsy without a municipal water system. The city makes occasional purchases from neighboring cities; mostly it relies on private pumping from ground aquifers. As population advanced, so did wells. And as drought followed drought, residents bored more—until the great, climactic heat wave and drought of 1988, when the aquifers gave out and neighboring cities grew parsimonious.[22]

The Beach's shortages were compounded by suburban culture. Many settlers here are migrants from the Middle West who have brought to sandy southeastern Virginia their affection for bluegrass lawns. This grass (called Kentucky but originally an introduction from Europe) thrives on wet clay soils, but even in Ohio it browns in August under heat and drought. In Virginia Beach, bluegrass consumes water outrageously—and then to little effect, as the blazing sun scorches plants and evaporates much of suburbanites' irrigation. The desert suburbanites of Las Vegas, Phoenix, and Tucson irrigate their lawns with federal taxpayer–subsidized water from the distant Colorado River. Virginia Beach—much of which approaches desert in summer—has no such luxury. A western-style solution to the Beach's dilemma, nonetheless, was well into plan by 1988.[23]

This solution was a proposed pipeline—sixty inches in diameter and eighty-four miles long, at a cost of $219 million—from Virginia Beach to Greensville County's Lake Gaston, an enormous flood-control and recreational project on the Roanoke. Because Gaston water lies in two states and the proposed pipeline would cross three counties and four cities, political and legal complications dwarfed the project's considerable engineering challenges. The Beach's representatives silenced some opponents along the pipeline path by promising allocations—ten million gallons to Chesapeake (another new city with uncertain supplies), and a million apiece to Franklin and Isle of Wight County. But Carolinians especially, and Virginia sportsmen and vacationers who used Lake Gaston, were unreconciled to the prospect of enormous drawdowns on the lake. Virginia Beach, it was reasonably asserted, had grown unjustifiably in relation to its own resources and now made unjustifiable demands on others.[24] But that had been said of Los Angeles, too.

The ending of the Cold War and draconian reductions in military spending quashed the Hampton Roads boom during the early 1990s. Completion of the great interstate highway circle and its intersectors, however, serves to fix for the foreseeable future the culture of suburban life and automotive commuting to work and recreation. The subregion approaches its fifth century of European and African settlement asymmetrically, then—still urban and still plantation. Virginia Beach's dreamed-of water pipeline would become only another linear connector, uniting and alienating at once.

The capacity to confound landscape accomplishes such a paradox. The dynamic called "development" begets more speed, more alienation. Wisdom of several sorts, then, pleads for thoughtful pause—a repose used to reconsider geologic morphology's own genius, perhaps especially to reconsider the slow-measured poetry of pocosins. What better reservoir is there than one midway in a landscape's profile, requiring no pumps or managers? And what other reservoir not only conserves but also filters and clarifies, regenerating life itself?

NOTES

The following abbreviations are used in the notes.

DSLCo. Dismal Swamp Land Company Papers, Perkins Library, Duke University
NCSA North Carolina State Archives, Raleigh
SHC Southern Historical Collection, University of North Carolina, Chapel Hill
SP *Southern Planter*
SPF *Southern Planter and Farmer*
VHS Virginia Historical Society, Richmond
VSLA Virginia State Library and Archives, Richmond

PREFACE

1. On the word, see Curtis Richardson, Rhonda Evans, and David Carr, "Pocosins: An Ecosystem in Transition," in Curtis R. Richardson, ed., *Pocosin Wetlands: An Integrated Analysis of Coastal Plain Freshwater Bogs in North Carolina* (Stroudsburg, Pa.: Hutchinson Ross Publishing Co., 1981), 3–19.

2. On carbon storage, see Charles Daniel, III, "Hydrology, Geology and Soils of Pocosins: A Comparison of Natural and Altered Systems," in ibid., 69–108.

3. Mark R. Walbridge, "Functions and Values of Forested Wetlands in the Southern United States," *Journal of Forestry* 91 (May 1993): 15–19; and Daniel, "Hydrology, Geology and Soils of Pocosins," especially 69, 82–84.

4. Norman Christensen, Rebecca Burchell, Annette Liggett, and Ellen Simms, "The Structure and Development of Pocosin Vegetation," in Richardson, Evans, and Carr, *Pocosin Wetlands*, 43–61; and Daniel, "Hydrology, Geology and Soils of Pocosins," especially 78–82.

5. See Christensen et al., "Structure and Development of Pocosin Vegetation," especially 48–49.

6. See Henry Wilbur, "Pocosin Fauna," in Richardson, Evans, and Carr, *Pocosin Wetlands*, 62–68—the briefest chapter in the volume.

7. On vagueness, see John Toliver, "What Are Wetlands: A Historical Overview," *Journal of Forestry* 91 (May 1993): 12–14; and Richardson, Evans, and Carr, "Pocosins," in Richardson, Evans, and Carr, *Pocosin Wetlands*, 406.

8. J. W. Gilliam and R. W. Skaggs, "Drainage and Agricultural Development: Effects on Drainage Waters," in Richardson, Evans, and Carr, *Pocosin Wetlands*, 109–24 (especially 110); and Curtis Richardson, "Pocosins: Ecosystem Processes and the Influence of Man on System Response," in ibid., 135–54 (especially 146).

PROLOGUE

1. See Carolyn Merchant, *The Death of Nature* (New York: Harper and Row, 1980); Robert Pogue Harrison, *Forests: The Shadow of Civilization* (Chicago: University of Chicago Press, 1992), especially 3–60 (including a discussion of humans' propensity for talking with trees).

2. Jeffrey Gray, "Consciousness on the Scientific Agenda," *Nature* 358 (23 July 1992): 277 (a report on Ciba Foundation Symposium No. 174 on Experimental and Theoretical Studies of Consciousness, London, 7–9 July 1992).

3. Sandra Blakeslee, "Finding New Messenger for the Brain's Signals to the Body," *New York Times*, 11 Aug. 1992, B5 (both quotations), B8.

4. My use of *linear* and *linearity* may suggest to some readers an exaggeration of human immobility and isolation before all-weather roads, canals, railroads. Certainly people have always moved—themselves and their belongings, including some trade goods. Still, I do suggest that geologic morphology–defying transportation implied something more than incremental change, something culturally profound.

5. This and following paragraphs on geology and the indigenes are based compositely upon H. G. Richards, "Structural and Stratigraphic Framework of the Atlantic Coastal Plain," and R. Q. Oaks, N. K. Coch, J. E. Sanders, and R. F. Flint, "Post-Miocene Shorelines and Sea Levels, Southeastern Virginia," both in *Post-Miocene Stratigraphy: Central and Southern Atlantic Coastal Plain*, edited by Robert Q. Oaks, Jr. and Jules R. DuBar (Logan: Utah State University Press, 1974), 11–20, 53–87; Robert Q. Oaks, Jr. and Donald R. Whitehead, "Geologic Setting and Origin of the Dismal Swamp, Southeastern Virginia and Northeastern North Carolina," Donald R. Whitehead and Robert Q. Oaks, Jr., "Developmental History of the Dismal Swamp," and Edward Bottoms and Floyd Painter, "Evidence of Aboriginal Utilization of the Bola in the Dismal Swamp Area," all in *The Great Dismal Swamp*, edited by Paul W. Kirk, Jr. (Charlottesville: University Press of Virginia, 1979), 1–24, 25–43, 44–56; and U.S. Environmental Protection Agency, "Chesapeake Bay: Introduction to an Ecosystem" (Washington: GPO, 1982), 2–5 (microfilm).

6. This and following paragraphs on Woodland culture are based compositely upon Helen C. Rountree, *The Powhatan Indians of Virginia: Their Traditional Culture* (Norman: University of Oklahoma Press, 1989), especially 46–47; James Axtell, ed., *The Indian Peoples of Eastern America: A Documentary History of the Sexes* (New York: Oxford University Press, 1981), especially 130–33; William Cronon, *Changes in the Land: Indians, Colonists, and the Ecology of New England* (New York: Hill and Wang, 1983), especially 47–91; Stephen J. Pyne, *Fire in America: A Cultural History of Wildland and Rural Fire* (Princeton: Princeton University Press, 1982); Timothy Silver, *A New Face on the Countryside: Indians, Colonists, and Slaves in South Atlantic Forests, 1500–1800* (Cambridge: Cambridge University Press, 1990).

7. See Thomas Story, 1747 memoir (typescript), Thomas Story Papers, North Carolina State Archives (NCSA), Raleigh; Thomas J. Wertenbaker, *Norfolk, Historic*

Southern Port, edited by Marvin W. Schlegel (Durham: Duke University Press, 1962), 3–5; and Arthur Pierce Middleton, *Tobacco Coast: A Maritime History of Chesapeake Bay in the Colonial Era* (Baltimore: Johns Hopkins University Press, 1953).

8. Story memoir, p. 2. For context see also Rhys Isaac, *The Transformation of Virginia, 1740–1790* (New York: W. W. Norton, 1982).

9. Story memoir, p. 2.

10. Ibid., pp. 2 (quotation), 3–5.

11. See Luther Porter Jackson, *Free Negro Labor and Property Holding in Virginia, 1830–1860* (1942; reprint, New York: Atheneum, 1969); and Ira Berlin, *Slaves without Masters: The Free Negro in the Antebellum South* (New York: Random House, 1974), especially 20–21, 31–32; U.S. Census, 1850, county tables.

12. U.S. census of population and manufactures, 1850 (including a composite of censuses of 1840, 1850, and 1860); Legh R. Watts, *An Address Embracing a Historical Sketch of Norfolk County, Va., Delivered at Berkley, July 4th, 1876...*, edited by Charles B. Cross, Jr. (Chesapeake, Va.: Norfolk County Historical Society, 1964), 22–25; Col. William H. Stewart, ed./comp., *History of Norfolk County, Virginia and Representative Citizens* (Chicago: Biographical Publishing Co., 1902), 156 (on Cox and truck farming).

13. See Wertenbaker, *Norfolk*, 27–47, 82; Allan Kulikoff, *Tobacco and Slaves: The Development of Southern Cultures in the Chesapeake, 1680–1800* (Chapel Hill: University of North Carolina Press, 1986), 120–21.

14. Blow Family Papers, Virginia Historical Society (VHS), Richmond, especially Richard Blow Letterbooks (e.g., Letterbook for 1806, on canal construction by slaves); Alexander Crosby Brown, *The Dismal Swamp Canal* (Chesapeake, Va.: Norfolk County Historical Society, 1970), 45.

15. Brown, *Dismal Swamp Canal*, 46–49, 59–65 (quotation 65).

16. See Bland Simpson, *The Great Dismal: A Carolinian's Swamp Memoir* (Chapel Hill: University of North Carolina Press, 1990); and Oaks and Whitehead, "Geologic Setting and Origin," 8.

17. See George Blow to Robert W[aller] Blow, 25 Aug. 1819; Edmund Ruffin to George Blow, 18 Jan. 1820; George Blow, "Rough Plantation Memorandum Book for 1842—Tower Hill Plantation"; and Norbonne Blow to George Blow, 6 Mar. 1844, all in Blow Family Papers, VHS.

18. See M. B. Connolly, "Union Occupation of Norfolk and Portsmouth: Prelude to Reconstruction or Precursor to Violence?" (bound typescript, 1987), p. 3, Kirn Memorial Library, Norfolk; and Wertenbaker, *Norfolk*, 204–6.

19. Wertenbaker, *Norfolk*, 207–25.

20. See ibid., 211–12, and Wayne K. Durrill, *War of Another Kind: A Southern Community in the Great Rebellion* (New York: Oxford University Press, 1990), which relates class warfare in Washington Co., N.C., on the southern shore of Albemarle Sound.

21. See E. A. Wild to John T. Elliott ("Captain of Guerrillas"), 17 Dec. 1863 (threatening reprisals for hostage-taking); Col. Alonzo G. Draper (commander of

the Second North Carolina Colored Volunteers, based in Portsmouth) to Hiram W. Allen, 24 Dec. 1863; J. D. Stokeley et al. to Gen. Getty, 13 Jan. 1864, with copy of notice pinned to the hanged Union soldier; E. A. Wild to Capt. George H. Johnston, 28 Dec. 1863 (a summary of Wild's expedition), all in Edward Augustus Wild Papers, Southern Historical Collection (SHC), University of North Carolina, Chapel Hill. See also Ira Berlin, ed., and Joseph P. Reidy and Leslie S. Rowland, assoc. eds., *Freedom: A Documentary History of Emancipation, 1861–1867*, series 2: *The Black Military Experience* (Cambridge: Cambridge University Press, 1982), 114.

22. See Wertenbaker, *Norfolk*, 211–12; John Hammond Moore, "The Norfolk Riot, 16 April 1866," *Virginia Magazine of History and Biography* 90 (April 1982): 155–64.

23. Rountree, *Powhatan Indians*, 9, 14–15, 132–32.

24. *William Byrd's Histories of the Dividing Line Betwixt Virginia and North Carolina*, introduction and notes by William K. Boyd, new introduction by Percy G. Adams (New York: Dover Publications, 1967), 54.

25. On swine on the peninsula see Robert Beverley, *The History and Present State of Virginia*, edited by Louis B. Wright (Chapel Hill: University of North Carolina Press, 1947), 318. On diet see Elizabeth W. Etheridge, *The Butterfly Caste: A Social History of Pellagra in the South* (Westport, Conn.: Archon Books, 1972), which (among other virtues) reveals the corn-bean chemical symbiosis. The open range and its closing will be described further in a later chapter.

26. *Byrd's Histories*, 66, 92. See also David Bertelson, *The Lazy South* (New York: Oxford University Press, 1967).

27. *Byrd's Histories*, 56.

28. U.S. manuscript census, 1850, population schedule, Nansemond Co., Va.; shingle and pay records for 1840s and 1850s, Dismal Swamp Land Company Papers, Perkins Library, Duke University, Durham, N.C. (hereafter cited as DSLCo.).

29. *Byrd's Histories*, 68.

30. Ibid., 70, 84, 86. On the Dismal's healthful aspects see Simpson, *Great Dismal*, and David C. Miller, *Dark Eden: The Swamp in Nineteenth-Century American Culture* (Cambridge: Cambridge University Press, 1989), 23–46.

31. Charles and Eleanor Cross, *It Happened Here* (Chesapeake, Va.: Norfolk County Historical Society, 1964), 21–22; Edmund Ruffin, "Observations Made during an Excursion to the Dismal Swamp," *Farmers' Register* 4 (Jan. 1837): 519.

32. Brown, *Dismal Swamp Canal*, 50; Simpson, *Great Dismal*, 45–47, 50–51; and DSLCo. Jericho Ditch opened ca. 1810.

33. See Steven A. Cormier, *The Siege of Suffolk: The Forgotten Campaign, April 11 – May 4, 1862* (Lynchburg, Va.: H. E. Howard, 1989); and claims deposition, Sept. 1962, DSLCo.

34. Spanish moss at Hertford observed by the author (see photo). On the subregion's biological distinctiveness, see Kirk, *Great Dismal*, 1–25.

35. On ocean travel after the hurricane, see, for example, the Thomas Nicholson Journal for 1749 (typescript), p. 3, in Stephen B. Weeks Collection, SHC.

36. Nicholson Journal for 1746, pp. 24, 26, 28.

37. See undated "Considerations on Slavery," and Nicholson to "B. H." (the slave trader), 6 Nov. 1779, in Nicholson Journal, pp. 31–36.

38. John Early Diary (typescript), pp. 26–27, SHC.

39. William S. Leonard to Isam Leonard, 14 Sept. 1819, in William S. Leonard Papers, SHC.

40. William S. Leonard to Jacob Leonard (father), 7 Aug. 1819, Leonard Papers.

41. William S. Leonard to Isam Leonard, 28 Dec. 1819, Leonard Papers.

42. On corn, salt, and the stores in Hertford and Windsor, see William S. Leonard to Gamaliel Bryant, 19 Dec. 1820; William Leonard to Jacob Leonard, 14 Dec. 1820; William Leonard to Jacob Leonard, 20 Nov. 1822, all in Leonard Papers. On William's illness and death see Thomas Covington to Withington and Russell (Boston merchants), 14 Aug. 1825, Leonard Papers.

43. On the Skinner family generally, see the typescript introduction to the Tristrim Lowther Skinner Papers, SHC.

44. See Joshua Skinner, Jr., to Joseph B. Skinner, 23 July 1821, and Tristrim L. Skinner to Eliza F. Harwood, 5 Jan. 1841, Skinner Papers.

45. U.S. manuscript census, 1850, slave and manufactures schedules, Perquimans Co., N.C. On the Chowan Skinner fishery and the Perquimans stave business, see Tristrim L. Skinner to Joseph B. Skinner, 13 May 1838 and 10 Aug. 1848, Skinner Papers.

46. See "Address by the Honorable Colgate W. Darden, Jr., Southampton County Bicentennial Celebration, July 3, 1976" (Courtland: Southampton County Historical Society), *Bulletin No. 3* (unpaginated); Tyson Van Auken, John W. Knapp, and Richard O. Mines, "Navigation of the Blackwater River," typescript report for U.S. Army Corps of Engineers, Norfolk District (Lexington, Va., Sept. 1978), 34 pp.; and Tyson Van Auken, Richard O. Mines, and John W. Knapp, "Navigation of the Nottoway River," typescript report for U.S. Army Corps of Engineers, Norfolk District (Lexington, Va., Sept. 1978), 62 pp., all in Walter Cecil Rawls Library and Museum, Courtland, Va.; and John Crump Parker, "Old South Quay in Southampton County: Its Location, Early Ownership, and History," *Virginia Magazine of History and Biography* 83 (April 1975): 209–22.

47. W. L. Smith to Seth Smith, 24 May 1806; W. L. Smith to parents, 20 June 1806, in William Lay Smith Papers, NCSA.

48. Smith to parents, 20 July and 23 Aug. 1806, Smith Papers.

49. Ibid.

50. Smith to parents, 23 Aug. 1806, 17 Feb. 1808, 3 Dec. 1812, and 17 June 1813, Smith Papers.

51. See William D. Valentine Diary, SHC, especially typescript introduction.

52. See ibid., entries for 28 Nov. 1838 and 10 Mar. 1853.

53. See ibid., entries for 21 Apr. 1839, 9 May 1843, and 8 May 1852.

54. Bryant quoted in Parke Rouse, Jr., *The Timber Tycoons: The Camp Families of*

Virginia and Florida and Their Empire, 1887–1987 (Richmond: William Byrd Press for Southampton County Historical Society, 1988), 16.

55. Valentine Diary, entry for 23 Dec. 1845.

56. Rouse, *Timber Tycoons*, 16–17; Cecil C. Frost and Lytton J. Musselman, "History and Vegetation of the Blackwater Ecologic Preserve," *Castanea* 52 (1987): 16–46. The author has explored the Blackwater Ecologic Preserve several times. Fernald and subsequent botanists conjectured that feral hogs also played a role in the near-extinction of the longleaf, and this subject will be pursued later.

CHAPTER ONE

1. See family correspondence for the 1810s through the 1840s, including Tristrim L. Skinner to Joseph B. Skinner, 30 Oct. 1827 and 2 Jan. 1835, in Tristrim Lowther Skinner Papers, SHC.

2. See Skinner to Eliza F. Harwood, 5 Jan. 1841, Skinner Papers.

3. Tristrim Skinner–Eliza Harwood letters, 1841–46, and E. L. Skinner to Tristrim L. Skinner, 11 Jan. 1847, Skinner Papers.

4. See Tristrim–Eliza Skinner letters, 1850–62, and the 30 June 1862 telegram atop Box 1, Skinner Papers.

5. *The Diary of Edmund Ruffin*, vol. 2: *The Years of Hope, April, 1861 — June, 1863*, edited by William Kauffman Scarborough (Baton Rouge: Louisiana State University Press, 1976), 472–73.

6. Archie K. Davis, *Boy Colonel of the Confederacy: The Life and Times of Henry King Burgwyn, Jr.* (Chapel Hill: University of North Carolina Press, 1985), 8, 10, 22–29, 329–39 (especially 336). (This biography of a man dead at twenty-one consumes four hundred pages.) Griffith's film was first released in 1915.

7. Ibid., 71–90.

8. Ibid., 9–29; and Burgwyn Family Papers, SHC.

9. See Verner W. Crane, *The Southern Frontier, 1670–1732* (1928; reprint, New York: W. W. Norton, 1981), 40, 61, 129, 154; and Theda Perdue, *Native Carolinians: The Indians of North Carolina* (Raleigh: North Carolina Department of Cultural Resources, 1985), especially 1–24.

10. See various accounts of Henry King Burgwyn, Sr., and especially those of Thomas Pollok Burgwyn — the slave inventories of 1844 and 1863, mule and horse inventories of 1844 and 1847 (vol. 12 in the collection); and (on "Ditcher" Reed) the John Alveston Burgwyn Diary, 12 Jan. 1885, Burgwyn Family Papers.

11. Davis, *Boy Colonel*, 344–45.

12. John Alveston Burgwyn Diary, 8 July through 25 Oct. 1871.

13. Ibid., entries for 26 Oct. 1871 through June 1872.

14. Ibid., especially entries for 29 June, 1 and 27–28 Nov. 1885 and 12 Jan. 1886.

15. Ibid., entries for 4 July, 21 Sept. 1885, 11 July 1887, and 2 Jan. 1887. See

Roy Parker, Jr., "Mebane Burgwyn" (an obituary/essay), *Fayetteville Observer-Times*, 23 Aug. 1992.

16. Eppes Family Muniments, Richard Eppes Diary, VHS; see especially the diary entries for 4 Feb. 1859 and 18 July 1860.

17. Eppes Diary, 11 Nov. and 8 Dec. 1860.

18. Ibid., 4 Feb. 1861.

19. Ibid., 18 Apr. 1861. A fuller treatment of Eppes's dilemma and behavior is Shearer Davis Bowman, "Conditional Unionism and Slavery in Virginia, 1860–1861: The Case of Dr. Richard Eppes," *Virginia Magazine of History and Biography* 96 (Jan. 1988): 31–54.

20. See Eppes Diary, volume for 1859–62 (pp. 318–23 in the rear) on his plantations during the war; and the National Park Service's Civil War displays at Appomattox Manor, Hopewell, Va.

21. Eppes Diary, 1, 2, 3, and 7 Sept. 1865, 3, 5 Jan. 1866. On the restoration of the old order on the James, see also Gregg L. Michel, "From Slavery to Freedom: Hickory Hill, 1850–80," in *The Edge of the South: Life in Nineteenth-Century Virginia*, edited by Edward Ayers and John C. Willis (Charlottesville: University Press of Virginia, 1991), 108–32.

22. Regarding Eppes Family Muniments, see Eppes Diary, 2 Jan. 1853, on Eppes's management of his estate in 1847; see also Bowman, "Conditional Unionism," 45–46, 52.

23. Eppes Diary, 3 Sept. 1851.

24. See Lewis Cecil Gray, *History of Agriculture in the Southern United States to 1860*, 2 vols. (1933; reprint, Gloucester, Mass.: Peter Smith, 1958), 1:26–27; Robert Beverley, *The History and Present State of Virginia*, edited by Louis B. Wright (Chapel Hill: University of North Carolina Press, 1947), 143–45; James Axtell, ed., *The Indian Peoples of Eastern America: A Documentary History of the Sexes* (New York: Oxford University Press, 1981), 130–33; Carville V. Earle, *The Evolution of a Tidewater Settlement Pattern: All Hallow's Parish, Maryland, 1650–1783* (Chicago: University of Chicago Geography Department, 1975), especially 24–30; and Allan Kulikoff, *Tobacco and Slaves: The Development of Southern Cultures in the Chesapeake, 1680–1800* (Chapel Hill: University of North Carolina Press, 1986), especially 48.

25. On the conversion to grain see Earle, *Evolution of a Tidewater Settlement Pattern*, 128–30; Gray, *History of Agriculture*, 1:166–68; Harold B. Gill, Jr., "Wheat Culture in Colonial Virginia," *Agricultural History* 52 (1978): 380–93; David Klingaman, "The Significance of Grain in the Development of the Tobacco Colonies," *Journal of Economic History* 29 (1969): 268–78; and T. H. Breen, *Tobacco Culture: The Mentality of the Great Tidewater Planters on the Eve of Revolution* (Princeton: Princeton University Press, 1985).

26. On English farming see G. E. Mingay, ed., *The Agricultural Revolution: Changes in Agriculture, 1650–1880* (London: Adam and Charles Black, 1977), 1–68, 115–25; *Hopewell News*, 30 Oct. 1952 (on the building of Appomattox Manor); *The Diary of Colonel*

Landon Carter of Sabine Hall, 1752–1778, edited by Jack P. Greene, 2 vols. (Charlottesville: University Press of Virginia, 1965), 1:157–62, 172, 337 (on English farming methods), 2:611 (on an English-style rotation system that included turnips), and 2:753 (on the novelty of plows as late as the 1770s). One must beware the extent of agricultural "revolution," however, whether in Britain or America. See G. E. Fussell, "Science and Practice in Eighteenth-Century British Agriculture," *Agricultural History* 43 (1969): 7–18.

27. L. C. Gottschalk, "Effects of Soil Erosion on Navigation in Upper Chesapeake Bay," *Geographical Review* 35 (1945): 219–38; U.S. Environmental Protection Agency, "Chesapeake Bay: Introduction to an Ecosystem" (Washington: GPO, Jan. 1982), 2–5 (on subaquatic vegetation); John Capper, Garrett Power, and Frank R. Shivers, Jr., *Chesapeake Waters: Pollution, Public Health, and Public Opinion, 1607–1972* (Centreville, Md.: Tidewater Publishers, 1983), introduction and 7–8, 26, 28. On pests see *Diary of Colonel Landon Carter,* 1:168–69, 170–80, 185–86, 2:605–7; Hill Carter, "Causes of Failure of the Wheat Crop in Virginia," *SPF,* n.s., 5 (Dec. 1871): 726–29; and William B. Alwood, "Implements for Applying Insecticides, Fungicides, Etc.," *SP* 50 (Aug. 1889): 126–28.

28. See the Eppes Diary, especially 18 Oct. 1851 (on the rotation system) and 17 Mar. and 20 Sept. 1859 (on soil-enrichment additives), VHS.

29. Ibid., 12 Aug. 1859.

30. Ibid., 7 Nov. 1851, and Eppes Island map in vol. 1, p. 79.

31. See David F. Allmendinger, Jr., ed., *Incidents of My Life: Edmund Ruffin's Autobiographical Essays* (Charlottesville: University Press of Virginia for the Virginia Historical Society, 1990), especially 39–40, 79–85.

32. Ibid., especially 38–39, 79 (on reclamation); Hill Carter, "Account of the Embankment and Cultivation of the Shirley Swamp," *Farmers' Register* 1 (Aug. 1833): 129–31; Hill Carter, "The Progress of Sinking and Loss in the Embanked Marsh of Shirley," ibid., 5 (May 1837): 40–41.

33. See Helen C. Rountree, *The Powhatan Indians of Virginia: Their Traditional Culture* (Norman: University of Oklahoma Press, 1989), especially 38, 79, 87–88; and Stuart A. Marks, *Southern Hunting, in Black and White: Nature, History, and Ritual in a Carolina Community* (Princeton: Princeton University Press, 1991).

34. Eppes Diary, 29 and 30 Sept. 1851 and 2 Jan. 1860, VHS.

35. "The Duck Trade," *SP* 17 (July 1857): 418; and "Canvassback Ducks," ibid., 18 (Mar. 1858): 132–33.

36. See Jennifer Price, "When Women Were Women, Men Were Men, and Birds Were Hats: Gender Roles and Bird Conservation at the Turn of the Century," paper delivered at the American Society for Environmental History conference, Houston, 3 Mar. 1991; and the H. B. Ansell Books (2 vols.), 1:7–8, SHC.

37. "Injury from Destroying Birds" [from *Farmer's Cabinet*], *Farmers' Register* 6 (Aug. 1838): 280–83.

38. "C," "What has become of our Birds?" *SP* 20 (April 1860): 202–9; Eppes Diary,

6 Jan. 1860, VHS. (The boy was Beverly Carter, who "skated across the Appomattox to Bermuda and then across to Shirley today.")

39. "The Crow's Value to the Farmer" [from *Atlantic Monthly*], *SPF*, n.s., 3 (Aug. 1869): 464; and William F. Jackson, "Spare the Crow," ibid., n.s., 4 (June 1870): 336–37.

40. Ibid. [from Richmond *State*], 37 (July 1876): 482.

41. "Protection for the Birds" [from *Forest and Stream*], *SP* 47 (Mar. 1886): 122; Price, "When Women Were Women"; and on the emergence of Ducks Unlimited, see files with this title in the Dudley Warren Bagley Papers, SHC. On the larger, national context, see John F. Reiger, *American Sportsmen and the Origins of Conservation* (1975; reprint, Norman: University of Oklahoma Press, 1986), which grants hunters rather all-encompassing credit for conservation; and Thomas R. Dunlap, *Saving America's Wildlife* (Princeton: Princeton University Press, 1988), especially 5–33.

42. See Eppes Diary, 10 Mar. and 8 Apr. 1859.

43. Eppes Diary, 23 Mar. 1859.

44. "The Osage Orange," *SP* 6 (Nov. 1846): 246–47; and James Gowen, "Maclura or Osage Orange for Hedges" [from *Ohio Cultivator*], ibid., 6 (Dec. 1846): 269. (The author has had more than a quarter century of unhappy experience with Osage oranges, in Ohio.)

45. Eppes Diary, 12 Oct. 1851 and 15 Jan. 1852.

46. "Osage Orange Hedges," *SP* 17 (Feb. 1857): 71–72, quotation 71; this article summarizes *Boston Cultivator*'s criticism.

47. E. G. Eggeling, "Hedges—Osage Orange," *SP* 18 (Mar. 1858): 185–88. See also Yardley Taylor, "Osage Orange Hedging," ibid., 19 (Mar. 1859): 150–54 (another endorsement).

CHAPTER TWO

1. On Ruffin's and Ruffin family slaves see David F. Allmendinger, Jr., "Introduction: A Farmer's Life in Virginia," in David F. Allmendinger, Jr., ed., *Incidents of My Life: Edmund Ruffin's Autobiographical Essays* (Charlottesville: University Press of Virginia for Virginia Historical Society, 1990), 8; the quotation is from Allmendinger, *Incidents of My Life*, 91. On Ruffin's background, position, and early travels see (among others) David F. Allmendinger, Jr., *Ruffin: Family and Reform in the Old South* (New York: Oxford University Press, 1990), 8–56, 229 (n. 61).

2. Among the Ruffin biographers, Allmendinger, *Ruffin*, especially 8–22, best employs isolation as theme and explanatory device, both enlightening and reinforcing my own reading of Ruffin's life.

3. Allmendinger, *Incidents of My Life*, 28–29.

4. See Allmendinger, *Ruffin*, 15–21; and (on Ruffin's wish to emigrate) Allmendinger, *Incidents of My Life*, 194.

5. [Ruffin], "First Views Which Led to Marling in Prince George County," *Farmers'*

Register 7 (1839): 659–67, reprinted as Appendix 3 in Allmendinger, *Incidents of My Life*, 189–209. See also [William Boulware], "Edwin [*sic*] Ruffin, of Virginia, Agriculturist . . . ," *De Bow's Review* 11 (1851): 431–36. This biographical sketch, which Ruffin approved, is reprinted as Appendix 1 in Allmendinger, *Incidents of My Life*, 167–78. My summary of Ruffin's early career is based upon these sources unless otherwise noted.

6. Quotations from Allmendinger, *Incidents of My Life*, 193.

7. See Henry H. Simms, *Life of John Taylor: The Story of a Brilliant Leader in the Early State Rights School* (Richmond: William Byrd Press, 1932), especially 3–15 and 223–26 (a copy of Taylor's will, mentioning his estates and Kentucky lands); and Robert E. Stalhope, *John Taylor of Caroline: Pastoral Republican* (Columbia: University of South Carolina Press, 1980), especially 13–69, which emphasizes Pendleton's influence on Taylor. See also M. E. Bradford, introduction to John Taylor, *Arator: Being a Series of Agricultural Essays, Practical and Political: in Sixty-Four Numbers*, edited by M. E. Bradford (Indianapolis: Liberty Fund, 1977), 11–46, which is quite adequate on the principal events of Taylor's life (as well as his thought).

8. See Allan Kulikoff, *Tobacco and Slaves: The Development of Southern Cultures in the Chesapeake, 1680–1800* (Chapel Hill: University of North Carolina Press, 1986), especially 120–21; T. H. Breen, *Tobacco Culture: The Mentality of the Great Tidewater Planters on the Eve of Revolution* (Princeton: Princeton University Press, 1985).

9. See Taylor, *Arator*, or Avery Craven's excellent précis of Taylor's system in *Soil Exhaustion as a Factor in the Agricultural History of Virginia and Maryland, 1606–1860* (Urbana: University of Illinois Press, 1926), 99–103 (the quotation from letter to Jefferson appears on 101). Taylor declared (*Arator*, 130) that "Manures are mineral, vegetable or atmospherical."

10. On the publication history of *Arator*, see M. E. Bradford's introduction to Taylor, *Arator*, 31–32, 47–48. Taylor quoted Strickland in essay 1 (pp. 65–67 in this edition). (Bradford's edition recreates the 1818 version, which added three essays to Taylor's original 61, along with corrections and appendices.)

11. Ibid., 36–38 (quotation 38). Bradford presents a bibliography of Taylor's published works on p. 43. See also Louis Hartz, *The Liberal Tradition in America: An Interpretation of American Political Thought since the Revolution* (New York: Harcourt, Brace and World, 1955), especially 145–77, 192–93.

12. On grain culture east and west, see *Eighth Census of the United States, 1860 — Agriculture*, xxix–xxx, xlvi–xlix, lxiv–lxvi; Craven, *Soil Exhaustion*, 79–80, 142–43, 156; Morton Rothstein, "Antebellum Wheat and Cotton Exports," *Agricultural History* 40 (Apr. 1966): 91–100; Jack Temple Kirby, "Virginia's Environmental History: A Prospectus," *Virginia Magazine of History and Biography* 99 (Oct. 1991): 449–88 (especially 460–64).

13. Taylor, *Arator*, 127.

14. On soils east and west, see Kermit C. Berger, *Sun, Soil and Survival: An Introduction to Soils* (1965; reprint, Norman: University of Oklahoma Press, 1972), especially 137–66. On state rankings in grain production, see *Eighth Census of the United States,*

1860—Agriculture. On the persistence of the East's disadvantageous competition with the West, see Jack Temple Kirby, *Rural Worlds Lost: The American South, 1920–1960* (Baton Rouge: Louisiana State University Press, 1987), especially 1–24.

15. Ruffin, "Marling," in Allmendinger, *Incidents of My Life*, quotations 192.

16. Ibid., quotations 194–95.

17. Ibid., 24 (first quotation), 48 (second quotation); and Allmendinger, *Ruffin*, 35.

18. See J. E. Cirlot, *A Dictionary of Symbols*, translated by Jack Sage (New York: Philosophical Library, 1962), 280; Helen C. Rountree, *The Powhatan Indians of Virginia: Their Traditional Culture* (Norman: University of Oklahoma Press, 1989), especially 55–56, 71, 73, 102–3. Rountree does not acknowledge aboriginal recognition and use of "shelly" land, however. My source is Edmund Ruffin, "Hasty Observations on the Agriculture of the County of Nansemond," *Farmers' Register* 4 (Jan. 1837): 524–27 (especially 525–26). Ruffin visited "Stockley, the farm and residence of Willis Cowper, Esq. which was the site of the principal town of the Nansemond tribe of Indians." Cowper raised crops on the land without manure or marl, and Ruffin's soil test revealed high calcium content.

19. Ibid.; Stephen Calloway, "SHELLS: For centuries decorative motifs have washed ashore from the deep," *House and Garden*, Nov. 1992, 178–81, 198. (The original Chinese character for "money," portentously, was a simple, stylized shell, now updated and only slightly recognizable from the original.)

20. Calloway, "SHELLS," 198, finds only two American houses with shell art— one on Long Island, one in Florida. On New England gravestone carvings, see Francis Y. Duval and Ivan B. Rigby, *Early American Gravestone Art in Photographs* (New York: Dover Publications, 1978), 22, 35, and Allan I. Ludwig, *Graven Images: New England Stonecarving and Its Symbols, 1650–1815* (Middletown, Conn.: Wesleyan University Press, 1966), 68, 77, and Plate 7. On antebellum American discourse, I find no usage of shell-lore in my perusal of several scores of manuscript collections relating to the area under study. On Ruffin in South Carolina, see William M. Mathew, ed., *Agriculture, Geology, and Society in Antebellum South Carolina: The Private Diary of Edmund Ruffin, 1843* (Athens: University of Georgia Press, 1992), especially 29–30, 86–87, 112–13, 187–90, 206–7, 229–31 (quotation p. 207). My colleague Michael O'Brien, at work on an ambitious project on discourse in the Old South, maintains an enormous and accessible data bank on the larger region and beyond; and he, too, finds no reference to shells as symbols.

21. Quoted in Michael O'Brien, ed., *An Evening When Alone: Four Journals of Single Women in the South, 1827–67* (Charlottesville: University Press of Virginia, 1993), 12.

22. On Americans' divided mind—Rationalist/instrumentalist versus Romantic—see Robert Pogue Harrison, *Forests: The Shadow of Civilization* (Chicago: University of Chicago Press, 1992), especially 197–249.

23. Reference to the "The Pink Clam" appears in David R. Slavitt, "Short Stories Are Not Real Life," in *Writers and Their Craft: Short Stories and Essays on the Narrative*, edited by Nicholas Delbanco and Laurence Goldstein (Detroit: Wayne State Univer-

sity Press, 1991), 352. Other sexual references are my own observation and (I presume) common knowledge. On Royal Dutch/Shell see Kendall Beaton, *Enterprise in Oil: A History of Shell in the United States* (New York: Appleton-Century-Crofts, 1957), 1, 20–46.

24. Allmendinger, *Incidents of My Life*, 46–48 (on publishing *Farmers' Register*); Avery Craven, *Edmund Ruffin, Southerner: A Study in Secession* (1932; reprint, Baton Rouge: Louisiana State University Press, 1966), 66–71 (on the banking issue and disaffection); [William Boulware], "Edwin [*sic*] Ruffin, of Virginia, Agriculturist...," *De Bow's Review* 11 (1851): 431–36 (reprinted with notes in Allmendinger, *Incidents of My Life*, 167–78). See also Allmendinger, *Ruffin*, 23–56.

25. On the *Essay*'s influence in American soil science, see W. P. Cutter, "A Pioneer in Agricultural Science," in *Yearbook, Department of Agriculture, 1895* (Washington: USDA, 1895): 493–502; and U.S. Department of Agriculture, Soil Conservation Service, "Early American Soil Conservationists," Misc. Publication No. 449 (1941; Washington: USDA, 1990): 42–56. On evaluation of the *Farmers' Register*, see Virginius Dabney, *Virginia, The New Dominion: A History from 1607 to the Present* (Garden City, N.Y.: Doubleday, 1971), 280 (quoting John Skinner of the Baltimore *American Farmer*), and Craven, *Edmund Ruffin*, 62.

26. *Farmers' Register*, 1833–42. See also Allmendinger, *Ruffin*, 36–44.

27. On mid-eighteenth-century tensions and the depletion of hardwoods, see *The Diary of Colonel Landon Carter of Sabine Hall, 1752–1778*, edited by Jack P. Greene, 2 vols. (Charlottesville: University Press of Virginia, 1965), especially 1:382. W. J. D., "On the Law of Enclosures in Virginia," *Farmers' Register* 1 (Dec. 1834): 450–52; [Ruffin?], "The Law of Inclosures," ibid., 2 (Nov. 1834), 345–46; R. N., "A Commentary on the Law of Enclosures of Virginia," ibid., 346–47; [Ruffin?], "General Results of the Law of Enclosures in Virginia," ibid., 2 (March 1835): 610–11. On fence/antifence struggles ca. 1870–1900, see Forrest McDonald and Grady McWhiney, "The South from Self-Sufficiency to Peonage: An Interpretation," *American Historical Review* 85 (Dec. 1980): 1095–1118; J. Crawford King, Jr., "The Closing of the Southern Range: An Exploratory Study," *Journal of Southern History* 48 (Feb. 1982): 53–70; and Steven Hahn, *The Roots of Southern Populism: Yeoman Farmers and the Transformation of the Georgia Upcountry* (New York: Oxford University Press, 1983), especially 137–69.

28. "Petition of Stock-Owners. To the General Assembly of Virginia," *Farmers' Register* 2 (Dec. 1834): 425–26. See also Fencemore, "The Policy of the Law of Enclosures Defended," ibid., 3 (May 1835): 47–49.

29. [Ruffin], "Remarks," *Farmers' Register* 3 (May 1835): 49–50; and (last quotation) Ruffin, "The Oppression of the Fence Law, and the Dawn of Relief," ibid., 8 (31 Aug. 1840): 504–5 (quotation 504). See also Allmendinger, *Ruffin*, 117 (who is more inclined than I to credit Ruffin's concern about land aggrandizement).

30. Ruffin, "Oppression of the Fence Law," 504–5; *The Diary of Edmund Ruffin*, vol. 1: *Toward Independence, October, 1856–April, 1861*, edited by William Kauffman Scar-

borough (Baton Rouge: Louisiana State University Press, 1972), 150 (22 Jan. 1858). See also Allmendinger, *Ruffin*, 117.

31. See untitled report of a commission of the state agricultural society that had conferred with Governor Gilbert C. Walker, *SPF*, n.s., 5 (Jan. 1871): 52–55 (quotation 54).

32. See "The Fence Law," *SPF*, n.s., 9 (Nov. 1875): 653; advertisement by Watt and Call (agents for barbed wire sales), ibid., n.s., 41 (Jan. 1880): n.p.; "Stock Law in Georgia," ibid., n.s., 42 (Aug. 1881): 457; "No-Fence Law," *SP* 47 (Jan. 1886): 6; B. Puryear, "The Relations of Agriculture to Legislation—Fence Laws—III," ibid., 47 (Dec. 1886): 628–30; R. J. H. Hatchett, M.D., "Improving Condition of North Carolina," ibid., 48 (July 1887): 361–62; and "Fences," ibid., 50 (Sept. 1889): 155 (on the persistence of open-range hog foraging in tidewater Virginia near the end of the century).

33. Ruffin, "Sketch … An Address to the Historical and Philosophical Society of Virginia," *Farmers' Register* 3 (Apr. 1836): 748–60.

34. See Ruffin, "Observations Made during an Excursion to the Dismal Swamp," *Farmers' Register* 4 (Jan. 1837): 513–21; [Ruffin], "Curious Extracts from the Ancient Laws and Records of Virginia," ibid., 7 (31 Mar. 1839): 181–83; [Ruffin], "Publication of the Byrd Manuscripts," ibid., 9 (31 Oct. 1841): 577; Ruffin, "Report to the State Board of Agriculture, on the Brandon Farms," ibid., 10 (30 June 1842): 274–82.

35. Ruffin, "An Address … November 18, 1852" (Charleston: Steam Power Press of Walker and James, 1853), incomplete copy in Ruffin, "Incidents of My Life" (vol. 3/1853), in Edmund Ruffin Papers, VHS.

36. Untitled editorial note, *Farmers' Register* 3 (Feb. 1836): 602. For the publication history of Malthus's work, see T. R. Malthus, *An Essay on the Principle of Population*, edited by Patricia James, 2 vols. (Cambridge: Cambridge University Press, 1989), 1: ix–xv.

37. Ruffin note, 602. On Malthus and "Malthusians" see William Petersen, *Population* (London: Macmillan, 1969), 142–61.

38. Malthus, *Principle of Population*, 1:143.

39. Untitled editorial note, 602 (emphasis Ruffin's). On the United States' exceptionalism in the slave trade and African American demography see Philip D. Curtin, *The Atlantic Slave Trade: A Census* (Madison: University of Wisconsin Press, 1969), and C. Vann Woodward, *American Counterpoint: Slavery and Racism in the North-South Dialogue* (Boston: Little, Brown, 1971), 78–106.

40. Malthus, *Principle of Population*, 11–12 (quotation 12).

41. Ruffin, "Observations Made," 513–21 (quotations 513).

42. Ibid., quotations 516, 520–21; and William Byrd of Westover, "Proposal to Drain the Dismal Swamp," *Farmers' Register* 4 (Jan. 1837): 521–24.

43. Ruffin, "'Jottings Down' in the Swamps," *Farmers' Register* 7 (30 Nov. 1839): 698.

44. Ibid., 699.

45. Ibid., 700.

46. Ruffin, "'Jottings Down' in the Swamps," [continuation of Nov. travelogue], *Farmers' Register* 7 (31 Dec. 1939): 724–33 (quotation 728).

47. Ruffin, "Notes of a Steam Journey," *Farmers' Register* 8 (30 Apr. 1840): 243–54; J. R. Poinsett, "On Irrigation" [from *Southern Agriculturist*], ibid., 9 (31 July 1841): 409–10 (quotation 410).

48. Ruffin, "Address on the Opposite Results of Exhaustive and Fertilizing Systems of Agriculture," more or less repeated and elaborated in Ruffin, "Southern Agricultural Exhaustion, and Its Remedy," in U.S. Congress, Senate, *Report of the Commissioner of Patents for the Year 1852*, Part 2: *Agriculture* (Washington: Robert Armstrong, Printer, 1853), 373–89. Quotation from Allmendinger, *Ruffin*, 115.

49. *Diary of Edmund Ruffin*, 1:444–45 (quotation 444; 29 July).

50. Allmendinger, *Ruffin*, 171–72.

51. Ibid., 152–85 (especially 157–69).

52. On the failure of marling see especially William M. Mathew, *Edmund Ruffin and the Crisis of Slavery in the Old South: The Failure of Agricultural Reform* (Athens: University of Georgia Press, 1988), 110–28. On commercial fertilizers, see, for example, advertisements in *SPF* and *SP*, 1870–1900. On surviving and new postbellum river planters see the Richard Eppes Diary, 1866–95, VHS; Hill Carter, "Results of Fifty-Four Years' Experience in Farming," *SPF*, n.s., 4 (May 1870): 257–62; and Gregg L. Michel, "From Slavery to Freedom: Hickory Hill, 1850–80," in *The Edge of the South: Life in Nineteenth-Century Virginia*, edited by Edward Ayers and John F. Willis (Charlottesville: University Press of Virginia, 1991), 103–21.

53. On the postbellum persistence of grain culture see Carter, "Results of Fifty-Four Years' Experience in Farming"; Michel, "From Slavery to Freedom"; and the Eppes Diary, 1866–95. On wheat production and prices, see U.S. Bureau of the Census, *Historical Statistics of the United States, Colonial Times to 1957* (Washington: GPO, 1960), 297. On the shifting structure of U.S. grain culture see Harry D. Fornari, "U.S. Grain Exports: A Bicentennial Overview," *Agricultural History* 50 (Spring 1976): 137–50; Guy A. Lee, "The Historical Significance of the Chicago Grain Elevator System," ibid., 11 (Winter 1937): 16–32; and William Cronon, *Nature's Metropolis: Chicago and the Great West* (New York: W. W. Norton, 1991), 97–147. On doubts in the Chesapeake, see X—Virginia, "Is It Wise, in View of Western Competition, to Counsel Virginia to Curtail Her Wheat Production?," *SPF*, n.s., 8 (Oct. 1874): 185–87; and October meeting minutes, Garrison Forest Farmers Club Papers, Maryland Historical Society, Baltimore.

54. Eppes Diary, 28 Nov. 1889.

CHAPTER THREE

1. Daniel William Cobb Diary, VHS. See especially entries for Nov.–Dec. 1843, 16 Mar. 1846.

2. See Daniel W. Crofts, *Old Southampton: Politics and Society in a Virginia County, 1834–1869* (Charlottesville: University Press of Virginia, 1992), 39–41, 58–73, 77–78 (quotation 68), and Cobb Diary, 1842–61.

3. Elliott Lemuel Story Diary, VHS; see entries for 14 Feb. 1838, 9 Oct. 1846, 27 Feb. and 1 Mar. 1847, and 29 Aug. 1851. See also Crofts, *Old Southampton*, 41–58.

4. On making fence rails, see Cobb Diary, e.g., 23 Jan., 25 Mar., and 9 Apr. 1843, 15 and 26 Feb. 1857, 30 Jan. 1861, 7 Jan. 1866, and various entries during Jan. 1870 and Mar. 1872. On heaping and burning wood see ibid., e.g., 2 Feb. 1843, 6 Feb. 1846, 27 Mar. 1854, 16 Feb. and 30 Mar. 1857, 4 and 11 Mar. 1861, 6 Jan. 1866, and 3 Feb. 1870.

5. On Story's log-heaping and -burning see Story Diary, e.g., 1 and 24 Mar. 1847. On fertilizing, see, for example, Story Diary, 25 Feb. and 14 Nov. 1857, and 14 Apr. 1858, and his narrative entry for 1872; Cobb Diary, e.g., 24 Apr. 1846, 11 and 28 Apr. 1854, 14 Feb. 1866, and 2 Mar. 1870. See also Julian Calx Ruffin Diary, 9 Mar. 1846, in Edmund Ruffin Papers, VHS.

6. Robert Beverley, *The History and Present State of Virginia*, edited by Louis B. Wright (Chapel Hill: University of North Carolina Press, 1947), 318.

7. See Merrill K. Bennett, "Aspects of the Pig," *Agricultural History* 44 (April 1970): 223–35; and Lewis Cecil Gray, *History of Agriculture in the Southern United States to 1860*, 2 vols. (Washington, D.C.: Carnegie Institution, 1933), 1:206.

8. *The Diary of Colonel Landon Carter of Sabine Hall, 1752–1778*, edited by Jack P. Green, 2 vols. (Charlottesville: University Press of Virginia, 1965), 1:465 (quotations); see also 1:312–13, 246–47, 265.

9. See the Benjamin Cocke Account Book, 1826–34, entries for 21 Sept. 1826 and 3 Mar. 1834, in Eppes Family Muniments, VHS; and Richard Eppes Diary, 18 Mar., 19 and 21 Apr. 1852 (Eppes quotations), 2 Dec. 1867, 4 Mar. 1868, 8 Jan. and 26 Mar. 1875, 21 Nov. 1888, and 10 Feb. and 10 Dec. 1890, VHS. On the Poland-China, see ubiquitous advertisements in, for example, *SPF* and *SP*, during the 1880s.

10. Eppes Diary, 3 June, 20 and 25 Aug., 4 and 6 Sept. 1859.

11. Ibid., 19 and 27 Feb., 10 Mar. 1866.

12. Julian Ruffin Diary, 28 Dec. 1844, 16 Dec. 1845, and 23 Dec. 1847. (On the last date Ruffin "killed [an] old sow — 114 lbs.")

13. *The Ordinances of the Borough of Norfolk...* (Norfolk: T. G. Broughton and Co., 1845), 183–84; Parke Rouse, Jr., *The Timber Tycoons: The Camp Families of Virginia and Florida and Their Empire, 1887–1987* (Richmond: William Byrd Press for Southampton County Historical Society, 1988), 28.

14. Cobb Diary, 23 and 24 Jan. and 2 Apr. 1861. On Cobb's hogs ranging, see, for example, entries of 10 Apr. and 1 May 1846, 18 Jan. 1849, and 23 Dec. 1854.

15. Story Diary, 19 Feb. 1848 (first quotation), 8 Jan. 1853 (second quotation), 4 Nov. 1847, 9 and 20 Jan. and 14 Mar. 1857.

16. Gray, *History of Agriculture*, 1:210; Story Diary, 29 Jan. 1846. See also G. Melvin Herndon, "Elliott L. Story: A Small Farmer's Struggle for Economic Survival in Antebellum Virginia," *Agricultural History* 56 (July 1982): 516–27.

17. See Gray, *History of Agriculture*, 1:149, 210, 2:840–41, 883–84; and Forrest McDonald and Grady McWhiney, "The South from Self-Sufficiency to Peonage: An Interpretation," *American Historical Review* 85 (Dec. 1980): 1095–1118.

18. Census of Agriculture, 1860, tables for Bertie, Camden, Chowan, Currituck, Gates, Hertford, Northampton, Pasquotank, and Perquimans, North Carolina; and Isle of Wight, Nansemond, Norfolk, Prince George, Princess Anne, Southampton, Surry, and Sussex, Virginia.

19. U.S. manuscript census, 1850, schedules for population, slaves, and agriculture, Gates Co., North Carolina.

20. Ibid.

21. Censuses of population, 1790–1920, county tables.

22. See Cecil D. Eby, Jr., *"Porte Crayon": The Life of David Hunter Strother* (Chapel Hill: University of North Carolina Press, 1960), 3–102, especially 59–61.

23. Laura Wood Roper, *FLO: A Biography of Frederick Law Olmsted* (Baltimore: Johns Hopkins University Press, 1973), especially 1–123.

24. Olmsted to Charles Loring Brace, 22 Dec. 1852, in *The Papers of Frederick Law Olmsted*, vol. 2: *Slavery and the South, 1852–1857*, edited by Charles Capen McLaughlin (Baltimore: Johns Hopkins University Press, 1981), 92–93 (quotation 93). On Olmsted's itinerary see Roper, *FLO*, 86.

25. Olmsted, *A Journey in the Seaboard Slave States, with Remarks on Their Economy* (New York: Dix and Edwards, 1856), ix.

26. *New-York Daily Times*, 16 Feb. 1853, in *Papers of Frederick Law Olmsted*, 90.

27. *New-York Daily Times*, 20 Apr. 1853, in *Papers of Frederick Law Olmsted*, 140–43 (quotations 141–42).

28. Ibid., 141.

29. Olmsted, *Seaboard Slave States*, 64–68 (quotations 64–65, 68).

30. Ibid., 65.

31. See, for example, ibid., 69.

32. *New-York Daily Times*, 13 Apr. 1853, in *Papers of Frederick Law Olmsted*, 135 (emphasis added).

33. See William M. Mathew, ed., *Agriculture, Geology, and Society in Antebellum South Carolina: The Private Diary of Edmund Ruffin, 1843* (Athens: University of Georgia Press, 1992), 210; December 1852 summaries in Edmund Ruffin, Jr., Plantation Diary, Edmund Ruffin Papers, SHC; and Cobb Diary, 28 Apr. 1857, VHS.

34. On corn production in new fields, see Olmsted, *Seaboard Slave States*, 135.

35. See [Kedzie], "Wood Ashes in the Orchard," *SP* 46 (Jan. 1885): 31; "Wood Ashes as a Fertilizer" [from *Massachusetts Plowman*], ibid., 46 (May 1885): 233; Kedzie, "Manurial Value of Ashes," ibid., 47 (Aug. 1886): 418–21; and A. B. Stevens, "Analysis of Wood Ashes," ibid., 49 (Nov. 1888): 553.

36. For a literature review and research summary see Alton G. Campbell, "Recycling and Disposing of Wood Ash," *Tappi Journal* (Sept. 1990): 141–46; also Tsutomu

Ohno and M. Susan Erich, "Effect of Wood Ash Application on Soil pH and Soil Test Nutrient Levels," *Agriculture, Ecosystems and Environment* 32 (1990): 223–39; and Kermit C. Berger, *Sun, Soil and Survival: An Introduction to Soils* (1965; reprint, Norman: University of Oklahoma Press, 1972), 146–56.

37. Ibid. (especially Berger, *Sun, Soil and Survival*, 150); Lewis M. Naylor and Eric Schmidt, "Paper Mill Wood Ash as a Fertilizer and Liming Material: Field Trials," *Tappi Journal* (June 1989): 199–206; and B. R. Lerner and J. D. Utzinger, "Wood Ash as Soil Liming Material," *HortScience* 21 (Feb. 1986): 76–78.

38. See the Cobb and Story diaries for examples of fodder-making from corn tops and leaves; and on corn and peas, see Olmsted, *Seaboard Slave States*, 134–35, and Ruffin, "'Jottings Down' in the Swamps," *Farmers' Register* 7 (30 Nov. 1839): 698–703, especially 700 (on northeastern North Carolina). On corn/pea culture generally in the South, see Carville Earle, "The Myth of the Southern Soil Miner: Macrohistory, Agricultural Innovation, and Environmental Change," in *The Ends of the Earth: Perspectives on Modern Environmental History*, edited by Donald Worster (Cambridge: Cambridge University Press, 1988), 175–210, especially 201–10.

39. See Peter Novick, *That Noble Dream: The "Objectivity Question" and the American Historical Profession* (Cambridge: Cambridge University Press, 1988), especially 92–97.

40. W. P. Cutter, "A Pioneer in Agricultural Science," in *Yearbook, Department of Agriculture, 1895* (Washington: USDA, 1895), 493; "Agricultural Teachers and Writers of the Present Day," *SP* 65 (Jan. 1904): 1–18 (especially 2–7, on Ruffin). On the rise of agronomic education and professionalism see Roy V. Scott, *The Reluctant Farmer: The Rise of Agricultural Extension to 1914* (Urbana: University of Illinois Press, 1970), and Alfred Charles True, *A History of Agricultural Education in the United States, 1785–1925* (Washington: GPO, 1929).

41. Jack Temple Kirby, *Westmoreland Davis: Virginia Planter-Politician, 1859–1942* (Charlottesville: University Press of Virginia, 1968), especially 25–39.

42. See the Craven entry in *Directory of American Scholars*, 5th ed. (New York: Jaques Cattell/R. R. Bowker, 1969), 108; his obituary in *Journal of Southern History* 46 (Aug. 1980): 478; and Craven, "An Historical Adventure" [a reprint of his Mississippi Valley Historical Association presidential address], in his *An Historian and the Civil War* (Chicago: University of Chicago Press, 1964), 217–33. The first two sources listed (the first apparently at Craven's own direction) cite North Carolina as his birthplace. A longer and seemingly more authoritative sketch, which I follow, is John David Smith, "Avery Craven (12 August 1885 – 21 January 1980)," in *Dictionary of Literary Biography*, vol. 17, *Twentieth-Century American Historians*, edited by Clyde Wilson (Detroit: Gale Research/Book Tower, 1983), 126–31. Smith's birth-year for Craven is probably mistaken, however.

43. See Howard Lamar, "Frederick Jackson Turner," in *Pastmasters: Some Essays on American Historians*, edited by Marcus Cunliffe and Robin W. Winks (New York: Harper and Row, 1969), 79–110, especially 97–99; Avery Craven, "The 'Turner Theo-

ries' and the South," *Journal of Southern History* 5 (Aug. 1939): 291–314; and Craven, *Soil Exhaustion as a Factor in the Agricultural History of Virginia and Maryland, 1606–1860* (Urbana: University of Illinois Press, 1926), acknowledgments.

44. Craven, *Soil Exhaustion,* 9–10.

45. Craven, *Edmund Ruffin, Southerner: A Study in Secession* (1932; reprint, Baton Rouge: Louisiana State University Press, 1966); and Craven, "John Taylor and Southern Agriculture," *Journal of Southern History* 4 (May 1938): 137–48 (quotations 137).

46. "M," "The Farmer," *SP* 43 (Aug. 1882): 57–58.

47. The Taylor-Ruffin-Craven influence is vast. A sample, from the decades since *Soil Exhaustion* appeared, would include Gray, *History of Agriculture,* 2:779–810; William B. Hessentine, *The South in American History* (1936; reprint, New York: Prentice-Hall, 1943), especially 276–78; Clement Eaton, *A History of the Old South* (1949; reprint, New York: Macmillan, 1966), especially 216–17; and the introduction to *The Diary of Edmund Ruffin,* vol. 1: *Toward Independence, October, 1856–April, 1861,* edited by William Kauffman Scarborough (Baton Rouge: Louisiana State University Press, 1972), xviii, which declares that "Two centuries of soil exploitation under the one-crop system and poor agricultural practices had transformed the once-fertile region of eastern Virginia into a veritable wasteland." William Edwin Hemphill, Marvin Wilson Schlegel, and Sadie Ethel Engelberg, *Cavalier Commonwealth: History and Government in Virginia* (New York: McGraw-Hill, 1957), a popular school text, conveys nostalgia and restorationist sympathies by both title and text. A more recent state history, Virginius Dabney's *Virginia, the New Dominion: A History from 1607 to the Present* (Garden City, N.Y.: Doubleday, 1971), also follows Craven.

48. Censuses of agriculture, 1860–1930, county tables. Counties are the same seventeen employed in previous chapters.

49. On the persisting fence agitation see W. M. Evans, "Fence Laws—Adulteration—Referendum, etc," *SP* 57 (Jan. 1896): 29; "The Fence Law Case," ibid., 61 (Mar. 1900): 162; and "Smithfield Hams" [the USDA report], ibid., 58 (July 1897): 306–7. See also T. O. Sandy, "Can Farming Be Made to Pay in Southside Virginia?," ibid., 59 (Feb. 1898): 59–60. (Sandy described a similar system, in which he fenced his woods and ranged his hogs there, then fattened them in his pea field.)

50. Censuses of agriculture, 1890–1940, county tables.

51. *Twelfth Census of the United States, Taken in the Year 1900 ... Agriculture,* part 1: *Farms, Live Stock, and Annual Products* (Washington: U.S. Census Office, 1902), cxi–cxlii.

52. Olmsted, *Seaboard Slave States,* 156–57 (quotations 157). Wallaceton crop fields were later much enlarged, extending west of the canal, as well. Author's observation; but see also the U.S. Geological Survey map of the Lake Drummond Quadrangle, dated 1977.

53. See Dudley Warren Bagley Papers, SHC, especially page proof for a *Progressive Farmer* (Raleigh) profile of Bagley, dated 17 Apr. 1926; see also copies of profiles in *SP* (15 Apr. 1928) and *Country Home* (Mar. 1932), Bagley Papers.

54. See "Highland Farm" records (especially folders 240–96), Bagley Papers.

55. See the Bagley–Joseph P. Knapp correspondence and various political materials (especially folder 138), Bagley Papers.

CHAPTER FOUR

1. F. Roy Johnson, comp., *Oral Folk Humor from the Carolina and Virginia Flatlands* (Murfreesboro, N.C.: Johnson Publishing Co., 1980), 89.

2. Elizabeth Lay Green and Paul Green, "Folk Beliefs and Practices in Central and Eastern North Carolina" (typescript dated 1926–28), North Carolina Collection, University of North Carolina, 51 (first quotation); Johnson, *Oral Folk Humor*, 45 (second quotation).

3. Green and Green, "Folk Beliefs and Practices," 97 (first quotation) and 73; Johnson, *Oral Folk Humor*, 43–44, 61. See also James L. Leloudis II, "Tokens of Death: Tales from Perquimans County," *North Carolina Folklore Journal* 25 (Nov. 1977): 47–60.

4. See Eugene P. Odum, "The Value of Wetlands: A Hierarchical Approach," in *Wetland Functions and Values: The State of Our Understanding*, edited by Phillip E. Greeson, John R. Clark, and Judith E. Clark (Minneapolis: American Water Resources Association, 1979), 16–25.

5. See the Confederate Engineers' Maps of the Jeremy Francis Gilmer Collection, VHS. (I work from photographic duplications of the originals — e.g., No. 87, Surry, Sussex, and Southampton Counties, 1863 [2 of 2].)

6. Confederate Engineers' Map No. 27 (Prince George County, 1863).

7. Confederate Engineers' Map No. 91 (Bertie County, N.C., 1863 (2 of 2).

8. Confederate Engineers' Map No. 90 (Bertie County, N.C., 1 of 2).

9. See various U.S. Geological Survey quadrangle maps, especially for Southampton County and Suffolk (formerly Nansemond County); and North Carolina Department of Parks and Recreation, map and brochure for Merchants Millpond State Park.

10. U.S. Geological Survey quadrangle map of Runnymede, Va. (1968, photorevised 1986).

11. See review of John MacCulloch, M.D., F.R.S., *Malaria: An Essay on the production and propagation of this Poison . . .*, in *Southern Review* 2, no. 3 (Aug.–Nov. 1828): 152–92; Joseph V. Siry, *Marshes of the Ocean Shore: Development of an Ecological Ethic* (College Station: Texas A&M University Press, 1984), 30–33; Albert E. Cowdrey, *This Land, This South: An Environmental History* (Lexington: University of Kentucky Press, 1983), especially 20, 25–28; and David C. Miller, *Dark Eden: The Swamp in Nineteenth-Century American Culture* (Cambridge: Cambridge University Press, 1989), especially 13, 184–88.

12. Dr. Thomas O'Dwyer Diary, entries for 19 and 25 Oct. 1825, SHC (no. 766).

13. David F. Allmendinger, Jr., ed., *Incidents of My Life: Edmund Ruffin's Autobiographical Essays* (Charlottesville: University Press of Virginia), 25–26 (quotations 25).

14. Ibid., 86.

15. See William Cronon, *Changes in the Land: Indians, Colonists, and the Ecology of New England* (New York: Hill and Wang, 1983), especially 97–99, 105–7.

16. "Fact in Natural History" [reprinted from Richmond *Enquirer*], *Farmers' Register* 6 (June 1838): 174.

17. See the twin Norfolk newspapers, the *Virginian-Pilot* and *Ledger-Star*, during December 1992/January 1993.

18. Ruffin, [title illegible], *Farmers' Register* 5 (May 1837): 41–43 (quotation 42).

19. Ruffin, "On the Sources of Malaria, or Autumnal Diseases, in Virginia, and the Means of Remedy and Prevention," *Farmers' Register* 6 (July 1838): 216–28 (quotations in order: 217, 218, 222).

20. "Malaria and Millponds," *Farmers' Register* 8 (31 Mar. 1840): 141.

21. Ruffin, "Report to Board of Agriculture. III. Of mill-ponds, as producers of malaria and disease, both alone and in combination with other causes," *Farmers' Register*, n.s., 1 (28 Feb. 1843): 85–93. On Ruffin and the Board of Agriculture, see Allmendinger, *Incidents of My Life*, 63–64, 123, 176.

22. Dr. C. W. Dabney, Jr., "How to Avoid Malaria" [reprint from *Southern States*], *SP* 58 (June 1897): 278.

23. Richard H. Lewis, M.D., "Mosquitoes and Malaria," *Progressive Farmer* (13 Aug. 1901): 7.

24. See Will D. Campbell, *Brother to a Dragonfly* (New York: Continuum, 1977), 14–15.

25. Norman S. Beaton, *Boykins: One Hundred and Twenty Years* (n.p., n.d. [ca. 1956]), 2; and Cowdrey, *This Land, This South*, 5, 132 (quotation), 158, 170, 173. See also Rachel Carson, *Silent Spring* (New York: Houghton Mifflin, 1962), especially 5–8; Thomas Dunlap, *DDT: Scientists, Citizens, and Public Policy* (Princeton: Princeton University Press, 1981); and James Brooke, "Colombian Physician Challenges Malaria on the Home Front," *New York Times*, 23 Mar. 1993, B6.

26. Southerners' vaunted "laziness" is a subject larger than malaria, of course. See, for example, David Bertelson, *The Lazy South* (New York: Oxford University Press, 1967), and Shields McIlwaine, *The Southern Poor White: From Lubberland to Tobacco Road* (Baton Rouge: Louisiana State University Press, 1939).

27. H. B. Ansell Books (2 manuscript vols.), 1:3–4 (first quotation), 1:5 (second quotation), 1:2–3 (third quotation), SHC. On the demise of parakeets, see Mikko Saikku, "The Extinction of the Carolina Parakeet," *Environmental History Review* 14 (Fall 1990): 1–18.

28. Ansell Books, 1:8 (first quotation), 1:42 (second quotation).

29. Ibid., 1:44 (first quotation), 1:45 (second quotation).

30. Ibid., 1:126 (first quotation), 1:120–22 (next quotations).

31. Ibid., 1:54–56 (on fishing), 1:2 (quotation).

32. See Walton H. and George H. Riggs Papers, NCSA. On the Albemarle-Chesapeake Canal and the Dismal Swamp Canal's decline, see Betty Hathaway Yar-

borough, *The Great Dismal* (Chesapeake, Va.: Norfolk County Historical Society, 1965), unpaginated [ca. p. 8].

33. Edmund Ruffin, "Hasty Observations on the Agriculture of the County of Nansemond," *Farmers' Register* 4 (Jan. 1837): 524–27, especially 524 (first quotation), 525 (second), and 527 (third).

34. On Nansemond's timber resources and the federal market, see ibid., 527. On the shingle-getting business in the Dismal, see Edmund Ruffin, "Observations Made during an Excursion to the Dismal Swamp," *Farmers' Register* 4 (Jan. 1837): 513–21 (especially 515–15).

35. Edmund Ruffin to Charles Campbell, 13 Mar. 1834, and Charles Campbell to Elizabeth Campbell, 4 Jan. 1834, in Charles Campbell Papers, Swem Library, College of William and Mary, Williamsburg, Va.

36. Ruffin, "Observations Made," 513, 516 (quotation).

37. See early portions of the Dismal Swamp Land Company Papers, Perkins Library, Duke University, Durham, N.C.; John Byrd [Collector] Papers, SHC; and Bland Simpson, *The Great Dismal: A Carolinian's Swamp Memoir* (Chapel Hill: University of North Carolina Press, 1990), 6, 12.

38. Ruffin, "Observations Made," 515–16, 517 (quotation).

39. Thomas Moore, "The Lake of the Dismal Swamp," reprinted in Porte Crayon, "The Dismal Swamp. Illustrated by Porte Crayon," *Harper's New Monthly Magazine* 13 (Sept. 1856): 441–55 (quotations 443–44).

40. Crayon, "Dismal Swamp," quotations (in order) 446, 447.

41. Ibid., 448.

42. Ibid., quotations 446, 451.

43. See "Free Colored" list in population schedule, manuscript census return for Nansemond Co., 1850; and various reports, lists, and accounts, 1850–61, DSLCo.

44. Crayon, "Dismal Swamp," 451.

45. Olmsted, *A Journey in the Seaboard Slave States* (New York: Dix and Edwards, 1856), 153–56 (quotations 153–55).

46. Ruffin, "Observations Made," 518.

47. Crayon, "Dismal Swamp," 447; manuscript census for Nansemond Co., 1850, population and agriculture schedules; and shingle records, 1840s/1850s, DSLCo.

48. See manuscript census for Nansemond Co., 1850, population and agriculture schedules; and shingle records, 1843–60, DSLCo.

49. Crayon, "Dismal Swamp," 451–52.

CHAPTER FIVE

1. See Bland Simpson, *The Great Dismal: A Carolinian's Swamp Memoir* (Chapel Hill: University of North Carolina Press, 1990), 9–10 (quotation); and Thomas

Jefferson Wertenbaker, *Torchbearer of the Revolution* (Princeton: Princeton University Press, 1940).

2. Simpson, *Great Dismal*, 11–12 (quotations 11).

3. See (among many) Bruce Catton, *The Army of the Potomac: A Stillness at Appomattox*, 3 vols. (Garden City, N.Y.: Doubleday, 1953), 3:145–90; and T. Harry Williams, *Lincoln and His Generals* (1952; reprint, New York: Vintage, 1967), 318–23 — although neither emphasizes adequately (to my mind) the significance of Grant's Chickahominy-crossing achievement.

4. See, for example, David C. Miller, *Dark Eden: The Swamp in Nineteenth-Century American Culture* (Cambridge: Cambridge University Press, 1989), 77–104; Thomas Wentworth Higginson, *Black Rebellion* (1889; reprint, New York: Arno Press, 1969); and Richard Price, ed., *Maroon Societies: Rebel Slave Communities in the Americas* (1973; 2d ed., Baltimore: Johns Hopkins University Press, 1979).

5. On postbellum southern Appalachia's industrial ruin see Ronald D. Eller, *Miners, Millhands, and Mountaineers: The Industrialization of the Appalachian South, 1880–1930* (Knoxville: University of Tennessee Press, 1982). Discussion of swamps (here and elsewhere) is also influenced by the "postimperialist" school of literary criticism; see especially Edward Said, *Culture and Imperialism* (New York: Alfred A. Knopf, 1993).

6. A useful introduction to the phenomenon of slave-hiring is John B. Boles, *Black Southerners, 1619–1869* (Lexington: University of Kentucky Press, 1984), 122–23, 128–29. See also Clement Eaton, "Slave-Hiring in the Upper South: A Step toward Freedom," *Mississippi Valley Historical Review* 46 (Mar. 1960): 663–79; John H. Moore, "Simon Gray, Riverman: A Slave Who Was Almost Free," ibid., 49 (Dec. 1962): 472–84; Robert S. Starobin, *Industrial Slavery in the Old South* (New York: Oxford University Press, 1970). The numbers of slaves typically hired remains an open question.

7. See the antebellum volumes, Daniel Cobb Diaries, VHS.

8. John Fanning Burgwyn Diary, NCSA; for example, see entry for 3 July 1855. See also records of hiring slaves for work on Sunnyside (Southampton Co.), 1840s and 1850s, in Harrison Peterson Pope Papers, VHS. On annual hiring for principally agricultural labor markets, see the William Valentine Diary, SHC; for example, see entry for 5 Jan. 1846, in which Valentine attended various Hertford gatherings and noted high rates based on good prospects for corn and cotton.

9. Valentine Diary, 1 Feb. 1847; U.S. manuscript census, 1850, Gates County, N.C.

10. See Chesson's business correspondence with Baltimore merchants, 1840s, and J. A. Anderson (of Winton) to Chesson and Armstead, 3 Mar. 1849, in John B. Chesson Papers, NCSA. Other maritime slaves in the region are mentioned (e.g., in a list of Edenton slaves belong to the estate of Josiah Collins, 1 Apr. 1840) in the Josiah Collins Papers, NCSA.

11. On naval stores and cooperage see Timothy Silver, *A New Face on the Countryside: Indians, Colonists, and Slaves in South Atlantic Forests, 1500–1800* (Cambridge: Cambridge University Press, 1990), 123–29.

12. Dr. Thomas O'Dwyer Diary, especially entries for 5 and 6 June and 7 Sept. 1825, in Murfreesboro Collection, SHC.

13. Olmsted, *A Journey in the Seaboard Slave States* (New York: Dix and Edwards, 1856), 153–54.

14. Ibid., 155–56.

15. Crayon, "The Dismal Swamp," *Harper's New Monthly Magazine* 13 (June–Nov. 1856): 451.

16. Audubon, *Ornithological Biography, or an Account of the Habits of the Birds of the United States of America... Interspersed with Delineations of American Scenery and Manners*, 5 vols. (Edinburgh: Adam Black, 1831–39), 2 (1834): 27–32 (quotations 28–29).

17. Crayon, "Dismal Swamp," 452–53.

18. Ibid., 453–54 (quotations 453).

19. Audubon, *Ornithological Biography*, 32; and (on bear-killing with shotgun traps in the Dismal), Simpson, *Great Dismal*, especially 33.

20. Ruffin, "Observations Made during an Excursion to the Dismal Swamp," *Farmers' Register* 4 (Jan. 1837): 519.

21. F. Roy Johnson, comp., *Oral Folk Humor From the Carolina and Virginia Flatlands* (Murfreesboro, N.C.: Johnson Publishing Co., 1980), 13.

22. See F. Roy Johnson and Tom Parramore, "The Roanoke-Chowan Story," a vol. of clippings compiled from Murfreesboro's *Daily-Roanoke-Chowan News* (1960–62), 169–79, in F. Roy Johnson Collection, NCSA.

23. F. Roy Johnson, comp., *Myths and Legends of North Carolina's Roanoke-Chowan Area* (Murfreesboro, N.C.: Johnson Publishing Co., 1966), 59–64.

24. On whites' comfort in nonwhites' adoption of Christianity, see, for example, John Wheeler Moore, "Historical Sketches of Hertford County" (clippings and typescript, ca. 1880), chap. 63, in John Wheeler Moore Papers, SHC. For context see Albert J. Raboteau, *Slave Religion: The "Invisible Institution" in the Antebellum South* (New York: Oxford University Press, 1978), especially 163–65; and Eugene D. Genovese, *Roll, Jordan, Roll: The World the Slaves Made* (New York: Pantheon, 1974), 159–324.

25. Of the vast literature on the Turner Rebellion, a brief version is Stephen B. Oates, *The Fires of Jubilee: Nat Turner's Fierce Rebellion* (New York: Harper and Row, 1975); but for detail and illustration, I rely primarily upon Henry Irving Tragle, *The Southampton Slave Revolt of 1831: A Compilation of Source Material* (Amherst: University of Massachusetts Press, 1971), quotation 318.

26. Gray, "The Confessions of Nat Turner..." (Baltimore: Lucas and Deaver, 1831), in Tragle, *Southampton Slave Revolt*, 300–321 (quotations 316–17).

27. See Lawrence W. Levine, *Black Culture and Black Consciousness: Afro-American Folk Thought from Slavery to Freedom* (New York: Oxford University Press, 1977), 56–57, 67–74.

28. Gray, "Confessions."

29. Oates, *Fires of Jubilee*, 46–47.

30. Southampton Court of Oyer and Terminer, 3 Sept. 1831, in Tragle, *Southampton Slave Revolt*, 195.

31. On the Gabriel conspiracy of 1800 see Douglas R. Egerton, *Gabriel's Rebellion: The Virginia Slave Conspiracies of 1800 and 1802* (Chapel Hill: University of North Carolina Press, 1993), especially xi, 27–28, 38–39; and on the Vesey plot see Robert S. Starobin, ed., *Denmark Vesey: The Slave Conspiracy of 1822* (Englewood Cliffs, N.J.: Prentice-Hall, 1970), 57 (quotation).

32. Johnson, comp., *Oral Folk Humor*, 38.

33. Crayon, "Dismal Swamp," 454–55.

34. Among many sources on Irish-African-American conflict, see Sean Wilentz, *Chants Democratic: New York City and the Rise of the American Working Class, 1788–1850* (New York: Oxford University Press, 1984), 118–19, 264.

35. Tragle, *Southampton Slave Revolt*, 370–71.

36. Ibid., 11–13.

37. Tommy Bogger, oral history interview with Roy L. Watford, Portsmouth, Va., n.d. (1981), typescript in Portsmouth Public Library, quotations pp. 4–5.

38. Newspapers reproduced in Tragle, *Southampton Slave Revolt*, 35–36, 153.

39. Thomas C. Parramore, *Southampton County, Virginia* (Charlottesville: University Press of Virginia, 1978), 65–68; Egerton, *Gabriel's Rebellion*; and Moore, "Historical Sketches of Hertford County," Chap. 19.

40. Parramore, *Southampton County*, 70–71.

41. Johnson, comp., *Myths and Legends*, 103–7 (especially 103–5).

42. Civil War historians have largely neglected this subregion, probably because much of it was Union-occupied so early and because no important engagements took place there, except the Merrimack-Monitor battle in Hampton Roads. An exception, which treats Washington County, on the Albemarle's southwestern shore, is Wayne K. Durrill, *War of Another Kind: A Southern Community in the Great Rebellion* (New York: Oxford University Press, 1990). Washington's clear, then opaque white class warfare is more or less mirrored in the experience of the subregion north of the Sound.

43. Richard T. Barnes Notebook, typescript copy in SHC, pp. 2–4.

44. Ibid., 1–2.

45. Introduction to Creecy Papers; R. B. Creecy to Betty B. Creecy, 31 Aug. 1861; R. B. Creecy to Dr. Smedes, 31 Aug. 1861; and R. B. Creecy to Betty B. Creecy, 15 Mar. 1862, all in Creecy Papers, SHC.

46. R. B. Creecy to Betty Creecy, 13 Feb. 1862.

47. Ibid., 9 Feb. 1862.

48. Ibid., 12 Apr. 1862.

49. Ibid., 28 Apr. 1862.

50. See Durrill, *War of Another Kind*, especially chap. 7; John W. H. Porter, *A Record of Events in Norfolk County, Virginia, from April 19th, 1861, to May 10th, 1862...* (Portsmouth: W. A. Fiske, 1892), 33, 47–51; and R. B. Creecy to Betty Creecy, 1 Aug. 1864.

51. On the murkiness of allegiance see Durrill, *War of Another Kind*, especially chaps. 5 and 7. On "Scratch Hall" see Johnson, *Myths and Legends*, 96–102; on the goat man see Johnson, *Oral Folk Humor*, 92.

52. Jesse Forbes Pugh, *A Biographical History of Camden County: Three Hundred Years along the Pasquotank* (Durham: Seeman Printing, 1957), 160–66.

53. "Bradney," account of pursuit of eighty escaped Confederate officers, 28 June 1863, document in Virginia State Library and Archives, Richmond.

54. Ibid.

55. Durrill, *War of Another Kind*, 108, 119, 183; Ira Berlin, ed., and Joseph P. Reidy and Leslie S. Rowland, assoc. eds., *Freedom: A Documentary History of Emancipation, 1861–1867*, series 2: *The Black Military Experience* (Cambridge: Cambridge University Press, 1982), 114 and documents 47A, 47B, 47C (pp. 138–40) and 315B (pp. 729–30); and Ira Berlin, Steven F. Miller, Joseph P. Reidy, and Leslie S. Rowland, eds., *Freedom: A Documentary History of Emancipation, 1861–1867*, series 1, vol. 2: *The Wartime Genesis of Free Labor: The Upper South* (Cambridge: Cambridge University Press, 1993), 88–90.

56. Ibid.; and S. Smith to "Sir" [George W. Capehart], ca. 15 Nov. 1864, in Capehart Family Papers, SHC. On Union army reactions to runaways and blacks as spies, see Leon F. Litwack, *Been in the Storm So Long: The Aftermath of Slavery* (New York: Alfred A. Knopf, 1979), especially 104–66.

57. "Bradney" account, VSLA.

58. "Civil War Items Return to Virginia," *History Notes* (Newsletter of the Virginia Historical Society) 1 (Winter 1991): 1–2. (The Yates Co. [N.Y.] Historical Society donated the reassembled whipping post to the VHS in 1990.)

59. M. B. Connolly, "Union Occupation of Norfolk and Portsmouth: Prelude to Reconstruction or Precursor to Violence?" (bound typescript dated Fall 1987, in Kern Memorial Library, Norfolk); Ervin Leon Jordan, Jr., "A Painful Case: The Wright-Sanborn Incident in Norfolk, Virginia, July–October, 1863," M.A. thesis, Old Dominion University, 1979; and John C. Emmerson, Jr., comp., "Some Aspects and Incidents of Military Rule in Portsmouth … From the Letter Book of Captain Daniel Mersinger, Provost Marshal … " (1946; six-page bound typescript), and Bishop J. H. D. Wingfield to Bishop Quintard, 28 May 1907 (copy), both in Emmerson Papers, Portsmouth Public Library.

60. Ira Berlin, Barbara J. Fields, Thavolia Glymph, Joseph P. Reidy, and Leslie S. Rowland, eds., *Freedom: A Documentary History of Emancipation, 1861–1867*, series 1, vol. 1: *The Destruction of Slavery* (Cambridge: Cambridge University Press, 1985), document 16 (pp. 95–98). Wild was court-martialed for this act (and the killing of a white civilian), but Butler reversed the conviction and returned Wild to duty.

61. See Joseph B. Dunn, *The History of Nansemond County, Virginia* (Suffolk: *Suffolk Herald*, 1907), 49–51; and Steven A. Cormier, *The Siege of Suffolk: The Forgotten Campaign, April 11–May 4, 1863* (Lynchburg, Va.: H. E. Howard, 1989).

62. Giles L. Newsome, ed., *The Diary of Henry H. Ingalls, Sixth Regiment of Massa-*

chusetts Volunteer Militia... (Suffolk: Robert Hardy Publications, 1986), 9, 15, 35.

63. Solomon August Lenfest Diary, 1862–63, University of Virginia Library (quotations from entries for 15 Sept. 1862 and 7 Mar. 1863).

64. Frank B. Butts, *Reminiscences of Gunboat Service on the Nansemond* (Providence: Rhode Island Soldiers and Sailors Historical Society, 1884), 12–14 (quotations 13–14).

65. Eleanor P. Cross and Charles B. Cross, Jr., eds., *Glencoe Diary: The War-Time Journal of Elizabeth Curtis Wallace* (Chesapeake, Va.: Norfolk Co. Historical Society, 1968), 79.

66. Edward A. Wild to George H. Johnson, 28 Dec. 1863, Wild Papers, SHC.

67. Ibid.

68. Ibid.

69. See Wild Papers and Durrill, *War of Another Kind,* 207–8.

70. J. D. Stokeley et al. to Gen. Getty, 13 Jan. 1864 (with copy of notice on Jones' body), and Wild to Capt. George H. Johnston, 28 Dec. 1863 (quotation), Wild Papers.

71. Wild to John T. Elliott, 17 Dec. 1863.

72. Col. Alonzo G. Draper to Hiram W. Allen, 24 Dec. 1863, Wild Papers.

CHAPTER SIX

1. On Taylor's Confederate allegiance, see Taylor, report to shareholders, 9 May 1861, and W. S. Riddick to Tazewell Taylor, 1 July 1862, DSLCo.

2. Riddick to Taylor, 30 Sept. 1862 (quotations), 1 and 3 Jan. 1863, DSLCo.

3. Figures from Riddick's "Old Lumber" account, 1 Nov. 1865; Riddick to Dismal Swamp Land Co., 10 May 1865 (quotation); and undated Riddick memorandum (ca. May 1865), DSLCo. On Mahone and the company see copy of summons to managers, 9 July 1856; "Share-holders of the Dismal Sw. Ld. Co.," 17 Nov. 1859; and Riddick to Taylor, 26 Sept. 1865, DSLCo.

4. Riddick to Taylor, 12 Oct. 1865. On the labor market see Riddick to Taylor, 22 Mar. 1866.

5. Riddick to Taylor, 23 Aug. 1866 (quotations on second fire); Riddick to Taylor, 8 Sept. 1869 (third fire); and Riddick to Taylor, 16 Nov. 1969 (on Riddick's dismissal).

6. See Riddick to Taylor, 16 Nov. 1869, and copy of the new contract, dated 20 Nov. 1869; payrolls for Aug. 1870 and Apr. 1871; Taylor to stockholders, 7 Mar. 1871; and draft contract with Baird, Roper, and Gaskell, 15 Apr. 1871, DSLCo. On the demise of shingles and shingle companies, see "Guide to the Collection," DSLCo.; and "Composition Roofing. Its Growing Popularity with Farmers Everywhere. The Great Carey Plant," *Southern Cultivator* 64 (15 Aug. 1906): 29, on the Phillip Carey Co., manufacturers of "flexible cement roofing" in Cincinnati.

7. See introduction, lists of Revolutionary runaways, and sales records for the 1780s–90s, DSLCo.

8. See introduction to collection and sales and payroll records, DSLCo.

9. See (on the getting of shingles from fallen timber) Edmund Ruffin, "Obser-

vations Made during an Excursion to the Dismal Swamp," *Farmers' Register* 4 (Jan. 1837): 517.

10. See William Cronon, *Changes in the Land: Indians, Colonists, and the Ecology of New England* (New York: Hill and Wang, 1983), especially 120–21; Carville Earle, *Evolution of a Tidewater Settlement Pattern: All Hallow's Parish, Maryland, 1650–1783* (Chicago: University of Chicago Geography Department, 1975); quotation from Richard Beale Davis, ed., *William Fitzhugh and His Chesapeake World, 1676–1701* (Chapel Hill: University of North Carolina Press, 1963), 18. On the historical distribution of types of trees see John W. Barrett, ed., *Regional Silviculture of the United States* (2d ed.; New York: Holt, Rinehart, 1980), 10–11, 258–59; *Tenth Census of the United States, 1880: Forest Trees of North America* (Washington: GPO, 1884), 511–12.

11. *The Diary of Colonel Landon Carter of Sabine Hall, 1752–1778*, edited by Jack P. Greene, 2 vols. (Charlottesville: University Press of Virginia, 1965), 1:382.

12. On heaping and burning wood in winter, see, for example, Julian Calx Ruffin Diary, 9 Mar. 1846, in Edmund Ruffin Papers, SHC; Richard Eppes Diary (c. 1852–60), in Eppes Family Muniments, VHS; and the Daniel Cobb and Elliott Story diaries, also in VHS. On wooden fences in the age of barbed wire and the persistence of wooden chimneys, see the George Monier Williams Drawing Book (mainly Middlesex Co., Va.), VHS; Eppes Diary, 16 Dec. 1868, and Story Diary, 20 and 30 Jan. 1875. On coal heat see Eppes Diary, 23 Mar. 1868. On postbellum wooden field drains see Menalcus, "Underdraining—Clover," *SPF* 38 (May 1877): 306–7; John Washington, "Drainage," ibid., p. 309. (The articles concern Southampton and Caroline counties, Va., respectively.) See also M. W. Early, "Stoves or Fire-Places," *SP* 51 (Nov. 1890): 529–30 (quotations). During the late 1940s and early 1950s I observed effective cooking with pine fuel in rural King and Queen Co., Va.

13. See Timothy Silver, *A New Face on the Countryside: Indians, Colonists, and Slaves in South Atlantic Forests, 1500–1800* (Cambridge: Cambridge University Press, 1990), 116–21; Al Roberts, "On the Brink of a Timber Boom," *Norfolk Virginian-Pilot and the Ledger-Star Business Weekly*, 8 Apr. 1991, p. 12 (on Wrenn's Mill); and DSLCo. On a small Alabama farmer's winter timbering during the early twentieth century, see Theodore Rosengarten, *All God's Dangers: The Life of Nate Shaw* (New York: Avon Books, 1974), especially 40–42, 89–95, 182–87, 204–7.

14. On early turpentining see Silver, *New Face on the Countryside*, 116–21. See also U.S. Censuses of Manufacturing, 1840, 1860, 1880, county tables.

15. On a particular longleaf forest (and longleafs' susceptibility to ranging hogs), see Cecil C. Frost and Lytton J. Musselman, "History and Vegetation of the Blackwater Ecologic Preserve [Isle of Wight Co., Va.]," *Castanea* 52 (1987): 16–46. I am especially indebted to Musselman's former doctoral student, Allen Plocher, who (in 1987 and 1988) identified the turpentine distillery ruin, grass-stage longleafs, and longleaf stumps with turpentine box scars.

16. Ibid., and (I think) reasonable conjecture based upon my own field study.

17. On markets and timbering in the Great Lakes states, see William Cronon,

Nature's Metropolis: Chicago and the Great West (New York: W. W. Norton, 1991), especially 148–206; and Michael Williams, *Americans and Their Forests: A Historical Geography* (Cambridge: Cambridge University Press, 1989), especially 238–88.

18. Draft leasing contract with Baird and Roper, 15 Apr. 1871, DSLCo.; Col. William H. Stewart, ed/comp., *History of Norfolk County, Virginia and Representative Citizens* (Chicago: Biographical Publishing Co., 1902), 553–54; *Norfolk and Portsmouth Directory, 1872–73* (Norfolk: Chataigne and Boyd, 1872), 296; *Directory of Norfolk, Portsmouth, and Berkley, 1900* (Norfolk, Richmond, and Newport News: J. L. Hill Printing Co., 1900), 181.

19. Ursula Fogleman Loy and Pauline Marion Worthy, eds., *Washington and the Pamlico* (Raleigh: Edwards and Broughton Co., for Washington–Beaufort Co. Bicentennial Commission, 1976), 332–34, 336–37.

20. See Parke Rouse, Jr., *The Timber Tycoons: The Camp Families of Virginia and Florida and Their Empire, 1887–1987* (Richmond: William Byrd Press for Southampton Historical Society, 1988), 29–32.

21. Stewart, *History of Norfolk County*, 694–95.

22. See W. Scott Boyce, *Economic and Social History of Chowan County, North Carolina, 1880–1915* (1917; reprint, New York: AMS Press, 1968), 121–26; Rouse, *Timber Tycoons*, 141.

23. Loy and Worthy, *Washington and the Pamlico*, 346–47.

24. Kenneth W. Coker, *Waverly: The First One Hundred Years, 1879–1979* (Richmond: Whittet and Skepperson for Waverly Centennial Commission, 1979), 29–30, 71–73; "The Richmond Cedar Works: A Major Forest Industry," *Virginia Forests* 1 (Nov.–Dec. 1946): 10–11; Rouse, *Timber Tycoons*, 29–32, 130.

25. Rouse, *Timber Tycoons*, especially 15–33, Appendix B, "Jenny Camp Norfleet's Memoirs," 233–43, and Appendix I, "John M. Camp on Company History," 269–74.

26. John Camp quoted in ibid., 269–70.

27. J. C. Parker to H. L. Norfleet, 31 Oct. 1911, John C. Parker Papers, University of Virginia Library; P. D. Camp letter in Rouse, *Timber Tycoons*, 244–45.

28. John Camp quoted in Rouse, *Timber Tycoons*, 270–71.

29. Ibid., 129–30; Bland Simpson, *The Great Dismal: A Carolinian's Swamp Memoir* (Chapel Hill: University of North Carolina Press, 1990), 50–51; and—on various Camp Manufacturing operations—the following sample from the Parker Papers: P. D. Camp to J. Edward Cole, 5 June 1902; Giles County Lumber Co. incorporation charter, 25 Mar. 1903; R. H. Mann–Parker correspondence, 1904–9 (on Dinwiddie Co.); legal agreement to deliver Georgia cypress, 1 July 1903; Parker to M. C. Woods, 21 July 1904.

30. See Parker's opinion on a fire, 17 Mar. 1900; Camp Manufacturing Co.–W. R. Carpenter correspondence, 1908–10 (on Brunswick Co.); Parker to Hill Carter (attorney for creditors), 15 May 1909; and Parker to Camp Manufacturing Co., 19 Mar. 1910, all in Parker Papers; Simpson, *Great Dismal*, 50–51.

31. Legal agreement to cut Georgia cypress, 1 July 1903, Parker Papers; Williams, *Americans and Their Forests*, 193–288; Jack Camp quoted in Simpson, *Great Dismal*, 53.

32. See Edward L. Ayers, *The Promise of the New South: Life after Reconstruction* (New York: Oxford University Press, 1992), 127–28 (quotation 128).

33. Simpson, *Great Dismal*, 54–55 (quotation 54). Simpson writes that families used company housing "not infrequently" (54), but this seems dubious, especially considering Ayers, *Promise of the New South*, especially 67–69.

34. Ayers, *Promise of the New South*, 68–69. (Between 1880 and 1915, 25 to 30 percent of black urban households were headed by mothers—double the rate for rural black households.)

35. Simpson, *Great Dismal*, 55–56 (quotations); Rouse, *Timber Tycoons*, 20 (on John Stafford Camp, alcoholic and storekeeper). On the extent of company stores in the Camp empire, see J. C. Parker to Camp Manufacturing Co., 1 July 1918, Parker Papers.

36. Simpson, *Great Dismal*, 57 (all quotations).

CHAPTER SEVEN

1. See introduction to Benjamin Wesley Kilgore Papers, NCSA, and Kilgore correspondence in Dudley Warren Bagley Papers, SHC.

2. See Standard Turpentine Co. files (especially brochure in 1903 file), Kilgore Papers.

3. I am indebted to Professor R. C. Peterson of Miami University's Department of Paper Science and Engineering for this information and analysis.

4. Thomas Dixon to Kilgore, 19 Aug. 1903 and 5 Apr. 1904, Kilgore Papers. On Dixon see Joel Williamson, *The Crucible of Race: Black-White Relations in the South since Emancipation* (Oxford: Oxford University Press, 1984), part 3; and Jack Temple Kirby, *Media-Made Dixie: The South in the American Imagination* (1978; reprint, Athens: University of Georgia Press, 1986), 1–22.

5. See Kilgore Papers; Kilgore's Standard Turpentine files end in 1908. On forests in ancient myth, see Robert Pogue Harrison, *Forests: The Shadow of Civilization* (Chicago: University of Chicago Press, 1992), especially 1–58.

6. Maryland State Board of Forestry, *Report for 1910 and 1911* (Baltimore, Jan. 1912), 5 (Besley quotation). A useful introduction to Pinchot and modern forestry, in appropriate context, is Michael Williams, *Americans and Their Forests: A Historical Geography* (Cambridge: Cambridge University Press, 1989), 411–21.

7. *Tenth Census of the United States, 1880: Forest Trees of North America* (Washington: GPO, 1884), 511; Maryland State Board of Forestry, *Report for 1906 and 1907* (Baltimore: State Board of Forestry, 1907), 3–5.

8. Maryland Board of Forestry, *Report for 1906 and 1907*, 4–8.

9. (Maryland) State Board of Forestry, *Report for 1908 and 1909* (Baltimore, 1909), 6; ibid., *Report for 1914 and 1915* (Baltimore, n.d.), 30–31 (quotation); ibid., *Report for 1918–1919* (Baltimore, n.d.), 33–39. See also F. W. Besley, "Maryland's Forest Resources (A Preliminary Report)," Forestry Leaflet No. 7, Maryland State Board of Forestry (Baltimore, 31 Dec. 1908); and Besley, *The Forests of Maryland* (Baltimore: Maryland State Board of Forestry, 1916).

10. Cope, *Loblolly Pine in Maryland* (1925), especially 3; State Board of Forestry, *Report for Fiscal Years 1924 and 1925* (Baltimore, n.d.), 22 (quotation); Neal P. Kingsley and Thomas W. Birch, *The Forest-Land Owners of Maryland*, Forest Service Resource Bulletin NE-63 (Broomall, Pa.: USDA/Forest Service, 1980), 2–4, 41; and Marie Van Deusen et al., "Terrestrial Ecological Survey of the Elms Property, St. Mary's County, Maryland," Special Report 71, Chesapeake Bay Institute, the Johns Hopkins University, Apr. 1971 (pamphlet at University of Maryland Library), 21, 41–42.

11. *Tenth Census...Forest Trees of North America*, 511–12; W. W. Ashe, "The Forests, Forest Lands, and Forest Products of Eastern North Carolina," N.C. Geological Survey, Bulletin No. 5 (Raleigh, 1894), 18 (first quotation), 29–30 (second quotation, 30), 52–59.

12. North Carolina Forestry Association, Report of Seventh Annual Convention, held in Raleigh, 24–25 Jan. 1917 (Chapel Hill: n.p., 1917), 8 (quotation).

13. Ibid., 15 (quotation); W. Darrow Clark, "The Forest Problem in North Carolina," N.C. Geological and Economic Survey, Circular No. 1 (Chapel Hill, 1922), 5; and Fred B. Merrill, "Forest Fires and the Boll Weevil," N.C. Geological and Economic Survey, Circular No. 7 (Chapel Hill, 1923), 1–4.

14. Seth G. Hobart, George W. Dean, and Edwin E. Rodger, "The History of the Virginia Division of Forestry, 1914–1981" (bound typescript, Virginia Polytechnic Institute and State University Library, 1981), 2–12. On the Weeks Act, see Williams, *Americans and Their Forests*, 308, 322.

15. James E. Fickle, *The New South and the "New Competition": Trade Association Development in the Southern Pine Industry* (Urbana: University of Illinois Press for Forest History Society, 1980), 63, 126–27.

16. Ibid., 126–27; Hobart, Dean, and Rodger, "History of Virginia Division of Forestry," 21–24, 29–34; Stephen J. Pyne, *Fire in America: A Cultural History of Wildland and Rural Fire* (Princeton: Princeton University Press, 1982), 71–83, 143–60.

17. Alonzo Thomas Dill, *Chesapeake, Pioneer Papermaker: A History of the Company and Its Community* (Charlottesville: University Press of Virginia, 1968), 1–55; Inman F. Eldredge (retired forester, interviewed in 1959) quoted in *Voices from the South: Recollections of Four Foresters*, edited by Elwood R. Maunder (Santa Cruz, Calif.: Forest History Society, 1977), 45; Thomas D. Clark, *Three Paths to the Modern South: Education, Agriculture, and Conservation* (Athens: University of Georgia Press, 1965), 87; and Williams, *Americans and Their Forests*, 287–88. Dr. Herty's championship of southern papermaking was but his second victory for the region. At the beginning of the century, he successfully refined the process of collecting resin from longleaf pines, for

the turpentine industry. See Edwin Mims, "The South Realizing Itself: Remakers of Industry," *World's Work* 23 (Dec. 1911): 203–19 (especially 204–6, 209).

18. Dill, *Chesapeake*, 60–141; "Elis Ollson: A Biographical Sketch," *Virginia Forests* 1 (Sept–Oct 1946): 3, 10.

19. Dill, *Chesapeake*, especially 140–47; *Sixty Years of Progress* (Franklin, Va.: Camp Manufacturing Co., 1948), unpaginated; Union Camp Community Relations, "Union Camp at Franklin — A Short History" (typescript), 2.

20. William E. Cooper, "Virginia Forests, Incorporated — and how it grew!," *Virginia Forests* 22 (Winter 1967–68): 8, 22, 24, 26; Cooper, "Virginia Forests … and how it grew [continued]," *Virginia Forests* 23 (Spring 1968): 16–24. See also various lists of officers and activities, *Virginia Forests* 9 (Jan.–Feb. 1949): 3; *Virginia Forests* 23 (Fall 1968): 10–14; *Virginia Forests* 24 (Apr. 1969): 12–16.

21. NCFA, "Minutes of Conference Called by the NCFA to Consider Forestry Legislation," (Chapel Hill, 1944); Hobart, Dean, and Rodger, "History of the Virginia Division of Forestry," 46–48; "Garland Gray: 'Man of the Year in Forestry,'" *Virginia Forests* 24 (Winter 1970): 7, 11.

22. Thomas Lotti and R. D. McCulley, "Maintaining Loblolly Pine," *Virginia Forests* 10 (May–June 1955): 8–11, 14.

23. Hobart, Dean, and Rodgers, "History of the Virginia Division of Forestry," 95–97.

24. Kenneth B. Pomeroy, "Can Hardwoods Be Controlled?," *Virginia Forests* 4 (Mar.–Apr. 1949): 6–7, 11, 13 (quotation, 6); and Pyne, *Fire in America*, 112, 118, 172.

25. Maunder, *Voices from the South*, 150; Hobard, Dean, and Rodgers, "History of Virginia Division of Forestry," 99 (quotation); Tree-ject advertisement, *Virginia Forests* 20 (Spring 1965): 2; "Spreading Infection: Guest Editorial" (against EPA bannings), ibid., 27 (Fall 1972): 5, 24.

26. See William C. Osborn, *The Paper Plantation, Ralph Nader's Study Group Report on the Pulp and Paper Industry in Maine* (New York: Grossman/Viking, 1974).

27. U.S. censuses, state and urban tables.

28. Ibid., county tables.

29. Virginia, Division of Industrial Development and Planning, "Economic Data, Sussex County, Virginia," 9; ibid., "Economic Data, Surry County, Virginia," 7; and ibid., "Economic Data: Isle of Wight County, Virginia," 11 (all n.p., 1962, typescripts in Norfolk Public Library); "Virginians Plant 54.7 Million Seedlings in 1969: Second Highest Record for Tree Planting," *Virginia Forests* 24 (Summer 1969): 14–15, 20.

30. On business during the 1980s, see "What's in store for Virginia industry, sector by sector," *Norfolk Virginian-Pilot and Ledger-Star*, 26 June 1988, E4. On small owners and reforestation, see Jim Conrad, "Southern Pines and the Small Landowner: A Down-Home View," *American Forests* 91 (Mar. 1985): 17–19, 58; plus James P. Jackson, "Nonindustrial Private Forests: New Look at an Old Problem," ibid., 90 (Feb. 1984): 25–27; and J. Walter Myers, Jr., "Outlook for Southern Forests," ibid., 90 (July 1984): 45–49.

31. "Virginia timber: Where it's growing, where it's not" [map/chart based on 1985 U.S. Forest Service survey], *Norfolk Virginian-Pilot and Ledger-Star Business Weekly*, 8 Apr. 1991, p. 13.

32. Al Roberts, "Chesapeake Corp.: Sowing the seeds of its own future," *Norfolk Virginian-Pilot and Ledger-Star Business Weekly*, 8 Apr. 1991, p. 13 (first quotation); ibid., "Sawmills: Split by competing interests," *Norfolk Virginian-Pilot and Ledger-Star Business Weekly*, 8 Apr. 1991, 14 (following quotations).

33. Parke Rouse, Jr., *The Timber Tycoons: The Camp Families of Virginia and Florida and Their Empire, 1887–1987* (Richmond: William Byrd Press for Southampton Historical Society, 1988), especially 1–10.

34. Union Camp, "Union Camp at Franklin—A Short History"; ibid., "An Overview of Union Camp Corporation" (bound eight-page brochure, n.d. [ca. 1987]); author's tour of Franklin mill, 7 Aug. 1987.

35. Ibid.; Bland Simpson, *The Great Dismal: A Carolinian's Swamp Memoir* (Chapel Hill: University of North Carolina Press, 1990), 59 (on the tax significance of the swampland donation); John Holusha, "Union Camp Turns a Cleaner Page," *New York Times*, 20 Oct. 1993, C1, C5; Cecil C. Frost and Lytton J. Musselman, "History and Vegetation of the Blackwater Ecologic Preserve," *Castanea* 52 (Mar. 1987): 16–46.

EPILOGUE

1. William Valentine Diaries, 10 Mar. (first quotation) and 11 May 1853, SHC.

2. Valentine Diaries, 11 May 1853.

3. Louise Vann Boone, "Historical Review of Winton," in *The Ahoskie Era of Hertford County*, edited by J. Roy Parker (Ahoskie: Parker Bros., 1955), 146–47.

4. John J. Alford, "The Role of Management in Chesapeake Oyster Production," *Geographical Review* 63 (Jan. 1973): 44–54; and R. F. Pharr, "Large-Scale Shell Production from Hampton Roads," *Virginia Minerals* 11 (Nov. 1965): 41–43. See also John R. Wennersten, "The Almighty Oyster: A Saga of Old Somerset and the Eastern Shore, 1850–1920," *Maryland Historical Magazine* 74 (Mar. 1979): 81–93; and James Tice Moore, "Gunfire on the Chesapeake: Governor Cameron and the Oyster Pirates, 1882–1885," *Virginia Magazine of History and Biography* 90 (July 1982): 367–77.

5. Valentine Diaries, 30 Dec. 1841. On Hertford's soils, see data provided by ex-county agent E. W. Gaither in Parker, *Ahoskie Era*, 79–80.

6. "Green-Sand Marl as a Fertilizer," *SP* 51 (Sept. 1890): 409 (on Eppes); and W. C. Knight, "Two Rural Visits," ibid., 48 (Oct. 1887): 548–52 (especially 550–52, on Ruffin); "The Fertilizer Law," ibid., 51 (Apr. 1890): 184–85; and *Census Reports*, vol. 5: *Twelfth Census of the U.S., Taken in the Year 1900 ... Agriculture*, part 1, *Farms, Live Stock, and Annual Products* (Washington: U.S. Census Office, 1902), cxl–cxlii.

7. Gaither quoted in Parker, *Ahoskie Era*, 82–83. On county agents generally, see Roy V. Scott, *The Reluctant Farmer: The Rise of Agricultural Extension to 1914* (Urbana: University of Illinois Press, 1970).

8. See editor Clarence Poe's annual diatribes against North Carolina state and county fair midway exhibitions, *Progressive Farmer* (usually midsummer), ca. 1899–1909; "Tidewater Agricultural and Mechanical Society's Fair, at Franklin, Va.," *SP* 50 (Dec. 1889): 330; and on southern fairs generally, see Ted Ownby, *Subduing Satan: Religion, Recreation, and Manhood in the Rural South, 1865–1920* (Chapel Hill: University of North Carolina Press, 1990), 182–93.

9. Kermit Hobbs and William A. Paquette, *Suffolk, A Pictorial History* (Norfolk and Virginia Beach: Donning Co., 1987), 103 (on the peanut machine); Helen H. King, "The First Peanut King," Isle of Wight County Historical Society, typescript newsletter (Sept. 1987), copy in Norfolk Public Library.

10. Norman and Willie Bosselman oral history, 15 Dec. 1986, Suffolk, Va., by LuAnn Jones, in National Museum of American History, Washington (Nansemond quotations); Martin Knight oral history, 14 Dec. 1986, Corapeake, N.C., by LuAnn Jones, ibid. ("total division" quotations). See also (by LuAnn Jones in the same repository): tape index to John F. and Gretchen Willey oral history, 7 Dec. 1986, Gates, N.C.; A. C. and Grace Griffin oral history, 8 and 10 Dec. 1986, Edenton, N.C. The labor of cleaning, sorting, and removing peanuts from shells remained unmechanized a very long time, the dubious preserve of black women. See Norman and Willie Bosselman oral history, 15 Dec. 1986, Suffolk, Va., by LuAnn Jones, ibid.

11. See John L. Shover, *First Majority — Last Minority: The Transforming of Rural Life in America* (DeKalb, Ill.: Northern Illinois University Press, 1976); W. Herbert Brown, *Peanut-Cotton Farms: Organization, Costs, and Returns, Southern Plains, 1944–1960*, Agricultural Economics Report No. 7 for the Farm Economics Division, Economic Research Service, of USDA (Washington: GPO, 1962); and Jack Temple Kirby, *Rural Worlds Lost: The American South, 1920–1960* (Baton Rouge: Louisiana State University Press, 1987), especially 334–55.

12. On farm subsidies see Kirby, *Rural Worlds Lost*, 348–49. Data from censuses of agriculture, 1940–70, county tables.

13. Susan McKerns, "Cotton comeback continues with gin," *Tidewater Review* (Franklin), 23 May 1991, 1A, 8A; Patrick K. Lackey, "Acreage of hardy crop triples in a year," *Norfolk Ledger-Star*, 14 Oct. 1991, D1, D4. On the antebellum Popes, see the Pope Family Papers, VHS.

A second cotton gin (called Commonwealth Gin) was built at Windsor, in Isle of Wight County, shortly after the Southside Gin. See "Cotton Comes in Early," in "The Citizen" section (for Isle of Wight and Surry Counties), *Norfolk Virginian-Pilot*, 29 Sept. 1993, 1, 7.

14. On the sale of Hopewell, see *Hopewell News*, 30 Oct. 1952 (clipping in Hopewell file, Norfolk Public Library).

15. Thomas B. Robertson, "Hopewell and City Point in the World War," in *Virginia Communities in War Time*, edited by A. K. Davis (1st ser.; Richmond: Dietz, 1926), 215–34; *Richmond Times-Dispatch*, 5 Oct. 1918.

16. *New York Times*, 30 Aug. 1975, p. 16; and Albert E. Cowdrey, *This Land, This*

South: An Environmental History (Lexington: University of Kentucky Press, 1983), 185–86.

17. *Richmond Times-Dispatch*, 10 June 1988, B1; U.S. Environmental Protection Agency, "Chesapeake Bay Program Technical Studies: A Synthesis" (Washington: GPO, Sept. 1982), i–iv, xii; and Christopher F. D'Elia, "Nutrient Enrichment of Chesapeake Bay: An Historical Perspective" (Washington: GPO, Sept. 1982), 45–100.

18. Bill Geroux, "Dirty but not dead, river throbs with both marine, industrial life," *Richmond Times-Dispatch*, 21 July 1991, A1, A4 (quotation); and "Who's Right? Study finds no PCBs in river's crabs," ibid., A4.

19. Geroux, "Dirty but not dead," A4 (quotations); Elizabeth River Project Survey, "Annual Report" [typescript report on river testing], by Daniel G. Borick (Portsmouth: I. C. Norcom High School, n.d. [1992]); and author's observation.

20. See John Capper, Garrett Power, and Frank R. Shivers, Jr., *Chesapeake Waters: Pollution, Public Health, and Public Opinion, 1607–1972* (Centreville, Md.: Tidewater Publishers, 1983), 144–52; and EPA, "Chesapeake Bay Program."

21. On the Virginia Beach water crisis see Betty Booker and Pamela Stallsmith, "Left to their own devices, localities forge own plans," *Richmond Times-Dispatch*, 9 July 1990, A1, A8–9; and Pamela Stallsmith, "Transfer of water between basins can cause conflict," ibid., 11 July 1990, A6. On Mulholland and Los Angeles see Marc Reisner, *Cadillac Desert: The American West and Its Disappearing Water* (New York: Penguin, 1986), 54–107.

22. Ibid.; and *Norfolk Virginian-Pilot* for July 1988, on the heat wave and drought. On water law, see Reisner, *Cadillac Desert*, 45, 48; and Donald Worster, *Rivers of Empire: Water, Aridity, and the Growth of the American West* (New York: Pantheon, 1985), especially 88–96, 104–11, 331–32.

23. Observations on lawns are mine.

24. Pamela Stallsmith, "Pipeline struggle points to need for compromise," *Richmond Times-Dispatch*, 9 July 1990, A8. The Virginia Beach city council approved the pipeline in 1982 and won clearance from the Corps of Engineers in 1984.

INDEX

African Americans: as conjurers,
173–75; culture, 26–27; as ditchers,
43; as forest workers, 155–61; as soldiers, 16, 191–94 passim. *See also* Civil
War; Free people of color; Slaves
Agriculture: chemistry of, 66–67, 69–71;
cotton, 240–42; crop pests in, 51–52,
56–58; decline of, 241–42; drainage,
53–54; East Anglian influences,
50–52; grain culture, 11–12, 23–27,
30–31, 50–55, 69, 87–91; Green Revolution, 241, 243; historiography,
114–19; Indian, xiii, 6–7, 114; labor
costs, 121–23; peanuts, 240–41; tenancy, 121–22; tobacco, 8, 201, 240,
242; "truck farming," 11, 104, 122
Agriculture, U.S. Department of, 115,
120, 217, 238–39
Ahoskie Swamp, 173
Albemarle, Assembly of, 162
Albemarle-Chesapeake Canal, 146
Albemarle Paper Co., 225
Albemarle Sound, xi, 4, 6, 12, 17, 23–26,
37, 69, 84, 162, 246; in Civil War,
183–84
Albemarle Swamp Land Co., 199
Alick, Uncle, 177–79
Allen, William, 208
Allied Chemical Corp., 243
Alligator River, 23
American Forestry Association, 232
American Peanut Corp., 240
Ansell, H. B., 56, 142–44
Appomattox Manor, 43–44, 46–47, 55,
58
Appomattox River, 43, 57, 100
Aquifers, 128, 246, 249

Arsenic, 52
Ashe, W. W., 221–22
Audubon, John James, 57, 168–69, 172

Back Bay, Va., 141
Bacon, Nathaniel, 163
Bacon's Castle, 203
Bagley, Dudley Warren, 123–25, 144,
217
Barnes, Richard T., 182
Barron, James, 150
Bears, 172
Beavers, 137–38
Beckwith, Julian, 87
Beechwood plantation, 85
Benthall, Jesse Thomas, 240
Berkeley, William, 163
Bermuda Hundred (farm), 44, 46, 100
Bertie County, N.C., 25, 27, 31–32, 103,
122, 132–33, 173–74; in Civil War,
187; forests of, 204
Besley, Wilson, 219–20
Beverley, Robert, 98–99
Birds, 56–58, 141
Blackwater Ecologic Preserve, xv, 34,
205–7, 234
Blackwater River, 4, 29, 33, 84, 210–12,
225, 234
Blow, George, 13–15, 37
Blow, Richard, 13, 37
Boxing, 145
Boykins, Va., 141
Bradford, M. E., 68
Brandon (plantations), 49, 58, 79,
87–88, 105
Brantley, Etheldred T., 177
Bright, Daniel, 16, 193

285